Pacifism

Also available from Bloomsbury

Citizen Killings, Deane-Peter Baker
On Resistance, Howard Caygill
The Ethics of Nonviolence, Robert L. Holmes
Violence, Pamela Stewart

Pacifism

A Philosophy of Nonviolence

Robert L. Holmes

Bloomsbury Academic
An imprint of Bloomsbury Publishing Plc

B L O O M S B U R Y
LONDON · OXFORD · NEW YORK · NEW DELHI · SYDNEY

Bloomsbury Academic

An imprint of Bloomsbury Publishing Plc

50 Bedford Square
London
WC1B 3DP
UK

1385 Broadway
New York
NY 10018
USA

www.bloomsbury.com

BLOOMSBURY and the Diana logo are trademarks of Bloomsbury Publishing Plc

First published 2017

British Library Cataloguing-in-Publication Data
A catalogue record for this book is available from the British Library.

ISBN: HB: 978-1-4742-7982-6
PB: 978-1-4742-7983-3
ePDF: 978-1-4742-7981-9
ePub: 978-1-4742-7984-0

Library of Congress Cataloging-in-Publication Data
A catalog record for this book is available from the Library of Congress.

Typeset by Newgen Knowledge Works (P) Ltd., Chennai, India
Printed and bound in India

For Veronica

Now it is an interesting, if obvious, fact that nobody who talks bravely about war has ever been killed in war.

—A. A. Milne

Yet the dust, the thunder, the carnage, and the ruin of war seem to make visible some deeper disorder, some suicidal madness in the human race.

—George Santayana

Contents

Acknowledgments

Some of what follows, rewritten and integrated into the text, has been drawn from previous publications of mine: Chapter 1: "Absolute Violence and the Idea of War," from *In the Interests of Peace*, ed. Kenneth H. Klein and Joseph C. Kunkel, Longwood Academic, pp. 25–32, 1990; Chapter 3: A few paragraphs from "The Philosophy of Political Realism in International Affairs," *The Ethics of Nonviolence: Essays by Robert L. Holmes*, ed. Predrag Cicovacki, Bloomsbury Academic, 2013; Chapter 4: "St. Augustine and the Just War Theory," *The Augustinian Tradition*, ed. Gareth B. Matthews, University of California Press, 1999, pp. 323–345; Chapter 7: "Pacifism for Nonpacifists," *Journal of Social Philosophy*, Vol. 30, No. 3, Winter 1999, pp. 387–401; *Social and Political Philosophy: Contemporary Perspectives*, ed. James Sterba, Routledge, 2001, pp. 391–407; and "Pacifism and the Right to Life," *Filozofska Istradivanja*, God. 17, Sv.1, 1997, pp. 61–70; Chapter 10: "Kosovo and NATO Intervention," from *Rising India: Friends and Foes*, ed. Prakash Nanda, 2007, Lancer publishers, pp. 190–207; Chapter 11: "On Pacifism" from *The Monist*, Vol. 57, No. 4, October 1973, pp. 489–507, Open Court Publishing Co.; Chapter 12 "The Metaethics of Pacifism and Just War Theory," from *The Philosophical Forum*, Vol. LXVI, No. 1, Spring 2015, pp. 3–16. © 2015 The Philosophical Forum, Inc., published by Wiley Periodicals, Inc.; "Pacifism, Just War and Humanitarian Intervention," *Pazifismus*, ed. Bleisch and Strub, 2006, Haupt, Berne, pp. 145–162; Earlier versions of Chapter 14 appeared in *Peacework*, a publication of the New England Branch of the American Friends Service Committee; *The Acorn: Gandhian Review*; Joseph Kunkel and Kenneth Klein (eds), issues in *War and Peace*, Longwood Academic, 1989; and *Metaphysical Research of St. Petersburg*, Russia, in 2005. Appreciation to these publishers for use of the material.

Epigraphs, in order of their appearance, are from the following:

A. A. Milne, *Peace with Honor* (New York: E. P. Dutton, 1934), p. 108.

George Santayana, *Dominations and Powers: Reflections on Liberty, Society and Government* (New York: Charles Scribner's Sons, 1951), p. 439.

Rajiv Gandhi, Speech before UN special session on disarmament, June 9, 1988.

Carl von Clausewitz, *On War* [1832], ed. Anatol Rapoport (Baltimore, MD: Penguin Books, 1968), p. 386.

Steve Morse, unpublished essay, smorse2@charter.net.

Augustine, Letter CCXXIX (AD 429) to Darius.

James M. Lawson, *Fellowship*, Vol. 78, No. 4–6, Summer/Fall 2014, p. 26.

Steven P. Lee, *Ethics and War: An Introduction* (Cambridge: Cambridge University Press, 2012), p. 33.

Michael Walzer, *Just and Unjust Wars* (New York: Basic Books, 1977), p. 128.

Robert W. Brimlow, *What about Hitler? Wrestling with Jesus's Call to Nonviolence in an Evil World* (Grand Rapids, MI: Brazos Press, 2006), p. 69.

Anonymous, *The New York Times*, May 15, 1966.

Philip Caputo, *A Rumor of War* (New York: Henry Holt, 1977), p. xix.

Daniel Yergin, *The Prize: The Epic Quest for Oil, Money & Power* (New York: Simon & Schuster, 1991), p. 200.

William G. O'Neill, *Kosovo: An Unfinished Peace* (Boulder, CO: Lynne Rienner, 2002), p. 54.

Hugo Grotius, *The Rights of War and Peace*, Book I, chapter II.

Richard Werner, "Pragmatism for Pacifists," *Contemporary Pragmatism*, Vol. 4, No. 2, December 2007, pp. 93–115.

James P. Sterba, *Justice for Here and Now* (Cambridge: Cambridge University Press, 1998), p. 163.

Jeff McMahan, "Aggression and Punishment," in Larry May (ed.), *War: Essays in Political Philosophy* (Cambridge: Cambridge University Press, 2008), p. 78.

Barry Gan, *Violence and Nonviolence* (New York: Rowman & Littlefield, 2013), p. 48.

Jessica Stern, *Terrorism in the Name of God: Why Religious Militants Kill* (New York: HarperCollins, 2003), p. xxviii.

Muhammad Ali, *The New York Times*, June 21, 2013.

Mark Twain, *Mark Twain in Eruption*, ed. Bernard DeVoto (New York: Grosset & Dunlap, 1940), p. 69.

Lin Yutang, *Between Tears and Laughter* (New York: Blue Ribbon Books, 1945), p. 130.

I would like to express appreciation to Predrag Cicovacki, Barry Gan and Richard Werner for valued conversations over the years on many of the topics of this book, as well as for helpful comments on portions of the book itself. Most of all, I thank my wife, Veronica, for her patience, support and encouragement throughout and for reading and providing valuable comments on the entire manuscript, a true act of supererogation.

Introduction

Nonviolence in international relations … is the only available basis for civilized survival, for the maintenance of peace through peaceful coexistence, for a new, just, equitable and democratic world order.

—Rajiv Gandhi, 1988

The most stunning international event of the last decade of the twentieth century was the collapse of the Soviet Union. In little more than a moment by historical standards, a state whose rivalry with the United States had shaped the international scene for nearly fifty years, ceased to exist, and along with it an empire forged in the name of a global Marxist ideology. This set the stage for the emergence of a new world order. What precisely that order will be remains unclear well into the twenty-first century. But how America uses its vast economic, political and military power will be a major determinant of that order. This fact does not make America exceptional in terms of entitlement or moral standing. It does, however, give it unusual potential for transformative world leadership. That potential carries with it a challenge to chart a wise and humane course through the twenty-first century. For this reason, I shall focus in Part III on issues centering largely, though not exclusively, on the role of the United States. Parts I, II, IV and V will focus on topics essential to critiquing the moral underpinnings of that role. These issues center on the problem of war.

America has not, since its founding, fought a major war against a foreign power on its own soil, and it has never suffered the devastation from war that countries like Russia have. Even the destruction of the Civil War, which claimed the most casualties of any American war, was largely limited to the South.[1] Whether this has made Americans readier to engage in foreign wars is debatable. But it surely means that the role war has played in shaping the American character has been determined by

---

[1] For a good discussion of these issues, see David M. Kennedy, "War and the American Character," *The Stanford Magazine*, Vol. 3, No. 1, Spring/Summer 1975, pp. 14–18, 70–73. Abridged version published in *The Nation*, Vol. 220, No. 17, May 1975, pp. 453–468.

a limited understanding of the nature of war and the moral issues it raises. Much the same might be said of the understanding of peace, which is often mistakenly taken to be no more than the absence of war. Positive peace exists only when the conditions of a good life are present and sustainable. These presuppose physical survival, of course, but preoccupation with physical survival not only cannot guarantee the realization of the other conditions, it can actually obstruct their attainment. It does so in nations that squander their resources on armaments to the detriment and sometimes impoverishment of their own people. Absolute security is an illusion. It is no more attainable by a country than by individuals.

The conditions of a good life for a people include social justice, trust and respect for persons. These require cooperation, not only among members of one's own society, but also with members of other societies as well. In the end, the well-being of all peoples is interconnected. No people's lasting security can be achieved at the expense of others. The exploitation, domination, or oppression of others eventually victimizes the victimizer as well, if only through the moral corruption it works in the oppressor's national character.

We think of military power as the best guarantor of security. But the collapse of the Soviet empire reveals the fragility of power understood primarily as the capacity to inflict death and destruction. A militarized state that could have been overcome, if at all, only at a horrendous cost if confronted head-on by military might, disintegrated once the true source of its power—the willingness of its people to continue acquiescing in the rule of a government in which they had lost confidence—was removed. That happened once people lost their fear, as they did, not only in the Soviet Union, but also in the essentially nonviolent revolutions of Eastern Europe: from the ten-year struggle of Solidarity in Poland, to the six-week inspired uprising in Czechoslovakia. Perhaps most notable was the case of Lithuania, the first of the Soviet Republics to declare its independence. Mobilizing a system of nonviolent defense against the Soviet military, volunteers from throughout the country converged on Vilnius, setting up shacks in the newly christened Independence Square, site of the parliament building, and establishing communications networks. Lithuanians responded by the thousands when called out to confront Soviet troops nonviolently when they moved against key governmental and communications centers. To be sure, the Soviets could have taken the parliament building—the seat of the new government and symbol of Lithuanian defiance of Moscow—in a few hours had they chosen to; and had not the Soviet government collapsed when it did, the Lithuanian struggle for independence would have been a protracted one of less certain outcome. But these considerations only highlight the fact that any successful nonviolent action, like any successful military action, presupposes conditions in whose absence the action might not have succeeded. Nonviolence did not succeed in Tiananmen Square. It did in Lithuania.

At no time has a country committed itself wholly to nonviolence. Nevertheless, it is in this direction that creative thinking must go in the quest for an alternative conception of security. A radically new conception of world order was set forth on June 9, 1988 by Prime Minister Rajiv Gandhi of India in an address to the UN Special Session on Disarmament. For the first time in history, to my knowledge, it was proposed that the nations of the world work toward creation of a nonviolent world order.[2] Though the details of such an order were not spelled out, the idea calls for fresh thinking of both a moral and political sort. It is toward helping point the way to a nonviolent world order that this book is addressed.

This book will not explore the many dimensions of nonviolence. That is a topic for further study. But central to understanding nonviolence is to confront the issue of war. The acceptance of war (and in some cases its glorification) is at the heart of the world orders that have dominated for ages. It is also at the heart of the conceptions of world order that have predominated in discussions since the collapse of the Soviet Union. For this reason it is with the issue of war—specifically with the moral issue of whether war is morally justifiable in today's world—that I shall be concerned.

It is commonly assumed with little or nothing in the way of argument that some wars are justified. When arguments are given, they are a mix. Some concede that war is wrong but argue that we must be prepared to fight wars anyway. That we do so is a matter of necessity or because wrongdoing is inescapable. Others argue that pacifism, the principled opposition to war, is self-contradictory or self-defeating, which means that one cannot even coherently oppose war. In neither case need one look at the actual reasoning of pacifists. In the first case, the arguments are given lip-service, but since war is justified anyway, the arguments against it need not be taken seriously. In the second case, pacifism is conceptually confused, so arguments for it are irrelevant. Either way, one is then free to refine the rationales for war without taking seriously the moral case against it.

The standard approach to the moral assessment of war is the just war theory, which typically starts from the assumption that some wars are just and proceeds from there. In so doing, it sidelines pacifism from the outset, dismissing it as an extreme position, at the opposite end of the spectrum from realism, terrorism and jihadism. By focusing on the entitlements of collectivities (notably nation states) as opposed to the well-being of individuals, the just war theory frames a rationale for war that omits the central moral issue in war, which is whether the massive, systematic and deliberate killing of human beings can ever be justified. That, in my judgment, puts the cart before the horse. One does not start by placing the highest value on states and then justify killing human beings to serve the interest of states. One starts by placing the highest value on human beings and evaluates the behavior of states in that light.

This book presents an argument for pacifism. Whether it will be ignored, refuted, defended or elaborated is beyond my control. If the argument should be sound, however, then those who support war—from government, religious and military leaders to intellectuals and ordinary citizens—are perpetuating a practice that is a detriment to

---

[2] The principles of the Holy Alliance promulgated by Czar Alexander I in 1815 were an ultimately futile attempt in this direction, committing Russia, Austria and Prussia to act in both domestic and foreign affairs according to Christian principles and calling upon other European powers to do the same. A more limited, and perhaps more serious, attempt, as it lasted for seventy-four years, was the so-called Holy Experiment initiated by William Penn in what is now Pennsylvania to establish a Quaker colony, which, in the words of historian Peter Brock, would be "a blueprint of a world to come, a new society from which war would be banished." Peter Brock, *Pacifism in the United States: From the Colonial Era to the First World War* (Princeton, NJ: Princeton University Press, 1968), p. 81.

humankind, and very possibly a threat in the long term to its very survival. My hope is to encourage reflection on that possibility. The essence of the argument is simple, though its elaboration is complex. It is that there is a moral presumption against war, and unless that presumption is defeated, war is wrong. That presumption, I contend, has not been defeated.

I have previously argued that war is wrong principally on the ground that it kills innocent persons.[3] In what follows I shall argue that what renders war wrong is the killing and harming it entails, whether of innocents or noninnocents. The elaboration of the argument requires both theoretical and practical dimensions. On the theoretical side, some of the arguments (especially in Chapters 6, 7 and 11) require close philosophical analysis, which may understandably try the patience of general readers. But I believe that such discussion is important to a thoroughgoing examination of the moral issues of war. On the other hand, some philosophers will no doubt find the treatment of particular wars such as Vietnam and the Gulf and Iraq wars out of bounds of what is properly considered philosophy. Be that as it may. If each academic field confines itself to what the mainstream professional consensus takes to be proper to it, issues like war, which span virtually every aspect of human life, remain examined only in fragmented ways and yield only limited understanding.

So that the reader will know where my reasoning is headed, here is a sketch of its main points, without qualification and elaboration.

1. Killing persons is presumptively wrong.
2. War entails killing persons, hence entails the performance of presumptive wrongs.
3. Thus war is presumptively wrong.
4. Unless that presumption is defeated, war is morally impermissible.
5. That presumption has not been defeated.
6. Therefore: War is morally impermissible.

All of these steps require clarification. Most people, I am assuming, would accept (1) and (2) and many, though by no means all, would accept (3) and (4). Step (5), however, is contestable, and almost everyone would reject (6). That is, almost everyone believes that some wars are justified, hence morally permissible. As I deny this, it is important that I explain why. Some of the explanation will involve clarification. Some of it will involve subsidiary arguments for the contestable portions of (3), (4) and (5). The full argument is summarized in Chapter 11.

---

[3] In *On War and Morality* (Princeton: Princeton University Press, 1989), reissued as part of the Princeton Legacy Series in 2014. For a thoughtful critique of that argument, see Mark Vorabej, 'Pacifism and Wartime Innocence,' *Social Theory and Practice*, Vol. 20, No. 2, Summer 1994, pp. 171–192.

Part I

1

Reconceptualizing War

[S]ince the time of Bonaparte, war... has assumed quite a new nature, or rather it has approached much nearer to Its real nature, its absolute perfection.
                                                                    —Carl von Clausewitz

1.1 Absolute war

Viewed from one standpoint, wars are simply happenings, events that occur along with others in the world. They are, in this view, particularly unfortunate events, to be sure, considering the death and destruction they wreak, but they are more or less inevitable given the nature of things.[1] But wars can also be viewed as products of human actions and intimately linked to human purposes and values. It is only when we view war in this broader connection that we can see why the *idea* of war is important. For whatever war actually is, as exemplified in the world, it is how we conceptualize it that determines how we think about it. And that in turn determines how we prepare for it, how we wage it and, perhaps most importantly, how seriously we seek alternatives to it.

The context of modern war shall be our starting point.[2] As Clausewitz points out, wars in the eighteenth century were mainly wars of governments, or at any rate of those who held power. It was their interests, not those of the people, that governed the recourse to war. This situation was an outgrowth of the centralization of power that

---

[1] See Anatol Rapoport's introduction to the abbreviated version of Clausewitz's, *On War* (Baltimore, MD: Penguin Books, 1968), in which he distinguishes political, eschatological and cataclysmic philosophies of war (the above epigraph is from p. 386). On the issue of whether war is inevitable, see Christopher Coker, *Can War Be Eliminated?* (Cambridge: Polity Press, 2014). Although he does not categorically say that war cannot be eliminated, Coker details strong evolutionary, cultural and technological forces tending to its perpetuation. Michael Allen Fox, after examining research on peaceful societies and human nature, concludes that war is not inevitable. See Michael Allen Fox, *Understanding Peace: A Comprehensive Introduction* (New York: Routledge, 2014), chapter 2.

[2] I shall confine myself to war in the Western world, mindful that it represents but one tradition among many.

gave rise to the nation state.[3] Much of armed conflict through the late Middle Ages had been diversified among kings and wealthy landowners, who fielded their own militias and were often guided in their use of violence more or less by prestige and honor as enshrined in the Chivalric Code.[4] The Napoleonic Wars of the nineteenth century changed all that. Whole peoples were mobilized and patriotism was harnessed in the interests of the state. Rulers were no longer dependent upon expensive professional armies which they could ill-afford to lose in reckless adventures or costly battles of uncertain outcome. They now had a renewable and practically limitless resource in the people. The people, who previously had been mere spectators to war, if they were lucky, or its victims, if they were unlucky, became its fighters. They became the war machine's source of energy. Accordingly, the prudential constraints upon rulers in initiating and waging war largely slipped away. It was no longer their personal treasuries and troops paid by them that were expended in warfare. It was the people themselves and their resources that were expended. They, rather than exclusively professionals, became the dogs of war. This made possible what Clausewitz calls absolute war.

Absolute war, for Clausewitz has as its natural end the complete subjugation of the enemy. And it has its own logic in pursuing that end without moderation. The limitations and uncertainties of actual wars represent departures from this absolute conception. Clausewitz even suggests that wars cease to be fully wars to the extent that they depart from it. However, the notion of absolute war is not purely theoretical. Napoleon, he thought, achieved its realization in the real world, with his mobilization of vast armies drawn from the populace, fighting over issues presumed to be of importance to the people.[5] This leads Clausewitz to ask: "From now on will every war in Europe be waged with the full resources of the state, and therefore have to be fought only over major issues that affect the people? Or shall we again see a gradual separation taking place between government and people?"[6] Without answering these questions, Clausewitz adds that "once barriers…are torn down, they are not so easily set up again." This was prophetic. The world wars of the twentieth century were more or less absolute wars.[7] They drew upon virtually all of the human and material resources of modern states, and hurled them against one another in titanic confrontations.

---

[3] Usually dated from the Treaty of Westphalia in 1648.

[4] Historian Richard Kaeuper writes: "Maintaining the peace in the emerging medieval state was a problem of significant dimensions because of the existence and the idealization of a noble code of violence; it is the violence of the powerful and privileged classes which so sharply differentiates the medieval from the modern problem of order." See Richard Kaeuper, *War, Justice and Public Order: England and France in the Later Middle Ages* (Oxford, UK: Clarendon Press, 1988), p. 188.

[5] As Clausewitz says, "one might wonder whether there is any truth at all in our concept of the absolute character of war were it not for the fact that with our own eyes we have seen warfare achieve this state of absolute perfection. Bonaparte brought it swiftly and ruthlessly to that point." Carl von Clausewitz, *On War*, ed. and tr. Michael Howard and Peter Paret (Princeton, NJ: Princeton University Press, 1976), p. 580. Subsequent references will be to this translation of *On War*.

[6] *On War*, p. 593.

[7] Chris Bellamy even entitles his account of Soviet Russia in World War II, *Absolute War* (New York: Vintage Books, 2007).

1.2 The interests of the people, the interests of the state and the interests of the people who rule the state

The modern nation-state enables today's rulers to have it both ways. Through the coercive apparatus of government, technology and management of information, they can detach the interests of governments from those of the people, but at the same time appropriate the resources of the people in the service of war. With modern technology, fewer and fewer people are needed to cause greater and greater destruction. At one time, every sword required an arm to wield it, every musket an eye to aim it. There was a close correlation between the physical effort of individual persons and the resultant power accruing to the machinery of war. Men wielded weapons by hand against one another, to vanquish or be vanquished according to circumstance, skill or luck. Today the relevant units are not individuals, or even weapons, but weapons systems—complex configurations of humans, computers, robots and conventional and nuclear explosives. These systems themselves are but part of even larger war systems that most industrial societies are becoming. With the advent of the nuclear age and more recently the cyber age, one person (or at most a few) can activate weapons systems capable of killing millions. The people still make all of this possible, of course. It is, after all, the scientists among them who do the research for these weapons, the engineers who design them and the workers in military industries who produce them. But they do so without having to put on uniforms or strap guns to their shoulders. By doing nothing more than paying taxes or putting in eight hours of honest labor in the military industry, ordinary people help make possible the absolute war of which Clausewitz wrote.

Once a government has nuclear weapons, misgivings, reservations and even outright opposition from other elements in society become largely irrelevant. Once war breaks out, these weapons are under nearly absolute control of a handful of people in a democracy as well as in a dictatorship. It has been said in modern warfare, speed is critical, making democratic processes virtually impossible.

In a democracy, of course, a government purports to be acting in the national interest, which is often vaguely associated with the interests of the people. But in times of crisis it is the government that defines what those interests are. In the absence of a clear accounting of what the national interest consists in, and *why* a particular course of action is in the national interest, governments have virtually a free hand in using military force as they see fit.[8] And, of course, it is important not only to distinguish the interests of the people from those of the government, but also to distinguish the interests of the government from those of the particular individuals who make up the government (or administrators of the government) at any given time. Rulers in authoritarian regimes often use their power to amass vast personal fortunes. But even in a democracy, leaders' interests are often controlling: pride, prestige, and personal

---

[8] When there were congressional challenges to the president's authority to commit troops to hostile arenas, the Office of Legal Council (OLC) of the Justice Department wrote: "the structure of the War Powers Resolution (WPR) recognizes and presupposes the existence of unilateral Presidential authority to deploy armed forces 'into hostilities or into situations where imminent involvement in hostilities is clearly indicated by the circumstances.'" http://www.justice.gov/olc/haiti.htm.

aggrandizement. At the least, their policies are often tailored to maximize their chances of being re-elected. Although they no longer need to wage war over what Clausewitz calls "the major issues that affect the people," they can, through skilful use of rhetoric and manipulation of the media, always represent their wars as serving those purposes.

In short, the coincidence of the interests of the government and the interests of the people that Clausewitz took to be required for the realization of absolute war is no longer necessary. Whether or not a government pursues the interests of the people, it has the people in its service. The people may or may not have consented to this. They may not even be fully aware of it. But these simply mark relatively minor differences between democratic and nondemocratic states. In democratic and nondemocratic states alike, the efforts and resources of the people help to create and sustain the power of their leaders. In the worst case of the misuses of that power, the efforts of the people help maintain a threat to their own very survival, the ultimate form of alienation.

1.3 Absolute violence

The quest for absolute security during the Cold War fuelled an arms race and the proliferation of nuclear weapons. The violence that became possible in an all-out confrontation between the United States and the USSR would no longer have constituted mere war; nor would such a confrontation between the United States and Russia in the twenty-first century. It is idle to speculate about whether such a cataclysm would destroy every last person on earth. It is enough that if it were to occur, most people would likely not know how it began or whether it was deliberate or accidental.[9] Further, it is likely they would not know what its outcome was. No rational purpose would likely have governed its initiation, neither courage nor honor its course, and neither victory nor defeat its conclusion. It would be a volcanic eruption of violence without rational purpose, proportion or moral effect. It would be what I shall call, in the spirit of Clausewitz, absolute violence. Absolute war is still war. Absolute violence is not. Increasing the destructive power of weapons endlessly does not give you bigger and bigger wars endlessly. At some point in the all-out use of those weapons you get something that transcends war. Not only is absolute war now possible without serving the "great interests" of the people and without the direct participation of large populations, what is also possible is a transcendence of war itself to something beyond it: cataclysmic nuclear violence. The idea of war is embedded in an historical-conceptual-moral context that has been transformed by the nuclear age. Unless we recognize this, we will persist in trying to assess absolute violence in terms of just causes, proportionality, historical processes, winning and losing—categories unsuited to understanding or appreciating the threat it poses.

---

[9] Those who have close to absolute control over their nuclear war systems have largely relinquished the final stages of that control to computers. In systems designed to deter a surprise nuclear attack, the reaction time necessary to determine whether an attack has been launched, and if so whether it was intentional or accidental, and then to make a determination about whether to retaliate, is so short as to preclude fully rational decision making by humans. It also precludes democratic control in any meaningful sense.

1.4 Between war and peace

Just as the very concept of war is inadequate for understanding the kind of violence represented by an all-out nuclear conflagration, it is also unsuited to characterize much of the lower-level violence of the twenty-first century.

In a prescient 1972 article, Elisabeth Mann Borges argued that we have moved into a period which conceptually stands somewhere between peace and war. She contended:

> Modern war is no longer a war between one sovereign nation against another, fought by national armies. It is a struggle conducted by one nation against a part of another, usually supported by internal factions or regions within that nation. Modern war has become an international civil war without boundaries, where regular armies fight alongside or against partisans, Vietcong, or other "non-governmental" units; a war of terror against civilian diplomats, businessmen, athletes, and airline passengers.[10]

Contributing to this blurring of the distinction between war and peace, as Borgese puts it, is what she calls the disintegration of the concept of a "weapon." Devices fashioned directly from raw materials into instruments of war are increasingly being replaced by so-called dual-purpose (or "multi-purpose") agents that, whether originally produced for war or peace, can be used for either.

> Any scientific discovery or, for that matter, any technological development is a dual-purpose agent in this sense. It can be used constructively or destructively. In a way of course this is nothing new. Dynamite, if you wish, has always been a dual-purpose agent. In the past, however, the dual-purpose agent was, so to speak, a raw material. This was then put through a process of specialization to fashion it for either peace or war. Today, instead, the stage of specialization is omitted. By "direct conversion," lasers, computers, tracking devices, remote sensors, satellites, and breeders can constitute a formidable arsenal.[11]

The lance, the broadsword, the machine gun, the tank and the fighter plane are clearly designed for warfare. Lasers, computers, herbicides, microwave radiation, meteorology and environmental engineering are not. But all can be used for purposes of warfare or instruments in violent conflict. This possibility was exploited extensively in the sanctions imposed upon Iraq before and after the Gulf War.[12]

---

[10] Elisabeth Mann Borgese, Twilight Zone: Between Peace and War, *The Center Magazine*, Vol. V, No. 6, Nov/Dec 1973, p. 25.

[11] Borgese, "Twilight Zone: Between Peace and War," pp. 25–26.

[12] As Joy Gordon writes, the sole concern of the United States in its dominant role in the application of UN sanctions against Iraq following the Gulf War "was to prevent Iraq from rebuilding its military. The first strategy was simply to bankrupt the nation as a whole to prevent the state from rearming. The second was disarmament, which included a prohibition on 'dual use' goods … Invoking 'dual use' the United States unilaterally blocked goods including child vaccines, water tankers during a period of drought, cloth, the generator needed to run a sewage treatment plan, radios for ambulances—any

War in the twenty-first century is also being transformed by so-called humanitarian intervention, the struggle against terrorism, and the promotion of democracy through regime change. In none of these cases is the idea of war, in its standard sense, forged over centuries, readily applicable. In each case, the use of violence assumes a different form from the classic idea of war. In the case of humanitarian intervention and forcible regime change, the violence conforms more or less to the tactics of conventional warfare. But in the case of terrorism, it involves a multifaceted combination of military violence, covert operations, surveillance, high-tech robotics—asymmetric or irregular war as it is called—with a nation state on one side, a decentralized, loosely organized network of individuals and groups on the other. The term asymmetric war has also been used to characterize conflict between a militarily weaker state and a substantially stronger state.[13] Though it was not called such at the time, much of the fighting by North Korea (prior to the introduction of Chinese "volunteers") in the Korean War, and by the Vietcong (prior to the introduction of North Vietnamese regulars) in Vietnam was asymmetric warfare, as were Israel's conflicts with Hamas and Hezbollah. And Iran purportedly has devised naval strategies to offset and neutralize America's superior military power in any conflict in the Persian Gulf.[14] Speed, mobility and swarming tactics by small units on land and sea are among the features of asymmetric warfare on the weaker side. Since the military power of the stronger state cannot be defeated in a head-on confrontation, the aim is to engage that power in ways that maximize the cost to the stronger state in economic and political terms.

Asymmetric war departs from the standard conception of war between states.[15] That standard conception of war gave way after the 1980s.[16] Some find encouragement in this. Indeed, noting that standard, interstate wars appear to be in decline (with the notable exception of the Iran/Iraq War, the Gulf War and the Iraq War there were no major interstate wars between the end of World War II (WWII) and the second decade of the twenty-first century), they feel that wars are becoming obsolete.[17] This,

goods that could even conceivably be used by the military, for any possible purpose." See Joy Gordon, *The Invisible War: The United States and the Iraq Sanctions* (Cambridge: Harvard University Press, 2010), p. 4.

[13] China reportedly is making preparations for such possible conflict with the United States. Their 1999 publication, *Unrestricted Warfare*, reportedly contains a "blueprint for how weaker countries can outmaneuver status quo powers using weapons and tactics that fall outside the traditional military spectrum." See Richard A. Clarke and Robert K. Knake, *Cyber War: The Next Threat to National Security and What to Do about It* (New York: HarperCollins Publishers, 2010), p. 50.

[14] See Jeremy Binnie, "Revolutionary Navy: Iran's Asymmetric Maritime Threat," *Jane's Defense Weekly*, Vol. 50, Issue 6, February 6, 2013, pp. 34–40.

[15] On the face of it, the just war theory might seem to be irrelevant to asymmetric war. For a revision of just war theory to take account of asymmetric, or irregular, warfare, see Nicholas Fotion, *War and Ethics: A New Just War Theory* (New York: Continuum, 2007).

[16] It was observed during the 1980s that "the assumption that only legally constituted states can make war, and that they do so for rational ends, is fundamental to the western view of war, and consequently to western foreign policy and western military organization, strategy and thought." Robert B. Killebrew, "The Role of Ground Forces in Conflict Termination," in Stephen J. Cimbala and Keith A. Dunn (eds) *Conflict Termination and Military Strategy: Coercion, Persuasion, and War* (Boulder, CO: Westview Press, 1987), p. 126.

[17] See, for example, John Mueller, *Retreat from Doomsday: The Obsolescence of War* (New York: Basic Books, 1989) and more recently, Steven Pinker, *The Better Angels of Our Nature: Why Violence Has Declined* (New York: Viking, 2011).

they contend, is a sign of progress. Perhaps. But we should be cautious on two counts. As far back as 1838, Emerson said much the same thing. He wrote that "as all history is the picture of war … so it is no less true that it is the record of the mitigation and decline of war."[18] At that time the most recent American war was the relatively minor War of 1812, which had few casualties and was sufficiently indecisive that it is unclear who even won it. Europe, moreover, was in the midst of a fifty-year absence of war following Napoleon's defeat at Waterloo. Not long after Emerson's optimistic judgment there followed the War with Mexico, the American Civil War, the Crimean War, the Prussian War with Austria, the Franco Prussian War, the Spanish American War, the two Balkan Wars, World Wars I and II, and more recently the Korean War, the Vietnam War, the Gulf War and the wars in Iraq and Afghanistan, to mention only some of the more noteworthy Western wars that took place. When viewing the world in broad historical terms, it is not easy to be sure that the absence of this or that phenomenon over a limited time frame is adequate evidence of a long-term trend. It may be that interstate war is a thing of the past, but it is difficult to be confident of that claim. The same is true of such claims as, democracies do not wage war against one another. The frame of history that is cited as evidence for them is too brief. The other cautionary note is that, even if it should prove true that standard wars are in decline, it does not follow that *warfare*—the systematic use of military violence—is in decline. The global arms trade and the speed of travel and communication, combined with the flourishing mercenary industry (so-called private contractors) have increased the potential for permanent warfare.

1.5 Cyberwar and robotics

Complicating matters further, the growing prospect of cyberwar and the use of robotics, particularly in the form of Unmanned Aerial Vehicles (UAVs),[19] threaten to change the face of even non-nuclear war dramatically. One might even speak of "cyberbotic" warfare on the horizon, to signify the component of future wars that will rely heavily upon information technology, robotics and bio-radiological weapons.[20] Already there has been a cyberattack on Estonia in 2007, the source of which has not been established but which some Estonians believe came from within Russia. The 2007 cyberattack on Estonia illustrated the power of botnets, a robotic network of computers (so-called zombies) that are under remote control.[21] When Russian tanks rolled into Georgia in 2008, their

---

[18] Ralph Waldo Emerson in a lecture in Boston entitled, "War," reprinted in "Aesthetic Papers," ed. E. P. Peabody in 1849 and in Ralph Waldo Emerson, *Miscellanies* (Boston, MA: Houghton, Mifflin and Company, 1885). The quote is from the latter, p. 185.

[19] It is estimated that the United States has more than 7,000 UAVs, with more in the production line, including new versions of the Predator and Reaper.

[20] A new rail gun is being tested that would use electromagnetic force to fire projectiles at previously unsurpassed speeds. Richard Scott writes that the "US Navy sees the high-energy EM railgun as a transformational weapon system that could revolutionize naval strike operations by delivering hypervelocity projectiles with pinpoint accuracy over extended ranges." *Jane's Defense Weekly*, Vol. 49, Issue 07, February 15, 2012, p. 8.

[21] See Clarke and Knake, *Cyber War*, p. 14.

advance was reportedly "greatly eased by cyberattacks on Tblisi's command, control, and communications systems, which were swiftly and nearly completely disrupted."[22] China is already alleged to be engaging in cyberwarfare.[23] Perhaps most significant was the assault by the malicious software program Stuxnet on Iran's nuclear facility in 2009, which reportedly involved the infection of 100,000 computers throughout the world. Israel and the United States are assumed to be responsible for the attack, which signals a potential for military grade cyberweapons.[24] Accordingly, terms like "logic bombs" are entering into the nomenclature. The United States established a US Cyber Command in 2009, and NATO has taken steps to detect cyber threats at NATO sites in twenty-eight countries. Actions through cyberspace differ from the use of the kinetic force of standard military violence, in that they are nonlethal in themselves. But they are capable of interrupting or destroying power, water and chemical facilities and causing mass casualties. Such hostile attacks, however, need not be by a government or on behalf of a government. Hackers, building upon the knowledge gained from the discovery of the Stuxnet worm, can do so. And if they cannot be identified or located, the concept of deterrence becomes irrelevant. It has been pointed out that "the most sophisticated cyberattacks, like Stuxnet, rarely leave clear fingerprints … But the concept of deterrence depends on the threat of certain retaliation that would cause a rational attacker to think twice. So if the attacker can't be found, then the certainty of retaliation dissolves."[25] Predictably, in light of these accounts, various and sometimes inconsistent definitions of cyberwarfare are emerging.[26]

---

[22] John Arquilla, 'Cyberwar Is Already upon Us,' *Foreign Policy*, 192, March/April 2012, p. 85. Arquilla and David Ronfeldt reportedly were the first to warn of cyberwar in a 1993 Rand paper.

[23] 'Equally disturbing is the aggressive cyberwarfare undertaken by China's intelligence services to steal technical data and other information that has national security value.' *Jane's Defense Weekly*, Vol. 40, Issue 10, 7 March 2012, p. 6.

[24] Iran reportedly has retaliated for the attacks with cyberattacks of its own against US banks, according to a document written in 2013 by the head of the National Security Agency, General Keith B. Alexander, but not released until 2015. According to the *Times* account, 'for the first time, the surveillance agency acknowledged that its attacks on Iran's nuclear infrastructure, a George W. Bush administration program, kicked off the cycle of retaliation and escalation that has come to mark the computer competition between the United States and Iran'. *The New York Times*, February 23, 2015. Kaspersky Labs reportedly detected in 2015 a cyber espionage operation, called the Equation Group, that is significantly more sophisticated than Stuxnet and has infected computers in more than thirty countries.

[25] David E. Hoffman, "The New Virology: The Future of War by Other Means," *Foreign Policy*, 185, March-April 2011, p. 78.

[26] Cyberwarfare has been defined as "the unauthorized penetration by, on behalf or, or in support of, a government into another nation's computer or network, or any other activity affecting a computer system, in which the purpose is to add, alter, or falsify data, or cause the disruption of or damage to a computer, or network device, or the objects a computer system controls." Clarke and Knake, *Cyber War*, p. 228. Similar definitions have been proposed of so-called information warfare, which has been called "a generic term that refers to hostile attack against the important information technology systems and networks of a nation (as compared to a criminal act) that is intended to damage that nation and actions taken to defend these information technology systems and networks." Herbert Lin, "Policy Consequences and Legal/Ethical Implications of Offensive Information Operations and Cyberattack." Computer Science and Telecommunications Board, The National Research Council of the National Academy of Sciences, February 17, 2006, p. 1. Lin defines offensive information warfare more specifically as "the application of digital force against military or civilian information assets and systems, against computers and networks which support the air traffic control systems, stock transactions, financial records, currency exchanges, internet communications, telephone switching, credit record, credit card transactions, the space program, the railroad system, the hospital systems that monitor patients and dispense drugs, manufacturing process control systems, newspaper and publishing, the insurance industry, power distribution and utilities, all of which rely heavily on computers."

Although there is a potential for nonlethal weapons as well as lethal cyberbotic weapons,[27] it is the destructive potential that will almost certainly be paramount. The line between civilians and combatants will become blurred because civilians can readily be trained to operate UAVs. A few people can enter a control booth in the morning, direct drones in the killing of persons thousands of miles away, then return home to their families in the evening.[28] To wage war they no longer need to march off to distant lands, separated from parents, children and loved ones. The killing becomes sanitized. Whatever natural reluctance the ordinary person has to killing other human beings is much more readily overcome than if it were done face to face. The familiarity and acceptance of video games transfers readily to weapons systems.[29] Many civilians, heavily armed and trained in the use of weaponry, serve in war zones as private contractors. If cyberbotic warfare emanates from the heartland of America, one can predict that those who are fighting against cyberbotic warfare will come to consider such installations legitimate military targets.[30]

1.6 Toward an ontology of war

As a systematic analysis of the morality of war presupposes an ontology of war, let me explain what I mean by war. It is instructive to begin by looking at the range of considerations different definitions of war highlight:

> "War is the State or Situation of those … who dispute by Force of Arms."[31] (Grotius)
> War is "a just and public contest of arms."[32] (Gentili)

[27] "For some strange reason, a few people have concerns about super-smart robots carrying machine guns that can shred entire buildings. Many believe that if a robot is going to have a weapon, it should be a nonlethal one." P. W. Singer, *Wired for War: The Robotics Revolution and Conflict in the 21st Century* (New York: Penguin Books, 2010), p. 83. Ralph Langer, the security expert who detected the Stuxnet worm, has said of Stuxnet: "It's certainly going to change the world. It already has in ways that not many people would recognize. The bottom line is that now we have a much better idea of what the future of war will look like—and what it would look like if certain military systems were a primary target." He claims that the Stuxnet worm could be considered a classic "just war" approach, since it did not kill anyone. Mark Clayton, "Warning of a New Kind of War," *The Christian Science Monitor*, October 17, 2011, p. 18.

[28] As one Predator squadron commander is quoted as saying, "You are going to war for twelve hours, shooting weapons at targets, directing kills on enemy combatants, and then you get in the car, drive home, and within twenty minutes you are sitting at the dinner table talking to your kids about their homework." Singer, *Wired for War*, p. 347.

[29] P. W. Singer writes: "While video games are widely derided as a waste of time, they are actually incredibly influential, both in the economy and in the way they shape the soldiers of today and tomorrow … The result is that while the younger enlisted troops are taking over more roles through robotics, they aren't coming into the military completely unprepared. Rather, argues one U.S. military journal, 'The Army will draw on a generation of mind-nimble (not necessarily literate), finger-quick youth and their years of experience as heroes and killers in violent, virtually real interactive videos.'" *Wired for War*, p. 365.

[30] Thomas Rid is skeptical of any realistic prospect of cyberwar, partly on factual grounds and partly on conceptual grounds. He writes: "Indeed, there is no known cyberattack that has caused the loss of human life. No cyberoffense has ever injured a person or damaged a building. And if an act is not as least potentially violent, it's not an act of war." "Think again: Cyberwar," *Foreign Policy*, 192, March/April 2012, p. 81.

[31] Hugo Grotius, *The Rights of War and Peace*, Book I, ed. Richard Tuck (Indianapolis, IN: liberty Fund, 2005), p. 134.

[32] Alberico Gentili, *De Jure Belli: Libri Tres*, in *The Classics of International Law*, ed. James Brown Scott, trans. John C. Rolfe (Oxford, UK: Clarendon Press, 1933), p. 31.

"[T]he nature of war consisteth not in actual fighting, but in the known disposition thereto during all the time there is no assurance to the contrary."[33] (Hobbes)

"War is … an act of force to compel our opponent to do our will."[34] (Clausewitz)

War is "a state of armed hostility between sovereign nations or governments."[35] (Lieber)

War is "the expression of a difference of opinion … THE OBJECT OF WAR IS TO CHANGE THE ENEMY'S MIND."[36] (King-Hall)

War is "a legal condition which equally permits two or more hostile groups to carry on a conflict by armed force."[37] (Wright)

War is "the use of proportionate and discriminate armed force by legitimate public authority in order to secure certain worthy public goods."[38] (Weigel)

"War is a situation or process of openly hostile (and generally armed) struggle between two or more organized groups whose premeditated intention is to inflict damage and/or death upon each other's members and destroy each other's territory in the interest of achieving a desired end."[39] (Fox)

When we add expressions such as "war on poverty," "war on crime," "war on drugs," we see that the term "war" admits of many uses. Some are fairly standard, such as those in the quotes from Lieber and Wright. It is war in the standard sense that I have argued has been transcended at one extreme by the prospect of nuclear war and at the other by the open-ended campaign against terrorism. Others are nonstandard, such as those by Hobbes and King-Hall. Gentili defines war in a normative way, as a just contest, as does Weigel who does not count something as war unless it is intended to secure "worthy public goods." Wright, on the other hand, defines war as a legal condition. The uses in expressions like "war on poverty" and "war on drugs" are clearly metaphorical. One of the controversial issues that arose after 9/11 was whether the so-called War on Terrorism was literally a war, as many of its proponents seemed to want it to be, or simply a metaphorical use of the term to signify a major, concerted effort to defeat terrorism. In one sense, it is of little consequence how war is defined. If one is clear about all of the factual, legal and moral issues surrounding it, then the definition reduces to a linguistic matter. But it is of considerable consequence how war is defined when different definitions are used to justify actions that otherwise would be considered unjustified. If, for example, war is a condition holding among states, and al-Qaeda is not a state, then the so-called War on Terror (initially directed mainly against al-Qaeda but now including the Islamic State and its affiliates) is not literally a war, and Osama bin Laden was not literally a combatant. But if the War on Terror is taken

---

[33] Thomas Hobbes, *Leviathan*, ed. Michael Oakeshott (New York: Collier Books, 1966), p. 100.

[34] Clausewitz, *On War*, p. 75.

[35] Francis Lieber, cited in William W. Bishop, Jr., *International Law: Cases and Materials*, 3rd ed., (Boston: Little, Brown and Company, 1962), pp. 947f.

[36] Stephen King-Hall, *Defense in the Nuclear Age* (Nyack, NY: Fellowship Publications, 1959), p. 23.

[37] Quincy Wright, *A Study of War*, 2nd ed. (Chicago: University of Chicago Press, 1965), p. 8.

[38] George Weigel, *Against the Grain: Christianity and Democracy, War and Peace* (New York: The Crossroad Publishing Company, 2008), p. 233.

[39] Fox, *Understanding Peace*, p. 4.

literally to be a war, and if bin Laden was properly understood to be an enemy soldier, and Pakistan and Afghanistan, or perhaps even the whole world, were combat zones, then his killing in 2011 arguably was an act of war and (it is commonly supposed) therefore permissible, at least legally.[40] Definitions of war that include moral, political or legal evaluations that divide advocates and opponents on the many issues war raises are persuasive definitions. They attempt to resolve the normative issues raised by war (whether, e.g., it is legal or morally permissible) by definition rather than by argument.

The practical implications are important, however, when it comes to legally defining war. The Vietnam War was not a declared war, nor was the Korean War before it.[41] If one conceives of wars as conflicts that are formally declared by recognized state authorities, then there have been no wars since World War II and may never be again.[42] Indeed, there may have been relatively few such wars in history.[43] While philosophically this may be of little consequence, and to the average person it may seem to be "just semantics," the practical effects are significant. While the legal issues involved in war are not my primary concern, it is worth noting that they arise in both domestic and international law. I shall discuss some of the issues in international law in connection with the Gulf War and the intervention in Kosovo, insofar as they relate to the moral issues that are my primary concern. For the present I shall only note that the domestic issues generated by the Vietnam War posed a threat to democratic rule in the United States. The war gave rise to the War Powers Resolution (WPR), often referred to as the War Powers Act because it has the force of law. I shall only touch upon the main features of the Resolution. In seeking to limit the extension of presidential war powers with regard to the use of military force, Congress passed on November 7, 1973 the WPR requiring that the president either seek to declare war or seek congressional approval before sending troops into hostilities—except in the case of a national emergency created by an attack upon the United States, in which case the president could unilaterally commit troops provided he report to Congress within 48 hours, detailing the circumstances, the constitutional and legislative authority for the action, and the expected scope and duration of the hostilities. The president is required to withdraw the troops within 60 days unless receiving authorization for the deployment from Congress. Since then, US presidents have sent troops into hostilities (or used military force, such as air power, missiles or drones that do not always necessitate ground troops) in Vietnam (1975), Iran (1980), El Salvador (1981), Lebanon (1982–83), Honduras (1983),Grenada (1983),

---

[40] As the *New York Times* editorialized on May 17, 2011, a new bill in Congress, within days of the killing of Osama bin Laden, would "expand, rather than contract, the war on terror" and "authorize the military to pursue virtually anyone suspected of terrorism, anywhere on earth, from now to the end of time. This wildly expansive authorization would, in essence, make the war on terror a permanent and limitless aspect of life on earth, along with its huge potential for abuse."

[41] The Korean War was considered a "police action" by the UN. The Vietnam War, as we shall see in Chapter 8, metamorphosed gradually into war, as financial backing, military aid, advisors and finally combat troops serving supposedly defensive roles led eventually to a full combat role for the United States.

[42] North Korea declared itself to be in a state of war with South Korea in 2013 but did not commence warfare thereupon.

[43] Gerhard von Glahn reports that between 1700 and 1870 a total of 107 conflicts took place without a declaration of war. See his *Law among Nations*, 2nd ed. (New York: Collier-Macmillan limited, 1970), p. 559.

Libya (1986), Persian Gulf (1987), Panama (1989), Somalia (1992), Haiti (1993), Libya (2010), Eastern Africa (2010). In 2015 President Obama indicated that he would seek authorization to fight the Islamic State of Syria and Iraq (ISIS), including associated forces, without geographical limits.[44] As I say, I am leaving aside for the moment the Gulf and Iraq wars[45] and the Kosovo intervention, which I shall discuss in greater detail later.

The issues regarding the definition of war arose in connection with the 1993 deployment of US troops in Somalia, which was done without congressional authorization. The Office of Legal Counsel (OLC) of the Department of Justice advised the president, George H. W. Bush, that the WPR was irrelevant, because the United States was supporting the provision of humanitarian aid (which had been authorized by the UN), and that this mission would not involve military action other than in self-defense or maintaining safe corridors for the provision of aid. The mission further extended the notion of national interest to include protecting the lives and properties of Americans abroad, defending the lives and property of foreign nationals, maintaining the credibility of UN Security Council decisions, and ensuring the effectiveness of UN peacekeeping operations. In Haiti, Bertrand Aristíde, after being deposed by a military coup in 1991 following his election as president, appealed to the United States to help him reclaim power. As it turned out, the US invasion (Operation Uphold Democracy) did not involve bloodshed. But what is important, again, was the opinion rendered by the OLC, which argued again that the WPR was irrelevant. More specifically, it argued that the invasion of Haiti was not war. "War," it reasoned, "does not exist where United States troops are deployed at the invitation of a *fully legitimate government* in circumstances in which the nature, scope, and duration of the deployment are such that the use of force involved *does not rise to the level of 'war.'* "[46] They seem to have quantitative as well as qualitative criteria for the definition of war in mind. And they note that force had been used unilaterally by presidents in the past.

While Congress sought to structure and regulate such unilateral deployments, its overriding interest was to prevent the United States from being engaged, without express congressional authorization, in major, prolonged conflicts such as the wars in Vietnam and Korea, rather than to prohibit the president from using or threatening to use troops to achieve important diplomatic objectives where the risk of sustained military conflict was negligible.

US presidents since the passing of the WPR in 1973 have either rejected its constitutionality or proceeded to use military force as they saw fit with no more than lip-service to the resolution. If one defines war in such a way that it must be declared between states, then if a president uses military power without such a declaration such uses do not constitute war. If one then acknowledges that conflicts like Korea and Vietnam constituted wars even though they were undeclared, then one has begun to import other criteria into the definition, such as duration and scope and casualties.

---

[44] *The New York Times*, February 11, 2015.
[45] As I shall argue later, the so-called Gulf War and the Iraq War were in actuality two phases of one war.
[46] The circularity of this claim seems to have eluded the OLC.

But then the waters become muddied. With a little ingenuity, as shown by the OLC opinions, almost any use of force by a president can be represented as falling short of war; and if it does not fall short of war, then some prior action, express or implied, by Congress can be represented as having sanctioned the war. On the other hand, if a president wants to avail himself of the powers of a commander in chief during wartime, then it is to his advantage to represent certain situations as constituting a war, even though they may conspicuously fail to meet the standard criteria of war. The so-called War on Terrorism is a case in point. If the campaign against terrorism is militarized in such a way as to enable one to represent it as a war, then a whole array of actions—from the treatment of prisoners, the definition of combat zones, the definition of "enemy combatant"—become arguably permissible. The concept of war can then be expanded or contracted to suit the aims of the president. Increasing power then becomes centralized in the hands of one person. The differences between a democracy and a dictatorship, while they do not disappear, become vanishingly thin where it comes to the use of military power.

In light of these considerations, I want to propose definitions that can be agreed upon by all sides of the moral issues. But this requires sorting out some of the misleading aspects of our language about war.

There is an ambiguity in the notion of war, particularly when people speak of war as being just or unjust. When people speak of a particular war as just they do not mean that the whole war is just. They mean that the warfare on one side is just. So when they say, for example, that World War II was a just war, they do not mean that the entire phenomenon, commencing with Germany's invasion of Poland in 1939 and ending with the surrender of Germany and Japan in 1945, was just. They mean that the participation of the United States and its allies was just. The war as a whole included the participation of Germany and Japan (and their allies), and their participation, in this view, was unjust. Ours was a just war, theirs unjust. But there were not two wars, one just and one unjust. There was only one war. It was (by hypothesis) just in some respects, unjust in others.[47]

Language often obscures this distinction. When we speak of war we sometimes mean war in its entirety. But sometimes we mean a limited aspect of war, such as our participation in it. This second way of speaking makes it easy to think of war as "us" against "them" and to approach the morality of war from the perspective of one side only. When we think of war in this way we are thinking of simply one aspect or, if you

---

[47] Michael Walzer seems comfortable with a proliferation of wars, as when he says: "There isn't one war going on in the Middle East, and there isn't a single opposition of right and wrong, just and unjust. Four Israeli-Palestinian wars are now in progress.

The first is a Palestinian war to destroy the state of Israel.
The second is a Palestinian war to create an independent state alongside Israel…
The third is an Israeli war for the security of Israel within the 1967 borders.
The fourth is an Israeli war for Greater Israel, for the settlements and the occupied territories.
It isn't easy to say which war is being fought at any given moment; in a sense, the four are simultaneous." See Michael Walzer, *Arguing about War* (New Haven and London: Yale University Press, 2005), p. 113. This way of speaking can effectively make certain points, but it is unnecessarily confusing if taken literally.

like, a part of war. I shall call this partial war. To better understand partial war, let me first define warfare:

> *Warfare*: The deliberate, organized and systematic use of force to harm or kill persons.

The force will typically take the form of military violence but may include any form of technology, including cyberspace, robotics and chemical-biological-radiological elements, all of which can be weaponized. It can even include rape and torture, which can be used as weapons of war. Even if many uses of cyberwar are nonlethal in themselves, they are meant to be destructive, hence to cause harm either to individuals or their societies or states. We may now define partial war more specifically as follows:

> *War1* (partial war): Warfare by a collectivity against one or more other collectivities engaged in warfare against it.

By collectivities here and in what follows I do not mean simply collections but groups that have some measure of cohesion and exhibit planning and coordination in their use of destructive power. For our purposes there need not be a sharp delineation among such groups. Nation states clearly qualify, as do some guerrilla bands. Paramilitaries, urban gangs and terror groups might sometimes qualify, although that is more problematic and would require close examination of particular cases. Multinational mercenary companies, euphemistically called "private contractors," almost certainly would qualify.[48] When there are vast disparities among the collectivities involved, we have asymmetric war. But there is the potential for abuse in that term. When there exists a qualifying collectivity (e.g., a state) on one side and a nonqualifying group on the other (such as a smattering of guerrillas or terrorists), the use of the term "war" to characterize such a conflict can be used to justify the full use of military force by the qualifying collectivity in ways that would otherwise be considered unjustified. And it can be used to justify the treatment of individuals suspected of ties with such groups in ways that would otherwise be considered unjustified (as by labeling them "enemy combatants"). It should be understood that according to this definition warfare must be sustained, so as to rule out the occasional skirmishes between states that never rise to an extremely serious level.[49] The use of cyberspace, which can be expected to

---

[48] Although their numbers and global reach is so secretive that it is difficult to establish with certainty, it has been reported that 54,700 such contractors worked for the Defense Department in the Middle East, Pakistan and Afghanistan, with 40,000 in Afghanistan alone. China reportedly engages the services of such contractors in its expanding economic role in Africa. Blackwater, the best known of the groups because of the conviction of four of its former security guards for killing civilians in Iraq, has reportedly been renamed Academi, sold, resold and merged with the Constellis Group. *The New York Times*, April 15, 2015.

[49] In the tensions that surfaced between Pakistan and NATO following the killing of Osama bin Laden, which Pakistan considered a breach of its sovereignty, gunfire was exchanged between NATO and the Pakistan military near the border with Afghanistan. But it was not sustained and no one considered it a war. The frequent military exchanges between India and Pakistan over Kashmir are another example. The conflict between Britain and Argentina over the Falkland Islands in 1982 is a borderline case, which I shall comment upon later.

figure prominently in future wars, may for our purposes be considered either a form of military force or a form of nonmilitary force.

I want to ask whether the whole of war is morally justified—the event in its entirety, comprising the warfare of all of the participants.[50] I shall, for the sake of simplicity, speak here of states, although what I say is meant to cover other collectivities as characterized above. I shall call this whole war,[51] which may be defined as follows:

War2 (whole war): The entirety of a particular occurrence of wars$_1$.

Whole war[52] is the entirety of the warfare waged by collectivities against one another during a particular time frame (such as exemplified by the world wars). Some whole wars are readily individuated in this sense. But some are not, owing to the fact that warfare may continue through transformation of at least some of the collectivities involved. Thus the Gulf War clearly pitted the United States against Iraq, but even after that war ended with the withdrawal of Iraq from Kuwait, warfare against Iraq continued by the United States at a low level until the invasion of Iraq in 2003.[53] The war that commenced with the invasion of Iraq, what is called the Iraq War, ended swiftly, but fighting continued between the United States and various militias until the war was declared ended in 2011. Violence continued, however, and intensified with the emergence of the Islamic State of Iraq and Syria (ISIS) and the use of US air power against it, assisted by that of various other states, including notably Jordan. In any event, whole war in this sense is deliberately undertaken. It represents a choice by two or more collectivities. In the case of states, which I shall focus upon, it represents a choice by those who control military power and have the resources of the collectivities at their command. Once war is underway, the choices and decisions of countless other persons come into play—from the soldiers who pull the triggers on the frontlines to

---

[50] In discussing unjust killing, Cheney Ryan writes that "the more common response is to conclude that a certain amount of unjust killing is permissible if the war as a whole is just, and the unjust killing is inadvertent and incidental to the enterprise." "Democratic Duty and the Moral Dilemmas of Soldiers," *Ethics,* Vol. 122 No. 1, October 2011, p. 25. But he uses "whole war" here to refer to the warfare of one side only, not to the entirety of warfare by all sides. Jeff McMahan recognizes the ambiguity in "War" but says that "[w]ar as the sum of the fighting of all the belligerents can be neither just nor unjust." See Jeff McMahan, *Killing in War* (Oxford: Clarendon Press, 2009), p. 5. This claim is correct given the perspective of just war theory but doubtful if "just" and "unjust" are taken as equivalent to morally permissible and impermissible. My contention is that whole war can be morally assessed as right or wrong, even though that mode of assessment stands outside of the just war theoretic framework.

[51] Clausewitz makes clear that at times this is his concern, as when he says at the outset of Book Eight of *On War*: "the chapters that follow will deal with the problem of war as a whole" (p. 577). Michael Walzer, in his original preface to *Just and Unjust Wars: A Moral Argument with Historical Illustrations*, 4th ed. (New York: Basic Books, 2006), says that he "did not begin by thinking about war in general, but about particular wars, above all about the American intervention in Vietnam" (p. xix), but most of his discussion centers around the perspective of what I am calling partial wars.

[52] One might speak instead of total war, but that term is often used to designate unlimited warfare that draws upon all of the military and nonmilitary resources of a country. Whole war may not be total war$_1$ in this narrower sense.

[53] I am ignoring here the fact that coalitions were put together by the United States in these undertakings and that, at least on the face of it, these were cooperative undertakings on the US side, even though the preponderance of military action was by the United States.

workers in the munitions factories back home—in support of a massive effort to prevail by inflicting death and destruction on adversaries. Any particular War_1 is always part of a War_2.

1.7 Paradoxes of war

Paradoxically, whole war in this sense is a cooperative undertaking.[54] When two nations go to war, they have agreed—expressly, if they declare war, tacitly if they simply begin fighting—to try to resolve their differences by warfare. In this sense, war is the ultimate form of conflict resolution. *War cannot take place if either side refuses to cooperate with the other in this way.*[55] The paradigm of this type of situation is a duel, in which both parties explicitly agree to deal with a perceived offense by a formalized manner of trying to kill one another. If one party does not challenge the other or the challenge is not accepted, a duel cannot take place. Although wars (by which I shall mean whole wars in the sense indicated) are sometimes attended by declarations of war, most of them are not and probably will not be in the future. But they are all, by the very nature of war, cooperative undertakings.[56]

I am speaking of war in a philosophical and moral sense. Legally, it is sometimes supposed that an act of war can give rise to a state of war without being regarded by both states as so doing. The use of force might fail to give rise even to a state of war if neither side regards it as an act of war:

> If there is no declaration [of war], the state of war is regarded as commencing with the commission of the first act of force by a state with the intention of making war, or with the first such act of force committed without intent to make war but which is regarded as an act of war by the state against which it is directed. Thus, war may begin by formal declaration or by ultimatum which is not complied with or by acts of force which either party regards as constituting war.[57]

---

[54] War_1 presupposes that at least one other collectivity is engaged in warfare against it. But war_1 does not include the war_1 of another collectivity. War_1, is part of a larger whole, namely war_2, but can also be considered a whole in itself.

[55] As Julien Lider notes: "To be war, military action must be taken by both sides. A one-sided employment of military force is not enough to constitute war, for it may occur when the attacked object is unable or unwilling to resist." *The Nature of War* (Saxon House, UK: Swedish Institute of International Affairs, 1979), p. 187. By analogy, what each boxer does – considered in the abstract – does not constitute a boxing match. It is simply one part of the match. A boxer engaged in shadow boxing could throw exactly the same punches without an adversary. A boxing match occurs only if both sides willingly engage in fighting.

[56] Sometimes the ending of war is a cooperative undertaking as well, if both sides agree to an armistice or sign a peace treaty. But it need not be. One side can unilaterally end a war by surrendering or simply ceasing to fight. If it does so, it might then be occupied, enslaved or in the worst case annihilated. It might also become the beneficiary of reconstruction so that it emerges better than ever fifty years later, as with Germany and Japan following WWII. It takes two to start a war but only one to end it. For philosophical discussions of this topic, see "Symposium on Ending Wars," *Ethics*, Vol. 125, No. 3, April 2015.

[57] Editorial Note, *International Law: Cases and Materials*, 3rd ed., ed. William J. Bishop, Jr. (Boston, MA: Little, Brown and Company, 1962), p. 948.

But this understanding is at variance with others, which define an act of war as "an action by one country against another with an intention to provoke a war or an action that occurs during a declared war or armed conflict between military forces of any origin."[58] According to the first view, an act of force is equated with an act of war. But an act of force might fail to give rise to a state of war if neither party regards it as an act of war.

Further complicating matters is the possibility that a state of war might exist between two states but no warfare exist between them. Theoretically, two states might declare war against one another, and thereby bring into existence a state of war, but terminate the state of war peacefully before actually coming to blows. The so-called Phony War bore at least some of the marks of the distinction between a state of war and actual war (involving warfare) when England and France declared war on Germany in September of 1939 after Germany attacked Poland, but serious hostilities (at least on land, not on sea) did not begin until the following spring. During that time, of course, the countries were preparing for full-scale war, and it commenced seven months after the declarations. North Korea and South Korea fought a war but remain in a state of war, reaffirmed by North Korea in 2013, more than fifty years after the active warfare ceased.

Be that as it may, a state of war is a legal condition, and our concern is with the moral issues. But the different understandings of the notion of an act of war highlight the importance of distinguishing between aggression and war. Aggression, even with the intent to initiate a war, fails to initiate a war if the party aggressed against does not respond in kind. Even if the aggression constitutes a *casus belli*, and legally the state aggressed against has the right to wage war, if that right is not exercised, war does not occur.

There are further paradoxical consequences. If one country attacks another and a war ensues, common sense would say that the country that launched the attack started the war. From the standpoint of ordinary language this makes sense. But strictly speaking it is not true. The attacking country has committed aggression. But aggression, even though legally an act of war, does not constitute war. Aggression is transformed into war only if the country aggressed against fights back militarily.[59] What is further paradoxical is that, strictly speaking, it is the country that responds militarily that initiates the war, not the country that committed the aggression. War comes into existence the moment the country aggressed against fights back and not before.[60]

---

[58] http://definitions.uslegal.com/a/act-of-war. See U.S. Code, Title 18>Chapter 1138> 2331. The quotation in the text apparently intends "acts of force" to be synonymous with "acts of war." But an act of force might fail to give rise even to a state of war if neither side regards it as so doing.

[59] Clausewitz in effect recognizes this when he says: "It is only aggression that calls forth defense, and war along with it." *On War*, p. 370.

[60] Equally paradoxical is the fact that is the person who strikes back who initiates a fight, not the person who throws the first punch. An assault does not constitute a fight. It takes two to fight. This fact is not merely of conceptual interest but plays a central role in the moral psychology of nonviolence. As Richard Gregg puts it, "between two persons in physically violent combat there may appear to be complete disagreement, but in reality they conduct their fight on the basis of a strong fundamental agreement that violence is a sound mode of procedure." Richard B. Gregg, *The Power of Nonviolence* (Nyack, NY: Fellowship Publications, 1959), p. 44.

Another paradoxical consequence is that (if we assume for the sake of argument that there may be just wars) every just war brings into existence an unjust war. A whole war cannot be just in its entirety. What confers justice on one side entails injustice on the other. If one side has a just cause, it is because the other has committed a wrong that vitiates any claim it might make to a just cause on balance.[61] A war can be unjust in its entirety; there can be wrongdoing all around. But it cannot be just in its entirety.[62] One side can have justice on its side only if the other side has committed a wrong that gives the first a just cause.[63] In the just war tradition it is generally assumed that the wrong must have been committed against the state having the just cause. In more recent years, it is often assumed the wrong may have been committed against others who have no particular connection with the state claiming the just cause. It is the interest that a state has in the rights or well-being of those others, whether they be individuals or states, that is thought to give it a just cause.[64] In any event, when just war advocates speak of *jus ad bellum*, they are actually dealing with the conditions under which a state is justified in initiating warfare against a state that is either already engaged in warfare against it (as in the case of aggression) or can be expected to commence such warfare with the initiation of its own warfare. Part of what one does by commencing warfare—even assuming that one does so justly—is to bring into existence an unjust (partial) war, and with it all of the wrongful killing such a war entails. If one does not go to war justly, then the unjust partial war one brings into existence is one's own; if one does so justly, then the unjust war is one's opponent's.

Thus every whole war is either unjust in its entirety or unjust in part. That is, warfare is at best just only as waged by some of its participants. This means that just wars can exist only if unjust wars exist. Every just war presupposes an unjust war.

Not only does a state fighting a just war (still on the assumption that there are such wars) bring into existence an unjust war when it goes to war, it also helps bring into existence a whole war. The war-fighting by the just side is an essential part of that whole. The police can be justified in pursuing a suspect at high speed only if the resultant high-speed chase is justified. And that chase is something both the police and the suspect choose to engage in; they create the chase. Similarly, war is something two sides choose to engage in. Bringing a whole war into existence must be justified

---

[61] It is sometimes said by just war theorists that there may be comparative justice in war, and that before going to war a state must consider what measure of justice may lie on the other side. This may be granted. The issue of weighty but nondecisive moral considerations will come up in the next chapter in connection with the alleged inescapability of wrongdoing. The point here is that all of the conditions making for justice on the whole cannot intelligibly be met on both sides.

[62] While both sides in war frequently believe they are acting justly, they cannot both be correct, even if they should both have grounds for believing they are correct. Just war theorists like Grotius distinguish different senses of justice, allowing that in some of those senses (e.g., ignorance that what one is doing is unjust) both sides may justly go to war even though their actions considered apart from the situation of the agents who perform them cannot both be just. See Hugo Grotius, *The Rights of War and Peace*, Book II.

[63] James Turner Johnson, for example, says in discussing just war concepts that "for a just cause to exist, the purpose of war must be to redress in some way a wrong done by the enemy." *Can Modern War Be Just?* (New Haven, CT: Yale University Press, 1984), p. 20.

[64] Jeff McMahan includes in the notion of a just cause that "those against whom the war is fought have made themselves morally *liable* to military attack," where what makes one liable is not limited to a wrong against the state having the just cause. See *Killing in War*, p. 5.

by the side whose participation represents a just (partial) war. More specifically, the partial war represented by the participation of the side that has the just cause can be just only if the war in its entirety that is brought about by that side's collaboration with its adversary is justified.

1.8 War, warfare and warmaking

A just war also presupposes the justifiability of warmaking. By warmaking I mean not only the fighting of wars, but also the creation and maintenance of a war system. A war system comprises the constellation of social, political, economic, religious and ethical practices and values necessary to being able to wage war effectively.[65] The recruitment and training of youths, the financing of the military, the design and production of armaments, the teaching of military values in schools, colleges and military academies, the trade in armaments to other countries all are part of the war systems of modern states. In this sense, warmaking is an integral part of virtually all modern states. Armies, tanks, planes, missiles, battleships—the elements of warfare—do not materialize overnight when a country decides to go to war. They are the product of a collective effort over a long period of time.[66] By analogy again, the police can effectively engage in high-speed car chases only if they are trained and have well-equipped cars at their command. They can be justified in engaging in such chases only if it is justifiable for others to train them, still others to provide and maintain such cars and for still others to maintain a system of law enforcement that authorizes them to engage in such chases. For just wars to exist, not only must the whole wars they create be justified, the warmaking that creates and maintains the war systems that make whole wars possible must also be justified.

   In deference to the just war tradition, as well as to fairly well-established linguistic practice, I shall sometimes speak of wars as being just or unjust. But it should be understood, that in so doing (except where I am talking specifically about the just war theory) I am using just and unjust as synonyms for right and wrong and not elevating justice to a privileged position in the moral assessment of war—a substantive

---

[65] Andrew Alexandra puts much the same point in his discussion of the institutionalization of war: "[W]ar as a political institution consists not simply of episodes of armed conflict between states and the rules and norms governing such conflicts, but also the whole complex of activities and organization that lead up to and make possible such episodes." Andrew Alexandra, "Political Pacifism," *Social Theory and Practice*, Vol. 29, No. 4, October 2003, p. 594.

[66] This process arguably has transformed America into a warfare state. As Paul Koistinen writes: "Once military spending began to escalate rapidly from 1950 onward, the nation simply lacked the policies, the institutional structures, the traditions, and the experience for controlling its war machine. The voice of the armed services would grow in the formulation of foreign policy, the military's influence would become pervasive throughout society, and various industries, whole communities, and entire regions would become economically dependent upon military spending for their prosperity … Once that occurred, America would become a warfare state." See Paul Koistinen, "Toward a Warfare State: Militarization in America during the Period of the World Wars," ed. John R. Gillis, *Militarization of the Western World* (New Brunswick, NJ: Rutgers University Press, 1989), p. 64. For a more recent examination of the influence of WWII specifically in this transformation, see James T. Sparrow, *Warfare State: World War II Americans and the Age of Big Government* (Oxford: Oxford University Press, 2011).

philosophical issue we shall take up later. I shall also, for the present, disregard differences between asking whether some wars are justified and asking whether some wars are just or right.[67]

1.9 Synoptic war

Finally, in addition to partial war and whole war it is important to recognize what I shall call synoptic war. By synoptic war I mean not only all of the fighting and killing on all sides but also the totality of the bravery, heroism, patriotism, profit, glory, pride, propaganda, deception, lies, fear, pain, rape, suffering, depression, death, despair and grief that war occasions, as well as the psychological and physical harms inflicted in the way of post-traumatic stress disorder (PTSD), domestic violence, drug and alcohol abuse and suicide that would not have occurred but for the war. The outcomes of synoptic war include all the deaths resulting from the war: those from starvation, disease,[68] the elements, deaths of the unborn, animals and the "moral injury" suffered by survivors. These are among the casualties of war, even if they are not all the result of killing. They are on balance unquantifiable with any certainty. Although the positive elements are frequently brought to bear on the side of the benefits of war—and they are considerable in the areas of medical and technological advances—the negative elements are rarely reckoned among the costs of war. Synoptic war, unlike partial war and whole war, in itself is neither right nor wrong. Right and wrong apply only to actions, practices or policies of rational beings,[69] and although synoptic war includes the actions and practices of rational beings, it is not itself the action of a rational being. It is a complex phenomenon supervening upon the actions of rational agents but also upon psychological states, physical events and often vast social and political movements over a period of years, and encompasses death and destruction, sometimes of tens of millions of people, and the destruction of whole cities. It is likely that this is something Tolstoy had in mind when he represented war in *War and Peace* as beyond human control. It is a perspective that invites comparison of war with natural disasters, a view that has aptly been called a cataclysmic philosophy of war.[70] But if synoptic wars are neither right nor wrong, just nor unjust, as I shall argue in Chapter 2, the notions of right and wrong apply fully to the actions and practices of the multitudes of persons who cooperatively engage in partial and whole wars. Part of what must be reckoned in assessing the morality of what they do is the nature of what they produce in the form of whole war and synoptic war. Many of the characteristics of synoptic war

---

[67] I shall understand "right or "permissible" to mean, at the minimum "not wrong." Accordingly I shall understand "obligatory" to mean "wrong not to do."

[68] The largest number of deaths in any of America's wars occurred during the Civil War, but more than half of those deaths were from disease.

[69] While the concepts of just and unjust do not apply to synoptic war when they are used synonymously with right and wrong, they may apply in a broader sense to whole societies or communities. When we speak of just and unjust societies, the terms just and unjust represent pervasive qualities of collectivities rather than properties of specific actions.

[70] See Anatol Rapaport's introduction to *Carl Von Clausewitz On War*.

are inherent in whole war, as we shall see in Chapters 2 and 11. Even if right and wrong do not apply to synoptic war, value concepts do. Synoptic war is good or bad in varying degrees, its value determined by the value of its constituent parts. Warfare nests inside of war_1 and war_1 inside of war_2. All three nest inside synoptic war.

1.10 Conclusion

In sum, a just war presupposes an unjust war. Two or more partial wars, just or unjust, make up a whole war. That whole war must be justified in order for participants in it to be justified in waging warfare. Leaving aside the just war perspective, we can make the same point by saying that a permissible (partial) war presupposes and helps bring into existence a wrongful (partial) war. And in order to be justified in so doing, the whole war it thereby helps create must be justified.

Thus, to say that some wars are permissible is to say that some whole wars are justified.[71] And that is to say that the world is *morally better* with them than without, that there is no available alternative that would be morally preferable. And it means further that the warmaking that renders whole wars possible is justified. There cannot be wars (by which I mean modern wars) in the absence of warmaking, which includes, as we have seen, the maintenance of war systems. For warmaking to be justified, that justification must be consistent with the possibility that sometimes it will lead to whole wars which are thoroughly wrong. So, for there to be just wars, that is, for some partial wars to be just, the world must be better with whole wars than without, even though some of them will be unjust in their entirety and the best of them will be unjust in part; and all of them will be part of synoptic wars, which, while they will be neither just nor unjust in themselves, will be either good or bad on balance.

This way of conceptualizing war, roots the moral issues in the organized use of violence (or the threat thereof) to harm, kill and cause destruction as a means to one's ends. The question of the definition of war, though it still has practical and legal importance, and some philosophical interest, is in the end of secondary importance morally. The use of violence that rises to the level of warfare is essential to war but not limited to war. So if one were to understand the War Powers Resolution as limiting the president's ability unilaterally to engage in warfare, then it would matter little whether the cases in which he does so represent war in a standard sense. What would be prohibited (with the stated qualifications) would be warfare, whether or not it eventuates in war (either war_1 or war_2). In what follows I shall, for the most part, so as to remain within the general context of contemporary discussions, focus upon the question of whether war is justified. It should be understood, however, that I see the central issue to be whether or not warfare is justified.

---

[71] I am for the present disregarding differences between saying that a war is just (or right or obligatory) and saying that it is justified. There are some senses of 'justified' in which an unjust war (objectively speaking) might be justified, if available evidence to the state waging the unjust war pointed reasonably to its being just. For a discussion of some of these issues, see Deane-Peter Baker, "Epistemic Uncertainty and Excusable Wars," *The Philosophical Forum*, Vol. 46, No. 1, Spring 2015, pp. 55–70.

2

The Presumption against War

It's axiomatic that the immediate purpose of war is to kill people.

—Steve Morse*

2.1 The ends of morality and warfare

Morality has as its end the fostering of understanding, harmony and happiness among peoples. That end is good. Indeed, it is often taken to be the *summum bonum*. Warfare has as its end the causing of harm, death and destruction. That end is bad in itself and its pursuit epitomizes some of the worst in human behavior. In other words, morality and warfare are both teleological, and their ends are antithetical. That morality and warfare are antithetical does not mean that morality and war are necessarily antithetical.[1] Warfare is not the whole of war.

Warfare is the organized use of violence, typically in the form of military force, to cause harm, death and destruction.[2] This may be undertaken in low-intensity conflict and punitive expeditions against nonresisting peoples that fall short of war. It may also be undertaken in asymmetrical conflicts, in which one side is a nation state, the other a smaller loosely organized group or less powerful nation state. But both war and warfare cause death and destruction. In addition, war often produces selflessness, discipline and heroism. These are arguably good and have even been alleged to ennoble the human spirit. War may also be waged for self-defense, protection of the innocent

---

[*] *"Goodbye Old Man," A Short Essay on Horses in War*, unpublished essay by Steve Morse, smorse2@charter.net.

[1] Michael Allen Fox contends more directly that "… given the problems with just war Doctrine … and the fact that any universalized ethics is meant to embrace strangers as well as friends, it is not difficult to see that war is incompatible with morality." *Understanding Peace*, p. 121.

[2] The harm, death and destruction of warfare are directed primarily against human beings but often against animals and the environment as well, often incidentally, but sometimes intentionally insofar as the targeted human beings depend on them. Destruction is directed against property such as civilian or military equipment and structures on which the targeted persons depend.

and even, as Augustine says, for peace itself,[3] and these objectives are almost universally deemed to be good as well. In addition, war often contributes to technological progress and medical advances, sometimes in dramatic ways.[4] Even if these are not conscious aims, they are functions that war sometimes serves. Thus war, as well as warfare, is also teleological, and at least some of the ends for which it has been waged, and some of the functions it serves, are arguably good. Many think that these and similar considerations legitimize war. They believe that despite their essentially destructive nature, some wars are permissible or even obligatory.

The central moral question regarding war is whether morality, whose end is the promotion of the highest human goods,[5] can justify warfare, a practice whose end is to cause death and destruction.[6] For warfare is what Clausewitz aptly calls the essence of war.[7] The question whether war can ever be justified is often ignored. It is assumed that war is justifiable and that the only important questions are when it is justified and how to minimize its destructiveness.[8] Sometimes this assumption is rooted in a broader assumption that serious wrongdoing—actual or imminent—justifies violence in response. But a wrong done does not in itself justify any particular response to it. Much less does it justify a violent response. A wrong is one act, the response another.

---

[3] Augustine writes: "It is therefore with the desire for peace that wars are waged, even by those who take pleasure in exercising their warlike nature in command and battle. And hence it is obvious that peace is the end sought for by war." *The City of God*, Bk. XIX, chap. 12, *Nicene and Post-Nicene Fathers: A Select Library of the Christian Church*, Vol. 2, ed. Philip Schaff (Peabody, MA: Hendrickson Publishers, 1994), p. 407. Near the end of his life, Augustine speaks as though it is only good men who seek peace when they wage war. Letter CCXXIX to Darius, *Nicene and Post-Nicene Fathers*, Vol. 1, p. 581. For very different reasons, Edward Luttwak contends that the sole useful function of war is to bring peace and for that reason conflicts should often be allowed to run their course rather than being stopped prematurely. See Edward N. Luttwak, "Give War a Chance," *Foreign Affairs*, Vol. 78, No. 4, July/August 1999, pp. 36–45.

[4] It has even been claimed that war serves the social function of reducing inequalities in wealth. Thomas Piketty writes, "it was the chaos of war, with its attendant economic and political shocks, that reduced inequality in the twentieth century... In the twentieth century it was war, and not harmonious democratic or economic rationality, that erased the past and enabled society to begin anew with a clean slate." See his *Capital in the Twenty-First Century* (Cambridge, MA: The Belknap Press of Harvard University Press, 2014), p. 275.

[5] The reference to human good does not prejudge the issues between deontological and axiological theories (or, relatedly, between deontological and utilitarian or consequentialist theories) of moral rightness and obligation. Morality might be thought by its very nature to promote human good whether the rules, principles, virtues, etc. by which it does so are deontological or axiological.

[6] In Chapter 12 I shall refine the central moral question of war in connection with the issue of whether pacifism and just war theory converge.

[7] As Clausewitz says, "Essentially war is fighting, for fighting is the only effective principle in the manifold activities generally designated as war." *On War*, p. 127. See also p. 207. Clausewitz, however, understands warfare more broadly than I do here, saying that it "comprises everything related to the fighting forces—everything to do with their creation, maintenance, and use." (p. 95). Warfare in this sense is more akin to what I call a war system.

[8] Although their collection does not altogether disregard this question, Richard Sorabji and David Rodin, for example, write that the ethics of war "can be discussed in connection with two different questions: the question of when it is just to go to war (called in the just war tradition the *ad bellum* question), and the question of how it is just to behave in the course of a war (the *in bello* question)." See Richard Sorabji and David Rodin (eds), *The Ethics of War: Shared Problems in Different Traditions* (Aldershot, UK: Ashgate Publishing Limited, 2006), p. 3 This does not preclude asking, first and foremost, whether war can be justified, but it puts the question at best in the background.

All actions need justification.[9] So with war. That a state has committed a wrong does not in itself justify another state in waging war against it. To show that it does in any particular case requires argument. The justification must be produced. A study of the morality of war cannot begin by assuming answers to the fundamental questions of the justifiability of war and violence. These must be considered open questions. This is a topic to which I shall return in Chapter 12.

As warfare is at the heart of war, if it cannot be justified, then war cannot be justified. And as killing is at the heart of warfare, if it cannot be justified, then warfare cannot be justified. So it is with the morality of killing that we shall begin.[10]

2.2 War and killing

I assume that virtually everyone thinks that, all things being equal, deliberately killing people is wrong. They believe it can sometimes be justified, such as in self-defense, but the justification must meet strict conditions. I assume furthermore that most people think that war, even when they deem it necessary, is bad. It, too, in their view, can be justified, but only under certain conditions. Put a bit more philosophically, most people think deliberately killing people is prima facie wrong and that war, which pre-eminently involves killing people, is presumptively wrong. I say most people. Some deny that war is presumptively wrong, or at least they deny that the just war tradition begins with any such presumption.[11] They see that view as a misreading of the just war

---

[9] Meaning that all voluntary acts need justification if circumstances call them into question, which frequently they do not; not that justification must be provided for all acts irrespective of circumstances. In any event, as I shall argue, all presumptively wrong acts need justification.

[10] Some will demur at conceding that we should begin with killing, as it seems to them that to start there creates too strong a presumption against war. Thus Larry May says: "One normative difficulty is that if what makes war immoral is the killing of people, then all wars are immoral and there is no relevant moral distinction between aggressive wars and defensive wars. If one wants to maintain a distinction of this sort and punish people for waging aggressive wars but not for waging defensive wars, focusing on killing alone will not work." See his *Aggression and Crimes against Peace* (Cambridge: Cambridge University Press, 2008), p. 6. Though May does not quite do this, this comes close to saying that if one wants war to be justified, then one should not focus too heavily upon killing. In this spirit, the just war theory typically does not question the justifiability of killing. It concerns itself with the circumstances under which the organized killing of warfare is justified, the assumption being that it is sometimes justified and sometimes not. If I am correct that killing is the essence of warfare, then a systematic approach to analyzing the morality of war must begin there.

[11] For example, James Turner Johnson says: "What, then, of the claim made in *The Challenge of Peace* that just war doctrine begins with a 'presumption against war'? … The idea of such a 'presumption' seems to owe more to the influence of Catholic pacifists on the development of *The Challenge of Peace* and to a general uneasiness with the destructiveness of modern war and the venality of modern states than to the heritage of just war tradition. I would say it more emphatically: the concept of just war does not begin with a 'presumption against war' focused on the harm which war may do, but with a presumption against *injustice* focused on the need for responsible use of force in response to wrongdoing." *Morality and Contemporary Warfare* (New Haven, CT: Yale University Press, 1999), p. 35. In the same spirit, Daryl Charles says—apparently approvingly—that it is a mistake to "assume that the just-war tradition begins with a presumption *against war*. It does not. In its development, the Christian just-war tradition issues out of a presumption *against injustice*." See his *Between Pacifism and Jihad: Just War and Christian Tradition* (Downers Grove, IL: InterVarsity Press, 2005),

tradition, dating back as far as Augustine. Although such writers strictly make only an historical claim about the absence of such a presumption in the beginning of the just war tradition, they seem to agree that there is no such presumption. Others would deny that war is presumptively wrong because they believe that morality does not apply to war and that such judgments are either pointless or unintelligible. Whether or not the just war tradition begins with a presumption against war, there may be such a presumption, particularly in the modern world.

I shall throughout deal with the nonconsensual harming and killing of persons, by which I mean human beings who have, or have significant potential for, consciousness, rationality, ability to communicate and life plans. There may be nonhuman persons as well, such as some animals, angels and divinities, but I shall not deal with that possibility here. Nor shall I deal with the vexing issues surrounding the unborn or those in irreversible comas or permanent vegetative states. Suicide and voluntary euthanasia involve killing, but such killing is consensual. It may be also be prima facie wrong, but some would contest that. Some think that killing is prima facie wrong only if it is harmful. Others think that killing is in itself harmful.[12] Neither of these claims is obviously true. The process of killing—or alternatively, the process of dying—may be harmful. You may be worse off while the process is underway, which sometimes is prolonged. But in the absence of metaphysical or theological assumptions, killing (or dying) is not harmful per se. To harm someone, as Plato saw, is to make him worse off. But to be worse off as a result of something done to you presupposes some sort of continuing existence on your part. The totally nonexistent, even if they once existed, are neither better off nor worse off. The conditions for their being either better off or worse off no longer obtain. If there is no after life, or there is one but a person is not worse off (or is even better off) for having entered into it, then one has not been harmed by being killed.

So I shall consider it prima facie wrong to harm or kill persons. For the sake of simplicity, I shall for the most part speak of killing, but I intend what I say to cover harming as well. I shall take nonconsensual to mean without the consent of those whose lives are at stake. Where those whose lives are at stake are incapable of giving consent but are under the care of persons who are morally entitled to consent on their behalf, I shall take nonconsensual to mean without the consent of those responsible for their care. Most killing of animals and young children is nonconsensual in this sense. In stage B of the argument I shall qualify this further.

---

p. 19. Although he speaks here specifically of the just war tradition, he seems to be rejecting a presumption against war *simpliciter*. See also Henrik Syse, "Augustine and Just War," in Henrik Syse and Gregory M. Reichberg (eds), *Ethics, Nationalism, and Just War: Medieval and Contemporary Perspectives* (Washington, DC: The Catholic University of America Press, 2007), p. 37. Steven Lee, on the other hand, contends that it "seems reasonable, given the moral horror of war, to view just war theory as representing a *presumption against war." Ethics and War*, p. 102.

[12] For example, Jeff McMahan, in comparing the killing of persons and the killing of animals, writes: "One strikingly obvious difference … is that a person who is killed normally thereby suffers a significantly greater harm than an animal does if it is killed. And it seems obvious that there is a close connection between the wrongness of killing and the fact that killing normally involves the infliction of a grievous harm on the victim." See his *The Ethics of Killing: Problems at the Margins of Life* (Oxford: University Press, 2002), p. 190.

I shall also limit my concern to deliberate killing, by which I mean that which is either intended or foreseen. I shall not deal with the causing of accidental deaths. An intention is that which it is one's purpose to bring about. To intend to kill is to have as one's purpose to cause death.[13] But not everything that is foreseen, much less everything that is foreseeable, is intended. Normally one can foresee outcomes of an act that are not part of what one intends. I foresee that if I drive to work I will burn gasoline, but it is not my intention to burn gasoline. Foreseeable killing is that which is capable of being foreseen whether in fact foreseen or not. What is foreseen is obviously foreseeable, but not everything foreseeable is foreseen.

To kill deliberately is to kill knowingly. Death in that case is either intended or foreseen. If you do not foresee that what you do will cause death, then you do not kill knowingly. But if the death was foreseeable, then you could have known that what you did would kill. Sometimes the steps that would have enabled you to have that knowledge are obvious. If you accidentally kill a child when backing your car out of a driveway, the killing was not foreseen. But it was foreseeable if you would have seen the child had you looked before backing up. Sometimes the steps that would enable one to foresee a death will not be obvious. If you unwittingly kill someone by administering mislabeled medication, the killing was not foreseen. But it too was foreseeable. With enough effort, you could have had the medicine chemically analyzed before administering it or insisted on watching the pharmacist prepare it. Every death could in principle be foreseen with enough foreknowledge of causal connections. But people cannot always be expected to have such knowledge. If the steps that would have enabled you to foresee that what you did would kill someone are sufficiently extraordinary, you cannot reasonably be expected to have taken them. If a killing was foreseeable, however, there will always be steps you could have taken that would have provided such knowledge, whether or not it would be reasonable to hold you accountable for not having taken them. I shall limit my concern with foreseeable killing to cases in which killing, though unforeseen, could reasonably have been foreseen, and for which one is therefore arguably accountable.

In light of these considerations, we can now begin an elaboration of the argument, the first premise of which becomes:

A1. The deliberate nonconsensual killing of persons is prima facie wrong.

As I shall use the term, to say that an act is prima facie wrong means only that it has at least one significant wrong-making characteristic; in other words, that it is wrong

---

[13] Language can be misleading here, because we can properly be said to do many things intentionally that are not our purpose to do. These will include things we foresee that we must do in the course of achieving our purpose. I intend to return a book to the library, but in the process I intentionally take the book off the shelf, open my office door and walk to the library. I do not have one intention to take the book off the shelf, another to open the office door and yet another to walk to the library, any more than I have one intention to move my left foot forward, another to move my right foot forward and so on as I approach the library. When we do things intentionally that are not our purpose, "intentionally" is used roughly synonymously with "deliberately" or "knowingly." To insist that everything one does knowingly in the course of carrying out one's intention has a separate intention would lead to a needless proliferation of intentions.

in at least one important respect.[14] Wrong-making characteristics include but are not limited to:

> causing harm or death
> inflicting unnecessary pain or suffering
> violating rights
> being unfair or unjust
> deceiving
> degrading
> betraying trust
> dehumanizing
> causing unhappiness[15]

An act that is prima facie wrong is then actually wrong all other things being equal; that is, if there are no other moral considerations overriding its prima facie wrongness. For simplicity, we may say, following philosophical convention, that such an act is wrong *ceteris paribus*.

To call an act prima facie wrong implies nothing, however, about whether all other things are in fact equal. If some acts are prima facie right in some respect and prima facie wrong in some other respect,[16] then the distinction is unhelpful in those cases unless there is some way of weighting prima facie rightness and wrongness. For this purpose I shall speak of *presumptive* rightness and wrongness.[17] That an act is presumptively wrong I shall take to imply (though not to entail) that all other things *are* equal; that is, that the act is actually wrong all things considered. It does not assert that the act is actually wrong, since it may be that the presumption can be defeated. That an act is presumptively wrong implies only that it is highly likely that it is wrong (the same, *mutatis mutandis*, for presumptive rightness).[18]

The point is that moral experience does not always require that we determine rightness or wrongness from scratch. Acts often come weighted on one side or the other. It is not a tossup whether lying, dishonesty, cruelty and torture are right or wrong. They come heavily weighted on the side of wrongness. Kindness,

---

[14] In saying this, I am following in part the account of W. D. Ross, *The Right and the Good* (Oxford, UK: The Clarendon Press, 1930).

[15] Some might want to consider the first two of these as wrong-making only insofar as they are directed toward human beings. While I do not share that view, I will not explore whether it is a reasonable restriction. I shall assume that, properly qualified, these are unquestionably wrong-making.

[16] Ross says that every act is prima facie right in some respects and prima facie wrong in some respects, but this seems doubtful and risks trivializing the distinction. It is hard to see any respect in which putting my right shoe on before my left (or vice-versa) is prima facie wrong. It is for this reason that I am stressing that there must be an important or at least significant respect in which an act is wrong in order for it to be prima facie wrong.

[17] Sometimes prima facie wrong is used as though it meant presumptively wrong, but I believe it is important to distinguish the two.

[18] It might prevent you from being late for work to run over accident victims rather than drive around them or stop to help. But that respect in which it would be prima facie right would be more than offset by the avoidable harm to innocent accident victims.

compassion, truthfulness and honesty, on the other hand, come heavily weighted on the side of rightness. This weight creates presumptions of rightness or wrongness. A final determination of right or wrong in any given case must factor in such presumptions.[19]

2.3 Act types and act tokens

Before proceeding, we should note that the term "act" is ambiguous. It may refer to an individual act or to a kind of act (or, if one prefers more specialized terminology, to an act token or act type). What it means to call an act prima facie wrong then varies according to whether we are speaking of an individual act or a kind of act. I will consider it sufficient for a type of act to be presumptively wrong that it tends to be wrong, by which I mean that most instances of that type are actually wrong. But that is not necessary. All that is necessary is that instances of that type tend to be presumptively wrong.[20] For the sake of simplicity, I shall in what immediately follows use the stronger claim, and contend that most instances of deliberate nonconsensual killing are wrong, a claim I am confident is true but probably could not establish to the satisfaction of anyone who seriously doubted it. At the very least, if an act is presumptively wrong, there is good reason to believe that it is actually wrong. The practical import is that *if an act is presumptively wrong, the burden is upon anyone who wants to perform it to show that doing so would not be wrong.* Put a bit more formally, we may say of individual acts, or act tokens:

> An individual act is prima facie wrong if, and only if, and because, it possesses at least one wrong-making characteristic.
>
> An individual act is presumptively wrong if, and only if, and because,[21] it is prima facie wrong and there are no evident moral considerations offsetting its prima facie wrongness.

What constitutes actual wrongness in the case of individual acts can then be represented as follows:

> An individual act is actually wrong if, and only if, it is prima facie wrong and there are in fact no other moral considerations offsetting and overriding its prima facie wrongness.

---

[19] For a discussion of closely related issues, framed in terms of the classification of moral beliefs as unimportant, resolved and unresolved, see Richard Werner, 'Pragmatism for Pacifists,' *Contemporary Pragmatism*, Vol. 4, No. 2, December 2007, p. 106. Werner is here following Catherine Elgin's analysis in her *Considered Judgment* (Princeton, NJ: Princeton University Press, 1996).

[20] As Larry May represents Grotius's view, "most forms of killing violate the rights of others." See May, *Aggression and Crimes against Peace*, p. 29. Depending upon one's understanding of the relation between wrongness and the violation of rights, this could be taken to mean either that killing tends to be (actually) wrong or that it tends to be presumptively wrong.

[21] I shall henceforth not specify "and because" in connection with "if and only if," but it should be understood.

Accordingly, we may then say of kinds of acts, or act types (by which I shall include activities and practices):

> A kind of act is prima facie wrong if, and only if, the individual acts constitutive of that kind are prima facie wrong.
>
> A kind of act is presumptively wrong if, and only if, it is prima facie wrong and the individual acts constitutive of that kind are either presumptively or actually wrong.
>
> A kind of act is actually wrong if, and only if, the individual acts constitutive of that kind are actually wrong.

I shall henceforth for the most part simply refer to "act," leaving it to the context to disambiguate between act type and act token.

2.4 The presumptive wrongness of deliberately killing persons

We can then proceed with the argument as follows:

> 2. If the deliberate nonconsensual killing of persons is prima facie wrong and tends to be actually wrong, then such killing is presumptively wrong.

That is, if the deliberate nonconsensual killing of persons (a kind of act) is prima face wrong and most of the individual acts of that kind are actually wrong, then such killing (as a kind) is presumptively wrong. That suffices to render the kind wrong, though it is not necessary. It suffices to render the kind presumptively wrong that the preponderance of individual acts of that kind are presumptively wrong.

I take it to be a bedrock conviction of morality that the deliberate nonconsensual killing of persons tends to be wrong.[22] This does not mean that it cannot ever be justified. That is left open. Such killing includes, but is not limited to, the killing of innocent persons. Persons are innocent if free of wrongdoing. They are morally innocent if free of moral wrongdoing. And they are presumptively innocent unless shown to be guilty of wrongdoing. If the nonconsensual harming or killing of persons in general, and of innocent and presumptively innocent persons in particular, does not tend to be actually wrong,[23] then morality loses its moorings. If people killed one another with as little concern as they swat flies, social life as we know it would

---

[22] As expressed by C. A. J. Coady, "...the prohibition on intentionally killing innocent people functions in our moral thinking as a sort of touchstone of moral and intellectual health. To suspend his, for reasons of necessity or supreme emergency, is to bring about an upheaval in the moral perspective." C. A. J. Coady, *Morality and Political Violence* (Cambridge: Cambridge University Press, 2008), p. 297. Jeff McMahan makes a similar point powerfully: "There is no moral belief that is more universal, stable, and unquestioned, both across different societies and throughout history, than the belief that killing people is normally wrong." See McMahan, *The Ethics of Killing*, p. 189. Again, in his *Killing in War* McMahan writes: "If there is a standing moral presumption against the killing of a person, and in particular against the intentional killing of a person, it should be unsurprising if it takes more than a modicum of responsibility to override it" (p. 230).

[23] Unless otherwise indicated, by "wrong" I shall henceforth mean actually wrong.

be impossible. Respect for human life is a condition of social life, and that in turn is essential to some of the most prized of human values. These include morality, art, science, music, literature. Respect and trust go hand in hand. "The distinctively moral value of life," it has been said, "begins in the sphere of those who trust one another."[24] If most deliberate nonconsensual killing of persons were not wrong (and, of course, perceived to be such), such killing would probably abound to such an extent as to render harmonious communal life impossible. One might go so far as to say that the very existence of such communal life attests to the fact that such killing tends to be wrong.[25] Hence:

3. The deliberate nonconsensual killing of persons tends to be actually wrong.
4. Therefore: The deliberate nonconsensual killing of persons is presumptively wrong.

This much I trust is relatively unproblematic. We are speaking of a shared conviction necessary to any community or social life. Indeed, something like this presumption underlies the central condition of the just war theory itself, that of just cause, a principal ground for which is national defense.[26] National defense is believed to be essential to national survival, which is widely taken to be the highest value of the state. If prevention of the destruction of the state from outside aggression justifies killing, then prevention of its disintegration from within should be equally as important. And if respect for human life is necessary to preventing that disintegration, then even if one takes survival of the state to be the highest value—a view which I shall challenge—there exists at least as strong a presumption against killing persons as can be urged in favor of national defense.

As Socrates reminds Crito, rational argument can proceed among people only if there is some common ground among them at the outset.[27] I would hope that (A4) would constitute such ground for the present argument. If for some it does not, then we are at odds from the start about what morality is all about.[28] As it would take a side track into metaethics to deal with such differences, I shall not engage such skepticism here.

---

[24] Nicolai Hartmann, *Ethics*, Vol. II (London: George Allen & Unwin Ltd, 1951), p. 294.

[25] There may even be an innate aversion within humans to killing other human beings, as maintained by psychologist Dave Grossman in *On Killing: The Psychological Cost of Learning to Kill in War and Society*, rev. ed. (New York: Little, Brown and Company, 2009).

[26] I speak here of a just cause in the modern world. Historically, such considerations as revenge or vindication of honor were sometimes paramount.

[27] Absent such common ground, philosophical discussion risks drifting into endless debate, in which all sides simply adjust their positions continually to accommodate what they are predisposed to believe. For an insightful exploration of this issue, see Werner, "Pragmatism for Pacifists," pp. 93–115.

[28] Paul Christopher reasons: "One might argue that if soldiers are not guilty, then they are innocent; and if they are innocent, then they should not be intentionally harmed. But, of course, it is permissible to harm enemy soldiers intentionally. Thus we must conclude that the *prima facie* obligation not to intentionally harm those who are innocent (where all those who are not guilty are innocent) is inappropriate when applied to soldiers." Paul Christopher, *The Ethics of War and Peace: An Introduction to Legal and Moral Issues*, 3rd ed. (Upper Saddle River, NJ: Prentice-Hall, 2004), p. 151. If I understand this correctly, it takes it as a given that it is not always prima facie wrong to harm innocent persons, namely when they are soldiers, which entails that it is not always prima facie

(A4) does not necessarily mean that killing people cannot ever be justified. Whether that is so, as I have said earlier, is left open. It means only that the burden is upon those who would deliberately kill people (or support those who kill on their behalf) to defeat this presumption; that is, to show that doing so in the circumstance they propose would not be wrong. Many who support killing of various sorts readily assume that burden. Those who favor the death penalty, for example, often provide extensive arguments in support of that conviction, as do pro-choice advocates on the abortion issue and those who support killing in self-defense.[29]

Some, however, do not accept the burden. They in effect concede that it cannot be met but contend that it need not always be met in warfare. They say that sometimes it is, in some sense, permissible to kill people even though it is wrong to do so. Instead of accepting the burden of proof to show that killing innocent persons is morally justified, they accept the burden of guilt for doing what is wrong. At the same time, they tend to argue that in those cases one has no other choice, which seems meant to absolve them of responsibility for such killing.

It is difficult to state fairly the reasoning behind this way of thinking, since it often emerges with little supporting argument. But it is important to confront it early on, even though it leads into a thicket of specialized philosophical issues. Most often it concerns the acceptability of killing innocent persons (not just killing persons in general), but the issues are the same. If there is a presumption against the nonconsensual killing of persons in general, then there is a presumption against the killing of innocent persons in particular. By extrapolating from the acceptability of killing innocent persons, proponents of this view conclude that war may be acceptable even if it cannot be morally justified. War, in this view, is for that reason tragic.[30]

2.5 Is some wrongdoing inescapable?

Let us try to understand the reasoning behind this approach. Consider the options if you have decided to do something that you know cannot be justified morally:

1. Bite the bullet and accept that what you are doing is wrong and that you are fully accountable for doing it.
2. Accept that what you are doing is wrong but convince yourself that you have no choice.

wrong to harm persons. This (if we take harm to include killing, as one assumes is intended) means that not only (A4) but (A1) as well would be rejected by this approach. If correct, that would mean there is no common ground with the argument of this book, which considers the permissibly of killing soldiers an open question.

[29] Abortion, by its supporters and opponents alike, is typically assumed to constitute killing. But although it almost always results in the death of the unborn, abortion per se (as noted earlier) is not feticide. It is the premature intentional termination of a pregnancy other than to facilitate a live birth. Nonetheless, for those who regard abortion as the killing of a human being, there is a presumption against killing, and some advocates of the right to abortion believe it can be defeated.

[30] For a thoughtful discussion of this issue, see Nicholas Edward Parkin, *Pacifism, Innocence, and Modern War*, ch. 7, "The Moral Tragedy of War," PhD dissertation, Centre for Applied Philosophy and Public Ethics, Department of Philosophy, The University of Melbourne, September 2012.

3. Accept that what you are doing is wrong but convince yourself that you ought (in some sense) to do it anyway.
4. Deny that what you are doing is wrong even though it cannot be justified morally.
5. Contend that there are two moralities, and that although what you are doing is wrong by one morality, it is permissible by the other.

Option (1) is refreshingly honest, but there is little of a philosophical sort to say to those who choose it, other perhaps than to suggest that they read Plato on wrongdoing from ignorance and think again. Most who take this approach opt for some permutation of (2) or (3). That is, they try to mitigate in some way the wrongness of what they do. Those who opt for any of the first three options, can also, if it is their inclination, lament the fact that they have "dirty hands." Those with a bent for philosophical analysis may opt for either (4) or (5), options I shall consider later.

Those who opt for (2) often appeal to "necessity" as creating the situation in which they have no choice. Augustine sets the stage for such an appeal, when he writes:

> Peace should be the object of your desire; war should be waged only as a necessity, and waged only that God may by it deliver men from the necessity and preserve them in peace. For peace is not sought in order to the kindling of war, but war is waged in order that peace may be obtained ... Let necessity, therefore, and not your will, slay the enemy who fights against you.[31]

If it is necessity and not your will that does the killing, then you are not sinning in the killing you do, as Augustine believes to be the case if you are otherwise a good Christian acting in obedience to your ruler. As Pufendorf puts it centuries later, "*Necessity* is said to *have no Law*."[32] We shall elaborate the underpinnings of Augustine's reasoning in Chapter 4. For the present, let us consider the more recent appeal to necessity by Michael Walzer:

> I have left the hardest question for last. What are we to say about those military commanders (or political leaders) who override the rules of war and kill innocent people in a "supreme emergency"? Surely we want to be led at such a time by men and women ready to do what has to be done—what is *necessary*; for it is only here that necessity, in its true sense, comes into the theory of war.

---

[31] Augustine, Letter CLXXXIX (to Boniface), in *Nicene and Post-Nicene Fathers*, Vol. 1, First Series, ed. Philip Schaff (Peabody, MA: Hendrickson Publishers, 1994), p. 554. See also St Thomas Aquinas: "[T]o have recourse to the sword (as a private person) by the authority of the sovereign or judge, or (as a public person) through zeal for justice, and by the authority, so to speak, of God, is not to *take the sword*, but to use it as commissioned by another, wherefore it does not deserve punishment." *Summa Theologica*, Pt. II-II Q. 40 Art. 1 (New York: Benziger Brothers, 1947), p. 1360. A somewhat similar absolving one of personal responsibility for wartime killing is found in the *Koran*, where it is written of the Battle of Badr in AD 624: "It was not you, but Allah, who slew them. It was not you who smote them: Allah smote them so that He might richly reward the faithful." *Koran*, ch. 8.

[32] Samuel Pufendorf, *The Whole Duty of Man, According to the Law of Nature*, ed. Ian Hunter and David Saunders (Indianapolis, IN: Liberty Fund, 2003), p. 91.

On the other hand, we cannot ignore or forget what it is they do. The deliberate killing of the innocent is murder. Sometimes, in conditions of extremity … commanders must commit murder or they must order others to commit it. And then they are murderers, though in a good cause … They have killed unjustly, let us say, for the sake of justice itself, but justice itself requires that unjust killing be condemned.[33]

Walzer seems to adopt all of the first three options. That one is a murderer for deliberately killing innocent people seems to be an acknowledgement that one acts wrongly in so doing (option 1). But the wrongness is mitigated because one acts from necessity and has no choice (option 2). Since the killing is done for the sake of justice—by people ready "to do what has to be done"—it would seem, that, in some inexplicable way, morality justifies the use of immorality, hence that one ought (in some sense) to do what is wrong (option 3).

What is the "true sense" of necessity, as Walzer conceives it? When people say they had no choice in doing something, they usually do not literally mean what they say. They mean that the choice they had was a difficult one, and that they did what almost anyone would have done.[34] Walzer seems to mean more than this. By "necessity" he seems to mean that what is done is, as Kant might have put it, an indispensable means to an end, and that the end is such that failure to pursue it is unthinkable. Augustine may also have had that in mind when he implies that war is a necessary means to peace. Walzer writes:

For the survival and freedom of political communities—whose members share a way of life, developed by their ancestors, to be passed on to their children—are the highest values of international society. Nazism challenged these values on a grand scale, but challenges more narrowly conceived, *if they are of the same kind*, have similar moral consequences. They bring us under the rule of necessity (and necessity knows no rules).[35]

Similar reasoning is available to others, of course. German Chancellor Bethmann-Hollweg said before the Reichstag at the outset of World War I (WWI):

Necessity knows no law. Our troops have occupied Luxemburg and have perhaps already entered on Belgian soil. Gentlemen, this is a breach of international law … A French attack upon our flank in the lower Rhine might have been disastrous. Thus we have been obliged to ignore the just protests of the governments of Luxemburg and Belgium. The injustice … that we are committing we will endeavor to make good as soon as our military aims have been attained. Anybody

---

[33] Michael Walzer, *Just and Unjust Wars* (New York: Basic Books, 1977), p. 323.

[34] In this spirit, Richard Norman writes: "I am suggesting that we can … make sense of the idea that in a particular social context the only available alternatives may be to submit or to fight, and that, submission being morally unthinkable, people can then intelligibly say that they have no choice but to fight." *Ethics, Killing and War* (Cambridge: Cambridge University Press, 1995), p. 221.

[35] Walzer, *Just and Unjust Wars*, p. 254.

who is threatened and is fighting for his highest possessions can think only of one thing, how he is to attain his end, cost what it may.[36]

The point, it appears, is that doing what is morally wrong may sometimes be the only means to preserve a political community. In those circumstances, necessity prevails.[37] It is puzzling, though, that both Walzer and the German chancellor say, in the spirit of Pufendorf, that necessity "knows no law (rules)." For necessity in this sense is rule-governed. It presupposes a principle, to the effect, that it is rational to choose the most efficient and effective means to one's ends. But the point of the principle is to *choose*. It is not as though, as Augustine says, it is necessity and not one's will that is acting. If one literally has no choice, then to speak of acting from necessity becomes vacuous. One can speak of responsibility, regret, guilt and "dirty hands" in such cases, but to do so is misguided. If you literally have no choice, you are absolved. It is morality or fate or the tragic scheme of things that is ultimately responsible, by forcing you to do what is immoral; or, to put it more bluntly, by forcing you to do what is wrong in order to do what is right. Morality, and the wars it would dictate that we fight, then becomes tragic. Less dramatically, it also becomes incoherent.

If, on the other hand, if the choice is difficult, perhaps even extraordinarily difficult, and one chooses to do what is immoral in order to achieve an objective one considers important, then one is responsible for the choice. Saying one had no choice is false and self-deceptive if one believes it.[38] Few want to be on record as advocating immorality, or confessing to supporting it themselves, so these options are hedged about with mitigating assumptions. One of these is the assumption that

A. There are some situations in which whatever one does is wrong.[39]

---

[36] Quoted by Charles Downer Hazen, *Modern European History* (New York: Henry Holt and Company, 1917), p. 617. The neutrality of Belgium, Luxemburg and Switzerland had long been recognized by international agreements and Germany's action was in clear violation of that neutrality. Somewhat similar events played out early in WWII when both Britain and Germany violated Norwegian neutrality. Hitler justified the invasion of Norway on the grounds that the action was necessary to preempt an Allied invasion of that country in order to obstruct essential iron ore shipments to Germany from Sweden. On the details of that phase of WWII, see Henrik O. Lunde, *Hitler's Pre-emptive War: The Battle for Norway, 1940* (Philadelphia, PA and Newbury, UK: Casemate, 2010), particularly chapters 1–3.

[37] For a penetrating critique of Walzer from a Christian pacifist perspective, see Robert Brimlow, *What about Hitler?* (Grand Rapids, MI: Brazos Press, 2006), especially pp. 66–77.

[38] Richard Norman enlists the notion of necessity in self-defense, saying: "I am ... inclined to say that the justification for killing in self-defense belongs more in the realm of *necessity* than in that of *justice*." *Ethics, Killing and War*, p. 128.

[39] Peter S. Temes puts this directly in the case of war: "The larger perspective, one that accepts responsibility for outcomes as well as for intentions, leads us to the essential Just War formulation: War is wrong, but we must accept the moral challenge not of life lived in some timeless ideal but of *our* lives in *our* times ... Thus we discover that a nation must sometimes choose not only between right and wrong but between wrong and wrong. Thus war, always wrong, always a sin, may nevertheless become at times the only decent option ... Indeed we are fools ... to have missed the chance to avoid war, but given the moment we find ourselves in, war may nevertheless be the least worst—indeed, the only—option. Wrong, but necessary." Peter S. Temes, *The Just War: An American Reflection on the Morality of War in Our Time* (Chicago, IL: Ivan R. Dee, 2003), p. 13.

If (A) were true, it would provide a rationale for at least some cases of (1) and (2). For then the concession of wrongdoing in (1) and (2) (once it is established that all available actions are wrong) would be unnecessary. It would be obvious that in such circumstances you are acting wrongly. And it would be necessary that you act wrongly (if you must act) and obvious that you have no choice (since there is no other choice but to do wrong). That would not suffice to show that it is necessary to perform any *particular* wrong act. You could choose any of those available to you. So once you have made your choice, it will not be true that that choice was necessitated. Nonetheless, wrongdoing of some sort in that situation would be inescapable. You can then proceed to kill innocent persons, overthrow governments, destroy cities, or support whatever morally unjustifiable acts you think the tragic nature of morality requires you to do.

If every available alternative is wrong, and you must act, then some wrongdoing is inescapable. But if there is an absolute and unconditional obligation to refrain from doing wrong, then one can equally say that in such situations every alternative is obligatory, hence that "rightdoing" is inescapable. Suppose *a* and *b* are absolutely and unconditionally wrong, and that they exhaust the options. Whether you do *a* or do *b*, you will be acting wrongly. But if *a* is wrong, and you have an obligation to refrain from doing what is wrong, then you have an obligation not to do *a*. Under the assumption—which I shall question later—that you must act, the only way not to do do *a* is to do *b*, which means that *b* is obligatory. The same reasoning, *mutatis mutandis*, establishes that you have an absolute and unconditional obligation to do *a* as well. Hence, you cannot escape doing what is obligatory. Rightdoing along with wrongdoing is inescapable. That you must do what is obligatory is not the grounds for regret that necessarily having to do wrong is, but it is no less a consequence of the situation as designed.[40] One might as well say with the extreme relativist, that some acts are both right and wrong—or in this case, both obligatory and prohibited—at the same time. And that makes nonsense of morality.[41]

In any event (A), so understood, immediately runs afoul of the thesis that *ought implies can*. It is incontestable (leaving aside hedging qualifications about prima facie and actual rightness, wrongness and obligatoriness) that what is wrong ought not to be done. That is part of the very grammar of morality. And *ought not* implies can as much as ought implies can. It requires that one refrain from doing what is wrong, and refraining is more than simply not doing something. It is choosing not to do it, and if morality requires that you choose not to do something, then it must be something that you *can* choose not to do. In the situations described by (A), you cannot choose not to do what is wrong. You can, as I have said above, choose not to do any *one* of the specific wrong acts confronting you by choosing one of the others. But you cannot choose not to do one of the acts you ought not to do. Therefore, the situations described by

---

[40] It is not, however, as implausible to say that rightdoing is inescapable as to say that wrongdoing is inescapable. I shall describe a possible situation shortly in which if one is an axiologist all alternatives are permissible. What is not possible, if I am correct, is a situation (as described above) in which all alternatives are obligatory.

[41] That there should be situations in which incompatible acts are obligatory is sometimes taken to define moral dilemmas. The impossibility of such situations can then be taken to be grounds for denying that there are such dilemmas.

(A) violate the thesis that ought implies can. As that thesis, properly understood, is part of the structural foundation of morality, any claim that would violate it should be rejected.[42]

But, the inadequacy of the above arguments notwithstanding, can there be situations in which all of the alternatives are wrong? I suggest not. With a little ingenuity one can contrive examples to try to show that there are. Fiendish villains put you in a situation in which if you push a button ten grandmothers will die, but if you do not push the button ten other grandmothers will die. You must, obviously, push the button or not. Do you not act wrongly in either case?

Not necessarily. Pushing the button is an act.[43] But not pushing the button need not be an act. Simply not doing something is not an act. I did not throw a rock through my neighbor's window this morning, or burn down the nearest barn or join the marines. But I did not choose not to do any of these things. Doing them did not enter my mind. My not doing them did not constitute acts (otherwise the indefinite number of other things I did not do would also constitute acts, as would all but a few of the things that I am not doing at the moment I write this). Even when the idea of doing something enters your mind, your not doing it does not necessarily constitute an act. You need to refrain from doing something for your not doing it to constitute an act. It is then an act of omission. In the case at hand, you need not choose to push the button or choose not to push it. You can refuse to cooperate with those who have put you in this diabolical situation. With sufficient (if admittedly extraordinary) presence you could turn your mind to other things. Their aim is not merely to see that ten grandmothers die. That, let us suppose, is easy to do. They do not need you to do it. The aim is to get *you* to do it. And this requires that you cooperate with them by choosing one of the options. If you do not cooperate with them in this way—if you turn your mind to other things[44]—ten grandmothers will die. But you will not have killed them. Whoever causes their death will have done that. Nor have you chosen their death, even though they die as surely as if you had. No one can *make* you make a choice, even though they can contrive situations in which the outcomes (nonmorally considered) will be the same as if you had.

---

[42] One can try to show that the thesis that *ought implies can* does not hold. If one assumes that "I ought to do *a*" and "I ought to do *b*," where I cannot do both *a* and *b*, and assumes further that this implies that "I ought to do *a* and b," then obviously one ought to do something one cannot do, namely both *a* and *b*. And if it would be wrong not to do *a* and wrong not to do *b*, then obviously wrongdoing is inescapable. But this "agglomeration principle" does not falsify *ought implies can*. It simply presupposes in its premises, and the stated condition that *a* and *b* are incompatible acts, what it purports to prove. Anyone who supports the thesis that ought implies can will deny from the outset that one can be obligated (without qualification) to perform incompatible acts. This example comes from Bernard Williams, "Ethical Consistency," in *Moral Dilemmas*, ed. Christopher W. Gowans (Oxford: Oxford University Press, 1987), p. 130. See Michael Neu's appeal to the Williams example in his argument against the so-called binary conception of morality, according to which every act is either morally justifiable or morally unjustifiable. Michael Neu, "Why there Is No Such Thing as Just War Pacifism and Why Just War Theorists and Pacifists Can Talk Nonetheless," *Social Theory and Practice,* Vol. 37, No. 3, July 2011, pp. 413–434.

[43] Assuming, among other things, that one does so intentionally, or at least knowingly, and not, say, by an inadvertent movement of one's hand.

[44] Which with sufficient presence one could do, say by reciting a mantrum or conjugating Latin verbs. The right to design silliness into far-fetched examples cuts both ways.

Suppose, however, that I am wrong. Suppose that not pushing the button, *simpliciter*, qualifies as an act. Suppose you must choose to push the button or choose not to push the button. Would all of the alternatives be wrong? Again, not necessarily. They would, to be sure, be equally bad, *ceteris paribus*. But even for an axiologist that does not mean that all the alternatives are wrong. While it makes no sense to speak of situations in which all of the alternatives are equally wrong, it makes sense to speak of situations in which all of the alternatives are equally bad. Deontic language and value language serve different functions and have different rules. For an axiologist, if all of the available alternatives are equally bad (or would bring about equal balances of bad over good), then all of the alternatives are equally permissible. For a deontologist, however, there will be a morally relevant difference between the two. If you push the button, you will (let us assume) be killing ten grandmothers to save ten others, and the same in reverse if you choose not to push the button. And it is always a morally relevant consideration—whatever weight should be attached to it—that you would have to kill one person to save another or to kill a certain number to save a certain other number. So there will always be a morally relevant difference between the options in such situations.

But even if there were situations like Walzer's supreme emergencies in which wrongdoing is inescapable, it would not follow that the actions and policies which lead to those situations are governed by necessity. It is voluntary actions that lead to supreme emergencies. If those actions are freely chosen, then the assumed necessary wrongdoing to which they lead is foreseeable. Such wrongdoing then becomes willful, even prideful, wrongdoing. For that reason, it is arguably morally wrong to cooperate in the creation of situations of supreme emergency.[45]

What of option (3)? The "ought" it contains cannot be a moral ought upon pain of rendering morality inconsistent. It could be a prudential ought. It is perfectly intelligible to say: I ought (morally) to do x, but I ought (prudentially) to do y, where x and y are incompatible.[46] It could also be the sort of "ought" implied by the kantian technical hypothetical imperative, pertaining simply to means and ends other than prudential (if you want your car to run, you ought to put gas in it). But there is nothing new or unusually interesting about this.

Perhaps the "ought" is what Bernard Williams calls a "deliberative ought," or it figures in a "deliberative question" to which it may provide an answer. Of this Williams says:

> For suppose I am in a situation in which I think that I ought (morally) to do *a*, and would merely very much like to do *b*, and cannot do both. Here, too, I can presumably ask the deliberative question "what ought I to do?" And get an answer to it. If this question meant "Of which course of action is it the case that I ought (morally) to do it?", the answer is so patent that the question could not be worth asking: indeed, it would not be a deliberative question at all. But the deliberative

---

[45] I am assuming for the present that so-called supreme emergencies arise in the case of interstate war$_2$. The point just made about cooperation in the production of such states of affairs would not necessarily apply in the case of perceived need for humanitarian military intervention. I shall deal with this later.

[46] This presupposes, of course, that morality and prudence are two different points of view, a claim which I believe is correct but will not argue for here.

question can be worth asking, and I can, moreover, intelligibly arrive at a decision, or receive advice, in answer to it which is offensive to morality … An answer to the deliberative question, by myself or another, can of course be supported by moral reasons, as by other sorts; but its role as a deliberative *ought* remains the same, and this role is not tied to morality.[47]

The "other sorts of reasons" that might support the deliberative ought might, one supposes, be prudential (or technical in the kantian sense alluded to earlier). But this does not seem to be what Williams has in mind. His use of "ought" to characterize the deliberative question obscures this. In the final (and in a way most important) two sentences of his article, he states:

> In fact … it is not even true that *the* deliberative question is "what ought I to do?" It may well be, for instance, "what am I to do?"; and that question, and the answers to it—such as "do *a*," or "if I were you, I should …"—do not even make it look as though decision or advice to act on one of the *oughts* in a moral conflict necessarily involves deciding that the other one had no application.[48]

It now appears that Williams is simply making the point that to conclude that you ought (morally) to do something is one thing, to decide *to do* it is another (and, he might have added, the actual *doing of it* is yet another). Aristotle recognizes this in his practical syllogism, the conclusion of which is not another normative judgment, but the doing of the act in question. R. M. Hare gives this a more sophisticated rendering by asserting that moral judgments entail imperatives. The judgment "I ought to do *a*" entails the imperative "Let me do *a*,"[49] and acting upon that imperative is the doing of *a*, not a reiteration of the "ought." One might make the same distinction among other sorts of oughts as well. It is one thing to conclude that 'I ought (prudentially, or legally, etc.) to do *x*," another to decide to do x. And in these, cases, too, it is a third thing actually to do x. If, having decided, that one ought (morally, or prudentially, legally or whatever) to do x one then is trying to make up one's mind about what to do, one might ask "what ought I to do?" as Williams usually puts it, but one would more likely ask "what am I to do?" or "what shall I do?"[50] It would avoid confusion if the issue were framed from the outset, not as though it were yet another normative question, but rather as an expression of indecision about whether in fact to do the morally right thing (or the prudential thing, or the legal thing, as the case may be), in the first place.[51]

Defenders of the inescapability thesis seem to have something stronger in mind. They seem to want to reject a so-called binary conception of morality, according to

---

[47] Williams, "Ethical Consistency," p. 135.
[48] Williams, "Ethical Consistency," p. 136.
[49] See R. M. Hare, *The Language of Morals* (Oxford: Oxford University Press, 1951).
[50] One might also ask "What kind of person am I to be?" and that, interpreted a certain way, might indeed be a normative question, one that eases the issue into the realm of virtue ethics. Although I shall not argue it here, I believe that the same conclusions as I am drawing here with regard to the alleged inescapability of wrongdoing can be shown to apply there as well.
[51] The point can readily be adapted to accommodate virtue-ethics approaches, by saying that once one has decided what kind of person one ought to be (understood in terms of the cultivation of virtues),

which every act is either right or wrong. This conception can be thought to presuppose an unexceptionable claim:

B. Every act is susceptible of moral assessment.

With a few obvious qualifications, such as that an "act" is voluntarily performed by a rational agent, this would again seem to be an element in the basic chemistry of morality.[52] It has generally been assumed in the history of ethics that a corollary of (B) is:

C. Every act is either right or wrong.

C obviously does not mean that one always knows, or even can know, whether any given act is right or wrong. It does not necessarily even mean that one can know whether *any* act is right or wrong, as even an average skeptic can argue. It means only that these are the options when one morally assesses any act.[53] It is this which defenders of the inescapability thesis challenge. But it is unclear why. That every act is either right or wrong does not preclude that in some situations all available acts are wrong. If there were situations (as I claim there are not) in which all acts are wrong, it could still be true that every act is either right or wrong. It would just be that in some situations you could know for a certainty which they are. In any event, in rejecting the binary conception of morality, inescapabilists seem to have in mind a trinary conception, represented as follows:

D. Every act is right or wrong or both right and wrong.[54]

If the disjunction in (C) is inclusive, (D) would be consistent with (C), otherwise it would be its contrary.[55] If there should be some acts that are both right and wrong (or obligatory and permitted), then, as noted earlier, extreme ethical relativism is true. But this makes nonsense of morality. Walzer has been interpreted as holding D, though all that is clear is that he is holding (1), that sometimes one decides of necessity to do what is wrong. As Michael Neu puts it:

> Walzer insists that, paradoxically, we *must* apply the standards of ordinary morality

---

one can still meaningfully be undecided whether to perform actions which will contribute to the cultivation of such a virtuous character.

[52] In the next chapter I shall discuss the complications that arise when one tries to attribute actions in a literal sense to states.

[53] This does not, of course, preclude other ways of affirming the same point, but in different language; such as that every act is either moral or immoral, or morally permissible or morally impermissible, or morally good or morally bad. Nor does it preclude value assessments of acts as nonmorally good or bad.

[54] Someone might think that every act is either right or wrong, both right and wrong, or neither right nor wrong, but this does not appear to be the position of the inescapabilists, so I shall not consider it.

[55] In saying this, I am assuming for the sake of argument that we can assign truth-value to sentences about right and wrong acts, which is a contested issue in metaethics.

to war and at the same time *cannot* apply them, as we cannot help but adapt the moral theory of war to the reality it deals with. It is clear that Walzer does not glorify, let alone romanticize, war as a pure act of justice, then, but considers it a morally justifiable act that is inherently wrongful.[56]

I take it here that "morally justifiable" entails "permissible," so that one and the same act is both right and wrong. Whether this is in fact Walzer's view is uncertain. All that is clear is that he holds (1) and/or (2) or (3).

What may in part motivate defenders of the inescapability thesis is an understandable resistance to the view that if you morally ought to do one act, there can be no moral weight attaching to other acts. For if one holds that view, then there seems to be no room for remorse, guilt, dirty hands and for regarding justified wars as tragic. Williams seems to have something of this sort in mind following the earlier argument. What Williams seems to want to establish here is something different.

> It does not follow from this that I cannot correctly say then that *I ought to have done a*; nor yet that I was wrong in thinking earlier that it was something I ought to do. It seems, then, that if we waive the agglomeration principle, and just consider a natural way of applying to each course of action the consideration that I cannot do both it and the other one, we do not get an application of *ought* implies *can* that necessarily cancels out one or other of the original ought's regarded retrospectively. And this seems to me what we should want. As I have tried to argue throughout, it is surely falsifying of moral thought to represent its logic as demanding that in a conflict situation one of the conflicting *ought's* must be totally rejected.[57]

If we waive the agglomeration principle, there is no violation of thesis that ought implies can and no inescapable wrongdoing. What is left is a weaker and uncontroversial claim, to wit that in doing what one ought one may be overriding other weighty but nondecisive considerations on the other side. There are times that Neu seems to take the binary conception of morality to be denying this, which it does not. But that would be a different claim from (C). It is one thing to claim that every act is either right or wrong, but it is another to say that when an act is right or wrong there can be no weighty but nondecisive moral considerations on the other side. There is a ready vocabulary to describe this, in Ross's notion of prima facie versus actual obligations. In doing what I ought, on balance, with all things considered, I may choose an act over another, which also has elements of prima facie rightness about it. In fact Ross says at one point (perhaps implausibly) that every act is prima facie right in some respects and prima facie wrong in some respects. In situations of conflict, where one ought prima facie to do *a* and ought prima facie to do *b*, where *a* and *b* are incompatible acts, there is no reason to totally reject one of the oughts. Its prima facie rightness remains. What is incoherent is to say that one ought absolutely to do both of two incompatible acts, and that whichever of the ones one chooses, the other remains in full force. This would

---

[56] Neu, "Why there Is No Such Thing as Just War Pacifism," p. 422.
[57] Williams, "Ethical Consistency," pp. 133f.

represent inescapable wrongdoing. If it would make morality tragic, it is because it would make it irrational.

If this is correct, (D) must be rejected. Absent compelling arguments to the contrary, the binary conception of morality is sound. What defenders of (D) may have in mind is that there may be situations in which every alternative is bad. This indeed is true and happens fairly often. It presents what is commonly called a moral dilemma. But it does not imply that in such situations every alternative is wrong. For deontologists, there are other morally relevant features of acts and situations besides value realized, and these may well be decisive in rendering one alternative right and the other wrong. Even for axiologists, for whom value realized is the sole criterion for determining rightness, a situation in which the bad of all of the alternatives is equally distributed (or, if you like, the balance of good and bad) would not mean that all of the alternatives were wrong. Quite the contrary, it would mean that all of the alternatives are permissible and you can flip a coin if you like. The situation would be one of inescapable rightdoing.

In the absence of substantially more compelling arguments for the claim, I shall assume that there is no ground for saying that one sometimes has no choice but wrongfully to kill persons, or that wrongdoing is inescapable, or that there is some overriding sense of "ought" in which one ought to do what is immoral. So I shall take it that premise (4) stands. The deliberate nonconsensual killing of persons is presumptively wrong.

2.6 Intrinsic and extrinsic wrongness

If war$_2$ (whole war) is to be morally justified, it must be shown that such war is not actually wrong, either *intrinsically* or *extrinsically*, that is, either by virtue of its very nature or because of the circumstances in which it occurs. I shall take intrinsic wrongness to be that which is based solely on the intrinsic properties of what is wrong, and extrinsic wrongness to be that which is not intrinsic (which leaves open whether such wrongness is based solely on a thing's extrinsic properties or based on both its intrinsic and its extrinsic properties). Torturing a child is intrinsically wrong. It is wrong by its very nature, whatever the circumstances. Yelling "Fire!" is not intrinsically wrong. It is wrong if done in the proverbial crowded theater but not if done in your home to alert your family. The circumstances make it extrinsically wrong. Intrinsic properties are those constitutive of what possesses them. They include, but are not limited to, properties that (metaphysically speaking) make up the essence of a thing.[58] Extrinsic properties are those that are not intrinsic. Among war's intrinsic properties are that it involves deliberate killing. Among its extrinsic properties are its consequences.

So the question of whether war$_2$ is justified is tantamount to asking whether some wars$_2$ can be shown to be permissible. Some approach this question from the macro level, taking as givens the supreme value of collectivities such as states, or the preeminent value of an international system of states. Then the attention is focused primarily upon how to

---

[58] I take the nature of a thing to be more inclusive than its essence. Being a solid with six equilateral sides is part of the essence of a cube. But a cube also necessarily has twelve edges, which is part of its nature though not of its essence. Harming and killing are part of the essence of war. Killing innocent persons is not. Both, however, are part of the nature of war.

ensure the well-being of particular states (usually their own or those they approve of), or how to maintain the stability of the nation-state system.[59] This elevates to a position of first importance the concepts of aggression and self-defense. There is considerable precedent for this. As we shall see in Chapter 13, it represents the prevailing view of international law through the twentieth century, particularly as embodied in the UN Charter. But it is not, in my judgment, adequate as the starting point for a moral assessment of war. Neither states nor systems of states have intrinsic value. They are human creations that are valued as means to such ends as safeguarding human rights, minimizing violence and maintaining order. When one details why it is that these are valued, one is led back to the micro level, and to the lives and well-being of persons. No state and no system (other perhaps than biological) is conscious, and no entity that lacks consciousness, and the rationality that presupposes it, can be a moral agent. For these reasons, a microethics must be our starting point in the moral critique of war; and a macroethics—if one can plausibly be developed at all—must be framed around it. We shall return to this issue later.

Warfare also typically involves foreseeably, but not necessarily intentionally, killing innocent persons. The intentional killing of persons is intrinsic to warfare, the intentional killing of innocents is not. But the foreseeable killing of innocents is common to warfare and inevitable in war$_2$.

2.7 The presumptive wrongness of warfare

The killing in warfare is not merely nonconsensual, however. It is typically *against the will* of those killed. An act is nonconsensual if it is without the consent of those affected, as it will be if those affected had no opportunity to consent or had the opportunity but for whatever reason did not in fact consent.[60] That people did not consent is consistent with its being the case that they might have consented if they had been fully informed, unpressured and given the chance. But virtually all of the killing in warfare is not only nonconsensual, it is against the will of those killed (or, in the case of young children and animals, against the will of those responsible for their care). Those who are killed do not want to be killed.[61] In what follows, I shall take nonconsensual to mean not only without consent but also against the will of those killed.

---

[59] In the microeconomic theory of the state, the state is a profit-maximizing entity, providing protection (along with other services) in exchange for rent. Whether maximizing profit is included among the national interests of the state, or is considered an alternative to national interest as usually conceived, the analysis nonetheless proceeds at the macro level. See David A. Lake, "Powerful Pacifists: Democratic States and War," *American Political Science Review*, Vol. 86, No. 1, March 1992, pp. 24–38. For an analysis that argues for maintenance of the nation-state system, as based on the so-called Westphalian principles, see Henry Kissinger, *World Order* (New York: Penguin Press, 2014). Such a perspective is sometimes associated with realism, a topic to be discussed in the next chapter.

[60] While most nonconsensual killing is probably against the will of those killed, it need not be. In so-called suicide by cop, for example, people provoke the police into shooting and killing them. They apparently want to die. But they have not in fact consented to be killed (at least not in any minimally acceptable sense of consent; they might arguably be said to have tacitly consented to be killed, but evidence for that is circumstantial at the time of the killing). Nor have the police consented to kill them (which would be illegal on their part).

[61] Banzai attacks, and the attempt to crash planes into US ships (*Kamakazai* attacks) by the Japanese during WWII are arguably exceptions to this, although it may be more accurate to say of Kamakazai

B1. Warfare by its nature is the deliberate, organized and systematic nonconsensual killing of persons.

  2. Therefore: Warfare by its nature is the deliberate, organized and systematic performance of presumptive wrongs.[62]

  3. If warfare by its nature is the deliberate, organized and systematic performance of presumptive wrongs, then warfare by its nature is presumptively wrong.[63]

  4. Therefore: Warfare by its nature is presumptively wrong.

I have said earlier that warfare is at the heart of war (both war$_1$ partial war, and war$_2$, whole war) and killing is at the heart of warfare. Thus I take (B1) to be unproblematic, whether taken as a conceptual truth about the nature of warfare or as a factual claim. I take B2 to be relatively uncontroversial as well. Most warists[64] and pacifists alike can agree with (B2). (B3) is an inference from that claim and a presumably uncontroversial moral judgment in (A4), that the deliberate killing of persons against their will is presumptively wrong. Warists who accept the just war theory ("just warists," as we may call them) can agree, because they believe the presumption against killing people can be defeated. The just war theory, in their view, shows how.

---

attacks that they represent suicide. It is sometimes said that some warriors historically longed to die in battle. That may in some sense be true, but one assumes that, for the most part, they sought not to be killed so that they could carry on their own killing, else they could have allowed themselves to be killed straightaway, with no opportunity to exemplify the heroism they prized. It might be thought that volunteer soldiers, at any rate, consent to being killed by virtue of serving in the military, but that seems dubious. They agree, at least tacitly, to do things that risk being killed. But that is different from consenting to being killed. It has been alleged that even just combatants indirectly consent to be attacked. "Just combatants lose their right not to be attacked by unjust combatants because they subject themselves to a rule that disregards the distinction between just and unjust combatants. They do so because they know that it is in their interest that this rule would be commonly followed. In other words, they lose their title to life (in war) by virtue of their (very indirect) consent, just like boxers who, by agreeing on certain fair rules, lose their right not to be attacked by each other." Yitzhak Benbaji, "A Defense of the Traditional War Convention," *Ethics*, Vol. 118, No. 3, April 2008, p. 487. The overwhelming evidence would seem to be, in any event, that soldiers do not want to be killed. There are, however, important issues raised by this contention that I shall take up later in connection with the so-called moral equality of soldiers in Chapter 6.

[62] This does not mean that the acts are believed to be presumptively wrong. Most killing in warfare is probably believed by those doing it to be permissible or even obligatory. The point, rather, is that the acts of killing that are at the heart of warfare are in fact presumptively wrong, whether believed to be so or not. However, if my overall argument is correct, it is capable of being known that such killing is presumptively wrong, hence foreseeable that one will be performing presumptive wrongs by participating in warfare.

[63] It might be argued that warfare can also involve the performance of presumptively right acts, such as combating injustice, hence that the performance of presumptive wrongs does not suffice to render warfare presumptively wrong. This may be what James Turner Johnson has in mind when he says "the concept of just war does not begin with a 'presumption against war' focused on the harm which war may do, but with a presumption against *injustice* focused on the need for responsible use of force in response to wrongdoing." (*Morality and Contemporary Warfare*, p. 35). But warfare does not by its nature involve the systematic performance of presumptively right acts; at best it does so only on a side that, by hypothesis, is waging war justly. Warfare by its nature entails the systematic performance of presumptively wrong acts whoever engages in it and for whatever reasons.

[64] I use "warists" to stand for advocates of what Duane Cady calls "warism," which is the view that "war is both morally justifiable in principle and often morally justified in fact." See Duane Cady, *From Warism to Pacifism: A Moral Continuum*, 2nd ed. (Philadelphia, PA: Temple University Press, 2010), p. 17.

Pacifists can agree because they think the presumption cannot be defeated. Both can agree that many deaths in war do not fall within the scope of this presumption. The deaths of soldiers when military vehicles collide are accidental, as are those of civilians if they die when a warplane crashes. These events may sometimes involve negligence, but there is no wrongdoing in the events themselves (even if wrongful acts may have contributed to the situation in which the deaths occur). *That* there will be some such deaths in war is predictable. They are part of synoptic war. But they do not, *per se*, constitute presumptive wrongs.

This opens the door to a common objection, however. The objection points out that we build highways even though it is predictable that a certain number of people will be killed in auto accidents.[65] We build bridges, though some of them will collapse, and houses, though some of them will burn and some people die as a result. Since building highways, bridges and houses cannot reasonably be said to entail the performance of presumptive wrongs, why say that in the case of killing in war?

This is seductive reasoning. But there is a difference between deliberately killing people against their will and doing things from which it can be predicted statistically that a certain number of deaths will result, usually from voluntarily undertaken activities on the part of victims, the risks of which can be known in advance. It is indeed predictable that a certain number of persons will die as an outcome of building highways, bridges and houses. It is also predictable that a certain number of people will die as an outcome of going on picnics, taking vacations or reproducing (every live birth eventually results in a death). There are probably no human activities (including sleeping) that do not eventuate in some deaths. But most of these deaths are not intrinsic to the activities in question. Architects, highway engineers, construction crews do not kill people; causing death is not their job. Combat soldiers kill people. That is what they are trained to do. They do it intentionally and against the will of those killed.[66] Moreover, the activity of which they are a part when they do their killing is warfare, and warfare by its nature is killing. That is its point. It is, intrinsically, the business of systematically killing. This sets warfare apart from other activities from which a certain number of deaths predictably result.

---

[65] Richard Wasserstrom explores this objection, specifically with regard to the killing of children, in his ground-breaking essay, "On the Morality of War: A Preliminary Inquiry," in Richard Wasserstrom (ed.), *War and Morality* (Belmont, CA: Wadsworth Publishing Company, 1970), pp. 97–99.

[66] Although he represents killing as something of a badge of honor, which may go beyond how most soldiers view it, this is put forcefully by a Gulf War veteran, Anthony Swofford, who writes of his branch of the service: "To be a marine, a true marine, you must kill. With all of your training, all of your expertise, if you don't kill, you're not a combatant, even if you've been fired at … receiving fire is easy—you've either made a mistake or the enemy is better than you, and now you are either lucky or dead but not a combatant … you haven't, with your own hands, killed a hostile enemy soldier. This means everything … You consider yourself less of a marine and even less of a man for not having killed while at combat." See Anthony Swofford, *Jarhead: A Marine's Chronicle of the Gulf War and Other Battles* (New York: Scribner, 2003), p. 247.

2.8 Possible objections

If acts of killing are parts of warfare, and presumptive wrongness is a property of the acts, then one might object that the whole (warfare) need not have the salient property of the parts (hence be presumptively wrong), any more than an apple need be colorless because each of the atoms that make it up is colorless. To claim that it need do so is to commit a fallacy of composition.[67]

The fallacy of composition is not a formal fallacy, of course, and some inferences from a property of the parts to a property of the whole are perfectly warranted. If every part of something is made of tin, it is safe to conclude that the thing in question is made of tin. The deliberate nonconsensual killing of persons is intrinsic to warfare.[68] Likewise, the presumptive wrongness of such killing is an intrinsic property of such killing. If so, it cannot fail to characterize every such act. Hence it cannot fail to characterize the individual acts of killing that are in the nature of warfare. Not that every act involved in warfare is presumptively wrong intrinsically. Feeding soldiers, tending wounds, fueling tanks and loading guns are also typically involved in warfare. They may be presumptively wrong as well, but they need not be, and if they are, it is because of their contingent connection to the broader activity of warfare. Consistency is involved here, as part of the scaffolding of morality. If an act is presumptively wrong, then unless there are morally relevant dissimilarities between it and another act, the other act is presumptively wrong as well. Each and every act of deliberate nonconsensual killing that is part of the nature of warfare is presumptively wrong. If an act is presumptively wrong, then the systematic performance of that type of act is presumptively wrong. Thus warfare itself is presumptively wrong.

It might also be objected that an activity that involves the performance of presumptively wrong acts might also involve the performance of presumptively right acts. Sometimes these presumptive rights, as I shall call them, might offset the presumptive wrongs and render the activity as a whole (warfare in this case) presumptively right. For example, it might be argued that injustice is presumptively wrong and that the rectification of injustice is presumptively right, and that in a just war it is precisely the rectification of injustice that is the object.

There is a point to this objection.[69] War may indeed be undertaken to rectify an injustice—or in Augustinian terms, to avenge the violation of a right. But not all wars

---

[67] The fallacy of composition in its typical forms talks about natural or empirical properties. The objection under consideration regards moral properties, such as presumptive wrongness as natural or empirical properties. I do not believe that moral terms stand for such properties, in which case I believe that the objection fails to get off the ground in the first place. But as the exploration of this issue regarding the function of moral terms would take us too far afield into metaethics, I shall consider the objection on its own terms, proceeding as though the moral terms are property-referring, and specifically related to natural properties.

[68] I shall discuss the notion of intrinsic properties in greater detail later.

[69] A common philosophical representation of the point is that breaking promises is presumptively wrong and saving drowning children is presumptively right, and sometimes one must break a promise (say to return a book at a certain time) to save a drowning child, in which case it is right to do what is presumptively wrong. The assumption is that one can readily defeat the presumption that it is wrong to break a promise in situations of this sort.

are so undertaken and the rectification of a wrong is not intrinsic to war. Even less is the rectification of wrong intrinsic to war*fare*, which, as I have argued, has as its end the causing of harm, death and destruction. *Warfare by its nature entails the systematic performance of presumptive wrongs, whoever is waging it and for whatever reasons.*[70] The deliberate, organized and systematic performance of presumptively wrong acts renders any activity to which such acts are intrinsic itself presumptively wrong.[71]

As I have indicated, warfare is at the heart of war. We now need to relate the preceding to war in light of our distinctions from the preceding chapter.

C1. War$_1$ (partial war) consists of warfare by a collectivity against one or more other collectivities engaged in warfare against it.
2. If warfare by its nature is presumptively wrong, then war$_1$ by its nature is presumptively wrong.
3. Therefore: War$_1$ by its nature is presumptively wrong.

2.9 The presumptive wrongness of whole war

Whether or not one fully agrees with the above reasoning, the conclusion that war$_1$ is presumptively wrong is probably not extraordinarily controversial. Most warists think the presumption can readily be overridden in certain circumstances. The thinking of ordinary people would seem to be in accord. They believe that wars are to be avoided if possible but must sometimes be fought. However, the argument becomes somewhat more controversial as we move from the presumptive wrongness of war$_1$ to the presumptive wrongness of war$_2$. Here the argument proceeds as follows:

D1. War$_2$ (whole war) consists of two or more wars$_1$.
2. If war$_1$ by its nature is presumptively wrong, and war$_2$ consists of two or more wars$_1$, then war$_2$ by its nature is presumptively wrong.
3. Therefore: War$_2$ by its nature is presumptively wrong.

If the warfare of both sides (or all sides as the case may be) against one another is presumptively wrong, then war$_2$, which is the entirety of the warfare of both sides, is presumptively wrong. Even if the presumption of wrongness could be defeated on one side, and the war$_1$ on that side (considered in abstraction from the broader war$_2$ of which it is a part) be shown to be permissible—a possibility not ruled out by anything said so far—two presumptive wrongs melded into a joint undertaking do not make a presumptive right. At best, the whole war$_2$ would be permissible in part only (namely the war$_1$ waged by one side), but would be wrongful in the other part (the war$_1$ waged

---

[70] Rape and sexual assault, although not intrinsic to warfare, are sometimes used as weapons of warfare, and are, in any event, commonly associated with warfare. They are, more importantly, as I shall maintain in stage D of the argument, a part, though not an intrinsic part, of both war$_1$ and war$_2$.
[71] This does not mean that all of those performing such acts think of them as presumptively wrong at the time they perform them. Nor does it mean that every single act performed in the course of warfare is presumptively wrong. If a soldier is asked a question by a superior, it is (we may assume) presumptively right for him or her to answer truthfully rather than to lie.

by the other side). The just war theory, at best, can show only that the war_1 undertaken by one side is just, *ceteris paribus*.[72] It cannot, and does not attempt to, show that the whole war_2 created by both sides is just. Even if, by hypothesis, the presumptive wrongness of the war_1 waged by one side (again, considered in abstraction from the war_2 of which it is a part) could be defeated, that would not defeat the presumptive wrongness of the resultant war_2.

2.10 The burden of proof

Apart from the fact that it involves killing persons, war_2 involves the massive, systematic use of violence, and the use of violence always requires justification. This indicates part of what it takes to defeat the presumption against war_2.

> E1. To defeat the presumption that war_2 by its nature is wrong requires showing that the deliberate, organized and systematic nonconsensual killing of persons by all sides that is intrinsic to war_2 is justified.

This, again, I assume is not overly problematic, except to those who deny that war is presumptively wrong to begin with. It is important to note, again, that rape and sexual assault are also sometimes used as weapons of warfare. They are, in any event, a part of war_2 as is torture, in the sense that they regularly occur in such wars. In addition, war_2 causes destruction of property and the creation of refugees (sometimes in the millions) through forced dislocation. It also causes untold harm and death to animals, not only those used in war, but also those untended in zoos and those killed in bombardments and destruction of sanctuaries.[73] War_2 also causes harm to the environment in varying degrees, as in the use of Agent Orange in Vietnam and the use of uranium enriched munitions in more recent wars. And war_2 inevitably kills innocent persons, civilians and noncombatants. Although the killing of innocent persons, and certainly the intentional killing of innocent persons, is not intrinsic to warfare, it is part of the reality of war_2 in the modern world, hence inherent in war_2, as is the psychological harms to soldiers in the form of PTSD and moral injury. Hence:

2. Rape, torture, the killing of innocents, mistreatment of women, orphaning of chil-
    dren, destruction of property, creation of refugees and the causing of economic

---

[72] I stress the "*ceteris paribus*" clause here, because if a particular war_1 were actually right or just but the resultant war_2 to whose production it was essential was not, it would render the moral assessment of war incoherent. A war_1 can be just only if the war_2 it helps bring into and maintain in existence is just.

[73] It is estimated, for example, that more than a million horses and mules were killed in the Civil War, and more than eight million in WWI. Figures are not known for animals killed in war throughout history, including not only horses, but also camels, elephants, pigeons and more recently dogs. All of these have been used in war. It is unknown how many pets were killed. In England, at the outset of WWII, both pets and many zoo animals were deliberately killed because of the expected drain they would place on food supplies or inability to care for them or threats some of them might pose to the populace if freed.

dislocation, medical crises, PTSD, moral injury, unwanted pregnancies and harm to animals and the environment are inherent in war$_2$ in the modern world.

While not intrinsic to war$_2$, these practices are inherent in war in the modern world. Some of them are commonplace. That is documentable.[74] Sometimes all of them occur. They are part of what in Chapter 1 I called synoptic war. Synoptic war in itself, as I have said, is neither right nor wrong. But it is good or bad according to the value of its constituent parts. And such of those parts (like rape) that involve practices that tend to be wrong[75] are presumptively wrong. Choosing to go to war is choosing to bring into existence the negative value of the elements in (E2), which are among the outcomes of whole war. It is also choosing to bring about the presumptive wrongs represented by these practices. What is intrinsic to, and inherent in, war$_2$ in the modern world I take to be part of the nature of such war. I trust, furthermore, that the claim that these practices are presumptively wrong is not seriously disputable. Many of them constitute war crimes or crimes against humanity as well. Thus:

3. It is presumptively wrong to rape, torture, kill innocents, mistreat women, orphan children, destroy property, create refugees and cause economic dislocation, medical crises, PTSD, moral injury, unwanted pregnancies and harm to animals and the environment.

If, furthermore, my argument thus far is sound, the following claim follows:

4. Therefore: To defeat the presumption that war$_2$ by its nature is wrong in the modern world also requires justifying these practices in war$_2$.

This, it should be emphasized, does not necessarily mean that war$_2$ is actually wrong, either in general or in any particular case. That is left open. It means only that the burden is upon those who support such war to show that it is not wrong. Most warists think this can readily be done in the case of war$_1$ (if, e.g., the conditions of a just war are met). I shall argue later that just warists do not succeed even in showing that the presumption against war$_1$ is defeated, much less that of war$_2$. To deny that war is presumptively wrong is to deny that one needs to justify going to war, a view generally consigned to the dust bin of nineteenth- and early-twentieth-century history.

If war were intrinsically permissible, a view for which it is difficult to find arguments outside of social Darwinism and nineteenth-century militarism, then one could assume that the presumption against nonconsensual killing is always overridden in the case of war. Warists do not typically think this. Most of them are for peace. They

---

[74] The 1982 Falklands War between Britain and Argentina might be considered an exception to this claim, in light of the brevity of the conflict (two and a half months) and its confinement to remote sparsely populated islands (population 1820), and the relatively small number of casualties (3328 combatants and 3 noncombatants). It is arguable, however, that the conflict was not so much a war as a brief military engagement between the two countries. For a good discussion of the Falklands War, see Baker, "Epistemic Uncertainty and Excusable Wars," 63–69.

[75] I hasten to add that I say "tend" to be wrong in connection with rape only to conform to my definition of presumptive wrongness and not to imply that rape is not always wrong.

think it is wrong to kill in wartime unless stringent conditions are met (such as those of the just war theory). Even those like Treitschke who think that war is permissible (and perhaps even obligatory) do not appear to think that it is intrinsically permissible. They appeal, rather, to war's consequences (say, for the health of the state). But even if the presumption could be systematically defeated, it would still exist. There has to be a presumption for it to be defeated.

The following two claims, however, are highly contestable. It is for that reason that they provide the focus of the argument in the chapters that follow.

5. It has not been shown that the totality of the deliberate, organized and systematic nonconsensual killing of persons by all sides that is intrinsic to war$_2$, and the rape, torture and killing of innocents, etc. that are inherent in war$_2$ in the modern world, are justified.
6. Therefore: the presumption that war$_2$ by its nature is wrong in the modern world has not been defeated.

2.11 Conclusion

Since warfare by its nature involves killing, and warfare is at the heart of both partial war (on one side) and whole war (the totality of warfare on all sides), whole war itself is presumptively wrong. This is reinforced by the fact that although the rape, torture, killing of innocents, etc. are not intrinsic to war, they are inherent in war in the modern world, and must be justified if such wars are to be permissible. This does not by itself mean that war in the modern world is wrong. But it does mean that the burden is upon those who would support it to defeat that presumption.

In Part II, I shall examine what are arguably the most formidable theoretical attempts to defeat this presumption. The first consists of the claim that moral concepts simply do not intelligibly apply to war. That would not so much defeat the presumption that war is wrong as deny that there is such presumption in the first place. Some just war theorists likewise contend that there is no such presumption, but for different reasons. They argue that, historically at least, no such presumption is to be found in Augustine. But they argue that some wars are just, and in so doing bring morality to bear upon warfare. War realism, on the other hand, challenges the relevance of morality to warfare. As war realism represents a serious challenge to D3, let us begin with it.

3

Realism and War

The states claim, if I kill in the name of my government, it's okay … But I say, as an ethicist, that the ethical standards developed by the human family also apply to the states.

—James M. Lawson[*]

3.1 Hard and soft realism

The term "realism" has been used to stand for many different things, often with little attention to the differences among them. In its classical sense associated with Hobbes and sometimes Machiavelli it affirms the sovereignty of states.[1] More recently, this way of construing realism has evolved into an identification of realism with balance of power politics in international relations. Thus Scott D. Sagan writes that "[r]ealists advocate balance of power policies—*realpolitik*—because they see no other means to protect the state in an effective manner."[2] In a similar vein, Henry Kissinger associates realism with balance of power, which he sees originating in the Westphalian principles deriving from the Peace of Westphalia in 1648, a return to which he sees as key to world order. "To achieve a genuine world order," he writes, "its components, while maintaining their own values, need to acquire a second culture that is global, structural, and juridical … At this moment in history, this would be a modernization of the Westphalian system informed by contemporary realities."[3]

---

[*] As interviewed by Diane Lefer in *Fellowship*, Vol. 78, No. 4–6, Summer/Fall 2014, p. 26

[1] As Michael W. Doyle expresses it, according to this view "the state is and should be formally sovereign, effectively unbounded by individual rights nationally and thus capable of determining its own scope of authority." Michael W. Doyle, "Kant, Liberal Legacies, and Foreign Affairs," Part I, *Philosophy & Public Affairs*, Vol. 12, No. 2, Summer 1983, p. 218.

[2] Scott D. Sagan, "Realist Perspectives on Ethical Norms and Weapons of Mass Destruction," in Sohail H. Hashmi and Steven P. Lee (eds), *Ethics and Weapons of Mass Destruction: Religious and Secular Perspectives* (Cambridge: Cambridge University Press, 2004), p. 74.

[3] Kissinger, *World Order*, p. 373.

Political realism is narrower in scope. It has its roots in nineteenth-century German political thought and has been deeply entrenched in American thinking about international affairs since the mid-twentieth century. It includes *Machtpolitik*, the view that the conduct of states is governed by the expression, and pursuit, of power and *Realpolitik*, the view that morality does not apply to the conduct of states.[4] *Machtpolitik* is an extension of classical realism. *Realpolitik* is a metaethical thesis and may or may not be entailed by classical realism depending upon how the latter is understood.

The central idea of political realism is that morality is inapplicable to collectivities, or applicable but of little or no relevance. This is a metaethical thesis with wide implications for the nature of morality. Frequently, however, realism is identified with a second thesis, namely that collective self-interest either is or ought to be the governing norm for collectivities. This second thesis also has implications for the nature of morality but is a sociological thesis about the nature of collectivities rather than a metaethical thesis. As such, it has both descriptive and normative elements concerning how collectivities in fact act or about how they ought to act. If the "ought" in the normative component is taken to be a moral ought, then that component is not properly a part of realism. In fact, it would put the second thesis in conflict with the first, since it would mean that a moral judgment underlies the commitment to collective self-interest.

By "collectivities," as indicated in Chapter 1, I mean such entities as states, societies, peoples, classes and perhaps paramilitaries, mercenary companies and terrorist groups. Political parties and social groups are also collectivities, though of marginal interest to our concerns. What it is that supposedly renders morality inapplicable to them, and self-interest the only governing norm, may vary from case to case. One might be a realist about some collectivities and not about others.[5] Book clubs, string quartets and charities are collectivities, but neither of the above theses is typically thought to apply to them. For this reason, political realism in its broadest sense stands for a cluster of possible theories, each of which requires specific defense depending upon the character of the relevant collectivity in question.

Some collectivities (e.g. some political organizations and terrorist groups) pursue the interest of other collectivities rather than exclusively their own. Partly for that

---

[4] Julian Lider sums this up when he writes that the basic assumption for realists is "that war as a political act cannot be subjected to moral assessment; that statesmen act according to their interpretation of state interests, which are regarded as the highest value, and not according to some ethical principles; and that governments must strive for power and, if necessary, wage war in order to maintain the security of the nation and protect its way of life." See Lider, *On the Nature of War*, p. 142.

[5] Not that this exhausts the ways of understanding the much abused term "realism." Michael Lind writes: "To adopt the realist view of world politics as an arena of frequent (though not perpetual) and legitimate armed conflict, it is not necessary to reject the attempt to apply moral reasoning to warfare … Properly understood, realism is a distinctive theory of political morality, not a theory that posits the incompatibility of politics and morality." He then asks, and proceeds to answer in the affirmative, the following question: "Is there a Realist Morality of War?" Michael Lind, *Vietnam: The Necessary War: A Reinterpretation of America's Most Disastrous Military Conflict* (New York: Simon & Schuster, 1999), p. 220. Realism so understood does not preclude the relevance of morality to international affairs. But insofar as Lind takes realism to be a moral theory and the governing theory for the assessment of armed conflict, his understanding of realism is radically at variance with the views of most of those who call themselves realists. In any event, the moral realism he defines should not be confused with moral realism in ethical theory, which is a very different theory.

reason, and partly because it is states that standardly wage war, I shall focus upon nation states (or states for short), since national interest is closely tied to them. Such *statist realism*, as it might be called, is a species of political realism. For the sake of simplicity, I shall take it to constitute political realism, bearing in mind that with appropriate modifications, other forms of political realism can be generated from it. We can now define political realism as follows:

Political Realism:

A. Morality is either inapplicable to states or applicable but of limited or no relevance.
B. National interest either is or ought to be the governing norm for states.

Thesis (A) contains two disjuncts. The first, which I shall call *hard realism*, denies the applicability of morality to states at all. The second, which I shall call *soft realism*, allows that morality may apply to states but has only a limited role. Although there may be many varieties of hard and soft realism depending upon the nature of the collectivities involved, I shall, for the sake of simplicity, use these terms to stand for statist realism.

3.2 Descriptive, necessitarian and normative realism

Soft realism takes different forms depending upon the role it assigns to national interest, whether, that is, it asserts that nations always act from self-interest,[6] either necessarily or because of contingent facts about states and the international order, or asserts that they ought always to act from national interest.[7] Under national interest I include not only the usual notions of security and economic prosperity, but also less quantifiable factors such as national pride, prestige, honor and glory. National interest, in this sense, is national *self*-interest, a form of collective egoism. Accordingly, we may define hard and soft realism as follows:

> *Hard Realism*: Morality is inapplicable to states, and national interest either (1) in fact governs states (descriptive realism), (2) necessarily governs states (necessitarian realism), or (3) ought to govern states (normative realism).
>
> *Soft Realism*: Morality is applicable to states but (1) is irrelevant to decision-making, which is or ought to be governed exclusively by national interest; or

---

[6] Although he also at times clearly embraces a necessitarian realism, and sometimes even a normative realism, F. von Bernhardi gives a good formulation of descriptive realism when he says that the "political behavior of a State is governed only by its own interests, and the natural antagonism and grouping of the different Great Powers must be judged by that standard." *Germany and the Next War* (New York: Longmans, Green and Co., 1914), p. 274.

[7] Jeff McMahan labels this position strong realism. He says: "Strong Realism holds that states *ought* to be guided solely by a concern for the national interest in their relations with other states." In "Realism, Morality, and War" in Terry Nardin (ed.), *The Ethics of War and Peace: Religious and Secular Perspectives* (Princeton, NJ: Princeton University Press, 1996), p. 79.

(2) is relevant to decision making but is or ought to be subordinate to national interest.

Realists often do not distinguish among the above claims. But the typical realist position can be understood as hard or soft. They may disagree on the specific claims bound up in those two positions, but they typically agree in the denial of the claim that states ought always to act morally.[8] Some so-called realists appear to take the *ought* in (3) under hard realism or in (2) under soft realism to be a moral ought, in which case they are not, as at least some of them seem to think, really denying that states ought always to act morally.[9] They are rather, denying the relevance of certain attitudes they associate with morality. Although they call themselves realists, their position is actually a moral position.[10]

According to hard realism, as we have seen, morality neither has nor can have any bearing upon the conduct of nations. Not that war is therefore morally justified. Rather, its justification, if it has one, must be on nonmoral grounds, such as those of national interest. It is this which represents an elaboration of option (4) considered in the previous chapter in connection with the alleged inescapability of wrongdoing. It allows that one might concede that war cannot be morally justified but still deny that it is wrong on the grounds that war is neither right nor wrong. War, in this view, stands outside the scope of morality.

According to soft realism, as we have seen, moral considerations apply to the conduct of states. But they either do not have, or ought not to have, a decisive bearing upon the assessment of such conduct. A classic statement of this view is the following:

> The statesman who conducts foreign policy can concern himself with the values of justice, fairness and tolerance only to the extent that they contribute to or do not interference with the power objective. They can be used instrumentally as moral justification for the power quest, but they must be discarded the moment their application brings weakness. The search for power is not made for the achievement of moral values; moral values are used to facilitate the attainment of power.[11]

According to the stronger form, morality has, or should be given, no weight whatsoever in foreign affairs. It is a mode of assessment that is intelligible but naive or downright dangerous.[12] On the weaker version morality has (or may be given) a place in international affairs but only a secondary one.

---

[8] When realists deny that states ought to act morally, the assumption of course is that morality and national interest do not coincide.

[9] Brian Orend considers this a moral form of prescriptive realism, and calls it "morally prescriptive realism," *The Morality of War* (Toronto: Broadview Press, 2006), pp. 234f. He also seems, at least some of the time, to subsume what I am calling necessitarian realism under descriptive realism. See pp. 225f.

[10] Such a view is suggested by Scott D. Sagan when he writes that there is "a long tradition among realists in arguing that amoral *realpolitik* behavior is both strategically wise and morally preferred to its alternatives, because it is necessary to maintain even a modicum of peace and stability in a harsh world of rival states." See "Realist Perspectives on Ethical Norms and Weapons of mass Destruction," p. 74.

[11] Nicholas J. Spykman, *America's Strategy in World Politics: The United States and the Balance of Power* (New York: Harcourt, Brace and Company, 1942), p. 18. Quoted from Lin Yutang, *Between Tears and Laughter* (Garden City, NY: Blue Ribbon Books, 1943), p. 153

[12] In this spirit, Susan B. Martin writes: "The introduction of morality in the anarchic international system can be dangerous, especially when a state assumes that its particular moral and ethical views

3.3 Can it be immoral to act morally?

The denial that states ought always to act morally might be advanced on moral grounds. It would then amount to saying that, for moral reasons, moral considerations should be given no direct role, or at best a secondary role, in international affairs. In that case the denial would not strictly be a form of realism, just as thesis (3) in hard realism would not strictly be a form of realism if the "ought" is taken to be a moral ought. It would be denying only that one should expressly appeal to moral considerations in decision making. This is an intelligible position, albeit a paradoxical one. It is at least possible that morality would be better served if people did not act directly on moral considerations but rather on other considerations, such as those of prudence. The assumption would be that morality and those other considerations ultimately yield the same conduct. It would nonetheless be morality, in the end, that would ultimately determine what criteria should directly guide conduct. If, for example, the prescriptions of morality and prudence were extensionally equivalent, but those of prudence were easier to follow (and perhaps provided stronger motivation), one might think that people should directly pursue the end of prudence, personal happiness, and in so doing they would as a matter of course be acting morally.[13] Historically, self-interest functions this way, according to at least some interpretations of Adam Smith's "invisible hand," in which a common good is supposedly promoted by each individual's acting on self-interest. And Bishop Butler thought that, although God intends the best for humans, they would do better, not by aiming directly at good consequences, but by abiding by conscience. Morality, in this latter view, is deontological at the level of individual decision making but consequentialist in the broader scheme of God's design.

To show that following nonmoral criteria for judging conduct would have morally better consequences than following expressly moral criteria would, however, be difficult.[14] With regard to the foreign affairs of a state, it would presume that one could know what the consequences of acting on national interest would be, and know what the consequences of acting morally would be, and could then make an accurate comparative assessment of those consequences. To do this would require knowledge of counterfactual states of affairs that would be virtually impossible to come by.

---

are or should be universal. For example, a state may put its survival in jeopardy when it assumes that other states share its moral beliefs and then takes or refrains from actions on the basis of those beliefs. A state that refrains from fighting wars because it believes that the taking of human life is immoral is likely to soon find itself conquered by another state." See "Realism and Weapons of Mass Destruction: A Consequentialist Analysis," in Sohail H. Hashmi and Steven P. Lee (eds.), *Ethics and Weapons of Mass Destruction: Religious and Secular Perspectives*, p. 98. The Clausewitzean coloration to such views is evident if we compare Clausewitz himself, when he says: "The fact that slaughter is a horrifying spectacle must make us take war more seriously, but not provide an excuse for gradually blunting our swords in the name of humanity. Sooner or later someone will come along with a sharp sword and hack off our arms." *On War*, p. 260.

[13] Among twentieth-century realists, this view is hinted at by Robert Osgood. See Robert E. Osgood, *Ideals and Self-Interest in America's Foreign Relations* (Chicago, IL: University of Chicago Press, 1953).

[14] In the previous chapter we examined and rejected the view that it is sometimes moral to act immorally. The view now under consideration might be taken to hold that it is sometimes immoral to act morally. The most charitable interpretation of this second claim is to take "acting morally" to mean being directly responsive to moral considerations. Understood in this way, the position is coherent but difficult to establish (except perhaps where being responsive to moral considerations is equated with being moralistic—preachy, self-righteous and dogmatic). But if the claim means literally that it is sometimes immoral to act morally, that is, wrong to do what is right, then the position is incoherent.

It is *possible* that to adopt a moral point of view in the conduct of foreign policy would have bad consequences. But if I am correct that has not been shown to be the case, and this conclusion derives little support from the particular frame of history (largely twentieth century) to which realists often appeal. This in turn means that neither of the approaches we have been examining succeeds in making the case against the claim that nations should govern their conduct by moral considerations, and neither provides good reason for rejecting D(3) (from Chapter 2), that war$_2$ is presumptively wrong.

The preceding considerations apply primarily to soft realism. Hard realism presents a stronger challenge. Indeed, it can appeal to many of the preceding considerations in support of the idea that morality simply does not apply to the conduct of states. If it can make sense of the claim that states act, and show that the context in which they act lacks some of the necessary conditions for the existence of morality, then it could establish that the conduct of states (including the waging of war) is ungoverned by morality. In that case, it would be denying thesis B discussed in Chapter 2, to the effect that every action is susceptible of moral assessment, since the actions of states would be immune to such assessment.

If morality came into existence only through the institution of a state authority with power to make rules and enforce sanctions (as one finds in Machiavelli and Hobbes), then the absence of such a power over nations would entail that moral relations do not exist among them. In that case it would be true, as some writers claim, that the "preconditions for morality are absent in international politics."[15] But this reasoning confuses morality with what it is for individuals or groups to have *a morality*. It is one thing to claim, as the moral nihilist does, that there is no such thing as morality. It is another to claim that there is not *a morality* among states.[16] A morality consists of a set of values, practices, rules or principles that are generally recognized and more or less followed within a group. It is the group that is then said to have a morality, whether it be a group of individuals or a collectivity consisting of groups. It is largely an empirical question whether a group has a morality in this sense. Hobbes confuses morality with *a morality*. Any particular collection of people or groups might fail to have a morality.[17] In any event, that a particular collection of peoples or groups does not have a morality does not suffice to show that their behavior cannot be judged morally, any more than the fact that a particular individual is amoral (i.e., acts in disregard of moral considerations) means that his or her conduct cannot be judged morally.[18] If the existence of a morality among states presupposes conditions which at present are not met but which *could* be met in time and with enough effort, then it would be a merely

---

[15] Robert J. Art and Kenneth N. Waltz, "Technology, Strategy, and the Uses of Force," in Art and Waltz (eds), *The Use of Force*, 2nd ed. (Lanham, MD: University Press of America, 1983), pp. 6f. Quoted in Sagan, "Realist Perspectives on Ethical Norms and Weapons of Mass Destruction," p. 74.

[16] On this topic, see W. K. Frankena, "The Concept of Morality," *The Journal of Philosophy*, Vol. 63, 1966, pp. 688–696.

[17] The Dallas Cowboys, The Daughters of the American Revolution and the Libertarian Party do not have a morality in this sense, though they conceivably could come to have one, if they began to interact over a period of time in the appropriate (if wildly improbable) ways.

[18] I have elaborated this point in *On War and Morality*, chap. 3

contingent fact that there is no morality among states, and that fact would provide no grounds for not trying to bring about the conditions that would make a morality among states possible.

Hard realism might, of course, be grounded in moral nihilism. If there is no such thing as morality, then obviously it cannot be the case that morality applies to warfare. That would entail that there can then be no moral presumption against war. But hard realists need not take such an extreme view. They might concede that there is such a thing as morality but contend that it applies only to the conduct of individuals. As states are collectivities, and it is states that standardly wage war, morality would not apply to their conduct. This might be thought to be because of something about human nature or the nature of states or because of the character of the context in which states operate.[19] Of course, one might claim that the question of the bearing of morality on international affairs is not part of a scientific study of the international scene, and that such a study is the only proper methodological approach.[20] The first part of this claim is undoubtedly correct, but the second part represents a normative judgment and needs justification as such. As I am unaware of any strong arguments for the claim, I shall not pursue it.

3.4 War and morality

One might think that morality applies generally to the actions of states (assuming for the present that one can make literal sense of that claim that states act) but that there is something about the nature of war in particular that makes it immune to moral assessment. For this reason it is important to distinguish from political realism in general the following thesis:

War Realism: Morality is inapplicable to war or applicable but of limited or no relevance.[21]

It might be thought that there is something unique about war that makes it impervious to moral assessment even if morality applies generally to the conduct of states. Although war realism follows from hard realism and raises many of the same issues, it does not

---

[19] Susan B. Martin, discussing the so-called structural realism of Kenneth Waltz, says: "it is the structure of the international system, characterized by anarchy and the distribution of power (the number of great powers), that are the main explanatory variables in structural realism," in "Realism and Weapons of Mass Destruction: A Consequentialist Analysis," Hashmi and Lee, *Ethics and Weapons of Mass Destruction*, p. 97.

[20] As Susan B. Martin again puts it: "the goal of realism as an analytic theory is to understand and to explain international politics" in "Realism and Weapons of Mass Destruction, p. 97. If one assumes that understanding and explaining the international scene can effectively be done without taking a stand on the relevance of morality, then such "analytic realism," as we might call it, might simply suspend judgment on the question of the relevance of morality to international relations.

[21] I am following Richard Werner here in defining a sense of realism that applies specifically to war. See Werner, "Pragmatism for Pacifists," 93–115.

itself entail hard realism. For that reason in what follows I shall focus primarily upon war realism. If it is untenable, then hard realism is untenable.

3.5 Value language and deontic language

Let us consider how one might be led to embrace war realism. Note that our normative language, as it relates specifically to morality, comprises three kinds of concepts: *value* concepts, like good, bad, desirable, undesirable; *deontic* concepts, like right, wrong, duty and obligation; and *entitlement* concepts like rights, justice and claims. Value concepts obviously apply to war, whether we are talking about whole war or partial war. Wars can be evaluated as good or bad just as phenomena of nature can. But one might think that deontic and entitlement concepts, at least in their moral uses, do not apply to wars. And if they do not, then (on the assumption that such concepts are central to morality), morality does not apply to war. One might think this if one approaches war from the standpoint of a cataclysmic philosophy of war, according to which wars are happenings, not unlike phenomena of nature. Although they obviously involve the choices and decisions of many persons, often even millions of persons, they are not in any direct way the products of those choices and decisions; and if they are not, then we cannot apply deontic and entitlement concepts to them. We cannot intelligibly say that they are right or wrong, obligatory or prohibited, just or unjust. This is true of phenomena of nature but also of certain phenomena in human affairs. Economic recessions are bad, but we do not say that the economy acted wrongly by going into recession or that it was unjust to do so. More controversially, capitalist economies produce inequalities in wealth, but defenders of such economies contend there is no injustice represented by that fact. Economic trends do, of course, involve the decisions of choices of millions of individuals who are rational beings, but that does not make the economy itself a moral agent.[22] War realism need not deny that there is such a thing as morality; only that it applies to war.

3.6 Synoptic war neither right nor wrong

There is a measure of truth to war realism so understood. Indeed, its conclusion does indeed apply to what I have called synoptic war. It is just that it does not apply either to partial war or to whole war. Let us consider why.

Value concepts readily apply to synoptic war, as they do to phenomena of nature and human systems and institutions, but deontic and entitlement concepts do not. Synoptically considered, war cannot intelligibly be said to be literally right or

---

[22] The disagreement between liberals and conservatives over inequalities in wealth and income often reflects issues of this sort. Liberals contend that such inequalities represent social injustices that the government should seek to rectify, conservatives contend that they simply represent the outcomes of the functioning of a fair and rational system (along the lines of Rawls's conception of pure procedural justice). The difference between this case and the case of war is that conservatives typically argue that because the system is fair and rational, the outcomes, whatever they are, are just. They could just as easily argue that those inequalities are neither just nor unjust because the economy, though a rational system, is not a rational agent.

wrong, obligatory or prohibited. Remember that synoptic war comprises the entire phenomenon of war—all of the killing and destruction, the mobilization of resources, the heroism, cowardice, deception, honor, courage, grief, trauma—that whole war occasions. This phenomenon encompasses the decisions and choices of millions of individual moral agents but is not itself the action of a rational agent. It is not even the action of an easily identifiable subset of rational agents. The initiation and conduct of partial and whole wars are reducible to the actions of appropriately designated agents of the state, including soldiers, but synoptic wars are not. Because entitlement concepts include "just" and "unjust," the very categories of the just war tradition are inapplicable to synoptic war. Nonetheless, many of the elements intrinsic to synoptic war are inherent in whole war, hence part of its nature. As we saw in premise (E4) from Chapter 2, bringing them into existence must be justified if whole war is to be justified.

3.7 Warfare always subject to moral assessment

What is not impervious to moral assessment, however, is war_2. If our previous reasoning is correct, it is presumptively wrong, which suffices to establish the application of moral concepts to it. War_2 is not reducible to the conduct of moral agents on one side only. As we have seen, it is a cooperative undertaking by two or more parties; a collective action, if you like, by individual agents who choose to wage war. Clausewitz is correct in characterizing this as a rational choice and, on the part of heads of state, probably a political choice as well in the broad sense he has in mind. As with the car chase, once again, both the police and the suspect choose courses of action which result in an event that neither by itself could produce. By the same token, when nations go to war, they bring into existence a phenomenon neither is capable of producing by itself. They produce a war_2. And even if synoptic war in all of its comprehensiveness is not amenable to moral assessment, the warfare that each engages in, and which produces war (meaning now both partial war_1 and whole war_2), is subject to moral assessment. The actions of the individuals who plan, initiate and wage war are fully susceptible of moral evaluation.[23] This, if correct, falsifies war realism, and with it hard realism. Unless there is good reason to downgrade the importance of the relevant actions of individual moral agents, it undercuts soft realism as well. There is, however, one fairly

---

[23] Count Helmuth von Moltke, a leader of the Kreisau Circle that opposed Hitler in Nazi Germany, spoke against this personification of the state: "The state is abstract and, therefore, stands outside the sphere of moral philosophy … Just as there is no moral guilt on the part of the state, there is also no special moral justification for the actions of the state." But he followed this immediately by writing: "If the state is deprived of a possible Justification for its actions, the ethical responsibility of the individual remains entirely unaffected. There are only actions by individuals acting as agents for the state, for which they are fully responsible; they therefore cannot excuse what they have done by claiming that reasons of state made it essential: the state can provide no cover for the actions of an individual." "The Foundations of Political Science," Memoranda by Moltke, in Ger van Roon, *German Resistance to Hitler: Count von Moltke and the Kreisau Circle* (New York: Van Nostrand and Reinhold Company, 1971), p. 316. Interestingly, Moltke's views foreshadowed those of the Nuremberg Tribunal that convicted Nazi war criminals at the end of the war.

common line of reasoning which attempts to downgrade the actions of individuals in the relevant way, and we need to consider it next.

3.8 Micro- and macroethics

The line of reasoning in question trades on recognition of a distinction between macro- and microethics. The distinction between macro and micro, like Aristotle's distinction between form and matter, applies at various ontological levels. From one perspective, subatomic particles define a micro level, tables, chairs and trees a macro level. But tables, chairs and trees from another perspective define a micro level relative to a macro level of collectivities, and more specifically, societies and nation-states. Extrapolating from the metaphysical dimension to the ethical, one might suppose that there is a microethics and a macroethics, an individual morality that governs the conduct of individual persons and a collective morality that governs the conduct of groups. I shall limit my concern in connection with macroethics to states, although one might make similar judgments about other collectivities. When individual morality and collective morality conflict, frequently it is collective morality that is held to take precedence. A classic statement of this distinction is set forth by Treitschke in the nineteenth century:

> Every moral judgment of the historian must be based on the hypothesis of the State as power, constrained to maintain itself as such within and without, and of man's highest, noblest destiny being co-operation in this duty. Ethics must become more political if Politics are to become more ethical; that is to say that moralists must first recognize that the State is not to be judged by the standards which apply to individuals, but by those which are set for it by its own nature and ultimate aims … the most difficult question arises when we come to consider the extent to which the State, to attain political ends which for it are moral, may employ means which everyday life would reject … In public, as in private, life there are unfortunately too many cases where it is not possible only to have recourse to means which are absolutely above reproach.[24]

This passage could have been written by a contemporary realist or by some defenders of the just war theory. The corollary to it, however, which Treitschke adds, is not one that many realists would be comfortable with. It is that when the interests of the individual conflict with those of the state, it is the interests of the state that take precedence. Indeed, in this view, one of the highest virtues of the individual can be to sacrifice his interests, and even his life, for the higher good of the nation. This was manifestly the view of Hitler and those like Treitschke who extolled the state.[25]

One can see here many of the elements of contemporary realist and warist thought: the emphasis upon the nature of the state as power, the alleged distinction

---

[24] Heinrich von Treitschke, *Politics*, Vol. I, tr. Blanche Dugdale and Torben de Bille (New York: Macmillan Company, 1916), p. 99.

[25] Strictly, Hitler extolled the interests of the nation above those of the individual, where the nation was the Aryan people. It was this that distinguished Nazism from the Fascism of Mussolini. In either case, however, a macroethics was presumed, and the individual was deemed morally less important than the collective.

between the collective morality of the state and that of the individual, and the belief that sometimes what is right for the state conflicts with what is right by individual morality. In addition, the belief that there are cases "where it is not possible only to have recourse to means which are absolutely above reproach" may support the view considered earlier that sometimes wrongdoing is inescapable.[26]

3.9 Collective ethics a category mistake

It should be said, on the other hand, that one might recognize the distinction between macro- and microethics but hold that if they conflict it is individual morality that should hold sway."[27] However, if there are not two moralities to begin with, as I contend is the case, the necessity of choosing between them does not arise. There is no compelling reason metaphysically to assign anything more than abstract being to the entities supposedly governed by macroethics. To impute to collectivities a macroethics is to commit a category mistake. It is to transfer moral concepts that are meaningful in one category, that of human actions, to another category to which they do not belong, that of the so-called actions of states.[28] Common to both hard and soft realism, as we have seen, is the view that states—as a matter of fact, logic or metaphysics—act only (or primarily) on self-interest; or, if they do not, they ought to do so. But this, no less than the view that nations ought to act on moral considerations, assumes that states engage in rational conduct. Realists want to have it both ways. They want to represent states as engaging in rational behavior but deny that such behavior is susceptible of moral assessment. While it makes sense linguistically to speak of states acting as though they were superbeings, states are merely abstractions. Their conduct must always be understood in terms of the actions of individual human beings. An ontology of nation states would provide transformation rules by which one could systematically relate statements about the actions of states to the actions of individuals. One could then intelligibly speak of states acting, provided one could make the appropriate transformations. One could, with sufficient refinement, even render statements about the morality of the behavior of collectivities into judgments about the morality of the actions of individuals. What does not follow, however, is that one can literally speak of states as acting morally or immorally. Even if the language about state behavior

[26] Treitschke may mean that there are situations in which no available means are right by individual morality, in which case wrongdoing (from the perspective of individual morality) would seem to be inescapable. Or he may mean that in such situations there are such means but one, of necessity, cannot choose them, in which case he would be saying that there are situations in which we must choose to do what we know to be wrong (by individual morality).

[27] As did Woodrow Wilson when he wrote: "We are at the beginning of an age in which it will be insisted that the same standards of conduct and responsibility for wrong done shall be observed among nations and their governments that are observed among the individual citizens of civilized states. *The Messages and Papers of Woodrow Wilson* (New York: The Review of Reviews Corporation, 1924), p. 379. However much this might in hindsight appear to have been wishful thinking, it nonetheless implies, no less than the Treitschke passage, tacit acceptance of a distinction between individual and collective ethics.

[28] For an attempt to frame a contractarian view of the war convention around a conception of states' rights, see Yitzhak Benbaji, "The Moral Power of Soldiers to Undertake the Duty of Obedience," *Ethics*, Vol. 122 No. 1, October 2011, pp. 43–74.

is transformable into language about individual actions, states, as abstract entities, lack consciousness and rationality. And these are necessary conditions of their being moral agents. Absent such properties, they cannot intelligibly be said to act morally or immorally. This is the truth in both hard and soft realism. But if they cannot be rational moral agents they cannot be rational egoists either. What they do cannot be right or wrong from the standpoint of national self-interest any more than from the standpoint of morality. When we speak that way, we must always be prepared to render that language in terms of the actions of actual moral agents, persons with consciousness and intelligence. To do otherwise is to be beguiled by language and the convenience it affords in simplifying complex human and social interactions at the macro level for a representation of reality. Language is flexible enough that we can have the convenience without the mystification. I shall myself speak from time to time of states acting. But it should not be taken to invest states on the international scene with a separate morality, much less a higher morality. The actions of the state are the actions of individual persons appropriately credentialed and those actions are as morally assessable as any other actions by individual moral agents.

This does not mean that one cannot make sense of elevating the value of collectivities like the state or the community to the level of a great good or even the highest good. One can do that. But that can be accommodated within the framework of a single morality. It just means that the good of the state or the community must be understood ultimately in terms of the good of individual persons—not necessarily considered atomistically, but considered in all of the richness and complexity of their social life. This means further that (leaving the ethical and metaphysical views aside) ultimately it is the lives and well-being of individual persons that is of greatest moral importance. Even if it were not true that the good of the state must ultimately be understood in terms of the good of individual persons, that would not suffice to establish a collective morality. It would mean only that the state (and other collectivities as well) can have *value*. And that can be true without its being the case that the holders of value can *act*. It would not make of them conscious, rational moral agents. And that is the precondition of the existence of a macroethics. That states may have value, as I say, can be accommodated fully within an individual ethics. There is no need to postulate a collective ethics to understand this. Though it would be uncharitable to suggest that this is the underlying motivation for postulation of a collective ethics, the effect of so doing is to legitimize actions that are demonstrably wrong by ordinary moral standards.

3.10 Conclusion

In short, there are four distinguishable theses involved here: (1) that there is an individual and a collective ethics, (2) that sometimes they may conflict, (3) that when they conflict collective ethics overrides individual ethics, (4) that when they conflict individual ethics overrides collective ethics. All four are metaethical theses. They cannot be validated within morality itself. Moreover, (2), (3) and (4) presuppose (1). If there are not two moralities to begin with, then the issues raised by the remaining three theses do not arise. In the absence of a metaethical account to establish that there are two moralities, and an account of action to establish that it makes sense to say that collectivities can literally *act*—other than in the derivative sense which reduces the actions of states to those of individuals with authorization to represent the state in specific contexts—there is no reason to suppose that there is anything other than one morality, centered about the lives and well-being of human beings (and perhaps sentient beings in general).[29]

If the preceding is correct, neither war realism nor political realism provides compelling grounds for rejecting the presumption against war$_2$. Ultimately it is the lives and well-being of individual persons that is of greatest moral importance. By well-being I include psychological and moral well-being along with physical well-being. The social life of a people, as some realists rightly point out, can embody values that are important to individual persons. It is not merely the survival of the collectivity, but also the preservation of such values that often is important. But all of this, as I have said, can be accommodated within the framework of morality understood to govern the micro level. Neither states nor communities need be invested with transcendent metaphysical or moral reality to enable us, pragmatically, to make sense of the variety of conceptions of the good found in human experience.

If the presumptive wrongness of war stands, then, as I have said, the burden to defeat that presumption is upon those who wish to show that war$_2$ is permissible. As the just war theory is by far the most prominent approach to trying to show how that presumption can be defeated, I shall begin with it.

---

[29] For an opposing view that seems to presuppose two moralities, though not along the same lines as the individual and collective ethics we have been considering, see Steven P. Lee, who writes: "The distinction to go to war is a decision made outside of war where different moral rules apply than in war … Specifically, as the *ad bellum* criterion of just cause illustrates … decisions to go to war are morally governed by an idea of moral fault, and, as a result, *jus ad bellum* is morally asymmetric. But under the different moral system governing *jus in bello*, the rules are symmetric and moral fault is not considered." *Ethics and War*, p. 212.

Part II

4

Augustine on Ethics and War

But it is a higher glory still to stay war itself with a word, than to slay men with the sword, and to procure or maintain peace by peace, not by war.

—Augustine

4.1 Augustine and the just war tradition

The just war theory represents an admirable effort to bring moral considerations to bear upon one of the oldest, most pervasive and destructive of human practices, that of trying to achieve ends by war. Indeed, the just war theory has been called the "longest-continuing study of *moral decision making* known in the Western World."[1] The attempt to understand the nature and justification of political authority represents a longer tradition, but for the most part it deals with the justifiability of social and political systems rather than with specific, deliberate undertakings—as warfare represents—that are common to nearly all social arrangements.

The resurgence of interest in just war theory during the last half of the twentieth century brought a better understanding of the traditions from which it has evolved. It also brought a better appreciation of its religious and secular dimensions and the parallels among Christianity, Judaism and Islam with regard to war.[2] The closing decade or so of the twentieth century also saw increasing philosophical attention to just war theory as applied ethics acquired a solid footing within philosophy. Historians of ethics focus primarily upon the history of ethical theory. But some of the most important contributions to philosophical ethics, from Plato through the classical utilitarians, and more recently the pragmatists, have been in applied ethics. And it is to applied ethics that the just war theory belongs.

---

[1] Paul Ramsey, *War and the Christian Conscience: How Shall Modern War Be Conducted Justly?* (Durham, NC: Duke University Press, 1961), xxiii.

[2] See particularly John Kelsay and James Turner Johnson (eds), *Just War and Jihad: Historical and Theoretical Perspectives on War and Peace in Western and Islamic Traditions* (New York: Greenwood Press, 1991).

It is often thought that the just war theory is the default moral position from which to evaluate war, but it is not. As I shall argue in Chapter 5, it is simply one theory among many. One could evaluate war from a purely theological perspective, such as the divine command theory, or from a purely consequentialist perspective such as utilitarianism. These, and many other possibilities, are among the options. And discussions of the morality of war often proceed in a way which privileges the just war theory. It is common, for example, to see the options represented as political realism, at one extreme, and pacifism at the other, with the just war theory being the mean between the two.[3] This is misconceived. If the central issue is *whether* war is morally justified, then the basic choice is between militarism on one side and pacifism on the other. If we take "militarism" to stand for the view that war is permissible, either morally or nonmorally, then the basic issue is between militarism and pacifism, with warism and realism both falling on the side of militarism.

The prevailing view is that, at least within Christianity, the father of the just war theory is Saint Augustine. For example, Roland Bainton writes that Augustine's view "continues to this day in all essentials to be the ethic of the Roman Catholic Church and of the major Protestant bodies."[4] This view is supported by the medievalists' heavy reliance upon him.[5] It is also supported by the deference to him by both early jurisprudentialists and just war revivalists in the twentieth century. The extent of Augustine's influence is documentable. If all that is meant by his being called the father of just war theory is that he has had considerable influence, the claim is certainly correct. If one means more than that, the claim is problematic. For although Augustine clearly seeks to justify war, he offers little in the way of original thinking about war. Less clear also is whether his views hold together in a coherent and consistent fashion—both on their own and within the broader context of his overall thought, which is vast in scope and rich in social, psychological and philosophical insights. Less clear still, as I shall argue, is the accuracy of the way in which many recent just war theorists interpret Augustine in support of their revisionist renderings of just cause.

Whether Augustine is the father of the just war theory is, of course, of considerable historical or scholarly interest. But that is of secondary importance to understanding him correctly. There is a common misrepresentation of him among just warists. It is the attribution to him of the view that the justice of a cause for going to war is the protection of the innocent.

---

[3] As the tendency, at least since Aristotle, is to avoid extremes in favor of the mean, this creates a strong bias at the outset in favor of the just war theory.

[4] See Roland Bainton, *Christian Attitudes toward War and Peace* (New York: Abingdon Press, 1960), p. 99. For challenges to this interpretation, see particularly David Lenihan, "The Just War Theory in the Work of Saint Augustine," *Augustinian Studies*, Vol. 19, 1988, pp. 37–70; George J. Lavere, "The Political Realism of Saint Augustine," *Augustinian Studies* 11, 1980, pp. 135–145; and Reinhold Niebuhr, *Realism and Political Problems* (New York: Chalres Scribner's Sons, 1953), pp. 119–156. For a balanced analysis of the issue, see William R. Stevenson, Jr, *Christian Love and Just War: Moral Paradox and Political Life in St. Augustine and His Modern Interpreters* (Macon, GA: Mercer University Press, 1987).

[5] On Augustine and the medievalists, see Frederick H. Russell, *The Just War in the Middle Ages* (Cambridge: Cambridge University Press, 1975).

Most just warists assume that some wars are permissible and start from there. Many of them also assume that defense of the innocent is the paradigm of a just cause. With regard to protection of the innocent, the following are representative views:

> For love's sake (the very principle of the prohibition of killing), and not only for the sake of an abstract justice sovereign over the political realm in separation from the private, Christian thought and action was driven to posit this single "exception" … that forces should be repelled and the bearers and close cooperators in military force should be directly repressed, by violent means if necessary, lest many more of God's little ones should be irresponsibly forsaken and lest they suffer more harm than need be.[6]

> The proper action for the Christian, reasoned Augustine, is to intervene between the criminal and victim, defending the latter even at the risk of his own life against attack or threat of attack by the former.[7]

> Augustine can make this distinction between the defense of others and self-defense, because he, like Ambrose, believes that the defense of others is a charitable or altruistic act, whereas self-defense is a selfish one. The former could be done with "love in one's heart," while the latter would be motivated either by hatred or self-love.[8]

> Augustine serves to remind us that political judgments are at bottom moral judgments. Christian justification for coercive force is neighbor love that must be willing on occasion to protect the innocent third party. The law of love obliges us to use force in the aid of others.[9]

> The primary moral justification for war is to protect the innocent from certain harm. Augustine, whose early 5th century book, *The City of God*, is a seminal contribution to just war thinking, argues … that it is better for the Christian as an individual to suffer harm rather than to commit it. But is the morally responsible person also required, or even permitted, to make for *other* innocent persons a commitment to non-self-defense? For Augustine, and for the broader just war tradition, the answer is no. If one has compelling evidence that innocent people who are in no position to protect themselves will be grievously harmed unless coercive force is used to stop an aggressor, then the moral principle of love of neighbor calls us to the use of force.[10]

> Early Christian just war theory regarded the use of coercion, sometimes lethal, as justified if it is necessary to protect the innocent from injustice.[11]

This interpretation of Augustine is of more than just academic interest. Jean Bethke Elshtain, whose view is expressed in the next to the last quotation, was one of a handful

---

[6] Ramsey, *The Just War*, pp. 150–151. Ramsey does not specifically mention Augustine in this passage but has been understood to have derived the view expressed from Augustine.

[7] Johnson, *Can Modern War Be Just?*, p. 3.

[8] Christopher, *The Ethics of War & Peace*, p. 41.

[9] Charles, *Between Pacifism and Jihad: Just War and Christian Tradition*, p. 44.

[10] Elshtain, *Just War against Terror: The Burden of American Power in a Violent World* (New York: Basic Books, 2003), p. 189.

[11] Nigel Biggar, *In Defense of War* (Oxford: University Press, 2013), p. 160.

of scholars and religious leaders invited to meet with President George W. Bush as he was considering his response to 9/11. Her interpretation of Augustine—that one could not kill in self-defense but could and must do so in defense of the innocent—reportedly was of interest to Bush, and that notion, according to the *New York Times*, "became central to the Bush administration's justification of the war in Iraq as in large part a humanitarian project to free the Iraqi people from a tyrant."[12]

This, however, is not Augustine's view. To see why not requires a closer look at his ethical and theological views.

What makes these issues difficult to assess is that Augustine's discussions of war are brief, scattered and unsystematic.[13] Many who deal with topics in his writings to which war would seem to be relevant either do not discuss his views on war at all, or do so only in passing. At the same time, metaphors of war recur in his writing. Augustine, like Plato before him and many after him, uses the language of war to characterize what he sees as an ongoing psychological conflict within each person. Plato has Clinias say, "Why, here … is the field in which a man may win the primal and subtlest victory, victory over *self*, and where defeat, defeat by *self* is most discreditable as well as most ruinous. There lies the proof that everyone of us is in a state of internal warfare with himself."[14] Augustine, for his part, asks, "What war, then, can be imagined more serious and more bitter than a struggle in which the will is so at odds with the feelings and the feelings with the will, that their hostility cannot be ended by the victory of either …?"[15] Such passages suggest that whatever its role in shaping his beliefs about the actual practice of armed conflict, the idea of war has deep roots in Augustine's thinking. Plato, however, understood war in the context of the state, viewing it as an art of acquisition to facilitate expansion when expensive tastes create wants that outstrip needs. In this way he thought it sprang from the same causes as all of the evils of the state.[16] Aristotle added that some people were meant to be dominated by others, and when they refused to submit it was "naturally just" that war be made against them.[17] There was believed to

---

[12] This account of Elshtain's advisory role to George W. Bush following 9/11 is taken from a *New York Times* obituary for Elshtain, August 15, 2013. The account implies, though it does not specifically state, that Elshtain's account of Augustine was influential in providing one of Bush's justifications for the Iraq War.

[13] The principal passages in which Augustine discusses war have been usefully compiled by David A. Lenihan, in "The Just War Theory in the Work of Saint Augustine," *Augustinian Studies*, Vol. 19, 1988, pp. 37–70:

The Free Choice of the Will (*De Libero Arbitrio*), I, 5. Reply to Faustus, the Manichaean (*Contra Faustum, Manichaeu*), Bk. XXII.

Letter 138, to Marcellinus.

Letter 189, to Boniface.

Letter 222, to Darius.

Quaestiones, in Heptateuchum VI, qu. 10.

Sermon, 30.

City of God—De Civitate Dei.

[14] Plato, *Laws I*, Steph. 626, trans. A. E. Taylor, in *The Collected Dialogues of Plato*, ed. Edith Hamilton and Huntington Cairns (Princeton, NJ: Princeton University Press, 1971).

[15] *City of God*, Bk. XIX.28, trans. Henry Bettenson (New York: Viking Penguin, 1986). See also Bk. XIX.4,13; Bk. XXI.15,16; *Reply to Faustus*, Bk. XXII.22; and *Confessions*, Bk. X.

[16] See *Republic*, Bk. II.

[17] *Politics*, Bk. I, Ch. 8.

be a teleological order to nature and, at least for Aristotle, a natural justice to war when it conformed to this order.

Augustine, on the other hand, understands war in terms of a divine order and (as do writers in Judaism, Christianity and Islam alike) accordingly seeks war's legitimation in the relationship between God and humankind. The problem for Christianity, of course, is that Christ *seems* to proscribe violence in the commandment to love, particularly as that applies to enemies. I say "seems" because Jesus does not talk specifically about war. But what he says would seem to create a presumption against war. To defeat this apparent presumption against war is the central challenge to Augustine.[18]

It is a challenge I believe he fails to meet. Despite a complex and sophisticated attempt,[19] Augustine departs radically from the pacifism of the early church. As his biographer, Peter Brown, writes:

> In an atmosphere of public disaster, men want to know what to do. At least Augustine could tell them. The traditional pagans had accused the Christians of withdrawing from public affairs and of being potential pacifists. Augustine's life as a bishop had been a continual refutation of this charge. He knew what it was to wield power with the support of the Imperial administration. Far from abandoning civil society, he had maintained what he believed to be its true basis, the Catholic religion; and in his dealings with heresy, lawlessness and immorality, he had shown not a trace of pacifism.[20]

Augustine fused Christianity to a militarism that to this day is a hallmark of societies that profess to be Christian. Indeed, the most striking feature of his position is its *acceptance* of war, just or unjust, as an inevitable part of the human condition. Insofar as the just war theory is thought to provide moral criteria by which to judge whether to go to war (*just ad bellum*), and how to conduct war once in it (*jus in bello*), there is little of such guidance in Augustine, hence little ground on that score for representing him as the father of the just war theory.

4.2 Was Augustine a private pacifist?

A contrary view merits consideration, however. Not only does it contain a measure of truth, but it also highlights one of the central problems in understanding Augustine on war. Although the prevailing view is that Augustine is progenitor of the just war theory, he has also been read as a private pacifist, whose views are peaceful in essence and on

---

[18] On the moral presumption against war in recent Catholic thought, see *The Challenge of Peace: God's Promise and Our Response*, A Pastoral Letter on War and Peace, May 3, 1983 (Washington, DC: The American Catholic Conference, 1983). Some more recent just war theorists, as we have seen, deny this presumption.

[19] The attempt is motivated in part by the desire to respond to Christianity's critics who charged that its teachings had weakened the Roman state and thus made it vulnerable to attacks like that of the Visigoths in AD 410.

[20] Peter Brown, *Augustine of Hippo* (New York: Dorset Press, 1967), p. 291.

a continuum with pacifists of the early church.[21] In this view, Augustine's thought is distorted by later writers who obscure its essentially pacifistic character.

A private pacifist is one who is pacifistic in his own conduct but does not expect or require it of others.[22] He believes, for example, that it would be wrong for him to participate in war but not necessarily wrong for others. Augustine was almost certainly a private pacifist in this sense. He denies that private individuals may kill even in self-defense. Short of assuming the duties of an official of the state or an agent thereof (as he understands soldiers to be), one not only need not, but may not, on Augustine's view, engaging in killing. It should not be surprising that as a bishop of the church, and not an official of the state, Augustine would have been unwilling personally to participate in war. In later medieval writers, the prohibition of clergy from participating in war came to be thought consistent with the Christian sanction of war.[23] One can personally refrain from participating in war and yet believe in its justifiability as waged by others.

It is true that Augustine stands on a continuum in many respects with earlier Christian writers—certainly if one counts Saint Ambrose among those writers, since Ambrose expressly supports war and killing. In extolling fortitude, he says:

> Nor is the law of courage exercised in causing but in driving away all harm. He who does not keep harm off a friend, if he can, is as much in fault as he who causes it. Wherefore holy Moses gave this as a first proof of his fortitude in war. For when he saw an Hebrew receiving hard treatment at the hands of an Egyptian, he defended him, and laid low the Egyptian and hid him in the sand.[24]

And in the course of his defense of the divinity of Christ for the Emperor Gratian, who was about to go forth to fight the Goths in the Eastern Empire, Ambrose says: "I must not further detain your Majesty, in this season of preparation for war, and the

---

[21] See Lenihan, "Just War Theory in the Work of Saint Augustine."

[22] Eric Reitan defines the related concept of personal pacifism rather more broadly as "a purely personal commitment to nonviolence, one that is not adopted on the basis of a perceived general obligation to refrain from violence and … not intended to express the belief that all persons ought to oppose violence under every circumstance." See his "Personally Committed to Nonviolence: Towards a Vindication of Personal Pacifism," *The Acorn*, Vol. 10, No. 2 (Spring 2000), pp. 30–41. Frederick H. Russell speaks of private pacifism in connection with Augustine, writing, "Augustine bore witness to the pacifistic tendencies of the Early Church. Only rulers and officials acting in the line of duty were able to kill without giving vent to hatred and other sinful passions. Private pacifism was thus joined to a justification of public warfare that underscored the later medieval emphasis on the legitimate authority necessary to wage just wars." See *The Just War in the Middle Ages*, p. 18. On private pacifism, see also Douglas P. Lackey, *The Ethics of War and Peace* (Englewood, New Jersey: Prentice-Hall, 1989), pp. 16–18. I shall in Chapter 11 refine the distinction between private and personal pacifism and distinguish both from existential pacifism.

[23] St. Thomas Aquinas writes: "Warlike pursuits are altogether incompatible with the duties of a bishop and cleric," both because they hinder the mind from contemplation of divine things and because it would be more fitting for them to shed their own blood for Christ. *Summa Theologica*, Pt. II-II Q. 40. Art. 2 (New York: Benziger Brothers, 1947), trans. Fathers of the English Dominican Province, p. 1361.

[24] *Duties of the Clergy* I:36.179.

achievement of victory over the Barbarians. Go forth, sheltered, indeed, under the shield of faith, and girt with the sword of the Spirit; go forth to the victory."[25]

Even discounting Ambrose, and emphasizing those writers typically identified with the pacifistic sentiments of the early church, like Origen, Tertullian and Lactantius, there are many similarities. Augustine talks repeatedly about peace and love and laments the horrors of war. That is not in question. What is in question is whether, despite this, his thought places Christianity on a different path from what it was on in the view of most Christian writers prior to Ambrose and prior to its de facto militarization by Constantine.

What needs scrutiny is Augustine's interiority, as it is often called—his emphasis upon subjective inner states. For it is this that renders consistent his probable private pacifism with his justification of war. Augustine turns Christianity inward. He says that Christ's injunctions in the Sermon on the Mount do not apply to outward action but rather to inner attitude; the "sacred seat of virtue," he says, is the heart.[26] This, if it can be rendered both intelligible and plausible, does seem to open the door to one's being a pacifist in his heart and yet supportive of killing in warfare. And that in turn would be a step in the direction of enabling Augustine, at one level, to remain committed to the pacifistic testimony of the New Testament and at the same time, at another level, to reorient Christianity to the path of militarism.

4.3 Augustine's subjectivism

Augustine's subjectivism stands out in his statement that "not what the man does is the thing to be considered; but with what mind and will he does it." Contrasting God's giving up of his Son and Jesus' giving up of himself with Judas' giving up of Jesus in betrayal, Augustine says, "The diverse intention therefore makes the things done diverse." With regard to the acts of Jesus and Judas, "though the things be one [presumably a giving], yet if we measure it by the diverse intentions, we find the one a thing to be loved, the other to be condemned; the one we find a thing to be glorified, the other to be detested. Such is the force of charity. See that it alone discriminates, it alone distinguishes the doings of men."[27]

Here the thing done is presumed in some sense to be the same. Intentions supposedly determine whether it is praiseworthy or blameworthy. Augustine then speaks of cases in which the things done are different: a father beating a boy, a boy-snatcher

[25] *Exposition of the Christian Faith* 2.16.136. Both quotations are from *St. Ambrose: Select Works and Letters*, in Philip Schaff, ed., *A Select Library of Nicene and Post-Nicene Fathers of the Christian Church*, 2nd ser., Vol. 10 (Grand Rapids, MI.: Eerdmans, 1955).

[26] "If it is supposed that God could not enjoin warfare, because in after times it was said by the lord Jesus Christ, 'I say unto you, That ye resist not evil: but if any one strike thee on the right cheek, turn to him the left also,' the answer is, that what is here required is not a bodily action, but an inward disposition. The sacred seat of virtue is the heart" (*Contra Faustum* 22.76, in Saint Augustine, *Writings in Connection with the Manichaean Controversy*, in Schaff, *Select Library of the Nicene and Post-Nicene Fathers*, Vol. 4.

[27] Saint Augustine, *Homilies on the First Epistle of John* 7.7, trans. H. Browne, in *Select Library of the Nicene and Post-Nicene Fathers*, Vol. 7.

caressing one. The first represents "a man by charity made fierce," the other a man "by iniquity winningly made gentle." Here not only do the outward acts differ, they differ deceptively. The beating is an act of love, the molestation an act of evil. It is the "mind" or "will" with which the two acts are done that makes the difference.

In the latter two cases it is not merely that the intentions differ. The motives differ as well, love in the one case, concupiscence in the other. Neither Augustine nor Aquinas after him carefully distinguish motives and intentions. But the distinction is of the first importance for understanding Augustine's position.

At stake is the grounds for sometimes judging similar acts differently and different acts similarly, a recurring concern of Augustine's that he believes requires looking beyond the outward act. In one of his letters to Marcellinus he writes:

> For just as in the case of different persons it may happen that, at the same moment, one may do with impunity what another man may not, because of a difference not in the thing done but in the person who does it, so in the case of one and the same person at different times, that which was duty formerly is not duty now, not because the person is different from his former self, but because the time at which he does it is different.[28]

Augustine here appears to deny the universalizability of moral judgments, if that thesis is understood to require that similar acts be judged similarly. It is doubtful that he is denying the thesis, however, if it is interpreted more broadly to require that relevantly similar *cases* or *situations* be judged similarly. For he does think that there are relevant dissimilarities in the cases he would have us judge differently (as there will always be if, as Augustine seems to do, one takes time to be a relevant dissimilarity). And he is almost certainly not denying the thesis if it is understood to mean that acts or cases must be judged similarly unless there are relevant dissimilarities between them.

Although Augustine speaks as though a difference of time *simpliciter* were a morally relevant consideration, a more charitable understanding of him is as holding that motives and intentions, representing as they do "mind and will," as distinguished from outward acts, are morally relevant aspects of situations. They differ from outward acts, yet are transformative of the moral character of such acts. The implication is that without some difference in motives or intentions, or both, acts cannot differ morally.

Augustine emphasizes diverse intentions in the case of giving. But intentions do not suffice to reveal the "inward disposition" of the heart. One can intend good but do so from pride. One who fights the flames in a burning building may intend to save the child but do so from expectation of praise. A right intention, to be sure, is necessary for a rightly done act. Augustine sees a bad intention as sufficient to condemn Judas. But it is not sufficient. Indeed all of the acts of charity—from feeding the hungry to clothing the poor—can be done from pride. When they are, the intentions (to get the hungry fed and the poor clothed) will be the same as if they were done from charity. Not *acts*

---

[28] Letter 138.4, trans. J. G. Cunningham, in *Select Library of the Nicene and Post-Nicene Fathers*, Vol. I.

of charity but only the motive of charity can properly be the root of our conduct. "It alone," says Augustine, "distinguishes the doings of men."[29]

Thus while evil intentions can spring only from evil motives, good intentions can spring from either good or evil motives. This makes possible the seduction of "good deeds" against which Augustine cautions. With prideful motives concealed, we seek praise through outwardly good acts. Such acts can abound. We can easily identify them. Truly good works we cannot easily identify because they are done from love, and that motive is hidden from us.

This means that Augustine's subjectivism is rooted in motivation, not intention. Both motives and intentions can determine the moral character of acts (though intentions cannot do so invariably, since a well-intentioned act can yet be basely motivated). But motives are basic, because they determine the character of intentions as well as of acts.

4.4 Motives and right conduct

There remains, however question of the precise role of motivation in determining correct conduct. This is crucial to understanding the justification of war. It brings us to one of the most difficult areas of Augustine's philosophy. There arises here a problem that continues to plague love-centered ethics. It is found in one of Augustine's homilies on the Epistle of Saint John:

> See what we are insisting upon; that the deeds of men are only discerned by the root of charity. For many things may be done that have a good appearance, and yet proceed not from the root of charity. For thorns also have flowers: some actions truly seem rough, seem savage; howbeit they are done for discipline at the bidding of charity. Once for all, then a short precept is given thee: *Love, and do what thou wilt:* whether thou hold thy peace, through love hold thy peace; whether thou cry out, through love cry out; whether thou correct, through love correct; whether thou spare, through love do thou spare: let the root of love be within, of this root can nothing spring but what is good.[30]

Central to this passage is the directive: Love and do what you will. But the directive is ambiguous. It could mean, as it most readily suggests:

1. Love, then do whatever love moves you to do.

This would give full weight to love as a motive. Love is commanded. Obeying that command is to be motivated by love. To be motivated by love is to govern one's conduct

---

[29] *Homilies on the First Epistle of John*, 7.7. See also, *Homilies on the First Epistle of John*, 8.9, in which Augustine says: "But that, in the good that is done, it may not be pride that sets us on, who knows? where is it? The works we see: mercy feeds, pride also feeds; mercy takes in the stranger, pride also takes in the stranger; mercy intercedes for the poor, pride also intercedes … In the works we see no difference." *Select Library of the Nicene and Post-Nicene Fathers*, Vol. 7.

[30] *Homilies on the First Epistle of John*, 7.8 (italics added).

by love.[31] In that case, everything one does when one loves would represent right conduct. If (*per impossibile* for humans) love fully and completely motivated us, then all of our conduct (at least all of it that is voluntary) would, as it is, in Kant's view for rational beings with a holy will, invariably be right. Where for Plato to know the good is invariably to do it (provided one is able), for Augustine, on this interpretation, to love perfectly would be invariably to act lovingly, hence invariably to act rightly.

A second interpretation is suggested by that part of the passage that says, "whether thou hold thy peace, through love hold thy peace; whether thou cry out, through love cry out; whether thou correct, through love correct; whether thou spare, through love do thou spare." Here it looks as though the directive may actually mean:

2. Do what you will, but whatever you do, do it from love.

This suggests that what you do in the way of outward conduct may, in the end, be unimportant. What is important is that whatever you do, you choose to do it from the motive of love. Thesis (1) implies that love moves us to perform *certain* outward acts, presumably because there is something about them (e.g., their goodness) that makes them the appropriate objects of love. The implication then is that there is some sort of connection between love and certain states of affairs that we are capable of actualizing through our conduct. Thesis (2), on the other hand, implies that outward acts are indifferent in themselves and that it is only when they enter into the appropriate relationship with love—being selected (or rejected), as it were, by love—that they acquire their particular moral significance.[32] According to both (1) and (2) whatever is done from love is right. But according to (1), that is because love reliably guides us to perform only those acts that are independently right. According to (2), it is because any acts chosen by love thereby become right. The difference between (1) and (2) is akin to that involved in divine-command ethics. Whereas one can ask whether God commands what he does because it is right, or whether it is right because God commands it, here one can ask whether loves motives us to do what is right because it is right, or whether what is right is so because love motivates us to do it.[33]

---

[31] It is possible, of course, though Augustine does not seem to consider it, that one can love but not always be governed by love. That is, love, while always a motive, may not always be a sufficiently strong motive to govern conduct. If that were the case, then doing "whatever thou wilt" would authorize only doing those things actually impelled by love. This would leave open whether acts not effectively motivated by love (i.e., where the motive is not strong enough to determine conduct), should be foregone or judged by some other criteria.

[32] This interpretation would accord with what Augustine says about the seat of virtue being in the heart. It would also accord with the Stoic doctrine that, in the classification of all things as good, bad or indifferent, everything other than virtue (an intrinsic good) and vice (an intrinsic bad) is indifferent, including human actions. This appears to be the understanding of William R. Stevenson, Jr, when he says of Augustine's view, "So long as one truly loves, *what* one does does not really matter; any action based in and arising out of true love is by definition 'right,'" *Christian Love and Just War*, 107.

[33] There are further complexities I cannot fully explore here. It may be that love selects certain acts not because they are right but because they are good. The acts are then rendered right because of the good they promise to actualize (or perhaps, in fact actualize). This would make Augustine basically a divine-command deontologist, holding that we ought always and invariably to do as God commands

At times Augustine inclines toward the consequentialist view suggested by (1)—that love moves us as it does because that is the direction in which the good lies (and ultimately, of course, because that is what God has ordained). At other times he inclines toward the nonconsequentialist view suggested by (2), that what is done lovingly, whatever it may be, is thereby constituted good and hence right.[34]

The consequentialist rendering is suggested by Augustine's saying that "there is a certain friendliness of well wishing, by which we desire at some time or other to do good to those whom we love"[35] and that, when we are not situated so as to be able to do good, benevolence—the "well wishing"—must suffice. Loving, it seems here, means doing good (acting beneficently) when we can and wishing good (being benevolently disposed) when we cannot. By extension we may presume that acting beneficently when possible (and benevolently otherwise) is to do what is right. In this spirit Augustine contends that love of enemies has an end that is an obvious good: the transforming of them so that they are no longer enemies.[36]

The problem with this interpretation is that it seems to reduce love to benevolence, which, though a motive, is only a motive to do good. And this would leave unexplained why God commands love rather than benevolence.[37] Yet Augustine seems to regard love and benevolence as two different things. Indeed, love, beneficence (doing good) and benevolence (being motivated to do good) are three different things. He says, for example, that when one cannot act beneficently "the benevolence, the wishing well, of itself sufficeth him that loves"—suffices presumably for right conduct[38] If love and benevolence are not two different things, love becomes vacuous, its content emptied into the notion of benevolence.

For these reasons the second, nonconsequentialist interpretation, is most plausible. This is suggested by the final thought of the above passage in which Augustine says, "let the root of love be within, of this root can nothing spring but what is good." This suggests that love cannot fail to produce good. And if one is troubled by the possibility that some of what one does may seem harmful to others (and here we should be mindful that, as Augustine conceives of love, it can lead to war and killing), Augustine counsels: "Therefore hold fast love, and set your minds at rest. Why fearest thou lest thou do evil to some men? Who does evil to the man he loves? Love thou: it is impossible to do this without doing good."[39] If this meant only that love reliably

---

(namely love). At the same time he would be a pragmatic teleologist, holding that when we do as God commands (i.e., act lovingly in all that we do) we as a matter of fact do what is best, given God's ordering of things. As indicated in the previous chapter, this view is defended by Bishop Butler.

[34] Stricly speaking, both (1) and (2) would be nonconsequentialist if they are taken without elaboration and also are taken as basic principles. It is when one understands (1) to presuppose that love impels us to do good that it becomes consequentialist and axiological, for then it requires of us that we calculate the value of the consequences of our acts in the determination of what is right.

[35] *Homilies on the First Epistle of John*, 8.5.

[36] *Homilies on the First Epistle of John*, 8.10. It is theoretically possible that there is something else about the character of certain acts besides their goodness or rightness that leads love to move us to do them, but it is difficult to see what that would be for Augustine.

[37] On related topics, see William K. Frankena, "Love and Principle in Christian Ethics," in Alvin Plantinga, ed., *Faith and Philosophy: Philosophical Studies in Religion and Ethics* (Grand Rapids, MI.: Eerdmans, 1964), 203–225.

[38] *Homilies on the First Epistle of John*, 8.5.

[39] *Homilies on the First Epistle of John*, 10.7.

directs us to the good and invariably moves us to it, then it would be consistent with interpretation (1). But if it means, as Augustine seems to intend, that love cannot in a logical or conceptual sense fail to produce good, then it supports (2). It is not that the good is out there, so to speak, and love simply directs us to it. It is that something's being good simply consists in its issuing from love. It is not that love is an infallible guide to right conduct, it is that love transforms any conduct done from love into right conduct. Thus otherwise identical acts may have different moral characters depending upon whether they are done from love. Acts done from pride sometimes produce good and sometimes do not, but they are always wrong. Acts done from love necessarily produce good (given how God has ordered the world) and are always right.[40]

4.5 Private pacifism and clean hands

Let us now return to the question of whether Augustine stands more in the tradition of the church's earlier pacifism than in that of subsequent just war theorists.

A private pacifist, again, is one who is unwilling to participate in war himself but does not expect the same from others. Such a person might believe that wars sometimes must be fought but simply not want to be personally involved; in that case the maintenance of clean hands is paramount. Alternatively, such a person might believe that war is wrong but owing to humility or moral tolerance be unwilling to legislate for others, leaving it to them to make up their own minds about what to believe and how to act.

If Augustine held the second view, it would indeed put him closer to early Christian pacifists than to later just war theorists. He would then be a personal pacifist as opposed to merely a private pacifist, a distinction I shall elaborate in Chapter 11. But then we could make little sense of his determination to justify war, which represents an attempt to justify it for all Christians, and by implication at least for non-Christians as well. To render his position consistent we must view him as a pacifist of the first sort; as one who believes that wars are sometimes justified but who is simply unwilling personally to be involved in them; who, as a man of God, feels he must keep his hands clean.

If one reads him as a private pacifist, there is no difficulty in reconciling his position with the justification of war, hence no ground on this basis for challenging the standard view of him as progenitor of the just war tradition. If that is the case, the view that puts Augustine more in the tradition of the early Christian pacifists than in that of later Christian just war theorists derives little support from Augustine's private pacifism. Even if Augustine maintained that not only he but others as well should be pacifists, the situation would not change. His subjectivism would render even

---

[40] As Peter Brown writes, comparing Augustine's early works with his later support of the repression of the Donatists: "Even in his early works as a priest, Augustine will constantly attempt to define the messy boundary between severity and aggression ... 'Love wholeheartedly: Then do what you like' is one epigram which ... will appear in its harshest form, as a justification of persecution by the Catholic Church." *Augustine of Hippo*, p. 209.

universal pacifism consistent with the waging of war and doing so justifiably. If the precept to love is understood to require an inner transformation that is compatible with any outward conduct (nonmorally described), then turning the other cheek, loving one's enemies and not returning evil for evil become fully consistent with striking back, killing one's enemies, and returning suffering, death, and destruction for evil.

When one looks at what Augustine considers loving conduct (as opposed to simply motivation) one finds it repeatedly associated with notions like "severity," "discipline," "correction" and "chastisement." Love is not preserved by gentleness.[41] It can inflict terrible suffering and often does. The pain, suffering and death almost universally taken to be evil become good when inflicted by love. It may even be that Augustine thinks that love of enemies is a purer form of love even than love of the poor and needy. He points out that loving the poor and needy is fraught with pitfalls because of the risk of pride creeping into one's motivation. "With a truer touch of love," he says, on the other hand, "thou lovest the happy man, to whom there is no good office thou canst do; purer will that love be, and far more unalloyed."[42] When shortly later he discusses love of one's enemies, he says: "Thou lovest not in him what he is, but what thou wishest him to be. Consequently, when thou lovest an enemy, thou lovest a brother. Wherefore, perfect love is the loving an enemy: which perfect love is in brotherly love."[43] There are degrees of purity of love. Just as loving a happy person will likely be freer of pride than loving a needy and wretched person toward whom one can show outward charity, so love of an enemy is purer still. It requires overcoming the very preoccupation with the temporal self that pride cherishes.

Even though Augustine's private pacifism lends little support to the view that he belongs in the tradition of early Christian pacifists, nothing in the preceding compels placing him in the later just war tradition either. His subjectivism does not settle the question whether he belongs more to one tradition than to the other. The sharp inner/outer dualism of his subjectivism means that there is no inconsistency in representing him as both pacifistic and militarist in different respects. It then becomes a matter of emphasis which side of him one takes to be most important. Where that emphasis properly belongs requires a fuller consideration of his views on war. So let us turn to the specifics of those views.

Augustine says little about *jus in bello* beyond sanctioning ambushes, prohibiting vengeful cruelty and acknowledging the need for truthfulness in dealing with an enemy. He says more about *jus ad bellum* but even there without much elaboration. The exception to this is with regard to wars commanded by God. Like Ambrose, Augustine looks to the Old Testament for much of his justification of war. God directs the Israelites to conquer and in some cases annihilate various peoples. What is commanded by God for Augustine is absolutely obligatory. There is a sharp distinction between his treatment of wars approved by God, which are unquestionably just, and

---

[41] This may be partly explained by the fact that as a child Augustine suffered beatings at the hands of his father.

[42] *Homilies on the First Epistle of John*, 8.5

[43] *Homilies on the First Epistle of John*, 10.

those not approved by God, which may or may not be just.[44] To be justified in waging a war not approved by God one must have legitimate authority and a just cause. Sometimes it is thought that Augustine requires a right intention as well. Although, as I shall argue, this is true in a trivial sense, it is not until Aquinas that right intention is fully enshrined in Christian thinking about just war.

According to Augustine, just cause is provided by a state's having suffered a wrong at the hands of another state. The wrong can be either by direct action of the other state or by actions of its citizens for which it refuses to make restitution.[45] The war a just cause warrants is punitive, to avenge the wrong. It may involve self-defense (as it presumably would if the wrong were aggression against the state having the just cause). But even then, it is the wrong constituted by the aggression, and the need to punish that wrong, that provides the just cause, not the need to defend the state. Self-defense need not be involved at all. A just cause may entitle a state under a ruler with legitimate authority to *initiate* a war. This sets Augustine against those contemporary theorists who see self-defense as the only justification for war. It also sets him against the twentieth-century paradigm for a justified war, which is one fought in self-defense against an aggressor.

Legitimate authority is framed by Augustine's Christian worldview. According to that view, husbands dominate their wives, fathers their children and monarchs their subjects. God dominates all persons, who ought to be submissive and obedient to his will.[46] As war takes place between states, only persons with the appropriate authority within states may initiate war. And only their agents may fight. And when those agents kill, they do so with impunity.[47] William R. Stevenson, Jr, effectively summarizes this aspect of Augustine's thinking:

> For the subjects of rulers, the fact of the *providential voluntaria* means that they should obey, essentially without question. Whatever the content of a particular regime, it serves a purpose ultimately good and consequently should not be hindered through disobedience. God bestows power on representatives of all degrees of human perversion; nonetheless, Augustine asked rhetorically, "although the causes be hidden, are they unjust?" Consequently, subjects ought to be both passive and obedient in the face of superior human power. For them, too, power equals authority. If the subjects are soldiers, they are obliged to carry out the orders of their commanders even if those orders require fighting and killing. If they kill under military orders they are not guilty of murder; on the contrary, if they do not kill when ordered, they are guilty of treason. Soldiers ought therefore to obey even the possibly unrighteous commands of infidels, such as Julian the Apostate.

---

[44] I shall speak of "approved" here, because Augustine speaks of acts of killing—presumably including acts of war as well—that are permitted although not specifically commanded by God. See, for example, his treatment of Moses' killing of the Egyptian as recounted in Exodus 1.2 (cf. *Reply to Faustus the Manichaean*, 22.70).

[45] *Quaestiones in Heptateuchum*, 6.10, in John Eppstein, *The Catholic Tradition of the Law of Nations* (London: Burns, Oates and Washbourne, 1935), 74.

[46] See *Of the Morals of the Catholic Church*, 30.63. *Select Library of Nicene and Post Nicene Fathers*, Vol. 4.

[47] *City of God*, I.21.

Even in such a case, "the soldier is innocent, because his position makes obedience a duty."

   Within the framework of historical providence, then, the matter of authority is a simple one; the ruler, whoever he might be and whatever he might do, rules with God's sanction. He can do nothing without God's foreknowledge of the deed and, if the deed issues from a perverted will, without God's ultimate compensatory historical intervention. Rulers thus war at their discretion, and subjects fight in obedience to their rulers.[48]

One part of this is misleading, however. It is that which says that rulers war "at their discretion." As descriptive of the behavior of rulers, this is true. But as normative of what rulers may justifiably do, it is not true. Rulers are constrained morally by the requirement of a just cause. What is left to their discretion is the determination of what constitutes such a cause. As Augustine sees the matter, "it is the wrongdoing of the opposing party which compels the wise man to wage just wars."[49]

   What of right intention? It is true, in a relatively trivial sense, that Augustine expects there to be a right intention in war. This is because he believes that everyone who wages war—justly or unjustly—does so for the sake of peace.[50] It is merely that different rulers have different conceptions of what constitutes peace. The question is whether any particular "right intention" deserves to be achieved. And that goes back to whether that intention is in the service of a just cause. It will be useful to speak here of a formally right intention, by which I mean an intention that aims at the perceived good of a particular peace. Augustine recognizes right intention of this sort. But right intention of this sort characterizes the just and the unjust alike. Hence it can always be presumed to be present, hence cannot be normative of what constitutes a just resort to war.[51]

   This provides a preliminary account of the conditions Augustine lays down for *jus ad bellum*. But its full import can be understood only by seeing how it fits with our account of Augustine's subjectivism. For here the radical dualism of Augustine's metaphysics affects his ethics and social and political philosophy as well. We have seen earlier that a right intention can issue from either a good or a bad motive. It is the motive that ultimately determines the moral character of what one does; "it alone," Augustine says, "distinguishes the doings of man."[52] A formally right intention, since it will always be present, cannot be among the criteria that distinguish just from unjust wars.

   Because rectitude is tied to virtue and virtue to love, we can know whether someone acts rightly only by knowing his motivation. And that, according

---

[48] Stevenson, *Christian Love and Just War*, 69.

[49] *City of God*, 19.7, trans. Marcus Dods, in *Select Library of the Nicene and Post-Nicene Fathers*, Vol. 2.

[50] *City of God*, 19.12. Later in life, Augustine may have thought that it is only good men who seek peace when they wage war. Letter CCXXIX (AD 429) to Darius. Post Nicene Writers, Vol. 1, pp. 581–582.

[51] The American Catholic bishops, on the other hand, tie right intention specifically to just cause, saying, "Right intention is related to just cause—war can be legitimately intended only for the reasons set forth above [protecting innocents, preserving conditions of decent human existence and securing basic human rights] as a just cause" (*Challenge of Peace*, 30).

[52] *Homilies on the First Epistle of John*, 7.7.

to Augustine, is hidden from us. It is often hidden even in the case of our own actions. We presumably know when we are deliberately acting pridefully. But when we think we are acting lovingly, we may unwittingly be motivated by pride. So we can sometimes be certain that we are acting wrongly. But there is no sure way to determine whether we are acting rightly. If we extend this to the case of war, it means that there is no sure way to know that we are acting rightly in going to war. Even if we knew the consequences of our actions and their value (hence knew what beneficence calls for) we would remain unable to know whether our underlying motivation is correct. If we cannot know when we are motivated by love, we cannot know when we are acting rightly (the virtues of fortitude, prudence and justice being forms of love). Not only can we not love fully without divine grace, we cannot even have faith without divine grace.[53] As these are necessary to living virtuously, we cannot live morally without grace.

This means that we must recognize in Augustine a distinction between true virtue and temporal virtue. In the case of war, we must recognize a distinction between true justice and temporal justice. True justice is that which is actually just according to what God ordains both in broad historical terms and in particular circumstances. Temporal justice is that which humans warrantably *judge* to be just according to standards accessible to them in view of their cognitive and motivational deficiencies. Reliance upon temporal justice is necessitated by our inability to know both what true justice requires and to know, either in general or in any given case, whether our conduct accords with it.

The conditions of a truly just war in Augustine's thought can now be filled in. In addition to legitimate authority and just cause we may now include right intention, appropriately qualified. I have said that since rulers who go to war do so intending to achieve a peace of their choosing, both sides in war can be presumed to have a formally right intention. But in addition we can distinguish (though Augustine does not explicitly do so) a materially right intention—one that aims not only to bring about a perceived good but also to achieve a rightly chosen, just peace. Peace, for Augustine, entails order. A given temporal order can be just or unjust (though no temporal order can be completely just). A just peace is provided by a just order. One ought only to aim for a just peace. Not every ruler does this. Only those who do so have a materially right intention.

But aiming for a just peace does not suffice to constitute a materially right intention. Even the best of intentions, if measured only by the states of affairs it is their purpose to bring about, are not enough. For good deeds, as we have seen, can be done from pride. It is only when intentions issue from love that they are materially right. We have been assuming that by "love" is meant the love commanded by God. But sometimes Augustine speaks as though love in another sense is at the root of sinful conduct—the love of things that can be taken from us against our will.[54] Such temporal love (as we may call it) can always be presumed to be present when states go to war. Hence it cannot be normative of what constitutes true justice in war. Only love as prescribed

---

[53] *Enchiridian*, 31. *A Select Library of Nicene and Post-Nicene Fathers*, Vol. 3.
[54] *De libero arbitrio*, I.

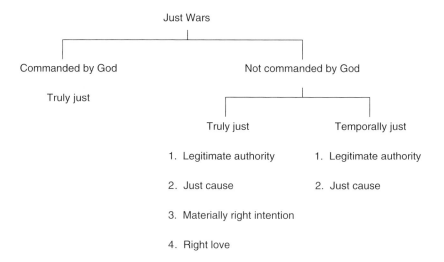

by Christ, that is, *agape*, is a proper love. This "right love," as Stevenson aptly calls it, must be the soil from which intentions spring if they are to be materially right. What forces us to rely upon the conditions of temporal justice is not that the conditions of true justice can never be met. It is that we can never know that they have been met. We can know when the conditions of temporal justice are met. When they are, we have a warrant for acting, if only because that is the best we can do. Such conduct is then actionably just.

The completed picture of the Augustinian view with regard to the justification of war is thus a complex one. It varies both according to the relationship of the war in question to God's express will (all wars ultimately accord with God's will in the sense that he allows them to take place and turns them, even when they are unjust, to his purposes) and according to the dichotomy between true justice and temporal justice. These interrelations can be represented as above.

God indisputably commands wars in the Old Testament, so there can be nothing intrinsically wrong with war. For early Christians this created a dilemma: how to reconcile the Old Testament's sanction of war with the New Testament's implied rejection of war. They resolved it by supporting the New Testament over the Old. Augustine resolves it by reinterpreting the New Testament to accord with the Old.

The result is a sharp division in his thinking between true justice and temporal justice.[55] We can on Augustine's view know when God commands us to go to war. Thus we can know when a war is truly just on those grounds. But absent a command (or express guidance) from God, whether a war is truly just cannot be known. The criteria are clear enough. But to know whether they are satisfied exceeds human capabilities.

---

[55] This dualism is probably prompted partly by Augustine's desire to reconcile the New Testament with the Old, but it almost certainly is facilitated by his Platonistic inclinations. For an account that alleges an expanded list of conditions for Augustine's account of war, see Stratmann, *The Church and War: A Catholic Study* (New York: P.J. Kennedy and Sons, 1928), chap. 3.

Thus we are left with the criteria of temporal justice as the only effective guide to going to war.

4.6 Augustine's authoritarianism

Despite the otherworldliness of his theological outlook, and the sharp dualism entailed by his subjectivism, Augustine seeks to understand and provide guidance for this world, not least of all in its social and political dimensions. Much of his work as bishop was devoted to providing such guidance. So were many of his letters, including those to men troubled by war and killing. How to provide such guidance in the face of the unknowability of true justice creates a continuing unresolved tension in his thought.

There are, however, grounds in Augustine's thought for partially bridging the gap between true justice and temporal justice. The direction in which they point is not, however, one that Augustine pursues. It would almost certainly have led him back to the early church's renunciation of war. But these grounds make of the commandment to love something more than the "impossible ideal" that it later becomes for Reinhold Niebuhr, the twentieth century's leading Augustinian in social and political thought.[56]

The first ground is broadly epistemological and is tied to Augustine's understanding of the state and its authority. The fundamental pragmatic imperative for Augustine is to obey the state. Even an oppressive state at least serves as the agent of God's chastisement for our sins and, moreover, provides order which is essential to peace. In its restraint of sinful conduct the state provides an opportunity for such transitory moments of happiness (or, perhaps more accurately for Augustine, relief from misery) mortal life affords. This same sentiment is echoed centuries later by Martin Luther, who says,

> Because the sword is a very great benefit and necessary to the whole world, to preserve peace, to punish sin and to prevent evil, he [the Christian] submits most willingly to the rule of the sword, pays tax, honors those in authority, serves, helps, and does all he can to further the government, that it may be sustained and held in honor and fear … Therefore, should you see that there is a lack of hangmen, beadles, judges, lords, or princes, and find that you are qualified, you should offer your services and seek the place, that necessary government may by no means be despised and become inefficient or perish. For the world cannot and dare not dispense with it.[57]

This need for obedience extends to participation in war. Even when the cause is unjust, one must fight when ordered to do so by the appropriate authority. One does so, in that case, with legal immunity from the standpoint of temporal justice. Moreover this gives soldiers on both sides in war—the just and the unjust alike—a kind of moral

---

[56] See Reinhold Niebuhr, *An Interpretation of Christian Ethics* (New York: Meridian Books, 1956).
[57] "Secular Authority: To What Extent It Should Be Obeyed," in *Martin Luther: Selections from His Writings*, ed. John Dillenberger (Garden City, NY: Doubleday & Company, 1961), pp. 373, 374.

immunity as well. Each has an equal right to kill.[58] As this view figures prominently in contemporary just war theorizing, we shall examine it more closely in Chapter 5.

In his early writings Augustine is troubled by this. He expresses uncertainty whether, by the eternal law, even those who kill with full legal sanction are free of sin.[59] But, as though resigned to the unfathomability of the answer to that question, he proceeds later to view the duty of obedience as nearly absolute (excepting only commands to do what is disrespectful of God), even when one is confronted with (temporally) unjust commands. Moral license, therefore, extends to soldiers on all sides in war, providing only that they are acting as agents of a legitimate authority.

Are those who must fight if commanded to do so by a legitimate authority free of guilt no matter with what inward disposition they do so? More specifically, if right love and intention are requirements of true justice, will not their absence mean that, whatever the standards of temporal justice, those who fight do so wrongly by the standards of true justice? It is hard to see how Augustine can consistently answer these questions other than by an affirmative. But he would contend that the unknowability of the presence of right love and intention makes temporal standards nonetheless actionable for practical purposes.

The problem with such a contention is that we can know, so it seems, and so Augustine gives reason to believe, when we are willfully and self-consciously acting from motives other than love—motives like selfishness, greed, malice and the like. Augustine reveals no skepticism on this score. It is not as though when we deliberately give rein to what we think are selfish, greedy or lustful impulses we may be mistaken and actually be acting from love. When we self-consciously act from these other motives we can be certain we are not acting from love, hence can know that our conduct does not accord with true rightness. When we strive to act from love, however, we can never be certain that we are in fact doing so. On the unproblematic assumption that when true justice and temporal justice conflict it is true justice that takes precedence, this means that in a limited way true justice then is practically as well as ideally normative for human affairs. It does not tell us in all cases what we ought to do, but it does tell us conclusively in some cases what we ought not to do.[60] In the case of war we can know that temporal justice when accompanied by illicit motives does not accord with true justice.

One would expect, for that reason, that it would at least be a necessary condition of the conduct of soldiers being truly just, and (assuming they are under the command of a legitimate authority) a sufficient condition of their being temporally just, that they not be acting from an identifiably evil motive. And indeed one can read at least one well-known passage in Augustine's reply to Faustus as consistent with this. In it Augustine asks:

> What is the evil in war? Is it the death of some who will soon die in any case, that others may live in peaceful subjection? This is merely cowardly dislike, not any

---

[58] As we shall see in Chapters 5 and 6, Michael Walzer defends the same view on different grounds, calling it the "moral equality" of soldiers.

[59] *De libero arbitrio* I.15.12, trans. Carroll Mason Sparrow (Charlottesville, VA: Dietz Press, 1947).

[60] It does not follow from this, of course, that acting from *any* motive other than love entails acting contrary to the requirements of true justice. Whether that is so depends upon whether those requirements require perfection in our motivation.

religious feeling. The real evils in war are love of violence, revengeful cruelty, fierce and implacable enmity, wild resistance, and the lust of power, and such like; and it is generally to punish these things, when force is required to inflict the punishment, that, in obedience to God or some lawful authority, good men undertake wars.[61]

Augustine runs together two issues here: first, that of what is evil *in* war; second, that of the evil that war is undertaken to punish. If these are the same evils, one could hardly say that one may go to war to punish such evils in others but tolerate them among one's own soldiers in the course of doing so.

What this suggests is that, in the broader context of Augustine's views, what is important in war, if one is being realistic, is not that we act from love, since we cannot do that without divine grace and cannot in any event ever know for certain that we are doing it, but that we be certain we are not acting from love of violence, revengeful cruelty, lust of power and the like. For whatever the obstacles to minimizing the power of these motives, we can at least know when we are consciously acting from them.

Thus in addition to the two interpretations of the precept to love considered earlier, we need to recognize another precept of more limited scope, applicable to the conduct of warfare:

3. Do as commanded (by a legitimate authority), but do it without cruelty, enmity, love of violence, lust for power and so forth.

To minimize the evils of war we should purge ourselves as nearly as possible of those elements of sin that can readily be identified. Death and suffering there will be. But their infliction, considered outwardly, is neither right nor wrong in itself. The determinant of which they are lies in our motivation. If one cannot be certain that he is ever acting from right love, that can only be because he cannot be certain that, even when he believes he is acting from love, he is not acting from some base motive like revengeful cruelty, and lust of power in disguise. Whether or not we are capable of fully extinguishing these motives, or at least of preventing them from controlling our conduct, it makes sense to view their removal as a requirement of nonculpable participation in war, hence as a condition of the moral license of soldiers on both sides to kill.

As for rulers, their legitimacy need have no more warrant by earthly standards than the power by which they enforce order. Even if harsh, that power is necessary to avoid the evils of license and disorder. The need for obedience is the Pauline spirit speaking here:

Every person must submit to the supreme authorities. There is no authority but by act of God, and the existing authorities are instituted by him; consequently anyone who rebels against authority is resisting a divine institution, and those who so resist have themselves to thank for the punishment they will receive … you wish

[61] *Contra Faustum*, 22.74.

to have no fear of the authorities? Then continue to do right and you will have their approval, for they are God's agents working for your good.[62]

Since rulers have no more privileged access to what constitutes true justice than anyone else—and arguably have even less if they are non-Christian—they can be guided at best by temporal justice. If they do not have sole moral discretion to do as they please, they at least have, as we have noted, sole discretion to decide what temporal justice requires of the state.

Given that opposing rulers in war are both seeking peace as they conceive it, and given that each may believe he acts justly, it can easily happen that wars are fought by sides equally convinced of their justice. And the killing that results is done by soldiers who, whatever they think of the justice of the cause they serve, enjoy legal and (temporal) moral immunity for their actions. But contrary to what some maintain,[63] there is no reason to suppose that Augustine believes that both sides in war can in fact be just, even from the standpoint of temporal justice. If not, then nothing in this aspect of Augustine's account is a bar to considering his account of the moral reality of war as fully coherent and consistent.

The second ground for bridging the gap between true justice and temporal justice in war relates to Augustine's denial of the right of self-defense. Properly understood, love can only be for that which we cannot lose against our will.[64] To cling to things that can be lost against our will—earthly possessions and even our own lives—is the way of sin. It represents trying to sustain ourselves other than in and through God, which is the essence of pride. Because we can have no assurance of preserving our own lives in this world, including saving them in the face of threats, we may not kill in defense of them. Not only may we not, in our capacity as private persons, kill another to save our own lives, we also may not even kill ourselves to prevent others from sinning against us, as in the case of threatened torture or rape.[65]

4.7 Killing out of obedience

If to kill in defense of our own lives is to try to cling to that which can be taken from us against our will, to kill in the defense of the lives of others is to do no less. We can no more prevent the lives of others from being lost against our (and their) will than we can our own. Indeed, we can do even less to prevent others from being killed if they are distant from us. Augustine does not expressly preclude killing in defense of others in the way he precludes self-defense. But his position entails it. The lives of friends,

---

[62] Romans 13.1–4, New English Bible.

[63] See, for example, Stevenson, *Christian Love and Just War*, 44–45. Paul Ramsey contends that, to be consistent, Augustine should have denied that one side only can be just in war, in *War and Christian Conscience*, 28.

[64] *De libero arbitrio* I.

[65] *City of God* I. 24–25. Martin Luther likewise writes, "No Christian shall wield or invoke the sword for himself and for his cause; but for another he can and ought to wield and invoke it, so that wickedness may be hindered and godliness defended." *Martin Luther: Selections from His Writings*, p. 381.

family, countrymen can be taken from us against our will. Natural disasters, wars, criminals do that all the time. Pride is involved in clinging to that which can be taken from us against our will. No harm can befall us simply because such things have been taken from us. Assailants can assault or kill us. But they cannot thereby truly harm us unless we allow fear or hatred to corrupt our wills as we try to cling to life or bodily integrity. They can do the same to others without thereby truly harming them either. Our intervening on behalf of others does not change that. An attacker may kill others but he cannot harm them by his act alone. We cannot prevent harm to others by our acts alone. Nor can we preserve others from harm by killing their attacker.[66]

The common view among recent just war theorists—that for Augustine a just cause consists in going to war in defense of the innocent—is mistaken. Just as we may not kill in defense of our own lives, we may not kill in defense of the lives of others. We may kill in wartime, but only as agents of the state, not as private persons, and when we do so, we do so from obedience. That does not mean that in killing in obedience to a ruler we may not *in fact* sometimes be killing in defense of others, innocent or not. Whether that is so will depend upon why the state has gone to war and what its objectives are. If the state has initiated the war, as it may for Augustine, then in that sense the state with the just cause will be the aggressor and will not be fighting in self-defense. If, on the other hand, the wrong which is being punished by the state is in the form of aggression by another state, then the state with the just cause may in fact be fighting in self-defense (though it would be defense of the state or kingdom, not personal self-defense of an individual). But punishment is the ground of the just cause, not self-defense or defense of others.

A passage sometimes cited in support of the view that for Augustine the justification for killing in war is defense of others is the following:

> As to killing others in order to defend one's own life, I do not approve of this, unless one happens to be a soldier or a public functionary acting, not for himself, but in defense of others or of the city in which he resides, if he act according to the commission lawfully given him, and in the manner becoming his office.[67]

Augustine here merely acknowledges that when one fights as an agent of the state, and in virtually absolute obedience to a ruler, one may, *inter alia*, sometimes in fact kill in self-defense or in defense of others. Rulers presumably want themselves and

---

[66] Augustine says: "For whatever man may do to thee, he shall not straiten thee; because thou lovest that which man cannot hurt: lovest God, lovest the brotherhood, lovest the law of God, lovest the church of God ... If no man can take from thee that which thou lovest, secure thou sleepest: or rather secure thou watchest, lest by sleeping though lose that which thou lovest" (*Homilies on the First Epistle of John* 10.6).

[67] Letter XLVII, p. 293. Grotius renders the passage somewhat differently: "*I do not approve of the Maxim of killing him, by whom one is apprehensive of being killed one's self; unless he happen to be a Soldier, or publick Officer, so that he does not do it for himself, but for others, by Vertue of a lawful Authority.*" Hugo Grotius, *The Rights of War and Peace*, I, p. 243. No mention here is made of defense of others, much less of the innocent, though it may be implied. It could, however, be read to refer to killing in the interests of others, perhaps even for their gain, as might well be in war, rather than in defense of their lives.

their kingdoms defended. One could scarcely stay alive and fight effectively, hence fully comply with orders, if one did not sometimes kill in self-defense. And could not defend the state without sometimes killing in defense of others. But one might with equal justification fight in an assault upon others. If obedience is required, one fights with justification in the service of whatever cause has led the ruler into war. It is perhaps because Ambrose before him and Martin Luther after him appeal to the defense of others as grounds for killing that many just warists take this also to be Augustine's view. It may also be that they fold back into Augustine their own conviction about defense of the innocent as the justification for going to war.

The only ground for love's inflicting pain, suffering or death upon others is for the others' sake. Punishment can only be inflicted to chasten offenders. If a ruler goes to war for this purpose, he has a just cause. But even if he does not have a just cause, it is the duty of the soldiers under his command to obey, and to kill those they are ordered to kill. This does not quite establish moral equality among soldiers, as it comes later to be called, if that means an equal moral right to kill, but it does establish moral immunity among them. But they must not, as we noted earlier, do so from those motives that constitute the evils in war—cruelty, lust of power and the like. An enemy is confronted, Augustine says, always as the brother he may become, not as the enemy he now is. It is only what he does that one may hate, not the person himself. If you truly love him, you act on his behalf, even to the point of killing him.[68]

From all Augustine says, however, love is hardly the motive governing the conduct of most persons. This is true of rulers and soldiers in war as well. Augustine speaks repeatedly as though he thinks it is greed, rapacity, desire for domination and conquest that is manifest in war. Even a (temporally) just cause provides no assurance that its prosecution is from love.[69] The desire to punish for the sake of punishing, to harm for the sake of harming, to satisfy desires for revenge—and throughout to profit from the spoils of war—ensures that even a temporally just war that has these characteristics cannot be truly just and indeed can be known not to be truly just.

If this is correct, it would provide grounds for supposing that virtually all of the wars prior to and during Augustine's time—including the sack of Rome by the Visigoths in AD 410 and the Vandal incursion into Africa that had Hippo Regius under siege at the time of his death in 430—were (by the standards of true justice) unjust. This may partly explain why warfare under Christianity, particularly during the Crusades, came increasingly to be justified on expressly religious grounds,[70] to help minimize the influence of self-consciously base motives in going to war and in its subsequent conduct. Later Christians have given insufficient attention to the Augustinian skepticism regarding our ability to certify love as a motive. If one gives credence to the more skeptical and pessimistic passages in Augustine, it may be that on a consistent Augustinian analysis no actual wars are in fact just. If so, whether or not Augustine was a personal pacifist, to be consistent he should have been a universal pacifist as well.

---

[68] *City of God* 19.17. It is but a short step from this, of course, to justifying the thinking behind the inquisition.

[69] See for example *City of God* 5.17.

[70] See Russell, *The Just War in the Middle Ages*, chap. 1.

4.8 Conclusion

The problem of war for these reasons is of the first importance to Augustine's thought. He never identifies it as such. Nor does he devote extensive attention to it. It is important because what is of concern to him, particularly in his later thought, is to define the implications of Christianity for life in the earthly city.[71] This requires understanding war, the social and political forces that bring it into existence and the divine purposes that allow it to endure. Perhaps no human practice flies more directly in the face of what seem to be the teachings of Christ than the organized, deliberate, systematic infliction of death and destruction.

Thus there is much in Augustine's philosophy that is important to understanding war; however, most of it is directly relevant to understanding the broader philosophy of war rather than to understanding the notion of just war in particular. Insofar as the just war theory is understood as a theory in applied ethics, meant to provide practical guidance in deciding whether to go to war and how to conduct war once in it, there is, as I have said, little in Augustine of such a theory. Such as there is shows limited concern with the complexities that have occupied subsequent just war theorists. There is more in the way of a theoretical account of the conditions that make for true justice in war. But even much of that is only implicit. Unless developed beyond Augustine's treatment, even that is of limited relevance to providing practical guidance to civil magistrates and individuals contemplating soldierhood.

When one looks at the practical import of Augustine's account, as opposed to his philosophy and theology of war, the picture is different. One finds an acceptance of war. It may be argued that there is in Augustine not even a presumption against war, though that view is questionable.[72] The pains he takes to interpret the teachings of Jesus in such a way as to make war permissible certainly suggest that he thought (as early Christians thought) that there was a presumption against war. And near the end of his life, he writes to the general, Darius, who had arranged a truce with the invading Vandals:

> But it is a higher glory still to stay war itself with a word, than to slay men with the sword, and to procure or maintain peace, not by war. For those who fight, if they are good men, doubtless seek for peace; nevertheless it is through blood. Your mission, however, is to prevent the shedding of blood. Yours, therefore, is the privilege of averting that calamity which others are under the necessity of producing. Therefore ... rejoice in this singularly great and real blessing vouchsafed to you, and enjoy it in God, to whom you owe that you are what you are, and that you

---

[71] As Peter Brown puts it, "the *City of God*, far from being a book about flight from the world, is a book whose recurrent theme is 'our business within this common mortal life'; it is a book about being otherworldly in the world." See *Augustine of Hippo*, p. 324.

[72] James Turner Johnson may be correct when he says, "I would say it more emphatically: the concept of just war does not begin with a 'presumption against war' focused on the harm which war may do, but with a presumption against *injustice* focused on the need for responsible use of force in response to wrongdoing." *Morality and Contemporary Warfare*, 35.

undertook the accomplishment of such a work. May God "strengthen that which He hath wrought for us through you." [Ps. Lxviii.29.][73]

Be that as it may, Augustine sets up only the frailest of constraints against entering into war, constraints that even optimists regarding human nature could hardly expect to restrain rulers from going to war practically whenever they want. And one finds virtually no constraints against individuals participating in war, provided only that they do so in obedience to their rulers and without otherwise forsaking God. The way is then prepared for Christians to lament the horrors of war and at the same time actively to support its perpetuation. Power on the part of rulers and submissive obedience on the part of subjects enable the state to run roughshod over the teachings of the Sermon on the Mount.[74]

In its practical import, then, as opposed to its theoretical and philosophical import, Augustine's account sets the stage more nearly for Hobbes, Machiavelli and twentieth-century political realists (some of the most prominent of whom were Christians) than for just war theorists. He provided the rationale for the permanent redirection of mainstream Christianity's course from pacifism to warism.[75]

---

[73] Augustine. Letter CCXXIX (AD 429) to Darius. *Select Library of the Nicene and Post-Nicene Fathers*, Vol. 1, pp. 581–582.

[74] Carried to an extreme that Augustine would never have imagined, Nazis like Adolf Eichmann pleaded absolute obedience to Hitler as the ground for their role in WWII and the Holocaust.

[75] It is arguable that Constantine, before Augustine, was largely responsible for effectuating the practical transition of Christianity from pacifism to militarism.

Anatomy of the Just War Theory

The institutionalization of just war theory … has ensured its practical universalization.

—Steven P. Lee

5.1 Just war tradition and just war theory

The just war tradition, as we have seen, is usually taken to refer to the evolution of the moral thinking about war from a perspective begun with Cicero and Augustine in the Western world, an approach that tends to ignore the thinking about war in Middle Eastern and far Eastern traditions. The just war tradition is of significant moral interest only if, explicitly or implicitly, it contains criteria for deciding when actual wars are just and when they are not. Even if Augustine has been widely misinterpreted in this regard and does not justify war as a means to defend the innocent, that does not in itself vitiate the just war theory (JWT). It simply means that it must have a different grounding than many of its advocates think they find in Augustine. Whatever criteria one distills from the just war tradition —whether they originate in Augustine or not—I shall take to constitute the JWT, and it is with the theory in this sense that I shall be concerned.[1]

5.2 Moral war theory

It is often assumed that if one is to assess war one is committed to doing so from the standpoint of the JWT. But, as I have said, that is not so. Any of the basic moral theories (e.g., consequentialism, kantianism, divine command theory) can in principle provide a basis for the assessment of war. The JWT is simply one ethical theory among many, a deontological theory with consequentialist elements, and is not even a basic moral theory in the sense of presenting a comprehensive perspective for deciding all moral

---

[1] In Chapter 12 I shall discuss whether the criteria of JWT are derived from an examination of purportedly just wars or are fashioned independently.

questions. To advance it as the preferred theory for assessing war requires supporting argument. Any such argument would have to show that the JWT is capable of showing that war$_2$, what I have in Chapter 1 called whole war, is morally permissible, and not simply that war$_1$, partial war, abstracted from the broader context of whole war and synoptic war, is morally permissible. The standard JWT does not even attempt to do this. It is framed from the perspective of one side only facing the possibility of war. Unless otherwise indicated, I shall in this examination use "war" to stand for partial war, the sense in which it is typically used in the JWT. Even if its conditions are met, the JWT would not suffice to show that even partial war is morally permissible. It would suffice if justice were the whole of morality, for then "just" might be taken as roughly equivalent to "right." But, as Aristotle noted, justice need not be taken to be the whole of morality. In fact, it is more often taken to be but one dimension of morality, an issue I will take up in Chapter 12. If justice is but one dimension of morality, it needs to be clarified which of many kinds of justice—for example, distributive justice, commutative justice, retributive justice—it is intended to signify.[2] It is a commonplace that justice, in at least some of its senses, may conflict with other moral considerations, such as utility.[3] Indeed, justice may be overridden by other moral considerations, so that the just act may not, all things considered, be the right act. That at least raises the possibility that a war might be just according to the JWT but nonetheless wrong on balance. To show that, in addition to being just, a particular war is morally permissible or obligatory, one would have to show that there are no other moral considerations offsetting and overriding the assumed justice of the war.

If the alleged permissibility of war from a moral standpoint is to be taken seriously, there must be at least the rudiments of a theory that explains why. We might call this, whatever specific form it takes, the moral war theory. The JWT is but one of many possible examples of a moral war theory. The moral war theory, as I understand it, sets forth conditions which, if satisfied, supposedly justify both the resort to war and the conduct of war. It might be formulated as follows:

Moral War Theory: One resorts to war permissibly if, and only if, conditions C are met, and one conducts war permissibly if, and only if, conditions C' are met.

Conditions C stand for whatever moral criteria are alleged to justify war. They might be the criteria contained in *jus ad bellum*, but they need not be. They might simply specify that resorting to war has the best consequences on balance or that war is divinely commanded. Conditions C', whether or not independent of conditions C, would be those whose satisfaction is necessary to render the conduct of war permissible. The conditions under C' might be the just war criteria contained under C, but they might

---

[2] It is worth noting that the idea of just cause for Cicero (the first, perhaps, to introduce the notion in Western thought) was a legal concept, grounded in contractual law. See Frederick H. Russell, Introduction, *The Just War in the Middle Ages* (Cambridge: Cambridge University Press, 1975), pp. 5–6.

[3] This is acknowledged by Nigel Biggar, who writes that "according to just war theory, war may not be waged simply in order to achieve a good, but only to rectify an injustice." *In Defense of War*, p. 123.

be very different, such as authorizing whatever means are necessary to achieve one's aims. Conditions C and C' could be derivative from any of the basic moral theories, such as consequentialism, kantianism, the divine command theory, as well as from a rights-based theory. As such they would provide alternatives to the JWT.[4] An example of a moral war theory extrapolated from the divine command would be that one resorts to war permissibly if, and only if, God commands it, and one conducts war permissibly if, and only if, in accordance with God's commands. Augustine holds that God's commanding war makes it not only permissible but also obligatory. But God's command, as we have seen, is not necessary to make war permissible. It is his showing how that might be so that constitutes Augustine's main contribution to just war theory. It is grafted onto a divine command theory.

Even if the JWT were shown to be the best theory by which to assess war, that would not in itself defeat the presumption that war is wrong. It would, at most, show that the presumption could in principle be defeated. To show that a presumption could be defeated is not to defeat the presumption. The JWT shows at best only what a just war would be.[5] One can define what a just war would be without knowing whether there are any such wars,[6] and even if one knew there were no such wars. To know whether there are such wars requires applying the theory to actual cases and showing that at least some of them qualify.[7] It is possible that this cannot be done.[8] It is possible that some hypothetical wars satisfy the conditions of the JWT but that no actual wars do. It is for this reason that the moral assessment of war can proceed only so far at the purely theoretical level and requires a substantial empirical dimension as well. I shall attempt to provide that in Part III.

---

[4] One might interpret just cause in terms of rights, as Fernando Tesón does in his *Humanitarian Intervention*. If it were interpreted in consequentialist or kantian terms, JWT would be grounded in a standard moral theory.

[5] Steven Lee writes: "Just war theory seeks to determine the conditions for distinguishing just wars from unjust wars." Lee, *Ethics and War*, p. 29. It is difficult to be certain whether he is saying, as many just war theorists seem to, that there *are* just and unjust wars and the JWT seeks to distinguish which are which, or simply that the JWT sets forth conditions for making the distinction, whether or not any actual cases satisfy the conditions of a just war. I shall say more of this later in Chapter 12 in connection with the question of whether JWT and pacifism converge.

[6] Similarly, one can define what a unicorn is without knowing whether there are any such things, or even while knowing that there are no such things.

[7] This would mean that even if it could be shown that some hypothetical wars₁ (partial wars) would be just, that would not suffice to show that any actual wars₁ are just, much less that any actual wars₂ (whole wars) are just.

[8] This possibility makes the idea of "just war pacifism" intelligible, a topic to which we shall return in Chapter 12. One might think that the JWT is the correct perspective from which to assess war—hence think that one can know what a just war would be in principle—but find that its criteria are never met, hence that there are in fact no just wars. On this issue, Andrew Fiala writes: "The sort of pacifism I want to defend here is primarily an antiwar position. For this reason it might be called *just war pacifism*: it reaches a pacifist conclusion from a stringent application of the just war theory." See Andrew Fiala, *The Just War Myth: The Moral Illusion of War* (New York: Rowman & Littlefield Publishers, 2008), p. 162. James Sterba, by somewhat different reasoning, calls his reconciliation of pacifists and just war theorists, just war pacifism. See James P. Sterba, "Reconciling Pacifists and Just War Theorists," *Social Theory and Practice*, Vol. 18, No. 1, Spring 1992, p. 35. Sterba contends that his view is similar to Richard Norman's in "The Case for Pacifism," *Journal of Applied Philosophy*, 1988, pp. 197–210. For a critique of Sterba's position, see Michael Neu, "Why There Is No Such Thing as Just War Pacifism and Why Just War Theorists and Pacifists Can Talk Nonetheless," *Social Theory and Practice*, Vol. 37, No. 3, July 2011, pp. 413–434.

Just war theorists tend to assume at the outset that some wars are morally permissible. In so doing, they assume an answer to the most basic moral question one can ask about war with little or no argument.[9] In holding that some wars are morally permissible, they attach to the theory a moral judgment that, if it is to be established, one would expect to follow from the application of the theory. The issue is a complex one, however, and we shall return to it in Chapter 12.

5.3 Just war internalism and externalism

It is important to understand what the JWT specifically says in contrast to the more general schema for the moral war theory. The two components of the JWT are JAB, conditions that purport to justify the resort to war$_1$ in the first place, and JIB, conditions intended to justify the conduct of war$_1$ once it has begun. It is sometimes thought that JAB and JIB are logically independent. The thought is that one might be justified in going to war$_1$ but fail to conduct the war$_1$ justly; or, conversely, that one might conduct a war$_1$ justly but be unjustified in having resorted to it in the first place.[10] I shall call JAB and JIB *externalist* theories if, and only if, according to them, justice in one area does not entail justice in the other; and I shall call them *internalist* if justice in either dimension entails justice in the other.[11]

One could, of course, stipulate that JAB and JIB are logically independent. They would then, in effect, represent separate theories about the nature of justice in war. Nothing that one did in the course of waging a war would or could change the fact that one had gone to war justly, and no measure of injustice in the resort to war could alter the fact that one might conduct the war justly. Each would have some claim to be a JWT, although each would deal with different aspects of war. If, on the other hand, the JWT is understood— as it usually is—to be a single theory, JAB and JIB would be two dimensions of that one theory, with JAB containing conditions applicable to the recourse to war and JIB containing conditions applicable to the conduct of war. It would be the overarching JWT that would prescribe what those conditions authorize or prohibit.

Let me make this clearer. A fairly standard rendering of the conditions contained under JAB is as follows:

legitimate authority
just cause

---

[9] Daniel S. Zupan, for example, writes: "I start with the assumption that some wars are just and that it follows from this that some killing in war is justified." See Daniel S. Zupan, *War, Morality, and Autonomy: An Investigation in Just War Theory* (Hampshire, UK: Ashgate Publishing Limited, 2004), p. 4. Another contemporary defender of the JWT writes, "the just war tradition recognizes that there are circumstances in which the first and most urgent obligation in the face of evil is to stop it. Which means that there are times when waging war is morally necessary." Weigel, *Against the Grain*, p. 207. A notable exception to this claim is Nigel Biggar, who offers explicit argument from a just war theoretic perspective to show that the Gulf and Iraq Wars were justified. See his *In Defense of War*, especially chapter 7.

[10] See Walzer, *Just and Unjust Wars*, p. 21.

[11] Steven Lee discusses this issue, though with a different terminology, in *Ethics and War*, pp. 97–102.

right intention
probability of success
comparative justice
last resort
proportionality

Without assuming that this is necessarily a complete or noncontroversial list, and without undertaking to interpret each of the conditions, I shall simply refer to these collectively as JC. If conditions JC are taken to be individually necessary and jointly sufficient to justify going to war, then JAB would assert:

JAB: One resorts to war justly if, and only if, conditions JC are met.

Similarly, JIB commonly is understood to consist of two conditions:

discrimination
proportionality

Where JW represents these conditions, JIB would assert:

JIB: One conducts warfare justly if, and only if, conditions JW are met.

Neither JAB nor JIB need make explicit reference to the conditions contained under the other. Unless there is a semantic or logical entailment between JC and JW, JAB and JIB are logically independent.[12] What we might call JWT_1 simply asserts the conjunction of JAB and JIB so understood.

JWT_1: One resorts to war justly if, and only if, conditions JC are met, and one conducts war justly if, and only if, conditions JW are met.[13]

According to JWT_1, one may be fully just in having resorted to war even if one conducts the war unjustly, and one may be fully just in the conduct of war even if one resorted to it unjustly.

The problem with this view is readily apparent. Consider two wars. In the first, a state justly resorts to war according to JAB but engages in genocide in the course of waging the war. The resort to war will have been permissible but what the state does once it goes to war will be wrong according to JIB. In the second, a state resorts to war

---

[12] Jeff McMahan in *Killing in War* seems to assume a semantic entailment between them, since the *in bello* requirement of discrimination is defined in terms of legitimate targets (p. 12). That is explicated by reference to just and unjust combatants, and that in turn is explicated by reference to just war and just cause (p. 5).

[13] There is nothing normative about the JWT_1 stated in this way. It simply conveys information about what is just or unjust in the way of the initiation and conduct of war. It can, however, readily be made expressly normative by being reformulated as: One may resort to war from the standpoint of justice if, and only if, conditions JC are met, and if one resorts to war, justly or unjustly, one may proceed with the conduct of war from the standpoint of justice if, and only if, conditions JW are met.

unjustly but conducts the war justly (it kills only combatants, treats prisoners well, respects the rights of civilians). The second state will have gone to war wrongly, but virtually everything it does in the course of the war will be permissible according to JIB. Would the first war be just, the second unjust? Or vice versa? Most just warists probably would say that egregious injustice in the conduct of a war offsets the justice of the resort to war, transforming what otherwise would have been a just war into an unjust war.[14] Whether they would say that exemplary regard for the constraints of JIB would offset the injustice of the resort to war is more problematic (though perhaps not totally problematic considering the growing support in the twenty-first century for aggressing against autocratic regimes to replace them with democracies).[15]

The point is that in addition to the moral assessments represented by JAB and JIB, a further assessment needs to be made of the war of which the dimensions they govern are a part.[16] It is that broader assessment that determines whether a war is just or unjust, all things considered (i.e., in full view of both JAB and JIB). Gross injustice in one dimension might offset justice in the other, transforming what otherwise would be a just war into an unjust war; and exemplary justice in one area might offset injustice in the other, transforming an otherwise unjust war into a just war. How one would balance justice/injustice in JAB against justice/injustice in JIB is unclear. If JAB and JIB were understood to be separate and logically independent theories, there would be no moral criteria, at least of a just-war theoretic sort, by which to make that determination. The two just war theories by themselves would be insufficient. If, on the other hand, one takes the JWT to comprise both JAB and JIB, then the theory itself would have to contain guidelines for adjudicating conflicting judgments resulting from the application JAB and JIB. If the JWT purports to be the proper moral perspective from which to make a comprehensive moral evaluation even of war$_1$, it must have a way of dealing with this issue.[17]

To render the JWT in such a way as to allow a comprehensive judgment of war, we need:

JWT$_2$: A war is just on balance if, and only if, conditions JC are met in the resort to war and conditions JW are met in the conduct of war.

---

[14] Gandhi, in this spirit, wrote in 1940, addressing the British in WWII: "I suggest that a cause that demands the inhumanities that are being perpetrated today cannot be called just." *Harijan*, June 7, 1940.

[15] For an exploration of some of these issues from a just war perspective, see Lee, *Ethics and War*, pp. 280–286. Among the possibilities are that an unjust war might become just in the course of fighting it. Of this, Lee writes: "Some think that the 2003 Iraq War is an example of this. On this understanding, the war was unjust at its beginning, but part way through it became clear (a reasonable expectation) that ending the war immediately would result in an all-out sectarian civil war within Iraq, causing much more harm than continuing the war would. If this is a correct understanding, then the unjust war acquired a just cause … which it lacked at the beginning" (p. 282). In support of this view, Lee cites Darrel Mollendorf, "*Jus ex Bello*," *Journal of Political Philosophy*, Vol. 16, No. 2, 2008, pp. 123–136.

[16] Remembering that by overall war we are referring to both dimensions of the partial war fought by one side.

[17] Bear in mind, once again, that we are here talking of the two dimensions of a partial war and the need for a comprehensive judgment of the whole of that partial war. There is still the need of a comprehensive judgment of the whole war of which such a partial war is a part.

To accord fully with the practice of some just war theorists, one would have to allow the possibility that not all of the conditions of JAB and JIB need be met in order for a war to be considered just. In particular, with regard to JAB, the conditions of last resort and proportionality are often questioned. Last resort is sometimes effectively scuttled and proportionality radically revised. Just warists also are willing to countenance some departure from the standards of JIB, so long as those departures are not too flagrant and frequent. The upshot is that they seem to be saying that a war is just if, and only if, the most salient of conditions JC are met in the resort to war and the conditions JW are met for the most part in its conduct. While there might well be disagreement over which conditions are salient, and how flagrant and frequent the violations of JIB might be, some just war theorists seem to think that the theory requires such qualifications. Such an approach represents what I shall call in Chapter 12, revisionist JWT. As it is difficult to assess this approach apart from a specification of the particular qualifications, and because revising the JWT in this way would seem to open the door to justifying virtually any war with enough tweaking of the relevant conditions,[18] I shall not discuss it further.

According to JWT_2, a war cannot be just overall, however justly it was entered into, if it is conducted unjustly; and however justly it is conducted, it cannot be just overall if it was not justly entered into.[19] Neither of these possibilities is precluded by JWT_1.

Also at stake in the issue between internalism and externalism is whether satisfying the conditions of JAB even suffice to warrant the resort to war.[20] If the internalist view is correct and one must conduct a war justly in order to have been justified in resorting to it, then one must wait to see how a war unfolds before concluding that one was justified in going to war. Indeed, if justice in the conduct of war can be transformed into injustice at any point during the course of a war—for example, by the annihilation of a civilian population—then one may not know until the war is ended, and perhaps even until long after it has ended, whether it was justly resorted to.[21] This possibility

---

[18] Richard Werner writes: "Simply stated, if we allow the principles of just war to be interpreted as *prima facie* rules then almost any modern war can be found morally just. If we require that the rules are each absolute then it is unclear that any modern war can be morally just. As already stated, we can find almost any war warranted if we allow a loose interpretation of just war principles and we can find the same war unwarranted if we apply a strict interpretation." See his "Pragmatism for Pacifists," p. 104. Steven P. Lee writes in a similar vein that "it seems likely that there are few wars that satisfy all of the *ad bellum* criteria, so that few would be overall just." See his discussion of permissive and restrictive interpretations of *jus ad bellum* criteria, *Ethics and War*, pp. 102–109. Werner focuses on how strictly the *jus ad bellum* criteria are to be interpreted, Lee upon how many of them need to be satisfied. Both issues need to be dealt with by defenders of the JWT.

[19] One might fine-tune this by allowing that some degree of injustice in the conduct of war is allowed without affecting the overall justice of a war that was entered into justly; and that unexpected turns of events might enable a just cause to emerge in the course of a war, and if it is otherwise conducted justly, transform it into a just war.

[20] Once again, as I shall for the most part be discussing partial war in what immediately follows, I shall drop the subscripts after "war," reintroducing them only when necessary to avoid confusion.

[21] I am ignoring for present purposes the question of how great an infringement of JIB is necessary to transform an otherwise just war—that is, one in which the conditions of JAB are met—into an unjust war. Presumably, for just war theorists, a single infringement by a single soldier would not suffice, but massive and systematic infringements—for example, genocide—would. Where is the line to be drawn in between these, and according to what sort of calculus, is unclear. Conversely, one might ask whether an overwhelming balance of justice on the side of JAB might transform an otherwise

may be part of the motivation for the growing tendency to recognize *jus post bellum* in addition to JAB and JIB. In any event, if justice in the resort to war requires justice in the conduct of war, one can never know at the moment one resorts to war whether one does so justly. The best one can do is intend to conduct the war justly. But since one can—let us assume for the present—know at the moment one goes to war whether all of the conditions of JAB are satisfied, those conditions cannot by themselves (if internalism is correct) suffice to justify the resort to war. They may be individually necessary but they are not jointly sufficient. In that case, the JWT cannot justify resort to war at the moment at which war is entered into. It can do so only retroactively.

Although it is tempting to regard JAB and JIB as logically independent considered in and of themselves (i.e., simply as lists of conditions), it is difficult to see how they would be logically independent as dimensions of a comprehensive JWT. For JWT aims to show that some wars (meaning overall on one side) are just and others unjust.[22] And to make those assessments requires weighing the justice or injustice of both JAB and JIB.

So there are three relevant areas of assessment. The first is that of the resort to war; the second is that of the conduct of war; the third is that of the overall justice of the war (taking into account the degrees of justice and possible injustice of both the recourse to war and the conduct of war). Since we are here talking only about a partial war, that is war$_1$, there remain the further issue of whether the resultant war$_2$ is just, an issue not addressed by the JWT.

5.4 What does *jus ad bellum* entitle one to do?

A minimalist interpretation of JAB would be the following, where JC, once again, stands for the various conditions of JAB (just cause, legitimate authority, etc.):

1. If, and only if, JC obtain, one may resort to war.

By "may" I mean permissibly from the standpoint of justice. I call this a minimalist interpretation, because JAB could not assert less than this and still purport to justify going to war.[23] According to (1), the satisfying of conditions JC entitles one to commence the organized violence of warfare; that is, to begin deliberately killing

---

illicit conduct of war in JIB into a just conduct of war overall. That is, what is at stake in these calculations is whether the partial war waged by one state—which is subject to evaluation according to the two dimensions of JWT, JAB and JIB—is just or unjust overall. And that requires assessing that war according to the criteria of JAB and JIB and then, if the war is just according to one set of criteria but unjust according to the other, deciding how to weigh those judgments in arriving at an overall judgment of the war (bearing in mind that this is still only the partial war).

[22] Again, in speaking of some wars "overall" as being just or unjust, I am not speaking of whole wars as defined earlier. Rather I am speaking of partial wars. It is the justice, on balance, of war as entered into and conducted by one side only that is at issue.

[23] I am assuming, for the sake of argument, that a minimalist interpretation sets forth both necessary and sufficient conditions for the resort to war. One could, of course, specify either necessary or sufficient conditions alone.

people against their will. But it does not say for what reason or against whom. We therefore need to expand upon (1).

1a. If, and only if, JC obtain, then one may resort to war in the service of a
　　 just cause.

The notion of just cause is, of course, already embedded in JC. This specifies that it must be in the service of that cause that you resort to war, not merely that you have a just cause, since you could have a just cause but go to war for reasons unrelated to it. Implied here is that one resorts to war against those whose conduct has given you a just cause. It does not entitle you to resort to war against others. Nor does it prescribe any limits in quantity or quality to the violence you may use. Usually if we say that people are morally justified in doing something, we mean that they are justified in trying to achieve the objectives encompassed by their purpose for doing that thing. (1) is silent on this issue. It says that you may commence warfare but does not say by what means or with what intensity. But what does that mean? To commence warfare is to begin deliberately causing harm, death and destruction. You cannot do this without using the weapons of warfare and without doing so with a certain intensity. One could commence warfare by firing the first shot, or by sinking a ship, bombing a city, or launching a nuclear attack. A *state of war* can exist without killing or destruction but warfare cannot. (1) tells you that you may resort to war—that is, commence warfare— when JC are met. But JAB is vacuous unless it tells you what you may when you resort to war. (1a) tells you that you may resort to war for a certain reason, or possibly with a certain motivation, but it also does not tell you what you may do. Given the presumptive wrongness of killing persons, you may not deliberately kill a single person unless such killing is justified. JAB, understood as asserting either (1) or (1a), does not establish that you are justified in killing. If JIB is logically independent of JAB, it renders JAB vacuous. Just as you can be justified in playing chess only if you are justified in moving the pieces, you can be justified in resorting to war only if you are justified in the killing of human beings that warfare entails. To be just in resorting to war according to JAB requires that you be justified in at least starting to kill and harm persons in accordance with JIB.

5.5 Intention, double effect and deliberate wartime killing

I have said that the deliberate nonconsensual killing of human beings is presumptively wrong, where "deliberate" covers both intentional and foreseeable killing. Warists often try to drive a wedge between intentional and foreseeable killing by means of the so-called principle of double-effect. The principle disallows intentional killing but sometimes allows foreseeable killing. The principle deals with actions which have both good and bad effects.[24] It requires that one intend only the good and never the bad,

---

[24] It is arguable that every action has both good and bad effects and that therefore the principle covers all actions and hence, in effect, constitutes a basic moral theory in and of itself.

even though the bad may be foreseeable and hence knowingly brought about. As I have dealt with this principle elsewhere,[25] I shall limit myself at present to a more recent defense of it.

The framing of the issue of double effect is suspect at the outset. If I kill you, your death is not an "effect" of what I do. It is part of what I do. Your death is integral to the act. Sometimes the act of killing can be broken down into subsidiary acts, and one can make sense of the resultant death being an effect of those subsidiary acts. John Wilkes Boothe killed Lincoln. Lincoln's death was integral to Boothe's act of killing. But one could decompose Boothe's act into subsidiary acts, such as moving his finger or squeezing the trigger of a gun, which had the effect of causing the bullet to be discharged from the chamber, which caused the bullet to enter Lincoln's brain, which had the still further effect of causing his death. It marks a departure from much of common sense to represent killing in that way, but I shall in what follows examine the principle of double effect on its own terms, granting for the sake of argument that the death as an act of killing is an effect of what one does rather than part of the act itself.

The relevance of the principle of double effect to warfare is evident. If killing a person is always bad, then there will be a "bad effect" to every act of causing death. If one may not intend such an effect, then a necessary condition of justifiable wartime killing is that one not intend to kill. The bad effect must be an unintended byproduct of a good the act is intended to achieve. This must be true of each and every act of killing by each and every soldier in war, if their killing is to be permissible. It must also be true of the act of initiating war by government leaders, since JWT requires a right intention as a condition of the permissibility of resorting to war in the first place. Since you can know that if you resort to war that you (or your armies) will kill people, then you can know for a virtual certainty that an undetermined number of "evils" will be among the consequences ("effects") of what you do. But you may not justifiably intend those consequences. You must merely tolerate them as a byproduct of the attainment of the good you intend.

So both heads of state[26] and individual soldiers are governed by the same requirement. The virtual certainty of the evil they knowingly do—often on a massive scale in the case of heads of state—must not be intended.

5.6 Right intention and the resort to war

Consider first the case of government leaders. Suppose you are such a leader trying to decide whether you may permissibly go to war. You know that to do so will cause harm, death and destruction and that this will be bad. If you know anything of history, you will also know that people in your position typically miscalculate the extent of the death and destruction. If you intend such effects, it would be wrong to resort to war.

---

[25] In *On War and Morality*, ch. 6.
[26] Recall that I am talking mainly about states, but that the relevant collectivities that conduct warfare include nonstate actors as well, such as militias, mercenary organizations and terrorist groups.

But if you intend a good and merely tolerate the bad, you have a green light so far as intention is concerned.[27]

Now what we intend is under our control. So in this case, you need only set as your intention the attainment of a good. If you have a just cause provided by a wrong done to you (meaning to your state), then you have a readymade good to aim at, the rectification of the injustice or vindication of the violation of a right. If, as is increasingly argued in the modern world, a just cause is afforded by wrongs done to or threatened against others, then you need only aim at ending those wrongs. There will nearly always be some perceived wrong that you or others have suffered or are threatened with whose termination or rectification can be held to be a good.[28] Even if you do not have a just cause, there will always be goods that you can aim at, such as a stable world order or a world safe for democracy. It takes only a little philosophical ingenuity to argue that justice and utility can conflict, and that sometimes the promotion of a greater good requires tolerating or even performing some injustice. If this is what you intend, then the harm, death and destruction you cause will be incidental byproducts. All other things being equal, your going to war will be permissible.

Some just war theorists are fairly strict deontologists and do not say that promoting a good, as opposed to rectifying an injustice, can provide a just cause.[29] This might seem to create a problem, since the principle of double effect requires that one aim at a good. But if one holds that the rectification of injustice constitutes a good, then one can have it both ways, saying that one can properly intend only a good and at the same time that promoting a good does not, at least ipso facto, give one a just cause.[30]

The upshot is that any head of state wishing to justify the resort to war according to JAB can easily satisfy the condition of right intention. This is true even where war is undertaken as punishment. Punishment is the intentional infliction of pain, suffering, deprivation or death for a perceived wrong. It might seem, therefore, that in punishing one unavoidably intends what is evil. But one can still argue even here that if the punishment is justified, one is in fact willing the good that retributive justice represents.[31]

In making right intention one of the conditions justifying resort to war, one puts in the hands of those who initiate war not only the power to wage war, which they already have by virtue of their command of armies, but also the power to determine (in part)

---

[27] Intending the good effects and merely tolerating the bad is a necessary but not a sufficient condition for justifying the act, according to most defenders of the principle of double effect. Additional conditions vary, but often include requiring that the act itself be good, or at least not bad, that the evil not be a means to the good, and that the good and evil be proportionate in the sense that the evil not outweigh the good.

[28] One can find issues in the recent or past history of almost any country, if only in the setting of boundaries, that can be thought to represent injustice and considered grounds for a grievance by that country.

[29] See, for example, Biggar, *In Defense of War*, p. 123.

[30] This matter is actually more complicated than this, and requires distinguishing between moral and nonmoral goods, as I shall do later in this chapter.

[31] In this case, the pain, suffering, deprivation or death in question are constitutive of the justice, hence of the alleged good. If, as is commonly required of uses of the principle of double effect, the evil involved may not be a means to the good, it is difficult to see how it can be permissible to undertake acts in which the evils are constitutive of the good.

whether their resort to war is right or wrong. JAB empowers them. Only a failure of imagination can prevent them from making use of that power. It is not merely that they will appear to have a good intention but fail to do so, which they might well do but with a little care can avoid doing; it is that they will in fact have a good intention, and by virtue of that will have fully within their control one of the necessary conditions of justifying the resort to war.

5.7 Right intention and individual combatants

What of the killing that individual soldiers do in wartime? Right intention is not typically a criterion of JIB, hence is not usually required by standard JWT. But if I am correct and if one must defeat the presumption against warfare and the killing of individual persons that warfare entails, then one might appeal to the principle of double effect for that purpose. Although he does not frame his analysis in precisely these terms, Nigel Biggar gives a thoughtful defense of the principle of double effect which, if sound, would serve that purpose. He defends the JWT from a Christian perspective, but, given a few assumptions, his defense of the principle of double effect would apply to the defense of a secular JWT as well. In any event, it highlights some of the relevant considerations in the assessment of double effect. Because his analysis seems particularly suited to the situation of those doing the actual killing in warfare (as opposed to that of state leaders who may be responsible for initiating war but rarely do any of the actual killing themselves), I shall examine it in that connection.

Biggar contends that insofar as "the life of any human being is a good and his death an evil, it is wrong to intend (or choose to want) to kill anyone."[32] At the conclusion of his discussion he asserts: "I continue to hold, therefore, that military personnel ought not to intend to wound or kill their enemy—insofar as 'intend' means to 'choose and want as a goal' rather than 'choose and accept with reluctance.'"[33] So I take his account to apply most naturally to the situation of individual soldiers rather than (or perhaps in addition to) that of state leaders making the decision whether it is permissible to go to war.

The key notions here are *intend* and *accept*. Given that every act of deliberately killing a person has an evil "effect" (the death of a human being), one must not intend that effect but only "accept" or tolerate it as a foreseeable side effect of what one does.

Biggar explicates what it is to intend something in terms of what one wants or desires, as opposed to what one accepts. But, he says, there are rational desires and sensual desires. Rational desires are for what one knows to be good or to do what is right. Sensual desires are "to be in a state of physical and emotional satisfaction; to avoid what is painful."[34] Rational desire is what makes for a good intention.

But there are two different dimensions to what Biggar identifies as a rational desire: (a) a desire for what one knows to be good, and (b) a desire to do what is right.

---

[32] Biggar, *In Defense of War*, pp. 100–101.
[33] Biggar, *In Defense of War*, p. 110.
[34] Biggar, *In Defense of War*, p. 95.

The second, however, risks circularity. Good intention is set forth as a criterion for determining the rightness ("moral quality") of an action as opposed to being solely a ground for a judgment of the person performing the act.[35] If one desires to do what is right and tries to determine what that is, it does not help to know that a proposed action would be right only if done with a good intention, and that a good intention is a desire to do what is right. Not only could an agent not determine what it is right in this way, a spectator could likewise never know whether the agent was doing what is right.

If the appeal to a rational desire is to be serviceable, it must be understood as (a), a desire for what is good, which is perfectly intelligible and involves no circularity. But, according to Biggar, the life of any human being is a good. In knowingly killing a person one knowingly destroys something of intrinsic value.[36] To do that is evil. But one can only accept that evil and not intend it. In producing that evil, one must be desiring another good and merely tolerating this destruction of what is good in the course of advancing, promoting or securing this other good. Precisely what that good is supposed to be is not altogether clear, but it may be justice.[37] It may be that in killing human beings in combat one is intending (i.e., rationally desiring) only to advance the alleged good of justice and merely accepting the evil of the death one causes.

The good that is represented by justice, however, is typically a moral good, not an intrinsic good. Consider distributive justice, which is fairness in the distribution of benefits and burdens. There is nothing of intrinsic value in any particular distribution of benefits and burdens. Taking a dollar from Donald Trump and giving it to a homeless person does not create intrinsic value. The value of such distributions is extrinsic, consisting of its contribution to the lives of those affected by it. Fair distributions are moral goods, in the sense that they are good on moral grounds, not in and of themselves. The same with retributive justice. Punishment, as I have said, is the deliberate infliction of pain, suffering, deprivation or death upon persons for alleged wrongs they have committed. With the exception of the death penalty, it is the effect upon their lives that supposedly constitutes the good, and perhaps upon the lives of those who know of or inflict the punishment. The good of the lives of those one kills, on the other hand, is intrinsic, according to Biggar (as are the lives of those one kills with the death penalty). One knowingly destroys that which has intrinsic value to achieve a desired extrinsic good.[38]

---

[35] As I maintain in *On War and Morality*, ch. 6. Biggar interprets me to be separating intention and action, which I do not do. Every action (at least understood for moral purposes) has an intention. What I maintain is that one and the same act can have different intentions at different times or as performed by different persons at the same time. One member of a firing squad may intend to contribute to the death of the condemned, and do so gladly; another may intend only to carry out an order, and do so reluctantly. They perform one and the same act, and though we may judge them differently as persons because of their different intentions, we must, on pain of inconsistency, judge what they do the same way.

[36] Biggar, *In Defense of War*, p. 96.

[37] Biggar, *In Defense of War*, p. 93.

[38] It is possible that Biggar is denying that one destroys something of intrinsic value in the killing of those who are "monstrously corrupt, such as Hitler, Stalin, and Pol Pot." See *In Defense of War*, p. 92. The thought that we can know who is "monstrously corrupt" or incorrigibly evil is at odds with Augustine who, in his later years, came to the view that although we know everyone is tainted with Original Sin, we simply cannot know whom God has chosen to be among the Elect. See *A Treatise on*

Although, in this view, those who kill in combat must do so reluctantly, and only accept and not desire the deaths of those they kill, they nonetheless are responsible (but not necessarily culpable) for those deaths. Accordingly, they must justify causing the evils they foresee but do not intend. In addition to not being intended, the evil caused by killing must be:

1. Not needless, in the sense that it could have been avoided;
2. Not in vain, in the sense of undermining the good effect "for whose sake it is tolerated";
3. Not disproportionate, in the sense of outweighing the good achieved;
4. Not against any strict obligations, as it might if it is unfair to others or "in breach of an obligation."[39]

But (4) also risks circularity. The aim, recall, is to lay down criteria justifying the nonconsensual killing of human beings in war. But to say that an act is not in breach of any obligations (or strict obligations, as the case may be) is to say that it is not (on that account at least) wrong. Quite apart from obligations, it is manifestly unfair to the families, loved ones and friends of those one kills to leave them widowed or orphaned or bereft for reasons that (for all one is likely to know at the moment one kills) confer no blame upon them. Some sense of this unfairness is perhaps at the root of the feelings some soldiers report experiencing when they come upon photos of wives or children on the bodies of soldiers they have killed. It is perhaps no less unfair to those who are killed if they are conscripts or volunteers who have been lied to by their governments or child soldiers who have been forced to fight upon pain of death for refusal. That represents unfairness to them by the authorities under whose control they are, and one contributes to that unfairness—indeed, might even be said to complete it—by killing them. It is virtually impossible for individual soldiers to know in advance whether those they will kill on a given day stand in relationships which render their killing unfair to others or to them. And if they cannot know that, they cannot justify causing the evil which they foreseeably do, and for which they are responsible, even though they do not intend it.

Nor can an individual soldier possibly know whether the evil he does is not disproportionate, that is, does not outweigh the good he hopes to achieve (condition (3) speaks of the good achieved, but the alleged good in question is not achieved until after the killing, and the rightness or wrongness of the act of killing must be determined before that occurs). If the person killed is a combat soldier in the army of a country with which one's own is at war, one can know that he or she is prevented forever after from harming or killing one's self or fellow soldiers, which he might well have tried to do had he lived. That, presumably, must be reckoned an instrumental good. But as such it must be weighed against the intrinsic good of this life that has been permanently eliminated, and against any unfairness to parents, spouse, children or friends who also

the *Predestination of the Saints, A Select Library of Nicene and Post-Nicene Fathers*, Vol. 1.5. Indeed, it would be a sin of pride in the Augustinian view to presume to have knowledge that only God can have.
[39] Biggar, *In Defense of War*, pp. 96f.

suffer a permanent loss by his death. Perhaps the person you kill loves warfare and delights in killing, in which case perhaps there is a considerable good achieved by his death. But in the fog and chaos of warfare such calculations of comparative good and evil are virtually impossible and perhaps even impossible after the war. Biggar stresses this himself elsewhere, when discussing proportionality as an express condition of JAB and JIB, when he says that such calculations cannot be made—indeed, are not calculations at all, but judgments.[40]

That the evil was not caused needlessly, meaning it could not have been avoided, is open to question, as we have seen in our earlier discussion of the alleged inevitability of wrongdoing. If the killing is a voluntary act, even if, by hypothesis, foreseen but unintended, then of course it could have been avoided. One simply need not have performed it. There is a commonsense perspective from which one "had no choice" if the circumstances are such that one's self or comrades will be killed if one does not kill first. This would be a variant on the type of situation considered in Chapter 2 in which one acts from necessity. But at some earlier stage in the sequence of events leading up to the situation in which one is face-to-face with an enemy soldier who is bent upon killing you and/or your fellow soldiers—the stage, for example, at which one volunteered for the military or answered a draft call—the situation could clearly have been avoided. That it could possibly have been avoided only at great personal cost can be granted but does not alter that fact.

This leaves the requirement that the killing not have been in vain, meaning that it not undermine the good effect "for whose sake it is tolerated." If the intended good effect is, say, to defend one's self or one's comrades, then such killing may not have been in vain. But great importance is commonly attached to the deaths that have already occurred. The resolve in that case is to ensure that those who are killed in combat not have died in vain, a topic to which we shall return in Chapter 15. This resolve can actually lead to sending more troops, engaging in more killing and suffering even more casualties. The scrupulous soldier tries to be careful that the killing he does is not in vain. But there remains the possibility that the killing he or she does will itself contribute to undermining the achievement of the good effect for which the evil effect is tolerated. Again, these are imponderables. It will almost certainly never be possible to conclude with confidence what these consequences will be and certainly not to do so before one engages in killing.

The upshot is that even if one is clear what the good is for which one kills and can keep that before one's mind in such a way that one can meaningfully be said to intend it, the further conditions that must be met in order for one to be justified in causing the evil one "accepts" but does not intend can at best only partially be met. In particular, if one cannot know that the evil one causes does not outweigh the good, then one cannot know that one is justified in causing that evil. And if one cannot know that, then one cannot know whether it is morally right to kill that fellow human being in the enemy uniform in front of you.

Biggar argues that soldiers in wartime do not (or at least do not necessarily) intend to kill. Their killing is foreseeable but done reluctantly and "beside" their intention.

---

[40] *In Defense of War*, pp. 140, 141, 147.

Even if that could convincingly be shown, it would not justify their killing because it would not show that one can meet the obligation that comes with responsibility for the evil they know they are causing.

One can imagine soldiers not intending to kill those they deliberately kill. They kill only reluctantly, accepting the evil they do without wanting it, and making as far as reasonably possible the necessary judgments that their killing is not needless, in vain or disproportionate and not unfair or in violation of obligations. Since what one does without intending one moment can become the object of one's intention the next, they do this repeatedly for each act of killing throughout the war. Then (assuming as I shall do for the sake of argument that the principle of double effect is the proper framework for analyzing wartime killing), one could conclude that the killing they do is permissible. But these conditions describe a fantasy world far removed from the reality of wars in the modern world.

Moreover, if these conditions could be met at all, they could be met on both sides in a war. Individual soldiers all around can have a rational desire for a good in what they do. To achieve that can be their intention. There is evidence that the German soldiers in WWII fought, not for the abstract causes the Nazi regime put before them, but primarily for their comrades.[41] If what one intends is within one's control, soldiers on all sides can, theoretically at least, intend a good and accept that the evil they do is not what they want, is done reluctantly, and is in need of justification. And unless soldiers on one side, but not on the other, are cognitively deficient, they can—again, in theory—make the judgments necessary to justify the evil they knowingly cause but do not intend. All sides, then, can kill both with moral impunity and with what Walzer calls moral equality.[42]

5.8 Just war theory's further implications

I have argued that, at the minimum, JAB entitles one to commence warfare, but that to do so entails killing, and that such killing must be justified if JAB is to be an acceptable criterion for going to war.

---

[41] See the account of the views of German prisoners of war during WWII by Sönke Neitzel and Harald Welzer, *Soldaten: The Secret WWII Transcripts of German POWS* (New York: Alfred K. Knopf, 2012): "Frontline soldiers felt an almost exclusive sense of duty to their comrades and their superiors who formed their social units ... Abstract concepts like a 'global Jewish conspiracy,' 'Bolshevist promotion of genetic inferiority,' or even the 'National Socialst *Volk* community' played only an ancillary role ... Most of them were fully apolitical ... In war, soldiers tended to behave alike, regardless of whether they were Protestants or Catholics, Nazis or regime critics, Prussians or Austrians, university graduates or uneducated people. In light of these findings, we should be even more skeptical of intentionalist explanations of Nazi atrocities" (p. 319).

[42] Biggar presents an alternative account which does not have the implication I am citing here. In it, he expressly justifies only the killing by soldiers in a just war. Then the killing that just warriors do is justified in part by the "objectively wrong" acts of their unjust adversaries, an account that bears similarity to that offered by Jeff McMahan in his *Killing in War*, which I shall examine later. It unclear whether this alternative account is intended to represent Biggar's own view or simply that of the later just war tradition which he is discussing. In any event, as we have seen in Chapter 4, that view is unsupported by Augustine, who holds that we must look to inner motives and intentions in our judgments, not to outward acts.

Let us for the present set aside the judgment that the principle of double effect does not suffice to justify the killing entailed by the recourse to war or by the acts of individual soldiers. Let us return to the question of what JAB entitles one to do. We have discussed the minimalist interpretation represented by:

1. If, and only if, JC obtain, one may resort to war.

Let us now consider a second interpretation of JAB which makes explicit what is sometimes assumed by (1):

2a. If, and only if, JC obtain, one may (i) resort to war in the service of a just cause, and (ii) do whatever is necessary to the war's successful prosecution.

In this interpretation, satisfying JC would not only entitle you to commence killing in the service of your cause, it would also authorize you to do whatever is necessary to succeed in your purpose for going to war. The purpose will often be to achieve victory, but it will sometimes be to achieve objectives short of victory. The necessity involved can be understood to be military necessity, even though the sort of effort required to achieve objectives in wartime will normally extend to civilian activities throughout society that are beyond what is normally covered by military necessity. This, recall, is the point of saying that warfare presupposes war making.

Interpretation (1) is externalist. It contains nothing to warrant saying that if a state justly goes to war it necessarily acts justly in the conduct of war. (2a) is more problematic. The permission represented by a just cause covers much of what one could expect to be done in the conduct of war. But while it might be taken to imply that one may do no more than what is necessary to achieve one's objectives, it does not say that. One might understand JIB to govern the whole of one's conduct of a war, not merely that part of it that is necessary to its successful prosecution. So, strictly (2a) is externalist as well. But if we expand (2) we get a position that is, at least implicitly, internalist:

(2b) If, and only if, JC obtain, then one may (i) resort to war, and (ii) do whatever is necessary to its successful prosecution, but (iii) do no more than that.

This says, in effect, that a state may cause death and destruction to the extent necessary to achieve its just objectives, but that is all that it may do. No area of the conduct of war is left ungoverned. Hence this can plausibly be regarded as internalist. If JAB authorizes doing what (2b) says, then it would appear that to fully comply with JAB a state would fully comply with any possible requirements for the just conduct of war. The only way one could fail to conduct a war justly under conditions justifying the resort to war would be if there were independent criteria of JIB which conflicted with the conditions of JAB. For example, if killing noncombatants were in some circumstances necessary to the successful prosecution of a war, and if an independent condition of JIB prohibited such killing, JAB would conflict with JIB. The overall JWT comprising JAB and JIB would then be inconsistent, because it would contain incompatible moral prescriptions. As this approximates a common characterization of extreme moral relativism, JWT would be relativistic on this interpretation. Another possibility would be to interpret the moral permission contained in (2b) to be subject to a clause. Satisfying JC would then yield a judgment of the rightness of doing what is asserted by (i) and (ii) only if all other things were equal. This could then be overridden by some requirement of JIB. While this is a possibility, I shall not so understand JAB, as the spirit of the theory seems clearly intended to specify when we are justified in resorting to war, not merely when we may be justified, all other things being equal. So, I shall take (2b) to be at least implicitly internalist. But JAB can be made explicitly internalist as follows:

(2c) If, and only if, JC obtain, one may (i) resort to war, and (ii) do whatever is necessary to its successful prosecution, but (iii) do no more than that, (iv) subject to the constraints of JIB.

If JAB asserts (2c), then the conditions of JIB cannot conflict with JAB because they are contained within it. One does not comply fully with JAB unless one at the same time complies with JIB. So, to take our earlier example, if killing noncombatants were necessary to the successful prosecution of a war, and JIB prohibited such killing, then JAB would entail that one may not engage in such killing. One may do what is necessary in war only up to the limits imposed by JIB.

A third set of positions can be specified governing military utility rather than military necessity. Then the relevant consideration is what is useful in war rather than what is necessary. Thus:

3(a) If, and only if, JC obtain, one may (i) resort to war, and (ii) do whatever is useful to its prosecution.
 (b) If, and only if, JC obtain, one may (i) resort to war, and (ii) do whatever is useful to its successful prosecution, but (iii) do no more than that.
 (c) If, and only if, JC obtain, one may (i) resort to war, and (ii) do whatever is useful to its successful prosecution, but (iii) do no more than that, (iv) subject to the constraints of JIB.

The bombing of Hiroshima arguably was useful to the prosecution of WWII by the United States. It may have ended the war sooner. But it was neither necessary nor in keeping with JIB, in which case it would have been sanctioned by (3b) but prohibited by (2a) and (3c). As in the case of the various forms of (2), (3a) will be strictly externalist, (3b) will be implicitly internalist and (3c) explicitly so.

There remains a fourth position that deserves consideration. It gives unlimited license once one has satisfied the conditions of JAB

4(a) If, and only if, JC obtain, one may (i) resort to war, and (ii) do anything in the course of its prosecution.

This says, in effect, that if you have justice on your side, you may do whatever you want in the course of waging war, even exceeding the bounds of what is necessary or useful. Such a view authorizes the expenditure of lives and resources beyond what serves any useful military purpose. So far as rationality calls for the choice of the most efficient means to one's ends, and insofar as one's ends are understood in purely military terms, implementation of such a principle would not be fully rational. Nonetheless, it is likely that some wars of antiquity fit this description, considering the rampages of massacre, rape and pillage they entailed.

There is nonetheless some basis for such a view in traditional just war theory. As Frederick H. Russell writes, "[a]s total war the Roman just war countenanced capture of civilians, devastation of land and plundering of cities."[43] Augustine speaks as though the warrant to go to war is a warrant to punish wrongdoing, much in the way that punishment is administered within domestic society.[44] If punishing the enemy, instead of achieving victory or other ends, is a primary objective of war, there might be thought to be a warrant for unleashing punitive violence of whatever scale the just party chooses. If capital punishment is thought to be justified at the micro level, one might think that genocide is warranted at the macro level. If a commitment to violence justifies putting individuals to death for certain crimes, it might well be thought to justify annihilating a whole collectivity—a city, a state, or a people—for its alleged crimes at the macro level.[45] If one thought that the infliction of such punishment was just, and that its infliction was one of the purposes for going to war, then this possibility could be incorporated as a permutation of 2(b). Augustine, it should be said, does not himself so understand the warrant provided by JAB. But much of the history of warfare has unfolded as though some such principle were in effect, as armies often act without even the constraints of military utility or necessity. One might, of course, attach a constraint to such a principle, along the lines of:

4(b) If, and only if, JC obtain, one may (i) resort to war, (ii) do anything in the course of its prosecution, (iii) subject to the constraints of JIB.

This is an unusual position, as it bypasses any reference to the notions of military necessity or utility. But it stakes out a possible position: while one must recognize the constraints imposed by JIB, one need recognize no others. And as the conditions defining JIB normally do not include (and are not restricted to) those of necessity and utility, it is possible to impose constraints in the one area and not in the other.

Position (4a) is implicitly internalist. As it authorizes the doing of anything when one has justice on one's side, there is nothing in the way of the conduct of war that

---

[43] Russell, *The Just War in the Middle Ages*, p. 7.

[44] It is said, for example: "Catholic philosophy … concedes to the State the full natural right of war, whether defensive, as in case of another's attack in force upon it; offensive (more properly, coercive), where it finds it necessary to take the initiative in the application of force; or punitive, in the infliction of punishment for evil done against itself or, in some determined cases, against others." *The Catholic Encyclopedia* (1908), s.v., War.

[45] Rome's destruction of Carthage and the Nazis' attempted destruction of the Jewish people are but two examples historically.

is precluded. If, therefore, the conditions of JIB are consistent with those of JAB, to establish JAB suffices to establish JIB. It could be the case, however, that at least one condition of JIB conflicts with the conditions of JAB. In that event, either the JWT itself would be inconsistent (in the sense that one of its dimensions, JAB, would authorize actions that are prohibited by its other dimension, JIB), or it would be relativistic, in the sense of allowing that both conflicting moral judgments may be correct. Position (4b), on the other hand, is explicitly internalist, in that it makes the satisfaction of the conditions of JIB a necessary condition of the satisfaction of the conditions of JAB.

Can justice in the conduct of war be achieved independently of justice in the resort to war? It cannot. If a state is wrong to resort to war in the first place, all of the harm, death and destruction it deliberately causes will be wrong. Virtually all of it will be bad and there will be and can be no proper proportion between good and bad or satisfaction of the requirements of discrimination understood as a moral principle. A state fighting a wrongful war could be scrupulously careful to kill only combatants (just as a state fighting a war that satisfies conditions JC could deliberately kill noncombatants as well as combatants). From a moral standpoint, however, this would not be enough and would not meet the condition of discrimination. If a state wrongfully embarks on war, then all of the killing it does is wrongful.[46] This includes the killing of soldiers as well as civilians. Insofar as JIB does not address this issue, it fails to provide an adequate account of the morality of killing in warfare.

It is perhaps for this reason that attention has been given to the so-called "moral equality" of soldiers, a license to kill held equally on both (or all) sides, regardless of the justice of their participation in the war. If soldiers do not have an equal right to kill, it is virtually impossible for war (meaning war$_2$, whole war) to be morally justified.

5.9 License to kill

The argument is that soldiers have, in effect, a license to kill. The argument does not challenge the claim in A(4) that the deliberate nonconsensual killing of persons is presumptively wrong. It holds that, even if that claim be conceded, it can still be shown that war$_2$, which consists principally of such killing, is not presumptively wrong.

There is no problem for hard realism. On that view morality does not apply to warfare. Moral judgments about what soldiers do in warfare make no sense. It is not that what they do is morally permissible; it is that it is neither permissible nor impermissible. There is also no problem from a legal standpoint. International law immunizes combatants from prosecution so long as they do not commit war crimes or crimes against humanity. Domestic law countenances the killing that is done by soldiers on one's own side; indeed, military law requires it of them if they are under orders. At the moment one takes the appropriate oath and steps forward (or performs

---

[46] I have argued in *On War and Morality*, ch. 6 that, on the assumption that there are just and unjust wars, all of the killing done by soldiers on the unjust side is wrongful. McMahan argues that, with few exceptions, which he details, this is true. But he interprets unjust combatants in such a way that the killing of them by just combatants (those fighting a just war) is permissible, which I do not. See McMahan, *Killing in War*, especially chapters 1 and 2.

the comparable legal act in the army in question), one morphs from a civilian into a soldier. At that moment, as though by the wave of a magic wand, one acquires the license to kill. In fact I shall call it *The Magic Wand Theory*. It is not a license to kill any human being at any time or in any way, anymore than a hunting license is a license to kill any animal at any time or in any way. The killing is regulated. There are prescribed circumstances in which one may kill. The principal difference is that in the case of humans the killing is mandated. You can purchase a deer license and go hunting or not as you choose. You can get a deer in your sights and squeeze the trigger or not as you choose. But once in the military you go into combat when ordered to, with what weapons you are told to use and against whomever you are told to fight. And you kill when ordered to. All sides in war have this license. Warfare, as we have seen, is the essence of war. And killing is at the heart of warfare.

One possible argument to justify the claim that soldiers in wartime may permissibly kill one another rests upon the externalist view just criticized and rejected. It is that JAB and JIB represent logically distinct modes of assessment. That contention, in Walzer's words, is: "In our judgments of the fighting, we abstract from all considerations of the justice of the cause."[47] The remainder of the argument is not explicitly detailed, but it may be presumed to go as follows: guilt and innocence of soldiers cannot be established apart from judgments of the justice of the cause for which they are fighting. Therefore such guilt and innocence cannot be established in the case of soldiers, hence is irrelevant to judgments of the fighting they do. This institutes a version of war realism with regard to the actions of soldiers in war. If soldiers cannot be judged to be innocent or guilty, then they cannot be judged to be acting wrongly in killing one another. This implied argument rests heavily on the claim that in judging the conduct of war we abstract from the justice of the cause. Factually, this claim is probably true of the thinking of most warists, but as a metaethical claim, I shall argue, it is indefensible.

5.10 Conclusion

The JWT does not and cannot defeat the moral presumption against war$_2$ (whole war) because it does not deal with the issue of war$_2$. Its focus is almost exclusively upon war$_1$ (partial war), the warfare conducted by one side, and upon the considerations that enter into the conventional approach to war. It typically begins with the assumption that some wars$_1$ are justified and seeks only to refine the conditions warranting that assumption. Often the conditions of the JWT itself are adjusted or modified (particularly last resort, proportionality and discrimination) to rationalize war when those conditions would otherwise not do so. It privileges the point of view of those who believe themselves to be in the right in conflicts, and who think of themselves as victims, or potential victims, of aggression and wrongdoing by states. Because of this limited perspective, it does not defeat the moral presumption against the totality of the harming and killing that is at the heart of warfare. Even less does it defeat the presumption against the rape, killing of innocents, destruction of property, creation of refugees, economic dislocation, medical

---

[47] Walzer, *Just and Unjust Wars*, 4th ed., p. 127.

crises, and harm to animals and the environment that are inherent in war$_2$. And as we have seen, it becomes vacuous if it does not authorize the killing that embarking upon warfare entails. The same, it should be said, though I have not stressed it, is true of the moral war theory. Just as war$_2$ is a collaborative undertaking among collectivities, the actual fighting and killing it entails (of combatants) is a collaborative undertaking among individual soldiers. They tacitly agree to try to kill one another when ordered to by their respective authorities. Although in the heat of combat they may sometimes be fighting in personal self-defense in a minimalist sense, they are not—or have not been shown to be—fighting in self-defense in a justifiable sense. As I shall argue in the next chapter, the disanalogies between personal self-defense as normally understood and the situations of soldiers in combat are simply too great to warrant that inference. Even if personal self-defense, appropriately qualified, is considered morally justifiable, one cannot, as we shall consider in the following chapter, extrapolate from this that violent national self-defense is morally justified. Beyond this, soldiers cannot be thought to have forfeited their right to life simply by virtue of having joined the military and become dangerous persons.

Self-Defense and the Alleged Moral Equality of Soldiers

Neither man [soldiers in conventional combat] is a criminal, and so both can be said to act in self-defense

—Michael Walzer

Of course soldiers may kill one another; otherwise you couldn't have war.

—College student

6.1 War and self-defense

The moral presumption against war, as we have seen, is grounded in the presumption against *warfare*, and that presumption in turn is grounded in the presumption against harming and killing persons. The JWT does not defeat that presumption. It typically assumes from the outset that some wars are just, and assumes furthermore that the killing of human beings that is at the heart of warfare is permissible. *The judgment that soldiers may permissibly kill one another in warfare underpins almost the entirety of the modern JWT.*[1] It also almost certainly underpins any remotely plausible moral war theory.[2]

A major reason for claiming that soldiers may kill one another is that when they do so they justifiably act in self-defense. There is in that case a moral equality among

---

[1] As Jeff McMahan writes, "The doctrine of the moral equality of combatants, with its corollary that combatants on both sides in a war have, as Walzer says, an equal right to kill, is almost universally accepted among those who are not pacifists, and has been for many centuries." *Killing in War*, p. 38. Nigel Biggar, on the other hand, contends: "Since Christian tradition regards just war as basically punitive, it cannot logically espouse a general doctrine of the moral equality of combatants … just warriors are justified in killing insofar as that is a proportionate means of punishing wrongdoing, and unjust warriors deserve to be killed on account of the wrong that they do." *In Defense of War*, p. 172. Whether it is logical or not, war, for Augustine (as we saw in Chapter 4), may be punitive as undertaken by the state, but individual soldiers on both sides are free of blame if they fight in obedience to their rulers and without blaspheming God.

[2] Although to show that soldiers may not permissibly kill one another would suffice to show that the JWT is inadequate as a moral war theory, to show that soldiers may permissibly kill one another would be necessary but not sufficient to show that the JWT is the correct moral war theory.

soldiers.[3] The very circumstances of armed men being hurled against one another, so to speak, at the outset of warfare means that at that moment any and all of them are fair game to be killed by their opponents. *All* of their lives are at risk.[4] This has the effect, so the argument might go, of systematically defeating the presumption against killing in that context. It does not mean that there is no presumption against killing persons. It is just that it is sweepingly defeated in the case of warfare, as though by the wave of a magic wand. War$_1$ and war$_2$ both consist in their entirety—if all sides honor moral and legal constraints in the conduct of war—of morally permissible acts. That being the case, according to this reasoning, the presumptive wrongness of the killing of persons at the individual level does not carry over to the collective actions of states. The presumption can be granted at the micro level but denied at the macro level.

More specifically, if self-defense is permissible at the micro level, it remains permissible even in warfare. The argument is not the common one, that if self-defense is permissible at the micro level, it is also permissible at the macro level. That is, it is not the argument that if the individual is justified in killing in personal self-defense, then the state is justified in killing in collective self-defense. That view we shall consider shortly. It is rather that the permissibility of individual self-defense extends even to the case of warfare, where it is the self-defense of all of the individual soldiers on both sides that makes warfare permissible. It is an unusual claim. It means that states can throw soldiers at one another for any reason, whereupon those soldiers may then justifiably kill one another in self-defense.

That soldiers may kill in self-defense is sometimes used as a rationale for expanding military action. Prior to major US military intervention in Vietnam, US advisors would accompany South Vietnamese soldiers on patrol. They supposedly were not actively engaged in combat. But they were allowed to defend themselves if attacked. Predictably, they were attacked—or at least had reason to believe they were attacked—when the South Vietnamese they were accompanying were attacked. And, of course, they used their weapons in self-defense. Gradually and almost imperceptibly defense evolved into offense until the United States bore the brunt of the fighting. When Israeli commandoes rappelled from helicopters onto a Gaza-bound ship and became involved in a violent altercation with some of those on board (resulting in the deaths of seven members of the contingent on board), the Israeli military described the commandoes as acting in self-defense. When Navy Seals killed Osama bin Laden in 2011, initial reports said he was killed in a firefight, which would suggest that the Seals killed him in self-defense. When it turned out that there was no firefight (evidently only one shot was fired by one of bin Laden's compatriots outside the house), it was then reported that bin Laden, while standing in his bedroom, made a movement that could have been interpreted as reaching for a weapon (reportedly there was an AK-47 in the house, perhaps even in the bedroom). And when one of his wives was shot approaching the

---

[3] Michael Walzer uses this term in his *Just and Unjust Wars*. It is a misleading term, in that soldiers would equally have moral equality if it were wrong for them to kill one another, but I will use the term, with reservations, because it has gained some currency in the literature.

[4] Their lives are obviously not all equally at risk. Those of frontline combat troops are more at risk than support troops in the rear or office workers at military headquarters. The lives of high-ranking commanding officers are least at risk.

Seals in the bedroom, it was surmised that she may have had explosives strapped to her, hence been shot in self-defense as well. Although many details of the mission are unclear, it is possible that the intention from the outset was to kill him; that is, that the killing was an assassination. All adult males in the compound were apparently killed, whether armed or not. Highly trained special forces from thousands of miles away killed an unarmed suspect in his home in the middle of the night. To claim that the killing was in self-defense gives extraordinary elasticity to the notion of self-defense.[5]

There is a strong commonsense belief in the rightness of personal self-defense. To justify killing, one need only extrapolate from this to other arenas. This is often done by leaders as a way to manipulate those whose support they would engage. In their perceptive analysis of the views of German soldiers held as POWs during WWII, Sönke Neitzel and Harald Welzer write:

> The murder of Jews was also defined as an act of self-defense, at least by racial theorists and those who helped arrange the Holocaust … Killing under the guise of self-defense also occurs in other cultural and historical contexts. The genocide carried out by the Hutu against Tutsi in 1990s Rwanda was preceded by forms of perception and interpretation that American historian Alison Des Forges vividly described as "accusation in a mirror." In a kind of putative genocidal fantasy one side accuses the other of planning to completely annihilate it. This schema of mirror-image accusations is not just a psychosocial phenomenon. It is also an explicitly promoted propaganda method … The logical corollary to spreading fantastic fears of being threatened is to create a willingness for self-defense among the party that feels itself under threat. Every form of murderous attack and systematic annihilation can also be perceived as a necessary act of self-defense.[6]

In this way, self-defense has not only been extended to supreme emergencies, as discussed in Chapter 2, it has been extended to preemptive and preventive warfare as well as to genocide. When its definition is controlled by those who hold political and military power, its emotive force can be used to pull along those who might not otherwise have supported their policies.

6.2 A Walzerian argument for the "moral equality" of soldiers

The argument we want to consider goes well beyond this. Rather than appealing to isolated incidents of alleged self-defense by individual soldiers, and rather than

---

[5] I use the term suspect, because although it is widely assumed that bin Laden was responsible for the 9/11 attack; he reportedly denied responsibility at the time, and it is difficult to find compelling evidence that he was responsible. An adviser to bin Laden, Sulaiman Abu Ghaith, testified at his trial that after the 9/11 attack bin Laden said to him, "We are the ones who did it." But Abu Ghaith also acknowledged that, though he was an adviser, and allegedly a close associate of bin Laden, he did not know the attack was forthcoming. *The New York Times*, September 24, 2014. Abu Ghaith was sentenced to life in prison by a civilian court.

[6] Neitzel and Welzer, *Soldaten*, pp. 329–330.

utilizing the justification of self-defense on one side only, the argument holds that soldiers on all sides in war act in self-defense, and that their so doing renders their killing of one another permissible. This reasoning, if sound, would establish that one of the conditions of *jus in bello*, that of discrimination, would automatically be met by all sides in a whole war so long as they kill only combatants.

The arguments pertaining to self-defense are set forth in rudimentary form below. I shall first indicate their general form, then reconstruct them as a single argument intended to contain Walzer's central points.

A 1. The soldier is a dangerous man.[7]
   2. He has allowed himself to become a dangerous man.
   3. If one allows himself to become a dangerous man, he loses his title to life.
   4. Therefore: Soldiers have lost their title to life.[8]
   5. Therefore soldiers have an equal right to kill (one another).[9]
B 1. The soldier is a dangerous man.
   2. Therefore when soldiers fight one another, they are acting in self-defense.[10]
   3. Therefore soldiers have an equal right to kill (in self-defense).

Recast for the sake of simplicity into one argument, the reasoning is as follows:

1. If all soldiers forfeit their right to life, then the killing of soldiers by one another is morally permissible.
   a. Persons forfeit their right to life when they allow themselves to become dangerous persons.
   b. Persons allow themselves to become dangerous persons when they enter the military.
   c. Soldiers (by definition) have entered the military.
   d. Therefore soldiers are dangerous persons.
2. Therefore: Soldiers forfeit their right to life.
3. Those who have forfeited their right to life by becoming dangerous to others may permissibly be killed by those others in self-defense.
4. Therefore: The killing of soldiers by one another is morally permissible.

As this is intended to capture the spirit, if not the letter, of Walzer's argument, I shall call it a Walzerian argument rather than Walzer's. Notice that the argument has initial plausibility only if the moral rightness of killing is determined exclusively by reference to rights. There might be consequentialist or other deontological reasons why killing is wrong even if it does not involve violation of a right to life. In any event, rights-based theories are only one type of moral theory and should not be considered the default position for assessing the morality of killing, although I will for the present limit my

---

[7] *Just and Unjust Wars*, 4th ed., p. 145.
[8] *Just and Unjust Wars*, 4th ed., p. 136.
[9] *Just and Unjust Wars*, 4th ed., p. 41.
[10] *Just and Unjust Wars*, 4th ed., p. 128.

discussion to that framework.[11] Notice also that, to be plausible, (1d) should be taken to mean, not that each and every soldier is personally involved in threatening others, but that even those who do not do the killing themselves support those who do and are, for that reason, dangerous persons.[12]

The notions of self-defense and forfeiture of a right to life are central to the reasoning regarding the moral equality of soldiers. Let us consider first the alleged forfeiture of a right to life.

According to (1a), persons forfeit their right to life when they allow themselves to become dangerous persons. Although I shall not do so here, one might question how a right to life can be forfeited.[13] If a right to life is a human right, as it is commonly understood to be, and if a human right is one that each person has simply by virtue of being human, then one cannot lose the right. It can only be respected, violated or ignored. If one weighs consequences heavily in ethics, it can be argued—in the end, untenably in my view—that there are some circumstances in which the violation of a right to life is outweighed by other moral considerations. But the right in that case is not forfeited. It is simply overridden. But the claim is suspect for other reasons. Police are dangerous persons. They are armed with clubs, guns, mace and increasingly with military equipment. They sometimes kill and frequently cause harm. Experts in some martial arts are dangerous persons. They can kill with a single kick or blow. It is the same with professional boxers or mixed martial arts competitors. But they have not thereby forfeited their right to life. Soldiers themselves are either innocent or noninnocent. Walzer considers them innocent. If innocent, then innocent persons can forfeit their right to life and, in those circumstances, it is permissible to kill them. If they are not innocent, then the fact that they become noninnocent by entering the military would cast doubt on whether it is right for them to enter the military. Entering the military arguably does make combat soldiers dangerous persons. It is questionable whether it makes mechanics, chefs, medics, secretaries and the many others who rarely if ever do any killing particularly dangerous, other than by virtue of the support they provide in various ways to those who do the killing. Even in the case of combat soldiers, being in the military does not entail a forfeiture of a right to life or provide a moral license to kill. One is not immunized from responsibility for what he or she does upon entering the military, even though much of military training seeks to weaken that sense of responsibility by stressing the need for obedience and discipline.

---

[11] Jeff McMahan frames his critique of the moral equality of soldiers largely in terms of rights. It is unclear whether he thinks that is the only way to frame the issue or simply one way among others. He writes, in elaborating his contention that unjust combatants are liable to be attacked, that "Walzer explicates the generic sense of 'innocent' by reference to people's rights … The claims that I will make about liability can also be articulated in the language of rights and indeed it may be illuminating to indicate the relations between liability and rights." McMahan, *Killing in War*, p. 9.

[12] Gandhi, in explaining his role in the Boer War and WWI, in effect acknowledges the responsibility of those who participate in war in ways other than by killing, when he says: "I draw no distinction between those who wield the weapons of destruction and those who do red-cross work. Both participate in war and advance its cause. Both are guilty of the crime of war." *The Moral and Political Writings of Mahatma Gandhi*, Vol. 2, ed. Raghavan Iyer (Oxford: Clarendon Press, 1986), p. 464.

[13] For a ground-breaking discussion of this topic, and others related to self-defense, see Cheney C. Ryan, "Self-Defense, Pacifism, and the Possibility of Killing," *Ethics*, Vol. 93, No. 3, April 1983, pp. 508–525.

6.3 Personal self-defense

There probably are no violent acts more widely approved than those in self-defense. As personal self-defense is the usual springboard for arguments for national (or collective) self-defense—often with the unquestioned assumption that if the first is justified, the second is also—I shall begin with it.

Personal self-defense (PSD) is belief-related. You cannot know that someone is acting in self-defense apart from some knowledge of his or her beliefs. It is not an objectively determinable type of act independent of epistemic considerations.

Some forms of PSD are nonphysical. One might defend oneself in court, in a debate, or against accusations. Our concern is with physical self-defense. Let us say that one acts in physical self-defense only if the following conditions are met:

1. One's life or well-being is in imminent danger.[14]
2. One believes that his life is in imminent danger.

If one person shoots another thinking it is in cold blood, but in fact (unbeknownst to the first) the other was about to shoot him first, the first person's life was in fact in imminent danger but he did not know or believe it, hence did not act in self-defense. His act, however, though unbeknownst to him at the moment he shot the second person, was in fact one of self-preservation. You can unwittingly act in ways that preserve your life, but you cannot unwittingly act in self-defense. It is necessary to self-defense that one believe one's life is in imminent danger, but that belief must also be correct; one's life must in fact be in imminent danger. A US tank gunner in Iraq shot and killed a news photographer who was raising his camera to photograph the tank. The gunner said he thought the camera was a grenade launcher. He thought he was acting in defense (of himself and the rest of the tank crew). But he was not. There was no actual threat from the photographer. The perceived threat must also be imminent. If a sniper kills a man half a mile away who has a grenade launcher strapped to his back while eating lunch, the killing is not self-defense, even if after lunch, or at some time in the future, the man might have attacked him.

3. The source of the danger is human or animal.

A falling tree, a tornado or a tsunami sometimes presents imminent threats. But stepping out of the way, taking to the storm cellar or seeking high ground do not constitute self-defense, even though they are all ways of trying to protect yourself in the appropriate circumstances. Self-defense differs from self-protection, even though they both are forms of attempted self-preservation. Warding off threats posed by inanimate

---

[14] By threats to well-being, I mean threats to essential well-being, not minor threats to person or property, such as having one's hair mussed before going out to dinner or having apples stolen from one's tree. I take the threat of torture to be a threat to one's essential well-being. I shall focus upon threats to one's life but intend that to include essential threats to one's well-being.

things is not self-defense. Not that inanimate things may not be involved in threats that occasion self-defense. A gun is an inanimate thing, but if someone shoots at you and you shoot back, you are acting in self-defense. The same if you try to destroy a drone that is firing missiles at you. The source of the danger, ultimately, is human.

4. One tries to harm, kill, or incapacitate the source of that danger in the belief that so doing will (or may) remove or mitigate the danger.

While it is necessary that one hold the belief referred to in (4) to be acting in PSD, it is not necessary that this belief be correct. PSD can fail to counteract the perceived danger. Notice that one need not believe that harming, killing or incapacitating the source of the danger is *necessary* to counteract the danger, only that it would be sufficient. Nor need it even be true that harming, killing or incapacitating the source of the perceived threat is necessary to counteract the danger. If you choose to stand and fight against a drunken assailant whom you could easily outrun, you are still engaging in self-defense, even though doing so is unnecessary to counteract the threat.[15]

This latter point is particularly important. It suggests that, depending upon the circumstances, there may be alternative ways of safeguarding one's life or well-being besides PSD. If as a pedestrian you had turned a corner in Fallujah, Iraq, during the US assault on that city, and found yourself in the midst of a firefight between US troops and militants, you would have done well to avoid walking down that street. Avoidance of situations that would pose imminent danger to you is often, though obviously not always, an option. So is flight. Sometimes walking, running or driving away can put you out of harm's way. Similarly, self-protection, as noted earlier, differs from PSD. Your well-being is in imminent danger if you take the field with an NFL team without helmet and pads. You can protect yourself by putting them on, but your wearing them does not constitute PSD. If you are struck repeatedly by someone trying to provoke a fight, even if you do not walk or run away you can try to protect yourself with your arms or by maneuvering out of the way rather than by fighting back. Deterrence also is sometimes an option. Threatening to call the police might sometimes work. Nonresistance is also an option. In the animal world, during a fight or confrontation one animal will sometimes assume a submissive posture, whereupon the other will immediately cease the attack. There is no assurance that this will work (though it sometimes works in attacks by bears), but it is always an option, and one that has sometimes been held to be the only moral option. Augustine, as we have seen, though he defended war, opposed personal self-defense, as the attempt to cling to something (your earthly life) that could be taken from you against your will. St. Ignatius after him represents Christian love as actually a form of resistance. In a more secular, but still spiritual vein, the martial art of akido seeks to deal with imminent threats by rendering the attack harmless without harm to the attacker.

---

[15] The controversial "stand your ground" law in Florida allows one to engage in legal self-defense even if one could easily avoid the threat by other means.

In light of these considerations, in the most general sense, personal, physical PSD may be defined as follows:

> *Self-Defense₁*: To try to harm, kill or incapacitate anyone knowingly posing by his actions an imminent threat to your life.[16]

Is self-defense in this sense always morally justified? It is not. It is easy to imagine circumstances in which the imminent threat to you is of your own making, such as when you initially pose such a threat to someone else, and they respond in their own self-defense. If you attempt to rob a bank, you cannot justifiably plead self-defense in shooting at the police when they arrive and order you at gunpoint to drop your gun, even though it would be PSD in the sense just defined. Nor can you justifiably argue PSD if you prowl the streets at night hoping that someone will try to mug you so that you can shoot them. Again suppose a person challenges another to a duel, and the other accepts. They assemble at dawn with their seconds. They stand back to back, walk the specified number of paces, then turn and fire. If one kills the other, he can scarcely plead self-defense on the grounds that the other was trying to shoot him.

6.4 Self-defense as a moral concept

What most people presumably have in mind when they appeal to PSD as a justification for killing is actually a normative sense of the term. We can formulate this as follows:

> *Self-defense₂*: To try to harm, kill or incapacitate anyone knowingly posing by his actions an *unjustifiable* imminent threat to your life in circumstances for which you are not culpably responsible.

This means that in addition to knowing something about the beliefs of the person in question and the facts of a situation, one must make a moral judgment about the assailant and the circumstances. You are not, as a matter of fact, acting in PSD if you are mistaken in believing that your life is in imminent danger. And you are not justifiably acting in PSD even if your life is in imminent danger if the threat to your life is in response to an unjustifiable threat you have made to the life of the person now posing

---

[16] I am assuming throughout that this is done for the purpose of removing or mitigating the threat associated with the belief that the action will (or may) have that effect. I say "anyone" for the sake of simplicity, but, as indicated, self -defense can come into play in the case of animals as well. I stress "by their actions" to exclude so-called innocent threats, where, for example, someone is falling down a shaft and will land on you unless you vaporize the person with your laser gun. These are clear cases of self-preservation, and even self-protection, but I do not consider them examples of self-defense. Although some court cases have upheld pleas of self-defense where the threat has not been imminent (as in the killing of abusive husbands by their wives), those represent nonstandard cases, and, in any event, deal with the legal and not the moral justification of self-defense.

the threat to you.[17] You do not have license to harm or kill people who pose a threat to you irrespective of what you may have done to lead them to pose that threat.

Even that, however, does not necessarily justify one in killing in PSD. Further necessary conditions of any putative justification of PSD are that the threat be unavoidable and that the harming or killing be necessary to the preservation of your life or well-being. Avoidance, flight, deterrence, self-protection and nonresistance are, as we have seen, often options. Thus we need to recognize a third sense of PSD:

Self-defense$_3$: To try, as a last resort, to harm, kill or incapacitate anyone knowingly posing by his actions an *unavoidable and unjustifiable* imminent threat to your life in circumstances for which you are not culpably responsible.

By "last resort" here is not meant that all theoretical alternatives to harming or killing must have been tried and proved fruitless; if the threat is imminent there is unlikely to be time for that. It means, rather, that harming, killing or incapacitating may reasonably be thought to be the only effective means of counteracting the threat in that situation. But in many circumstances the means you choose to defend yourself may put other persons at risk, and those persons may pose no threat to you and be innocent of any wrongdoing in the situation at hand. You might kill someone and at the same time needlessly kill his spouse, children, grandmother and cocker spaniel in the process. There might be times when the only means that will effectively counteract a threat will harm or kill innocents. Perhaps only a hand grenade that will kill bystanders will counteract the threat to you. Be that as it may, we need to recognize yet a further sense of self-defense:

Self-defense$_4$: To try, as a last resort, *and without unnecessary risk to innocents*, to harm, kill or incapacitate anyone knowingly posing, by his actions, an unavoidable and unjustifiable threat to your life in circumstances for which you are not culpably responsible.

The conditions in PSD$_4$, I say, represent necessary conditions of justifiable PSD. They may not be sufficient. Just as it is possible to argue that PSD is never justified, as does Augustine, it is possible to argue that it is justified only under stringent conditions, which include not putting innocent persons at risk at all. In that case, one would want to recognize still a further sense of PSD:

Self-defense$_5$: To try, as a last resort, *and without foreseeable risk to innocents*, to harm, kill or incapacitate anyone knowingly posing, by his actions, an unavoidable and unjustifiable threat to your life in circumstances for which you are not culpably responsible.

Soldiers in combat sometimes fight in PSD$_1$. At least some of them report believing that. If I am correct that PSD is belief-related, it would require extensive research to

[17] McMahan stresses that one becomes liable to defensive attack if one is morally responsible for an objectively unjustified threat of harm. *Killing in War*, p. 35.

establish what percentage of soldiers actually are fighting in PSD (and not confusing self-defense with self-preservation).[18] It cannot simply be assumed that they all are or even that most of them are. Sometimes they are fighting on behalf of their comrades, as they are sometimes trained to do. Some of them, if they are sufficiently high-minded and have their wits about them, are fighting for God and country or the constitution, which they are sworn to defend.[19] Some of them may simply be doing what they are trained to do, without much thought regarding what justifies their actions or even whether they are justified. Indeed, it is sometimes said that one can be an effective soldier only if he or she does not think too much. But it is doubtful that soldiers firing artillery shells from 20 miles away from their target either believe that they are in imminent danger from those targeted or (much of the time, at least) are in fact in such danger. They could be, and they could believe that. But often neither of those will be true. As we shall see in Chapter 10, when US planes bombed Serbia in 1999 from altitudes they knew were beyond the reach of antiaircraft fire, they were not in imminent danger. And when US military personnel in safe command booths in the US control drones in Afghanistan or Pakistan, killing persons on the ground there with missiles, they surely are not themselves in imminent danger from those they kill, nor can it plausibly be thought that they believe that they are in such danger. In one of the more extraordinary appeals to self-defense, it has been argued that the United States was acting in self-defense, as authorized by Article 51 of the UN Charter, when the 2011 drone strike in Yemen killed Anwar al-Awlaki, an American spokesperson for al Qaeda, who allegedly was threatening to "wreak havoc" on the United States. So while it is undoubtedly true that some soldiers believe and believe correctly that they are fighting in PSD_1 when they kill, many are not in fact so acting and, in the absence of hard evidence to the contrary, do not believe that they are so acting.

6.5 Self-defense and the presumptive wrongness of killing

As we have seen, PSD_1 does not defeat the presumption against killing, much less the presumption against war. Whether any of the remaining senses of PSD sometimes defeat the presumption against killing (an issue I shall not try to decide here), they do not defeat the presumption against war. While the immediate situation that soldiers find themselves in, abstracted from its antecedents and the broader social and international context, may constitute an unavoidable threat, that soldiers find themselves in that situation is not unavoidable. Each had a choice whether to enlist (if they are volunteers) or to answer a draft call (if they are conscripts). Each had a choice, however difficult it may have been with the penalties attached to noncompliance,

---

[18] A former Tiger Force soldier in Vietnam reportedly said, regarding killings of civilians as well as combatants in Vietnam: "The way to live is to kill because you don't have to worry about anybody who's dead." We shall discuss Tiger Force practices in Chapter 8.

[19] McMahan says that "just warfare is much more than the mere exercise of rights of individual self-defense by just combatants … they deliberately put their lives at risk for a reason: to achieve their just cause." *Killing in War*, p. 196.

whether to travel the thousands of miles (if they are in a distant country) to be placed in harm's way. Each shares responsibility for the moral situation he is in. If, according to the Magic Wand Theory, soldiers have a right to kill in self-defense, it is because their adversary is justifiably trying to kill them in self-defense. One is a threat to an adversary only insofar as one is trying to kill the adversary (or, again, supporting those who are trying to kill him). If you are not trying to kill an adversary, then he has no moral ground to try to kill you in PSD. You are not the requisite threat. The same is true of the adversary. Each, by his deliberate acts, poses the threat to the other which entitles the other to kill him in PSD. Refrain from those acts, and the entitlement to kill disappears. Either or both may still try to kill the other in the belief that they are acting in PSD, but they will be mistaken. There is a systemic confusion that pervades the soldiers on both sides if this is their belief. Just as unavoidable wrongdoing, if such a thing were to exist, would characterize situations created by voluntary actions, so with the self-defense of soldiers. Each finds himself in need of defending himself against the other because of voluntary choices he has made.[20]

None of this entails that killing in PSD may not sometimes be justified. That is left open. The various senses of PSD distinguished above merely indicate the necessary conditions of such justification. Whether they are sufficient would have to be determined. Accordingly, none of what I have said entails that the presumption against killing cannot ever be defeated. That, too, is left open. All that follows, if the preceding is correct, is that entering the military does not provide a blanket license to kill. The Magic Wand theory is simply false. Soldiers do not automatically forfeit their right to life nor do they automatically acquire a blanket moral authorization to kill when ordered to. The killing they do requires justification.

Even if this were incorrect, and soldiers had an equal moral right to kill, that fact would have bizarre consequences for the JWT. It would mean, as we saw in Chapter 5, that a state could embark upon an unjust war, and yet all of the death and destruction it caused could be morally justifiable. And all of the killing both sides do would be permissible, so long as they abide by the constraints of JIB. The distinction between just war and unjust war would then become vanishingly thin. It is difficult to see how an activity can be wrong if every individual act of which it is made up is permissible,[21] hence difficult to see how any war can be unjust. More exactly, it makes it difficult to see why the fact that a war is unjust is of much interest. From the standpoint of the killing it does, it would be of little consequence whether a state went to war justly or not. The practical effect would be to reinstate the discredited view, held throughout much of the nineteenth century, that states can go to war whenever they choose and for whatever reasons.

---

[20] A former Japanese World War II pilot, turned pacifist, put it that what is dehumanizing about war is that it puts one in a situation where he must kill absolute strangers or be killed by them. *The New York Times*, April 4, 2015. As he seems to realize, judging from his antiwar activism, it is not merely the war that puts one in that situation, it is one's own choices.

[21] Even the proverbial straw that breaks the camel's back is not an exception. The activity of placing straws on a camel's back has at least one wrong act, the placement of the final straw. Some individual acts, such as crossing a lawn, considered in abstraction from what anyone else does, may be permissible even if the performance of that act (type) by 10,000 persons within a short time might be wrong because it would ruin the lawn.

Individual self-defense nonetheless plays an important role in common thinking about war. It is often thought that if the individual has a right to PSD, then the nation has a right to national self-defense. And if one may kill in the first instance, then the state, through its military, can kill in the second instance. Indeed, when one considers the condition of just cause in JWT, it is generally assumed that national SD constitutes a just cause. So this reasoning may be considered an important support to the principal condition under C above.

As attractive as this reasoning is, however, it breaks down. Individual self-defense and collective self-defense are insufficiently analogous to warrant extending the moral justification of the one (assuming that it can be established) to the other.

6.6 Personal and collective self-defense

David Rodin, in his book *War and Self-Defense*[22] questions whether a right of national self-defense (NSD) can be derived from a right of PSD and concludes that it cannot. He founds this conclusion on a careful explication and justification of a right of PSD, backed in turn by a detailed analysis of rights. The discussion is enriched with informed references to events in the contemporary world scene. Rodin's concern is with the right of NSD as found in international law and the JWT, which means that his account, if correct, is a devastating critique of much contemporary legal and moral thinking about war.

According to Rodin, not only can a right of NSD not be derived from a right of PSD, a right of NSD cannot be substantiated at all.[23] He does not, however, conclude that war cannot be justified. He says that military action against an aggressor "could potentially be justified, not in terms of self-defense, but as a form of law enforcement."[24] In that sense, his work can be viewed as a moral justification of war. It spells out (as JWT does) the conditions under which war allegedly would be morally justified.

At the same time, the conditions thought necessary to justifying war (or military responses to aggression akin to war) would require the creation of at least an ultra-minimal world state. Such a state would hold a "world monopoly of military force together with a minimal judicial mechanism for the resolution of international and internal disputes."[25] Since that does not exist today, his argument might also be thought to support a conditional pacifism (of a sort that holds that war is wrong in the world as it is today). But Rodin refrains from drawing this conclusion. He says that "[e]ven for those who are impressed by the thought that there are some forms of aggression which we 'must' fight, my arguments remind us that, if we do so, our action cannot be conceived in terms of right and justice."[26] Whether Rodin thinks there are some wars we *must* fight even though they are not morally justified one cannot be sure. But this is

---

[22] For a pacifist defense of the view that killing in self-defense may sometimes be permissible even though war is unequivocally wrong, see David Carroll Cochran, "War-Pacifism," *Social Theory and Practice*, Vol. 22, No. 2 (Summer 1996), pp. 161–181.

[23] David Rodin, *War and Self-Defense* (Oxford: Clarendon Press, 2002), p. 196.

[24] Rodin, *War and Self-Defense*, p. 163.

[25] Rodin, *War and Self-Defense*, p. 187.

[26] Rodin, *War and Self-Defense*, p. 199.

a conclusion that many realists would accept. Thus, even though Rodin's conclusions are clear on the questions of whether there is a right of NSD, and whether that right can be derived from a right of PSD, his position is less clear on the broader implications of this for the justification of war.

Rodin's justification of PSD is based upon a rights-based theory, which is in turn grounded in a moral theory of obligation. He situates the right of PSD within a more general defensive right, which includes the right "to defend third parties and to defend goods of differing value."[27] The importance he attaches to this account warrants letting his own words speak for themselves:

> A right of defense exists when a subject is at liberty to defend a certain good by performing an action which would otherwise be impermissible. The moral justification for this liberty invokes the following three considerations: (i) an appropriate normative relation exists between the subject and the end of the right, consisting either of a right *to*, or a duty of care towards the good protected, (ii) the defensive act is a proportionate, necessary response to an imminent threat of harm, (iii) the object of defensive force has an appropriate degree of normative responsibility for, and the subject is innocent of, the harm threatened.[28]

I will not discuss that part of his argument further, and will assume that we can speak intelligibly of a right of PSD, whether or not such a right can plausibly be thought to exist, or if it does exist, to be imprescriptible.

That NSD is justified if PSD is justified is often taken as obviously true. Rodin shows convincingly that this is not so. He takes the view to rest upon a moral principle (MP), namely:

> MP: [A] valid conception of international justice can be generated by treating states as unitary moral agents and ascribing to them … a system of rights and responsibilities generated in the context of interpersonal relations.[29]

MP looks rather more like a metaethical procedural principle than a moral principle per se. It makes a claim about a way of looking at international relations that enables one to make sense of the ascription to states of rights and responsibilities. Be that as it may, this way of looking at states considers them unitary moral agents. It seems to presuppose that states can intelligibly be spoken of as acting, having interests and being entities to which moral categories are applicable. That is, it presupposes what we have called a macroethics. This, in turn, would seem to be a precondition of speaking intelligibly of states as having rights, and *a fortiori*, of states as having a right of NSD.

Realists have long dealt with this issue, of course, though rarely systematically or convincingly. Hard realists, as we have seen, would deny that morality applies to states at all. Soft realists would allow that it applies but is of secondary importance when it

---

[27] Rodin, *War and Self-Defense*, p. 99.
[28] Rodin, *War and Self-Defense*, p. 99.
[29] Rodin, *War and Self-Defense*, p. 196.

comes to issues as momentous as war. At times it sounds as though Rodin may think that the stronger realist position is correct, at least where rights are concerned. He sometimes speaks as though the problem with the JWT is that the moral concepts it relies upon do not apply adequately to the case of state behavior. He says, for example: "But what I have been suggesting in the course of this book is the more fundamental critique that our moral concepts are terminally ill-fitted to their subject matter [presumably in the case of states]."[30] It is one thing to say that a right of NSD cannot be justified. It is another to say that we cannot even apply concepts such as that of rights at the level of states. Rodin seems to argue for the former conclusion, but there are times when he seems almost willing to concede the stronger conclusion to realists. He says, for example, that "there is a deeply moral response to international conflict which does not seek to contradict the Realist perception that the current mechanisms of international politics are irredeemably devoid of morality, but rather grows out of it."[31]

For the most part, however, Rodin does not seem to question that states may be considered unitary moral agents in the manner required for a macroethics, which a system of international morality requires. What he appears to insist upon is that states *must* also be viewed as collections of persons to whom moral notions unquestionably apply and who individually have a right of PSD. This dual aspect of the international situation is what Rodin believes creates the problems for attempts to infer a right of NSD from a right of PSD. He believes those problems cannot be surmounted.

The attempt to infer a right of NSD from a right of PSD will follow one or the other of two strategies. The reductive strategy seeks to justify a right of NSD as constructed out of the rights of PSD. The analogical strategy seeks to justify a right of NSD by analogizing it to a right of PSD. Rodin does not consider the possibility that the right of NSD may be *sui generis*, as Treitschke and his followers may have thought. He does touch upon Hegel and fascism but mainly to dismiss them.

The reductive strategy consists, in turn, of two substrategies. The first takes the notion of NSD to be grounded in the end of defending the lives of citizens. NSD is "an application, *en masse*, of the familiar right of individuals to protect themselves and others from unjust lethal attack." This, in his view, makes NSD a kind of "shorthand for a more complex way of exercising, what would remain in the final analysis, an individual right."[32]

Rodin believes this approach fails for three reasons: (1) the liberties enjoyed by soldiers of a defending state extend well beyond what could be justified in terms of PSD; (2) the requirement of necessity in the right of PSD requires people to retreat if possible, which is not a requirement of NSD; (3) in JWT, "the rights of war, including the right to kill enemy soldiers, are held equally by soldiers on both sides of a defensive war."[33] In short, there is an asymmetry between a right of PSD and a right of NSD. Perhaps most importantly, in situations of PSD there is a forfeiture of a right to life on the part of a

[30] Rodin, *War and Self-Defense*, pp. 195f.
[31] Rodin, *War and Self-Defense*, p. 197.
[32] Rodin, *War and Self-Defense*, p. 127.
[33] Rodin, *War and Self-Defense*, p. 128.

culpable aggressor.[34] Correlatively, the innocent defender acquires a right to kill.[35] While I consider both of these points problematic, I shall assume for the sake of argument that they are correct. As typically understood, however, states have a right of NSD irrespective of wrongs they may have committed, either against other states or against their own citizens. Both international law and JWT assume this. So a right of NSD cannot be a simple construct out of a collection of rights of PSD held by individuals.

Relatedly, and perhaps most importantly, Rodin focuses upon the so-called moral equality of soldiers in wartime, in which it is presumed by both international law and JWT alike that soldiers on all sides (both just and unjust) have an equal right to kill. I have argued in the previous section that this "moral equality" does not exist, and that the Magic Wand theory which allegedly would establish it is false. But, that aside, Rodin argues that the disanalogy between PSD and NSD is manifest. There is, he shows, a glaring asymmetry between the case of war and the case of PSD. The assailant threatening lethal harm against another individual does not have a right to kill equal with the person engaging in PSD. In the end, Rodin rejects the notion of the moral equality of soldiers, in which case this asymmetry would not hold. Aggressive soldiers (and presumably those only) "may be appropriate objects of force."[36] Thus, in one of his more provocative conclusions, he says "[i]t seems plausible to conclude that soldiers, and not just sovereigns, are responsible for the aggressive wars in which they engage."[37] The upshot seems to be that, just as the *right* of NSD cannot plausibly be claimed by a state in going to war, whether defensively or aggressively, *responsibility* for an unjust war cannot plausibly be disavowed by the individual soldiers conducting that war. Once much of the asymmetry between right of PSD and a right of NSD is removed, however, the way would appear to be open for a reductivist to try to justify a transition from the former to the latter. But without the moral equality of soldiers, the resultant account would not accord with the notion of NSD found in JWT and international law, which is perhaps the reason that Rodin does not explore this possibility.

The second substrategy in the reductive strategy contends that "the state has an obligation (and therefore a right) to defend its citizens in much the same way that a parent has the right to defend his or her child."[38] Rodin believes this strategy fails for two reasons.

The first reason turns on the notion of humanitarian intervention. He contends that if right of NSD were grounded in the end of protecting individual citizens, then "not only would national-defense and humanitarian intervention share an underlying moral structure but the latter right could be derived from the former."[39] His reasoning to show that a right of humanitarian intervention could be derived from a right of NSD might be paraphrased informally as follows:

1. If citizens of state A are threatened by the aggressive action of state B, then A has the right to wage defensive war against B.

---

[34] Rodin, *War and Self-Defense*, p. 88.
[35] Rodin, *War and Self-Defense*, p. 75.
[36] Rodin, *War and Self-Defense*, p. 180.
[37] Rodin, *War and Self-Defense*, p. 173.
[38] Rodin, *War and Self-Defense*, p. 129.
[39] Rodin, *War and Self-Defense*, p. 130

2. Similarly, any third party, state C, has the right to engage in war against B (hence to intervene in that state without the approval of its authorities) to protect citizens of A.
3. Humanitarian intervention "is simply the application of this general principle with respect to third party intervention on the assumption that states A and B are the same state."[40]

Thus:

4. "If a particular military action of state C is justified by the fact that it defends the endangered lives of the citizens of A, then it should make no difference to the morality of C's action whether the citizens of A are threatened by their own state or a third party."[41]
5. Therefore, if C has a right to intervene in B in defense of A's citizens, then C has a right to intervene in A in defense of A's citizens.
6. As any third party has the same right as C, a right of humanitarian intervention has been established.

Rodin points out that this conclusion is at odds with "common sense as well as the law and the moral theory of national-defense." Humanitarian intervention, as commonly understood, is precisely a right to intervene when NSD is not an issue. Indeed, if NSD were the only just cause for going to war (as the JWT is often erroneously supposed to maintain), then humanitarian intervention would fail as a moral justification for war. Far from humanitarian intervention being derivable from a right of NSD, the two are potentially in conflict with one another, as we shall discuss in Chapter 13.

But if (2) is assumed to follow from (1) *simpliciter*, then the argument would appear to contain a *non-sequitur*. It does not follow from the fact that A has a right to defend its citizens and that other states have a right to defend its citizens. After all, this second substrategy of the reductive strategy maintains that "the state has an obligation (and therefore a right) to defend its citizens in much the same way that a parent has the right to defend his or her child." It is the relationship of parent to child that is crucial. And that is a standard deontological consideration. If I have an obligation to feed, clothe and shelter my child, it does not follow that I have the same obligation to someone else's child across town or on the other side of the country or halfway around the world. Similarly, if my right to defend my child is thought to derive from the specific obligations I have to it, my right to defend my child does not extend to the defense of these others either. It would not preclude that there is such a right, but it would not suffice to establish it. Accordingly, the defender of this variant of the reductive strategy might argue that the morally relevant relationship in which the citizens of A stand to state A is different from the relationship in which those same persons stand to state C. The persons in question are citizens of A. They are not citizens of C. Insofar as the right to defend them grows out of that relationship (as it would seem to according to

---

[40] Rodin, *War and Self-Defense*, p. 130.
[41] Rodin, *War and Self-Defense*, p. 131.

this subvariant of the reductive strategy), A's right to defend them does not transfer automatically to C. It must be shown independently. If it is not shown, then it cannot be assumed that C has a right to intervene against B; hence it cannot be assumed that a right of humanitarian intervention can be derived from a right of NSD.

If, on the other hand, (2) is not thought to follow from (1), but to have a justification at least partly independent of (1), then the reductivist might understandably ask to see the justification. If the reductivist claim were that *any* state has a right to intervene to defend *any and all* persons anywhere in the world, and if that were the basis of the claim in (1), then (2) could plausibly be thought to follow from (1). Indeed, a right of humanitarian intervention would follow without the convolutions of (3). But there is no reason why the reductivist need make such a sweeping claim. Though it would suffice to ground a right of NSD, it would not be necessary. It is possible that Rodin believes that his notion of "duties of rescue"[42] suffices to ground this more general right. If so, then the issue between him and the reductivist on this point would be dependent upon the assessment of that account. These issues, of course, open the way to the whole question of the justifiability of humanitarian military intervention, which we shall take up in Chapter 13.

The second basic strategy to derive a right of NSD from a right of PSD Rodin calls analogical. It seeks to justify a right of NSD on the grounds that it is analogous to the right of PSD. As Rodin understands it, in this view the right of NSD is grounded in the end, "not of defending the lives of individual citizens, but of defending the common life of the community." It is the end that is important here. This leads him to consider three different ways of understanding the notion of a "common life' of a community: first, locating the value of common life in an account of state legitimacy; second, seeing the common life as the "embodiment of a particular cultural and historical heritage"; third, seeing common life as "the arena of collective self-determination and autonomy."[43]

6.7 Defending a common life

I shall comment only briefly on Rodin's handling of these ways of understanding the notion of a common life. Regarding the first, he appeals to the Hobbesian notion of a social contract, which supposedly justifies sovereign power "because the state of nature which it replaces is so very awful."[44] But he correctly observes that most aggressors do not seek to destroy all political association, that is, to produce a state of nature. Rather, they seek a different political association, or, as he might have added, simply to put the existing political association in their own hands. Regarding the second, if we seek to justify the defense, not just of any political association but of our own favored political association, we risk slipping into a relativism of values. This would be at odds with an objective value that would seem to be important to the traditional paradigm of NSD. That is, if *all* states are presumed to have a right of NSD (as international law

[42] Rodin, *War and Self-Defense*, p. 38.
[43] Rodin, *War and Self-Defense*, p. 142.
[44] Rodin, *War and Self-Defense*, p. 145.

and JWT seem to assume), then grounding a right of NSD on the part of one's state in a commitment to one's own particular cultural and historical heritage would fail to account for such a universal right. If each state proclaimed a right of NSD for itself but did not acknowledge a right of NSD on the part of other states, the bars to aggression would be down as much as if no right of NSD were recognized by anyone. Likewise, regarding the third, one might appeal to freedom, autonomy and self-determination as candidates for values that would warrant defending one form of common life rather than another but would not be so particular as to commit one to relativism.[45] The problem, again, is that if we make democracy the condition of grounding a right of NSD, then such a conception cannot ground NSD as found in international law and JWT. In both, nondemocratic states are thought to have a right of NSD.[46]

Rodin brings humanitarian intervention to bear in connection with the analogical strategy as well as the reductive strategy. He points out that the end of protecting a community can conflict with the right of NSD, which is a right of a state. Earlier, he had represented humanitarian intervention as grounded in the end of protecting particular individuals within another state. Now he represents it as having the end of protecting minorities or communities within another state.[47] The point, of course, is that rights of communities to autonomy and integrity cannot be the ground of a right of NSD if those rights conflict with that right. And unless communities are coextensive with states, which he correctly points out they are not in the real world, those rights can conflict.

Finally, as we have seen, the JWT, at least as found in Augustine, does not locate the notion of just cause in self-defense. It locates it rather in the avenging of the violation of rights.[48] A just war, in that case, could be an aggressive war, in the sense of one initiated by the aggrieved party. Wars, in short, were seen as punitive. In this sense, by claiming that justifiable military force against aggression is punitive, Rodin, despite a penetrating analysis of self-defense, ends up back where JWT began.

6.8 Self-defense and liability

Although he does not frame his argument in the preceding terms, McMahan, like Walzer, relies heavily, though not exclusively, on the notion of self-defense to justify the killing of unjust combatants in war. As he writes, "the view about the status of unjust combatants that I am defending parallels the common view about individual self-defense. It holds that unjust combatants are liable to attack because they are responsible for an objectively wrongful threat."[49] McMahan does not speak of an analogy here between individual self-defense and wartime killing of unjust combatants, so it is unclear how much of Rodin's account affects his analysis. In any event, his argument

---

[45] Rodin, *War and Self-Defense*, p. 155.
[46] Rodin, *War and Self-Defense*, p. 156.
[47] Rodin, *War and Self-Defense*, p. 160.
[48] Steven P. Lee notes the tension between saying that a just cause consists in avenging a wrong and saying that it involves self-defense. See *Ethics and War*, p. 43.
[49] McMahan, *Killing in War*, p. 193.

to justify wartime killing (which includes but is not limited to the killing of unjust combatants) is sufficiently complex that it is difficult to be certain that one is doing it justice. Nonetheless, the reasoning, as I understand it, proceeds as follows.

McMahan appears to start from the assumption that there are justified types of killing and extends the rationales for those to the case of war.[50] He also appears to assume that there are just and unjust wars and defines combatants according to their participation in one or the other.[51] Just combatants are those fighting a just war, unjust combatants those fighting a war without a just cause.[52] His contention is that the killing of unjust combatants by just combatants can be justified but that the killing of just combatants by unjust combatants cannot. Therefore there cannot be moral equality among soldiers.

I have previously argued that, on the assumption that there are just and unjust wars, all of the killing done by those on the unjust side will be wrongful,[53] so I am in essential agreement with McMahan to this extent. What I question is his reasoning to show that just combatants may kill unjust combatants. Indeed, I challenge that whole way of framing the issue of killing in war. As I have argued in Chapter 1, allegedly just and unjust wars are only partial wars, fought by one side only. The relevant question is whether whole wars, wars$_2$ as I have represented them, are permissible. Whole wars cannot be just or unjust, as McMahan acknowledges. The JWT cannot assess them and is not intended to. Unless the presumptive wrongness of those wars has been defeated, it is wrong to engage in such wars. The categories just and unjust as commonly used in JWT simply do not apply. For that reason no argument to show that one can justify killing in warfare can succeed so long as it is limited to a standard just war–theoretic framework. Since McMahan is critical of standard JWT, it is difficult to tell whether his analysis is intended to replace the JWT or simply to amend it. In any event, he retains the vocabulary of JWT, and seems to assume that at least many of its criteria—such as just cause, proportionality and discrimination—are appropriate ones with which to frame the moral issues of war. So I shall for the present suspend the judgment of the inadequacy of JWT and discuss his argument on the assumption that there may be just wars. I shall also accept for present purposes the labeling of the persons who are killed in warfare as either just or unjust combatants, even though I believe it biases the evaluation of the killing they do. Both groups have already been defined by reference to a just war–theoretic framework and have attached to them moral judgments about what they do and the roles they play. The same is true of the characterization of such persons as just or unjust "warriors," an emotively laden term with intimations of honor,

---

[50] As he writes, "one of the presuppositions of this book is that the justifications for killing people in war are of the same forms as the justifications for the killing of persons in other contexts." McMahan, *Killing in War*, p. 156.

[51] Though he also says that it is not by virtue of membership in a group that unjust combatants are legitimate targets for attack. McMahan, *Killing in War*, p. 209.

[52] At times he says that unjust combatants are those fighting a war that is unjust because it lacks a just cause. McMahan, *Killing in War*, p. 6.

[53] Meaning the combat-related killing. The claim is not meant to cover possible cases incidental to warfare in which an unjust combatant might kill someone, civilian or soldier, engaged in murder or rape.

respect, courage, all of which tends, if only imperceptibly, to render the enterprises they are engaged in when they kill one another as honorable ones.

Leaving these misgivings aside for the present, I understand McMahan to be arguing that, although both just and unjust combatants threaten harm in war, just combatants do so justifiably, unjust combatants do so unjustifiably. The threats that unjust combatants make are objectively wrong by virtue of the fact that they are fighting a war that lacks a just cause.[54] Given that unjust combatants are defined as those who are fighting a war without a just cause, this seems to mean that unjust combatants by definition are engaged in acts that are objectively wrong. This is important, because the sorts of harms they threaten could be done—and presumably are done—by just combatants in the performance of actions that are permissible, justified or required.[55] Unjust combatants make objectively wrong or unjustified threats to inflict wrongful harms, whereas just combatants presumably sometimes make justified threats to inflict harms. This, on the face of it, makes sense, since to threaten harm is one thing, to inflict it is another. Those are separate acts, and while one's assessment of the act of inflicting harm might understandably be taken to determine the assessment of the act that threatens that harm, the two assessments might differ.

It is not, however, simply that unjust combatants pose unjustified threats of wrongful harm. They are *morally responsible* for those threats.[56] Moreover, some persons who do not directly pose the threat that unjustified combatants do, may also be morally responsible for that threat. In any event (and ignoring the many qualifications with which this portion of McMahan's argument is hedged), those who are morally responsible for objectively unjustified wrongful threats of harm forfeit their right not to be attacked.[57] Accordingly, they are not wronged if they are attacked and their right not to be attacked is not contravened. For that reason, they are liable to be attacked, and are therefore legitimate targets. Since discrimination in *jus in bello* requires, as McMahan understands it, that intentional attacks be confined to legitimate targets, attacking unjust combatants accords with that requirement. Just combatants, on the other hand, when they attack unjust combatants, have the backing of a just war behind them according to *jus ad bellum* and accord with one of the two main requirements of *jus in bello*, that of discrimination when they attack unjust combatants. Because just combatants are not legitimate targets, attacks against them by unjust combatants violate the principle of discrimination.

Further, attacks on just combatants by unjust combatants also violate the *in bello* principle of proportionality as McMahan understands it. Noting that proportionality typically is a condition of *jus ad bellum* as well of *jus in bello*, he contends that in "both cases the relevant bad effects are generally assumed to include only intentional harms to the innocent ... Harms inflicted on those who are liable to suffer them have

---

[54] McMahan, *Killing in War*, p. 155.

[55] McMahan, *Killing in War*, p. 38.

[56] Mark Vorabej has usefully formulated what he calls a Thesis of Combatant Noninnocence as follows: "Combatants in a morally unjustified modern war are either guilty of or responsible for moral wrongdoing in virtue of their functional role within that war." See his "Pacifism and Wartime Innocence," *Social Theory and Practice*, Vol. 20, No. 2, Summer 1994, p. 173.

[57] McMahan, *Killing in War*, p. 16.

traditionally been assumed to have no role in determining proportionality."[58] Since, in McMahan's view, unjust combatants are legitimate targets, hence liable to suffer harm, the attacks on them by just combatants do not, all other things being equal, violate the condition of proportionality. Attacks by unjust combatants on just combatants do violate proportionality because just combatants are innocent and not liable to attack.[59]

The upshot is that—again assuming that the categories of JWT represent the proper perspective from which to evaluate war, and that, in those terms, there may be just and unjust wars—the killing of unjust combatants by just combatants is permissible, the killing of just combatants by unjust combatants impermissible. Accordingly, the thesis of the moral equality of soldiers is false.

6.9 Self-defense and just cause

I have said that McMahan's argument relies heavily, but not exclusively, on the idea of self-defense taken from the law. He also justifies the killing of unjust combatants by just combatants by appeal to the just cause which, by hypothesis, just combatants serve. As he writes

> For just warfare is much more than the mere exercise of rights of individual self-defense by just combatants … they deliberately put their lives at risk for a reason: to achieve a just cause … the incapacitation of unjust combatants, usually by killing them, is almost always a necessary means of achieving the just cause. That is the nature of war.[60]

Here the alleged *in bello* justification for regarding unjust combatants as legitimate targets appeals to the just cause for which just combatants supposedly are fighting. What a just cause is, beyond self-defense and defense of others, is hard to ascertain.[61] A just cause, rather than being a condition, or something that one has, is represented as an aim that may permissibly be pursued by war and is pursued against those who have made themselves morally liable to attack.[62] In any event, it appears to be assumed that there are just causes and just wars, and the justified killing of unjust combatants that takes place in them is in part justified by the just cause providing the justification for war. If that is not assumed, that part of the rationale for killing in war does not stand.

Notice that one need only show that war-related killing by unjust combatants is wrongful to falsify the thesis of the moral equality of soldiers. It is necessary in addition

---

[58] McMahan, *Killing in War*, pp. 18, 19.

[59] At least they are innocent in what McMahan considers a generic sense. McMahan, *Killing in War*, p. 16.

[60] McMahan, *Killing in War*, pp. 196–197.

[61] McMahan elsewhere gives the notion of just cause a decidedly Augustinian coloration when he writes that "the just cause for a war consists of the prevention, mitigation, or rectification of wrongs for which those whom it is necessary to attack in war are responsible." See McMahan, "Proportionality and Time," p. 714.

[62] McMahan, *Killing in War*, p. 5.

to show the permissibility of the killing done by just combatants to show that even a partial war can be just.

With regard to the understanding of proportionality in JIB, McMahan says that it is generally assumed that "harms inflicted on those who are liable to suffer them have traditionally been assumed to have no role in determining proportionality."[63] This, if true, means that unjust combatants are in systematic violation of the principle of proportionality as well as that of discrimination in the killing of just combatants, but just combatants violate neither of these principles in their killing of unjust combatants. It also means that the JWT is inadequate to evaluate whole war, since the totality of the effects of war$_2$ never enter into the calculus. Only the bad effects of the intentional killing of innocents would enter in, and only as assessed by one side. The total effects even of the partial war waged by one side would be irrelevant.

Without undertaking a review of the just war tradition with a view to determining the accuracy of the claim that proportionality is usually understood in this way, it is worth noting at least the following passages from recent and contemporary just war theorists.

> The calculus of proportionality in just cause is the total good to be expected if the war is successful balanced against the total evil the war is likely to cause.[64]
>
> In terms of the *jus ad bellum* criteria, proportionality means that the damage to be inflicted and the costs incurred by war must be proportionate to the good expected by taking up arms. Nor should judgments concerning proportionality be limited to the temporal order without regard to a spiritual dimension in terms of "damage," "cost," and "the good expected." ... Hence a nation cannot justly go to war today without considering the effect of its action on others and on the international community. This principle of proportionality applies throughout the conduct of the war as well as to the decision to begin warfare.[65]
>
> Yet proportion or prudence or judgments concerning the lesser evil among the ends of action have nothing to do with whether something is the direct object of the action's impact and something else the collateral side-effect unavoidably produced by the action. That depends on the verdict under the first test, the principle of discrimination ... Then one has to choose, from among actions that are morally tolerable because they are not indiscriminate, those actions that should actually be done because of an apt proportion between their good and evil consequences ... the principle of proportion takes all the effects for the first time into account.[66]

---

[63] McMahan, *Killing in War*, p. 19. McMahan elsewhere puts it more specifically that "just war theory has traditionally assumed that proportionality is concerned only with harms to the innocent—that is to those who are not liable to be harmed—and not with harms to those who are relevantly noninnocent, such as combatants on both sides." See McMahan, "Proportionality and Time," p. 698.

[64] William V. O'Brien, *The Conduct of Just and Limited War* (New York: Praeger, 1981), p. 39.

[65] *The Challenge of Peace: God's Promise and Our Response. A Pastoral Letter on War and Peace*, May 34, 1983, National Conference of Catholic Bishops (Washington, DC: United States Catholic Conference, 1983), p. 31. Although as a definition, this account is circular, it clearly intends a comprehensive understanding of the relevant effects in determining proportionality.

[66] Ramsey, *The Just War*, p. 431.

These passages suggest that at least some notable just war accounts (one secular, one Catholic and one Protestant) have a more expansive understanding of the relevant effects when it comes to calculating proportionality than does McMahan.

In any event, I want to focus upon the idea that self-defense is a major factor in the justification of the killing of unjust combatants in war. I have until now been granting, for the sake of argument, the assumption that the just war–theoretic perspective is the proper perspective from which to evaluate war, and that there may be just and unjust wars and combatants are properly designated as just and unjust. I now want to drop those assumptions and frame the issue differently. When one is discussing theoretical wars, one can stipulate whatever one wants. This war is just, that war is unjust. This combatant is just, that combatant unjust. Pragmatically, the reality is that most partial wars are believed to be permissible by those who wage them, and the partial wars against which they fight, impermissible; and the reverse on the part of their opponents. The killing that takes place is, for the most part, the killing of human beings by other human beings, all of whom are acting under orders, and many of whom have been placed in involuntary servitude through a process of conscription. In the United States, even when they have not been conscripted, they have been forced to become part of the system that renders them liable to such servitude at practically a moment's notice through registration with the Selective Service System. Every seventeen-year-old male as he approaches his eighteenthth birthday must register for the draft or face the possibility of five years imprisonment, a $250,000 fine and ineligibility for student aid or federal employment. Additionally, colleges and universities—and many high schools—entice young people, both male and female, into ROTC programs with the promise of expensive paid college education and possible careers as officers in the military. Largely for those not headed for college, there is an extensive advertising program glamorizing military service.

All of these considerations make it understandable why young people, at an impressionable age when they are still maturing, are easily led to commit themselves to militarism. They are born into, and nurtured by, societies shaped to a large extent by war systems and a culture of militarism. By that I do not mean a culture run by the military, or in which the authoritarianism of militarism prevails. A culture of militarism can exist and flourish within a democracy and a society that touts freedom and equality. It is not that people openly embrace militarism and a war system; it is that they simply do not see it. If it has evolved gradually over decades, seeping into the nooks and crannies of a free society, people can become oblivious to what is happening. They can acquiesce to what they would never accept were its full character evident to them—and particularly if its outcomes were unpredicted.

So with a society that forces young men to became part of a military system on pain of imprisonment or large fines for failure to do so, and once part of that system to confront them with risk of even more severe penalties if a draft should be instituted and they fail to report; and which subjects both young men and young women—particularly the economically disadvantaged—with continuous financial inducements to volunteer for the military; and when in the military trains them to kill and to obediently follow orders to kill whomever they are ordered to, whomever that may be and wherever they might be; a society that likewise empowers some persons to order others to kill, and empowers them to inflict severe penalties for refusal to do so. A society that allows some people to order other people to kill, and compels others to respond obediently to such orders, is a free and open society in name only. McMahan sees some of this, and puts it effectively in the following passage:

> In most military organizations, the ability of soldiers to engage in autonomous reflection and deliberation about the content of their orders is also deliberately and systematically sabotaged. They are subjected to intensive conditioning and indoctrination, to endless drills, and to processes intended to efface their individuality and subvert their autonomy. The suppression of individual identity is achieved in part through shaving of the heads of males and making all soldiers wear the same uniform. They are all to look and act in exactly the same way. Their wills are broken through intimidation, bullying, and humiliation by their instructors, through demands for repeated public displays of deference and submissiveness … The aim is to convert them into largely unreflective instruments of the wills of their superiors.[67]

6.10 Potential soldiers and their "epistemic duties"

But McMahan seems to think that soldiers can tend to their "epistemic duties" and think all of this through, as well as stay sufficiently informed to be able to judge what is happening in foreign affairs to be able to evaluate the justice or injustice of the wars their government would have them fight. In an ideal world that might be possible. But one cannot leave the values and practices of a militarized society intact and expect most young people to be able to make those judgments. And they must be made by both potential just combatants and potential unjust combatants. For every potential just combatant is also a potential unjust combatant, and vice versa; and every actual just combatant can become an actual unjust combatant in the next conflict.

Unjust combatants, as we have seen, do not merely pose threats. According to McMahan they are morally responsible for those threats. This requires that just combatants not only know what threatening actions unjust combatants are engaged in but also know what moral judgments are correct about those combatants. Given that there are degrees of responsibility, and that liability varies with responsibility, two soldiers fighting side by side may, even in McMahan's view, have different responsibilities for the wrongs they threaten and accordingly may warrant different treatment. But it is impossible to have that kind of knowledge about each and every person one attempts to kill in warfare, and impossible to make all of the necessary moral judgments. McMahan sees that one's response is a matter of distributive justice— in this case, fairness in the distribution of harms. But to have to make those judgments would be to make war impossible. McMahan says, "[n]o one would or could fight a war on the basis of a strategy that sought to apportion the harms suffered on both sides according to some formula for justice in the distribution of harm … So if unjust

---

[67] McMahan, *Killing in War*, p. 119.

combatants were Innocent Threats and that were the right way to deal with Innocent Threats, wars that we now regard as just wars would all have been fought in an unjust manner."[68] That, of course, is correct. Moreover, one could argue that all such wars would not only have been fought unjustly, they would have been unjust wars overall. In any event, if McMahan's analysis of responsibility and liability, and the degrees of each, is correct, as I believe it is, every war, virtually without exception, involves injustice from the standpoint of distributive justice. The sense of justice one has in mind when speaking of just and unjust wars needs to be explained, as does the systematic disregard of distributive justice in warfare.

It might seem that the case of German soldiers in WWII represents a clear case of soldiers who are fully responsible for the harm and killing they do. But an insightful study of the views of individual German soldiers reports:

> As we observed in examples of extreme violence, sexual attacks, racist convictions, and quasi-religious faith in the Fuhrer, *temporally specific contexts of perception* influenced the perspective, interpretations, and actions of soldiers … War was the arena in which soldiers exist, and it was from within this world that they perceived POWs, civilian populations, partisans, forced laborers, and everyone else they encountered.
>
> … The violence of war opened up an interpretive and behavioral freedom that did not exist in civilian life. The power to kill and rape others, to be cruel or merciful, as well as all the new possibilities soldiers had, can be traced back to the opening of an arena of violence and its accompanying interpretive paradigms.[69]

A Vietnam veteran, a physician, focusing on the deaths of soldiers rather than the deaths they caused, writes:

> Each day I was at work in the navy hospital, our government sponsored the killing of fifty to seventy Vietnamese soldiers, used bombs to kill two or three hundred civilians, and positioned twenty to thirty American boys to die … The killing in Vietnam was highly organized and sanctioned. It was far away and easy to ignore. If I could have found my voice I could have tried to explain the sadness and waste and horror surrounding the death of each soldier. Once the killing was classified as "war," it was removed from our common morality. It's not a part of us; it is less tragic and horrible. In fact, it may be brave, romantic, and patriotic.[70]

While there is room for far more understanding of the psychosocial framework of individual soldiers in war, this suggests that, but for the relatively few ideological warriors, most soldiers are ordinary human beings, who become capable of harming and killing, and in some cases of doing horrendous things, because of the all-enveloping war mentality that pervades their world when in combat.

---

[68] McMahan, *Killing in War*, p. 184. By an "innocent threat, McMahan means" someone who in objective terms acts impermissibly in posing a threat to another but also acts subjectively permissibly, or even with subjective justification" (p. 163).

[69] Neitzel and Welzer, *Soldaten*, pp. 318, 319.

[70] John A. Parrish, MD, *Autopsy of War: A Personal History* (New York: St. Martin's Press, 2012), p. 154.

But McMahan thinks that soldiers may sometimes be liable to attack even if they have done nothing wrong, hence are not morally responsible for an objectively unjustified threat of wrongful harm.[71] He considers the hypothetical case of soldiers who join the military for good moral reasons in a peaceful society whose present government, unbeknownst to them, conspires to launch an aggressive, unjust war against another country. Preventive war against that country "would involve attacking the potential aggressor's soldiers, who know nothing of their government's plans and are engaged exclusively in activities of the sorts in which soldiers engage in peacetimes … Are these soldiers *liable* to preventive attack? I think that even in this case, in which the soldiers have as yet done nothing wrong, there are grounds for holding them liable. They earlier made a voluntary choice that in effect committed them in a public way to obedience, and those to whom they owe obedience will, unless prevented, order them to fight in an unjust war in which it is reasonable to expect that they will participate."[72] The examples are not parallel, but similar reasoning seems to have led Maj. Nidal Malik Hasan, the so-called Fort Hood Bomber, to kill thirteen fellow soldiers and wound more than thirty others in 2009. He apparently felt an obligation grounded in Jihad to attack US soldiers engaged in what he viewed as an unjust war against Muslims in Afghanistan, even though the particular soldiers he killed had not as yet done anything wrong. If soldiers are liable for having voluntarily committed themselves to obedience, it is unclear why it should matter who attacks them to prevent their participation in what one takes to be an unjust war. That the war is already underway rather than merely contemplated, as in McMahan's example, should not matter either.

Much of McMahan's analysis proceeds at the individual level. He continually talks of "a person" being liable or not, of forfeiting rights or not, of being morally responsible or not. He has to get from that to the conclusion that "virtually all" unjust combatants are liable to attack, particularly since he denies that they are liable simply by membership in a group.[73] Yet as individuals they belong to a group, namely that of unjust combatants. They do so by virtue of their supposedly objective unjustified act of participating in a war without a just cause. They are legitimate targets for attack by virtue of their moral responsibility for the threats of wrongful harm they pose; or, in some case, simply by virtue of the earlier "voluntary choice that in effect committed them to obedience."[74] Unjust combatants are liable for the threats they pose (or are responsible for) to just combatants and others and may be attacked because of those threats. They are threats to people who are not liable, hence are not legitimate targets.

---

[71] In a similiar vein, James P. Sterba argues that "[i]n order for defensible action to be morally justified, it is not necessary that one's defense be directed only at persons who are *actually* engaged in or are *actually* preparing to engage in unjust aggression; rather it suffices if one's defense is directed at persons whom one reasonably believes are engaged in or are preparing to engage in unjust aggression." *Justice for Here and Now* (Cambridge: Cambridge University Press, 1998), p. 170. On this issue, see also Eric Reitan, "The Irreconcilability of Pacifism and Just War Theory: A Response to Sterba," *Social Theory and Practice*, Vol. 20, No. 2, Summer 1994, pp. 117–135, and James P. Sterba, "Reconciling Pacifists and Just War Theorists Revisited," *Social Theory and Practice*, Vol. 20, No. 2, Summer 1994, 135–143.

[72] McMahan, *Killing in War*, p. 183.

[73] McMahan, *Killing in War*, p. 188.

[74] McMahan, *Killing in War*, p. 183.

Unjust combatants are supposed to know all of this. Just combatants on the other hand need to know mainly that their war is just. As McMahan writes, "their epistemic obligations are primarily concerned with determining the moral character of their war, not with determining the moral status of individual adversaries on the battlefield."[75] There is an asymmetry here. Unjust combatants are accountable for knowing that their adversaries are not legitimate targets. They violate the principles of discrimination and proportionality if they attack them, even in self-defense. But to know this, they must know that their adversary's war is just. In waging war, just combatants are, according to this approach, constrained by both discrimination and proportionality. And if these presuppose an understanding of liability, and liability is an individual matter and not a collective result of membership in a group, then just combatants, as well as unjust combatants, kill those with varying degrees of responsibility, and do so unavoidably, since the requisite knowledge (including here under "knowledge" the correct moral judgments) is impossible to come by and would be impossible to act upon in the massive, systematic violence of warfare. When it is argued that soldiers with a just cause may justifiably kill those lacking a just cause, the wrongness of the behavior of the collectivity is transferred to the individuals that are part of that collectivity. Those individual men and women may be killed because what they are doing is "objectively wrong." Their guilt is by association. They may not know that what they are doing is wrong and what their adversaries are doing is right. Nor may the soldiers with the purportedly just cause know these things either. But the men and women on one side may nonetheless justifiably kill those on the other side, regardless of their individual innocence. A veil of guilt has been cast over them because of their membership in a collectivity deemed to have done wrong. They may be killed because of the wrongs of the government that put them in that position. More specifically, they may be killed because of the wrongs of those individuals in the government and military responsible for their being ordered to fight.

6.11 Conclusion

The JWT does not defeat the moral presumption against war because it does not defeat the moral presumption against killing persons that is at the heart of warfare. And as we have seen, *jus ad bellum* becomes vacuous if it does not authorize the killing that embarking upon warfare entails. The same, it should be said, though I have not stressed it, is true of the moral war theory. Just as war$_2$, is a collaborative undertaking among collectivities, actual fighting and killing is a collaborative undertaking among individual soldiers. They tacitly agree to try to kill one another when ordered to do so by their respective authorities. Although in the heat of combat they may sometimes be fighting in self-defense in the minimalist sense of self-defense$_1$, they are not—or have not been shown to be—fighting in self-defense in a justifiable sense. The disanalogies between individual self-defense as normally understood and the situations of soldiers in combat are too great to warrant that inference. Even if one assumes that personal

---

[75] McMahan, *Killing in War*, p. 188.

self-defense, appropriately qualified, is morally justifiable, one cannot, as Rodin shows, extrapolate from this that national self-defense is morally justified. Beyond this, soldiers cannot be thought to have forfeited their right to life simply by virtue of having become soldiers. Since this view underpins it, the JWT is inadequate to the moral assessment of war.

Just Cause and the Killing of Innocents

It is incoherent to say that it is both right and wrong to kill the innocent.
—Robert W. Brimlow

7.1 Killing innocents inherent in warfare

Even if it could be shown that it is morally permissible for combatants to kill one another, it would not show that it is permissible for any of them to kill innocents.[1] That, in turn, would mean that the presumption against war has not been defeated. Warfare, as I have argued in Chapter 2, intrinsically involves killing. That is one of its governing intentions. It does not intrinsically involve killing innocents. It is even possible, however improbable, that there have been instances of warfare (if not of war itself) that did not involve the killing of innocents, and one can easily conceive of hypothetical wars that do not.[2] But the killing of innocents is *inherent* in warfare. By that I mean that it is virtually inevitable. If soldiers are innocent, such killing is a certainty. And if the nonconsensual killing of persons in general is presumptively wrong, then the nonconsensual killing of innocent persons is presumptively wrong.

The difference between what is intrinsic to warfare and what is merely inherent opens the door, however, to possible attempts to defeat the presumption that war is wrong. While one cannot wage war without intending to kill combatants, one can do so without intending to killing innocents. Whatever may have been true of some wars in the distant past, in the modern world it can be known in advance that it is

---

[1] Unless, of course, combatants, or at least some of them, are themselves innocent in a relevant sense. Having dealt with the moral equality of soldiers, I shall limit my concerns in this chapter to the killing of innocent noncombatants.

[2] If warfare were wrongly undertaken by both sides, with every participant culpable for the wrong done by that side, and if none other than combatants were killed, then no innocents would have been killed. Of course, as McMahan notes, even if no one on either side were innocent, it would not follow that they were justified in fighting. See McMahan, *Killing in War*, p. 17.

a virtual certainty that innocents will be killed in war.[3] It will in fact be foreseeable that innocents will be killed in many of the specific operations of war.[4] For this reason, to justify war it is pragmatically (as opposed to logically or conceptually) necessary to justify killing innocents. This is a problem not only for the JWT but also for the moral war theory in general. For just warists, the issue, more specifically, is to show that it is sometimes morally permissible to kill innocents in the service of a just cause. Sometimes that killing may be intentional. As Jeff McMahan writes, "most just war theorists, or at least those outside the Catholic Church, do not believe that the requirement of discrimination is absolute. They believe instead that if the consequences of refusing to attack an innocent person or group of innocent people would be vastly worse than those of conducting the attack, it can be permissible, and perhaps even morally required, to violate the requirement of discrimination by intentionally attacking the innocent."[5] The issue is put forcefully in the following passage:

> It goes without saying that what happened at Hiroshima was unspeakable ... Oversimplifying only slightly, President Truman had to choose either the death of what turned out to be over a hundred thousand innocent civilians in Hiroshima or the death of perhaps several times that many people, both soldiers and civilians, both Americans and Japanese, in the invasion of the home islands ... To restate my argument summarily: making room for humane relationships in the world depends on a readiness occasionally to carry out inhumane actions: saving the lives of innocent people sometimes requires taking the lives of innocent people.[6]

Responsibility for accidental deaths that one could not have foreseen is not what concerns me. What concerns me is responsibility for killing innocents when that killing, though not intended, hence (arguably) not desired, was foreseen or foreseeable. It was foreseeable that dropping an atomic bomb on Hiroshima would kill innocent civilians.

I shall first consider a line of reasoning to justify the killing of innocents that is available to both the moral war theorist and the just war theorist, and then consider two arguments advanced specifically from a just war perspective.

---

[3] I am speaking here of standard interstate or asymmetric war. It is possible that no innocents are killed in at least some of the warfare of primitive tribes, such as the Dani of New Guinea, as depicted in the documentary *Dead Birds*, for whom warfare is a feature of their culture.

[4] Some armies and their sponsoring governments at least tacitly acknowledge the distinction between what is intended and what is foreseen when, after killing innocents, they announce—often with expressions of regret—that they do not target civilians, meaning pretty clearly that they do not intend to kill them. Blame is then shifted to the enemy for the deaths of innocents, saying that they are responsible because of their chosen manner of fighting or the positioning of their combatants. This is easily done in much of asymmetric warfare because guerillas or militias often fight from urban areas.

[5] McMahan, *Killing in War*, p. 22.

[6] Glenn Tinder, "Can War Be Just?" Prepared for delivery at the 1990 Annual Meeting of the American Political Science Association, The San Francisco Hilton, August 30–September 2, 1990. Copyright by the American Political Science Association.

7.2 Killing and letting die

The first line of reasoning trades on the claim that there is, in the end, no moral difference between killing innocents and letting innocents die. Even if one can foresee that warfare to protect innocents will inevitably involve killing innocents, such killing is justified, at least in cases in which the defense of the innocent is an aim. For to let innocents die (i.e., to let them be killed by others) is as bad as killing innocents. Pivotal in the reasoning is the distinction between killing and letting die, which is part of a more general distinction between doing and allowing.

Whether or not there is a moral difference between killing and letting die, there is a clear conceptual difference. To kill is to cause death. To let die is to refrain from preventing death. More specifically, to let die is to refrain from intervening in processes which if unchecked will cause death.[7] The processes can be human or natural. To withhold life-saving medication from a dying person is to let the person die from a natural cause (a disease, let us suppose). To withhold information that an assassin awaits a person around the next corner is to let him die from a human cause.[8] If killing and letting die are understood solely by reference to their minimally defining properties (causing death and refraining from preventing death), there is no moral difference between the two. They could as readily be applied to the killing or letting die of weeds as to persons. To relate them specifically to the issue at hand, let us say that to kill innocents in warfare is knowingly to cause their deaths in the course of pursuing the ends of war. To let innocents die in warfare, on the other hand, is to refrain from intervening in processes which if uninterrupted will cause their death. More plainly, it is to save them from being killed by others or by disease, starvation, or the elements.

Deliberately killing persons nonconsensually is presumptively wrong. Is letting die, as we may call it, presumptively wrong as well? It is doubtful. To be sure, there are many instances in which letting die is morally as bad as killing. Sometimes, in fact, letting die is integral to the process of killing. One kills a person by administering poison and then withholding the antidote or by locking someone up and then withholding food and water.[9] But letting die in general is morally distinguishable from killing. We let persons die every day whom, with sufficient effort, we could save. There may be countless persons of whom this is true. Not that we let them die collectively. We could

---

[7] The assumption, of course, is that the processes could effectively be interrupted to prevent death. Aging is a process which if uninterrupted will cause death, but there is no known intervention in the process which will prevent eventual death. For that reason we do not let people die when they die of natural causes associated with aging.

[8] The classic example in discussions of this problem is that in which one person drowns a child in a bathtub for financial gain (hence kills), another intends to drown a child in the same circumstances but instead merely stands by and watches as the child slips and falls and drowns (lets die); the argument being that there is no moral difference between these two. See James Rachels, "Active and Passive Euthanasia," *The New England Journal of Medicine*, Vol. 292, 1975. Republished in James Rachels (ed.), *Moral Problems*, 3rd ed. (New York: Harper and Row), 490–498.

[9] When the Mossad poisoned a Palestinian operative in Jordan and the assassination attempt was uncovered, Israel was compelled for political reasons to provide the antidote for the poison. The letting die that was to have been integral to the killing was thereby interrupted.

not save all of them if we tried.[10] To let die, recall, is to refrain from intervening in processes which if uninterrupted will result in death. Such processes are continually at work, every moment of every day with regard to countless people. We could not save all of those whose deaths are going to result from the continued operation of those processes. But there are many we could save (i.e., not let die) if we devoted ourselves to doing so. It is doubtful that morality requires that much of the ordinary person, though we admire those who make heroic efforts to save others, even at great sacrifice to themselves. Otherwise, simply by getting up and going to work in the morning, or looking after our children or visiting a sick grandmother, we would be responsible for deaths we could have prevented. It is doubtful that letting die in general even *tends* to be actually wrong, even though it surely is prima facie wrong. Thus, if I am correct that the deliberate nonconsensual killing of persons tends to be actually wrong—and presumptively wrong for that reason—then there is a moral difference between killing and letting die. As a kind of act, killing is presumptively wrong, letting die is not. This is consistent with there being instances of killing that are no worse than letting die, and instances of letting die that are as bad as killing.[11]

If knowingly killing innocent persons is presumptively wrong, can that presumption be defeated by showing that there is a morally relevant difference between intentionally killing innocents and merely foreseeably killing them? Perhaps intentionally killing innocents is presumptively wrong but knowingly killing them is not always wrong.

7.3 Intentional and foreseeable killing

One common argument to establish this claim turns on the distinction between intended and foreseen consequences, the idea being that while it is wrong intentionally to kill innocents, one may sometimes do so when that killing is merely foreseeable. This way of thinking is implicit, as I have said, in the pronouncements of governments or military commanders (after they have killed innocents) that they do not target civilians. A second general line of argument is to contend that sometimes it is necessary to kill innocents in order to save innocents; specifically, to save more innocents. On one understanding, this argument transforms the issue into one of utilitarian calculation, by reasoning that all other things being equal, it is better to kill a few innocents than to see a larger number die or be killed. I shall not deal with the consequentialist argument here, as my analysis of it turns on a distinction between mediated and unmediated consequences, which I shall introduce in Chapter 11. Finally, yet another line of argument shifts the frame of reference to a rights-based perspective. It concedes that

---

[10] If you could easily save any one (and only one) of ten drowning people, then while it is true that you have let each of the others die considered individually, it is not true that you have let all nine die considered collectively. Each day there are perhaps thousands of people who will die without intervention in the processes (whether disease, starvation, accident, warfare) that will kill them. While it may be true that with sufficient effort you could save some of them, it is not true that you could save all of them, hence not true that you let them all (understood collectively) die.

[11] It is possible, though I shall not argue it, that letting a person die a slow painful death from a terminal illness is worse than killing him by administering a drug that brings about a swift and peaceful death.

innocents have a right to life, and that killing them infringes that right to life, but that nonetheless sometimes such infringements are justifiable.

One of the most formidable arguments to try to show that it may be morally permissible to kill innocents if that killing is only foreseeable and not intended is advanced by James Sterba in his attempt to reconcile certain forms of pacifism with the JWT. Sterba distinguishes different forms of pacifism: "nonviolent pacifism," "nonlethal pacifism" and "anti-war pacifism." He singles out antiwar pacifism—the view that "[a]ny participation in the massive use of lethal force in warfare is morally prohibited"[12]—as the preferred type.

In arguing that pacifism and JWT can be reconciled (an issue to which we shall return in Chapter 12), Sterba focuses upon the distinction between intended and foreseen harm to innocents. He argues that we can sometimes justifiably harm or kill innocents so long as their deaths are merely foreseen and not intended; and we can sometimes even intentionally harm or kill innocents if the consequences of not doing so would be sufficiently grave. McMahan makes a similar claim when he writes

> [T]here can be a lesser-evil justification for intentionally harming an innocent bystander and the same kind of justification is available in some cases for harming a Nonresponsible Threat in self-defense … In one case, the Justified Threat is objectively justified in intentionally infringing the right of an innocent person, a person who has neither waived nor forfeited her right. These are cases in which the innocent person's rights are straightforwardly overridden by more important countervailing considerations—for example, a case in which it is necessary to kill one innocent person as a means of preventing a much larger number of other innocent people from being killed by someone else. Anyone who is not a moral absolutist must believe that there are in principle such cases.[13]

I shall focus upon Sterba's rather more complex argument. Although I agree with Sterba that we can intelligibly make the distinction between intended and foreseen consequences, I am uneasy with the way he makes it. Let us examine his reasoning.

7.4 The Counterfactual Test

Sterba considers a Counterfactual Test for distinguishing between intended and foreseen consequences and finds it wanting. The test asks two questions of acts that have both good and evil consequences:

1. Would you have performed the action if only the good consequences would have resulted and not the evil consequences?
2. Would you have performed the action if only the evil consequences resulted and not the good consequences?

---

[12] James P. Sterba, *Justice for Here and Now* (Cambridge: Cambridge University Press, 1998), p. 153.
[13] McMahan, *Killing in War*, pp. 170 and 173.

A *yes* to (1) and a *no* to (2) supposedly would show that the good consequences are intended and the evil consequences merely foreseen. Following Douglas Lackey,[14] however, Sterba concludes that the test is inadequate in a case like the bombing of Hiroshima, in which the good is the shortening of the war, the evil the killing of civilians. The Counterfactual Test would seem to indicate that the killing of civilians was merely foreseen, whereas in fact it was "self-evidently a means for shortening the war"[15] (hence, presumably, intended). To remedy this, Sterba adds a Nonexplanation Test:

Does the bringing about of the evil consequences help explain why the agent undertook the action as a means to the good consequences? If the answer is *no*, then the evil consequence is merely foreseen; if it is *yes* then it is "an intended means to the good consequences." This supposedly gives the correct result in the Hiroshima case by showing the killing of civilians to have been intended.

But let us now look at the use that is made of the distinction between intended and foreseen consequences. This brings us to Sterba's argument for a differential restriction (attaching moral weight to the distinction between intended and foreseen consequences) rather than a uniform restriction (which presumably does not recognize the distinction or does not attach moral weight to it).

7.5 A differential restriction

From the standpoint of innocents suffering the harm, he asks: "Don't those who suffer harm have more reason to protest when the harm is done to them by agents who are directly engaged in causing harm to them than when it is done incidentally by agents whose ends and means are good?"[16] And from the perspective of those causing the harm, he says "it would seem that we have more reason to protest a restriction against foreseen harm than we do to protest a comparable restriction against intended harm. This is because a restriction against foreseen harm limits our actions when our ends and means are good, whereas a restriction against intended harm only limits our actions when our ends or means are evil or harmful." He concludes:

> Consequently, because we have more reason to protest when we are being used by others than when we are being affected by them only incidentally, and because we have more reason to act when both our ends and means are good than when they are not, we should favor the foreseen/intended distinction that is incorporated into just means.[17]

The argument thus far is for placing a more severe restriction upon the intentional harming of innocents than upon the merely foreseeable harming of them.

---

[14] Douglas Lackey, "The Moral Irrelevance of the Counterforce/Countervalue Distinction," *The Monist*, Vol. 70, 1987, pp. 255–276.

[15] Sterba, *Justice for Here and Now*, p. 155.

[16] Sterba, *Justice for Here and Now*, p. 156.

[17] Sterba, *Justice for Here and Now*, p. 156.

But the more severe restriction is not an absolute one. Sterba believes that consequentialist considerations hold sway here. Such harm is permissible when it is trivial ("stepping on someone's foot to get out of a crowded subway"), easily reparable ("lying to a temporarily depressed friend to keep her from committing suicide") or greatly offset by consequences, particularly to innocents ("shooting one of two hundred civilian hostages to prevent, in the only way possible, the execution of all two hundred"). Notice that although Sterba usually uses the term "harm" when speaking of consequences for innocents, it is clear from some of his examples that his concern extends to the permissibility of both harming and killing. Thus the analysis of the intended/foreseen distinction, and the detailing of its bearing upon the relevant moral issues, is presumed to show:

1. There is a more severe restriction against intentionally harming or killing innocents than against merely doing so foreseeably.
2. It is sometimes morally permissible to foreseeably harm or kill innocents when it would be wrong to do so intentionally.
3. Despite the more severe restriction, it is also morally permissible to harm or kill innocents intentionally when that harm is greatly outweighed by the consequences, especially to other innocents.

As a minor point, it should be noted that (2) does not follow from (1). There might be a less severe restriction against merely harming innocents foreseeably than against doing so intentionally but one that is still sufficiently stringent to prohibit the harming of innocents. All that clearly follows from (1) is that it is morally worse to kill innocents intentionally than to do so foreseeably. And one action can be morally worse than another even though both are wrong (torturing an innocent person to death is worse than giving him a painless lethal injection). Let us assume, however, that if (1) is true, then (2) is true also. Then it will presumably be easier to justify harming or killing innocents when that is a merely foreseen outcome of what one does. The consequentialist consideration in (3) is sufficient (and perhaps even necessary) to justify harming or killing innocents when one does so intentionally. Sterba apparently believes there is no reason to think that advocates of antiwar pacifism would reject these conclusions.

Although I would reject (2) and (3), I shall concentrate on (1). Granted there is a distinction between intended and foreseen consequences, as we saw in Chapter 2, the problem is with the differential as opposed to the uniform restriction.

The reasoning favoring the differential restriction, once again, involves looking at the matter, first, from the standpoint of the innocents to be harmed and, second, from the standpoint of those causing the harm. Those harmed supposedly have more reason to protest "when the harm is done to them by agents who are directly engaged in causing harm to them than when it is done incidentally by agents whose ends and means are good" (I take it that being "directly engaged in causing harm" here means that the harm is intentional). Those causing the harm, for their part, have more reason to protest the restriction against the foreseen than against intended harm, "because a restriction against foreseen harm limits our actions when our ends and means are good, whereas a restriction against intended harm only limits our actions when our ends or means are evil or harmful, and it would seem that we have stronger grounds for acting when both our ends and means are good than when they are not."[18]

My first concern is with the apparently equal weight attached to the two alleged grounds for protest. Innocents protest being harmed or killed. Those proposing to harm or kill them protest a limitation of their freedom to do so. These do not seem comparable. Surely innocent persons have far stronger grounds to protest being harmed (I will speak for the most part of harm and assume that it covers killing as well)—whether intentionally or foreseeably—than perpetrators have to protest being prevented from foreseeably harming innocent persons. Indeed, I would turn the matter around. Knowingly killing innocent persons against their will is presumptively wrong. If it can be justified at all, it requires a compelling justification. On the other hand, having one's harmful or lethal conduct towards innocent persons restricted (to include prohibiting foreseeable as well as intended harm) is not presumptively wrong. In fact, such a restriction would seem presumptively right. In the absence of further assumptions, no one has grounds to protest being restricted in knowingly inflicting harm upon innocents. Even in the absence of further assumptions, every innocent person has grounds to protest knowingly being harmed by others (and even for unknowingly being harmed where that is a result of negligence). In other words, there is a moral asymmetry between the considerations appealed to in deciding the issue of how to assess the relative weights of intended and foreseen harms to innocents.

Moreover, those suffering harm are said to have more reason to protest when the harm is done intentionally "than when it is done incidentally by agents whose ends and means are good." And regarding those protesting limitations of their maleficent actions it is said that "it would seem that we have stronger grounds for acting when both our ends and means are good than when they are not."

7.6 Incidental harms

In both cases the means as well as the ends are described as good. Moreover, in the former case, the resultant harm—when merely foreseeable—is said to be only incidental. The supposed goodness of means and ends, and the incidental character of the harm, contribute to whatever plausibility the differential restriction may be thought to have. Leaving the postulated goodness of the end unchallenged, I question the ascription of goodness to the means and the use of the label "incidental" to characterize the harm to innocents.

When you knowingly harm innocent persons in pursuit of a good end—even if the infliction of such harm is not your intention—you are adopting means that cause harm, injury or death. It is this which, by hypothesis, constitutes the evil consequence of acts. The question, then, concerns what justification there is for calling the means in question good (unless one assumes that a good end somehow makes the means to it good as well). If one wanted to describe *bad* means to a good end, one could hardly

---

[18] Sterba, *Justice for Here and Now*, p. 156

do better than to describe means that involve harming innocent persons. My point is that there are obvious grounds for calling the means in question bad and no obvious grounds for calling them good.

Let us turn now to the second element in the characterization. It holds that the foreseen harm or death to innocents is only incidental. Harms might be incidental whether or not the means with which they are associated are good. It is plausible to say, as Sterba does, that sometimes such harms might be incidental. But is a foreseeable outcome incidental solely by virtue of the fact that it was not brought about intentionally? And if those harms are incidental, does that mean that the judgment that those harmed have fewer grounds for protest than they would if the harms were intended? Let us take these questions in turn.

Are the harms or deaths in question incidental in the sorts of cases Sterba describes? They certainly are not incidental in the example to try to show that the prohibition against intentionally killing innocents is not absolute. That example, recall, is the shooting of one out of two hundred (presumably innocent) civilian hostages to prevent, "in the only way possible," the execution of all two hundred. It looks here as though killing the one is the means to saving the remaining 199. To be sure, Sterba uses this example to show the permissibility of sometimes intentionally killing innocent persons and not to argue for the differential restriction. But the example lends itself to the other sort of case as well. If the only way possible to prevent the execution of the 199 is to shoot a beer can off a fence post, and the designated hostage is strapped to the fence post in front of the can, then one foreseeably kills the hostage even though the intention is only to save the 199. But the killing could neither be called good nor incidental.

7.7 Hypothetical cases

Be that as it may, let us now look at some of the hypothetical cases Sterba cites to which the intended/foreseen distinction is directly relevant.

1. "only the intentioned or foreseen killing of an unjust aggressor would prevent one's own death."[19]
2. "only the intentioned or foreseen killing of an unjust aggressor and the foreseen killing of one innocent bystander would prevent one's own death and that of five other innocent people."
3. "only the intentioned or foreseen killing of an unjust aggressor and the foreseen killing of one innocent bystander would prevent the death of five innocent people."
4. "only the intentioned or foreseen killing of an unjust aggressor and the foreseen killing of five innocent people would prevent the death of two innocent people."
5. "only the intentioned or foreseen killing of an unjust aggressor would prevent serious injury to oneself and/or five other innocent people."[20]

[19] Sterba, *Justice for Here and Now*, p. 158
[20] Sterba, *Justice for Here and Now*, p. 159.

6. "only the intentioned or foreseen infliction of serious harm upon an unjust aggressor and the foreseen infliction of serious harm upon one innocent bystander would prevent serious harm to oneself and five other innocent people."
7. "only the intentioned or foreseen infliction of serious harm upon an unjust aggressor and the foreseen infliction of serious harm upon one innocent bystander would prevent serious harm to five other innocent people."
8. "only the intentioned or foreseen killing of an unjust aggressor and the foreseen killing of one innocent bystander would prevent serious injuries to the members of a much larger group of innocent people."

(1) is a case of personal self-defense in which the infliction of harm or death upon an innocent person is not at issue. Two others—(4) and (8)—are cases in which Sterba thinks that the killing of innocents would not be justified.

In each of the remaining cases it is said that only the act against the aggressor *and* (or in the case of (5), and/or) the foreseen harming or killing of innocents would prevent the harm in question. Anything less would not achieve one's end. If, knowing this, one then harms/kills the innocent person(s), it would seem as though the bringing about of those consequences "helps explain why the agent undertook the action as a means to the good consequences." But this, by the Nonexplanation Test, would render those consequences part of what is intended. If, to take case (3) above, you know that the only way to save five innocent people is to kill two people, one of them innocent, and you make it your end to save the five, then killing the innocent person is part of the explanation of why you performed the act you did. If asked to explain why you killed that person, you would surely answer that you did it in order to save the five. Had you done anything less you would not have achieved your aim. It would appear, then, that by the Nonexplanation Test, the killing of the innocent person is intended. Now that may be a reason for reexamining the Nonexplanation Test as a way of distinguishing intended from foreseen consequences. One might argue that the innocent death is still, as hypothesized, merely foreseen. Be that as it may, the death is not incidental, even though it was not intended. It was inextricably bound up with the indispensable means to one's end and by hypothesis was known to be such.

But suppose it could be shown that these harms or deaths are nonetheless, in some meaningful sense, incidental. Would that show that those harmed or killed have less reason to protest what is done to them than if it were intentional? It is hard to see why. If what is at issue is whether you have less reason to protest foreseen harm to yourself than intended harm, then it should not make any difference what the intention is when the harm is merely foreseen. If it is something about an outcome's being merely foreseen that is relevant, then I should have less reason to protest being foreseeably harmed or killed even when the accompanying intention is bad.

Consider three hypothetical examples, in one of which the intention is bad, in two of which it is arguably good. In the first, you are a student about to detonate a bomb in the car of a professor who gave you a bad grade, but your best friend unexpectedly gets into the car with the professor at the last minute. Your intention is to avenge the bad grade but you foresee that in doing so you will kill your best friend as well. Does your friend have less reason to protest being killed simply by virtue of the fact that your intention is only to kill the professor? And would you have more reason to protest a restriction against harming your friend than against harming the professor simply on the grounds that the harm is merely foreseen and not intended? I think not in either case. The second example is similar except that your friend gets into the car of a person bent on stealing candy from a baby. Here the intention to prevent the theft is arguably good, even though both the chosen means and the foreseeable consequence (killing your friend and the potential thief) are bad. Does your friend have less reason to protest being killed simply by virtue of the fact that your intention is to prevent a theft? And would you have more reason to protest a restriction against merely foreseeably harming your friend than one against intending to harm the friend? It is doubtful.

In the third example, the person whose car you are about to blow up is about to assassinate the tax collector. Your intention is to prevent the assassination, but you foresee that you will kill your best friend in the process. Here again the intention is good and of greater moment than in the second example. But the foreseeable consequence of killing the friend is clearly bad. Your friend has as much grounds for protesting your killing him/her as if it were intentional, and you have no more grounds to protest a restriction against killing the friend simply because the death is merely foreseeable than you would if it were intentional.

If we are accurately to assess the respective merits of a differential restriction as opposed to a uniform restriction—and if the matter is to be decided by intuitions about hypothetical cases—then we should not limit our concern to cases in which the intended ends and means are as pure as snow and the resultant harm merely incidental. There are those cases, to be sure. But there are as many others in which the means and ends are problematic or clearly bad. Indeed, for every hypothetical case one can design in which the intended means and ends in the foreseeable harming of innocents are good one can design another in which they are not. And if it is our "intuitions" about such cases that are thought to be relevant, they seem to go in one direction at least as often as in the other. The moral weight Sterba and just war theorists would attach to the distinction between intended and foreseen consequences has not been established. This does not show that it cannot be established, though I doubt that it can. It shows only that the considerations centering around grounds for protest on the part of perpetrators and innocent victims do not suffice to establish it. If this is correct, then this argument does not succeed in defeating the presumption against the killing of innocents, hence does not succeed undermining the conclusion that war is presumptively wrong. This does not mean that the conclusion follows in the absence of evaluation of other serious efforts to defeat the presumption in question; only that Sterba's argument does not suffice to block it.

Suppose, however, that the differential weights to intended and foreseen consequences in the sorts of cases Sterba characterizes could be established? Would that bolster the case for the JWT? I want to suggest reasons for thinking it would not.

The reasons center about the fact that the eight cases Sterba characterizes all appear to involve interpersonal relations and, by implication, the actions of one agent. Case (1) set the tone. It is the case of personal self-defense in which "only the intentional or foreseen killing of an unjust aggressor would prevent one's own death." Case (2) likewise is one of personal self-defense, enlarged to include defense of five others.

In the remaining cases personal self-defense drops out. But in each case it sounds as though we are talking about the killing of *an* individual aggressor and doing so to prevent death or injury to varying numbers of other individuals (five at most, except in (8) where reference is to a "much larger group"). Just as there is a quantum leap, as we have seen in the previous chapter, from the permissibility of personal self-defense to the permissibility of war, so there is a similar leap from the affirmed conclusions in Sterba's examples (assuming they could be established) to the permissibility of war. As Sterba characterizes antiwar pacifism, its opposition is to "any participation in the massive use of lethal force in warfare." So, what remains to be shown is that we can make the transition from killing in the sorts of cases Sterba hypothesizes—even assuming such killing is permissible—to killing in the sorts of circumstances of concern to advocates of antiwar pacifism.

7.8 Does a just cause entitle one to kill innocents?

A second argument concedes that killing innocent persons in warfare infringes their rights but contends that such infringement may nonetheless be justifiable. As McMahan puts it, "I believe that there could *in principle* be circumstances in which it would be morally permissible for people with a just cause to act in ways now prohibited by law. It could, for example, be permissible for just combatants intentionally to harm certain civilians or prisoners of war."[21] The issue is whether just war theorists, if they operate within a rights-based framework, can justify infringing the right to life of innocent persons in wartime. If they can, that by itself would not show that war is justified. But it would show that the presumption against killing innocents can at least sometimes be defeated.

An influential argument relevant to the issue is provided by Jan Narveson.[22] He argues that "*if* we have any rights at all, we have a right to use force to prevent deprivation of the thing to which we are said to have a right." Having a right, moreover, involves the "right to do whatever may be necessary to prevent infringements of [one's] right."[23] Taken at face value, this would entail that if killing innocent persons were necessary to preventing such infringements, one has a right to do so. But that this is too strong a claim seems clear.[24] One need only hypothesize circumstances in which the only way to prevent infringement of an inconsequential right is to perform an act of appalling enormity to see that. In any event, even if sound, Narveson's position would rule out only certain forms of pacifism, specifically absolute pacifism, which I shall define in Chapter 11.

The argument I want to examine is a more complicated one by Daniel F. Montaldi.[25] Warists recognize the right to life but think it can be forfeited or justifiably infringed,

[21] McMahan, *Killing in War*, p. 108.
[22] Jan Narveson, "Pacifism: A Philosophical Analysis," in Richard Wasserstrom (ed.), *War and Morality* (Belmont, CA: Wadsworth), pp. 63–78; published originally in *Ethics*, Vol. 75, 1965, pp. 259–271. References will be to the former.
[23] Narveson, "Pacifism: A Philosophical Analysis," pp. 72f.
[24] For a more detailed critique of Narveson's argument, see Jenny Teichman, *Pacifism and Just War* (Oxford: Basil Blackwell, 1986), pp. 29–37.
[25] Daniel F. Montaldi, "Toward a Human Rights Based Account of the Just War," *Social Theory and Practice*, Vol. 11, No. 2, Summer 1985, pp. 123–162.

contravened, overridden or even violated in some circumstances. It is difficult to thread through all of these qualifications, and particularly to reconcile them with the idea that the right to life is a human right, if that is understood to be a right one has simply by virtue of being human. Montaldi, to his credit, devotes more time than most to detailing how he thinks innocents can sometimes be killed despite their right to life. He does not claim conclusiveness for his account, only that it makes plausible the claim that there may be just wars. He believes his account has an advantage over those[26] which hold that one can justify infringing basic rights if, and only if, so doing will minimize the infringement of such rights in the future. In such accounts, quantitative considerations predominate; it is the *number* of infringements that counts. And this, he thinks, commits one to a utilitarianism of rights, in which what is appealed to are the harmful effects of rights-violations. This he finds unsatisfactory. If to avoid such a version of utilitarianism one says that infringing basic rights is wrong per se, then it is hard to see how war can be justified. For as Montaldi concedes, war inevitably kills innocent persons, hence inevitably infringes basic rights.

Montaldi's argument, if successful, would not by itself justify war, of course. The fact that you might be justified in killing innocents if you went to war would be insufficient to justify going to war. But it would undermine the claim that the nonconsensual killing of innocent persons in wartime cannot be justified. It would show that the presumption against killing innocents can be defeated in many of the cases relevant to the assessment of war, particularly from a just war theoretic standpoint.

Montaldi contends that it is sometimes permissible to infringe basic rights. A condition of permissibility is that such infringement is necessary to prevent the disrespectful violation of basic rights (presumably as embodied in other persons than those whose rights one infringes by killing them).[27] Let us try to understand what this condition means.

7.9 The Nazi and the just warrior

To infringe a right, in this view, is to treat a person in a way in which he has a right not to be treated. And this, as Montaldi understands it, need not always be wrong. To *violate* a right, on the other hand, is always wrong. But not all violations are disrespectful. It is disrespectful violations that constitute the greatest evils. That is why we are sometimes justified in infringing basic rights by killing innocent persons: to prevent disrespectful violations of those rights. Such prevention, he believes, constitutes the only just cause in war, and the aim to prevent such violations constitutes the right intention essential to just warriorship. So the JWT is tethered to a rights-based approach to ethics, and the notion of right intention in turn is tied to this understanding of just cause.

---

[26] See in this regard, David Luban, "Just War and Human Rights," *Philosophy and Public Affairs*, Vol. 9, 1980, pp. 160–182. See also Charles Beitz, "Nonintervention and Communal Integrity," *Philosophy and Public Affairs*, Vol. 9, 1980, pp. 385–392, and Gerald Doppelt, "Walzer's Theory of Morality in International Relations," *Philosophy and Public Affairs*, Vol. 8, 1978, pp. 3–26.

[27] It is unclear how this avoids some sort of utilitarianism of rights, but I shall not pursue that issue.

In this view, both the Nazi and the just warrior infringe basic rights by killing innocent people.[28] But what the Nazi does is wrong whereas what the just warrior does is permissible (or even obligatory). What makes the difference between the two?

The issue, notice, does not concern the assessment of the two as persons. The Nazi, after all (as Montaldi represents him), deliberately kills innocent persons. He knows that in so doing he acts wrongly. In this he is opting for the first alternative detailed in Chapter 2: accepting the wrongness of what he does. The just warrior, on the other hand, at least believes that he is acting rightly. This arguably makes the Nazi a worse person. Most of the German soldiers in WWII were not Nazis, and probably were no worse as persons than their American, British and Russian counterparts, but I shall not pursue that point. What must be shown is that the Nazi's *actions* are worse. It is the wrongful infringement of a right that constitutes a violation, in this view.[29] And that requires doing something; it is not enough just to be a certain sort of person. Wrongful infringements, to be evil in the manner Montaldi represents the Nazi's as being, must in addition be disrespectful. An act can be worse than another even though both are wrong. Taking pleasure in unnecessary harm you cause is arguably worse than causing harm reluctantly when under orders. Violations of basic rights are supposedly worse than mere infringements, and disrespectful violations are supposedly worse than mere violations.[30] Thus this position supposedly does not depend upon the minimization of infringements (the "utilitarianism of rights") which Montaldi rejects.

But if the argument were only that what the Nazi does is worse than what the just warrior does, that would not show that war is justified. It would show only that both the Nazi and the just warrior should stop killing innocents. Not only must it be shown that the Nazi's actions are worse than those of the just warrior (and worse than those of what we might call crusaders, who merely violate basic rights), it must also be shown that the just warrior's actions are permissible. The Nazi both violates rights and is disrespectful of persons in so doing. The crusader violates rights but is not disrespectful of persons. The just warrior *infringes* basic rights but does not violate them, respectfully or disrespectfully. The key to understanding the argument lies in understanding disrespectful violations. What exactly are they?

---

[28] The labels "just warrior" and "Nazi" bias the discussion even more than the labels just and unjust "warriors," but I shall follow Montaldi in using them.

[29] Jeff McMahan likewise distinguishes between infringements and violations of rights along somewhat similar but distinguishable lines. He writes: "When one thus permissibly acts against a right, I will say that one *infringes* that right, whereas when one impermissibly does what another has a right that one not do, one *violates* that right. Even though an agent acts permissibly in infringing a right, the victim is nonetheless wronged ... See *Killing in War*, p. 10. This would seem to imply that it is sometimes right (permissible) to wrong a person. Frederik Kaufman likewise distinguishes between infringements and violations: "But *if* we really are morally justified in deliberately killing innocent people in a supreme emergency, then this would not violate their right to life; it is instead a permissible infringement of the right." See Fredrik Kaufman, "Just War Theory and Killing the Innocent," in Michael W. Brough, John W. Lango, Harry van der Linden (eds) *Rethinking the Just War Tradition* (Albany, NY: State University of New York Press, 2007), p. 107.

[30] Nigel Biggar's observation is pertinent here, that "the notion that it can be morally right to *violate* a right and to *wrong* its bearer surely jars logically ... if, in these circumstances and all things considered, it is morally right for me to harm you, how far does it make sense to say that *in these circumstances* you *still* possess a right to life—or, more exactly, a right not to be harmed?" Biggar, *In Defense of War*, p. 176.

Let us begin to try to understand the claim that the Nazi's actions are worse than the just warrior's.

Nonmorally, the two are equally bad. Innocent persons are as dead if killed by just warriors as if killed by Nazis. Afghan children are as dead if killed by a US drone as if by a Taliban roadside bomb. To say that their killing is worse in the second case than in the first must mean that it is worse on moral grounds.[31]

7.10 Infringement and disrespectful violation of rights

Wherein, then, lies the moral evil that makes the actions of the Nazi worse? What sets those actions apart from the supposedly permissible acts of the just warrior (who merely infringes basic rights) and the wrongful acts of the crusader (who violates basic rights but does not do so disrespectfully)?

Montaldi gives various characterizations of disrespectful violation. The following is representative:

> When a person violates someone else's basic rights consciously, or with the knowledge that he is violating these rights, he is treating his victim as being unworthy of having or enjoying rights … the absence of respect (disrespect) is not just some harmful state of affairs or a collection of actions that are wrong regardless of an actor's state of mind (or will). It is a wrong act done consciously for the sake of inclination. Acting without respect for others occurs when an actor actually makes choices on the basis of a regard for persons as being merely instrumental to him when he knows that they are not.[32]

In disrespectful violations one deliberately infringes basic rights in the knowledge that in so doing he treats the victim as a means.[33]

But the just warrior does this as surely as the Nazi. He uses innocent persons as a means to preventing the disrespectful violation of the very rights he himself infringes.[34] Indeed, on Montaldi's view, "infringements are permissible only if they are necessary to prevent violations *qua* willful."[35] Both the Nazi and the just warrior destroy the capacity for respectful action that is the source of a person's moral worth. That moral worth, in turn, is the source of the respect the person is owed.

---

[31] Montaldi's characterization of the Nazi's actions as evil implies this. What is evil is bad for moral reasons. Even if it should be intrinsically (hence nonmorally) bad as well, it is the moral ground that renders it evil. Accidentally causing someone unnecessary suffering is bad; deliberately causing it arguably is evil.

[32] Montaldi, "Toward a Human Rights Based Account of the Just War," pp. 140–141.

[33] Montaldi allows that there may be disrespectful infringements (by which he seems to mean violations) which are not deliberate, such as those resulting from "wanton negligence" or "criminal neglect" (p. 157, n. 24). However, it is the cases which are deliberate that he regards as paradigmatic. Since it is those in any event that are candidates for an enormous evil, I shall confine my attention to them.

[34] Montaldi, "Toward a Human Rights Based Account of the Just War," p. 137.

[35] Montaldi, "Toward a Human Rights Based Account of the Just War," p. 149.

It will not help to say that the Nazi kills innocent persons for the sake of a bad end whereas the just warrior kills them for the sake of a good end. There certainly is this difference, and some might take it to warrant different assessments of their actions (on the grounds that the end justifies the means). But to justify killing innocents for the sake of an end is to justify it on consequentialist grounds. And this is precisely the kind of justification Montaldi rejects and to which the rights-based theory supposedly provides an alternative. It does not matter what the end is. To aim to prevent the disrespectful violation of rights is to appeal to consequences as much as to aim to minimize the infringement of rights (the view Montaldi rejects as representing a "utilitarianism of rights"). What makes a line of justification consequentialist has nothing to do with what makes the end good or bad. It has to do only with whether the action whose rightness is at issue is instrumental to the promotion or attainment of that end.

Perhaps what makes the Nazi's actions disrespectful is that he treats innocent persons as means *only* whereas the just warrior treats them at the same time with respect. This would accord with Kant's second formulation of the categorical imperative, which calls upon us to treat persons as ends and not as means only. If this is what Montaldi intends, then although the justification of the just warrior's act would be partly consequentialist (by virtue of promoting an end), it would also have a deontological character to it (by virtue of calling for respectful treatment of persons).

But we need to inquire wherein consists the respect the just warrior supposedly shows his innocent victims and the Nazi does not.

The problem is that disrespectful action would seem to be treating one's victims "as being unworthy of having or enjoying rights." And the Nazi and the just warrior do this equally. They kill innocent persons knowingly, in full knowledge that in doing so they are destroying the capacity for respectful action that is the source of their (the victims') worth. It will not do to respond that only knowingly *violating* rights (which the Nazi does) is disrespectful, not knowingly infringing them (which the just warrior does). At least it will not do to reply to this unless one explains at the same time why infringing people's basic rights is not wrong. At issue is not whether the just warrior's killing, though equally wrong, is in some sense less bad than the Nazi's.[36] That is the status of the actions of what I have called the crusader. At issue is whether that killing is permissible in the first place. One does not resolve that issue simply by saying that the one is disrespectful, the other not. One could be disrespectful and the other (like the crusader's) not and yet both of them be wrong.

So let us assume that violating basic rights knowingly is not the criterion of disrespectful action. What other possibilities are there? One is contained in the following tantalizingly cryptic passage of Montaldi's:

> In any event, if a person's worth owes significantly to his capacity to act from respect, then it makes sense to say with Kant that right action done from respect is of greater worth than a right action simply being done, for example, by accident or by inclination only. The importance of treating a person both rightly and with

---

[36] Killing an innocent person arguably is less bad if you let him call his mother first than if you do not, but it does not for that reason become less wrong.

respect is thus greater than simply treating him rightly. The importance of treating a person respectfully would not then be derived simply from the utility this has for protecting and furthering his interests. It has additional moral importance. So the importance of respecting rights would not be derived from the importance of right-holders being able to enjoy them (or those interests they protect). Rather, it may be the importance of enjoyment that is (in some sense) derivative. It is derived from the prior importance of respecting rights, or respecting persons as worth limiting one's own pursuit of personal ends to the extent dictated by rights claims.[37]

The point seems to be that in addition to possessing interests (which rights are intended to protect), people also possess a capacity for respectful action. This is the source of the unconditional worth that makes them deserving of respect. If so, one could make sense of assigning priority to respect over interests. And one could see why Montaldi takes infringing or even violating rights to be less serious than disrespectfully violating them. For in infringing or violating rights one would only be harming interests, a consequentialist consideration. Treating people disrespectfully, on the other hand, supposedly is a greater evil because it ignores the unconditional moral worth persons possess by virtue of their capacity for respectful action.

Moreover, if protecting rights, and securing the interests those rights safeguard, were the only relevant consideration, there would be little basis for distinguishing the attacker from his victims. As Montaldi concedes,

> [B]oth the attacker and his potential victim possess interestedness and basic autonomy. If it is simply each person's interestedness and autonomy that make them worth respect, thus generating obligations with regard to their particular interests and choices, then there is no basis for the relative difference in importance of the interests of the attacker vs. those of his potential victim.[38]

If the harming of interests were the greatest evil, then one would inflict such evil by killing the attacker as surely as the attacker does by killing his victim. Supposedly one does not inflict such evil by showing respect based upon the preservation of unconditional worth.

But this does not avoid the problem. Unconditional moral worth is grounded in one's *capacity* for respectful action, not upon respectful action itself. And the Nazi (leaving aside psychopaths and those with severe mental or emotional disorders) presumably has the same capacity for moral action as anyone else. Adolf Eichmann, remember, professed to try to live by the categorical imperative and Heinrich Himmler carried with him a copy of the *Bhagavad-Gita,* a work revered by Gandhi. It is just that, on Montaldi's view, the Nazi chooses to act immorally, willingly choosing to destroy that which is of unconditional moral worth in his victims. But in killing the Nazi—along with innocent persons in the process—the just warrior does precisely the same

---

[37] Montaldi, "Toward a Human Rights Based Account of the Just War," p. 144.
[38] Montaldi, "Toward a Human Rights Based Account of the Just War," p. 146.

thing. He destroys the Nazi's capacity for respectful action. So if *that* is what constitutes disrespectful action, then not only does the just warrior himself act disrespectfully in killing innocent persons, he does so in killing the Nazi in order to prevent the Nazi from killing innocent persons.

If this is correct, it has not been shown how it can plausibly be said that in killing innocent persons the just warrior is at the same time treating them with respect. Nothing in the actions themselves distinguishes the conduct of the just warrior from that of the Nazi.

There remains only one other possibility that I can see. It lies in the differing motivation of the two.

7.11 Do good motives suffice?

In Kantian terms, if the Nazi acts from inclination and the just warrior from duty, then that marks an important difference between the two (if the issue is approached from a Kantian, deontological perspective). As an historical fact, of course, this is questionable. Much of Nazism as conceived by its adherents is a moral position of the highest order. Hitler's *Mein Kampf* bears this out. To represent Nazis—or, at any rate, all of them—as knowingly and deliberately acting immorally is to fail to see much of the appeal of their ideology.[39] As R. M. Hare shows in his *Freedom and Reason,* the Nazi's position becomes more formidable when it is recognized that his conduct may be as principled as that of those who oppose him. And, on the other side, there is no particular reason to believe that wars widely believed to have been just (such as WWII)[40] were waged by persons acting only from duty in a Kantian sense. National interest, support of allies, safeguarding of natural resources and the like—the sorts of reasons nations typically go to war and which typically are gathered under the label *realpolitik*—all arguably represent action from inclination, not duty, in a kantian sense.

Montaldi might say, of course, that he is not primarily concerned with historical fact; that the label "Nazi" simply represents a certain sort of person for purposes of showing the justification for war. He might say that his account shows that a just war is possible only if waged against those persons ("Nazis," whoever they are) who wage war from inclination in the Kantian sense.

If so, his argument faces a second problem. If we adhere to the Kantian perspective, we must take account of the fact that for Kant self-love is ultimately the spring of all conduct other than that done out of reverence for the moral law. Inclination and duty are the operative motives in human conduct. In Kant's view we can never know for certain that our own or anyone else's conduct is in fact motivated by duty. If duty is taken as the criterion of respectful action, this would mean that we can never know that any action is genuinely respectful, hence can never know that any war is just. In

---

[39] If one is to credit prideful wrongdoing of the sort discussed in Chapter 2 on the part of warists, one has to be prepared to credit it in the case of Nazis as well.

[40] Recalling that we are speaking only of the partial war waged by the allies and not the entirety of WWII.

addition, the fact that an act is from inclination does not mean that it is disrespectful of persons as ends in themselves; only that it is not done *from* respect for them as ends. Much of our friendly, charitable, even loving conduct is of this sort. It is not wrongful. It simply confers no moral worth upon the agent because it is not done from the motive of duty. Conduct that is not done from respect is not necessarily done from disrespect. So the presence of inclination as a motive cannot suffice to render such actions evil. And if those actions are not evil (in addition to violating rights), their prevention cannot constitute the just warrior's just cause.

But suppose we say that, rather than acting from inclination, the Nazi acts from a motive that is the mirror image of the just warrior's. Whereas the just warrior does what he believes is right because he believes it is his duty, the Nazi does what he believes is wrong because he believes it is wrong. Sometimes it sounds as though this may be what Montaldi intends. To assume this makes it even more plausible to suppose that manifest evil characterizes the Nazi. If so, then in addition to the motives of inclination and duty, we would have a third motive, what we might call malevolence—the performing of wrong acts because one believes them to be wrong. And it would indeed seem worse that this motivation exists than simply those of duty or inclination.

The problem with this line of defense is that it subjectifies the account to such an extent that it deprives it of its plausibility as an account of why the Nazi's *actions* are worse than those of the just warrior. We must remember that what is at issue is not whether as persons the two are to be judged differently. That can easily be shown once one turns from properties of the acts themselves to the motivation behind the acts. What must be shown is that the killing of innocents done by the Nazi is wrong and the killing of innocents by the just warrior is permissible.

One might think that in characterizing the Nazi's actions as vicious, we are saying that he believes that what he is doing is wrong and is doing it for that reason. That would presuppose that there exist some criteria of wrongness to which he thinks his act conforms and which motivate him to perform it. But if it is the motive that *makes* the act wrong, this account is circular. One cannot be motivated to do an act because it is wrong, if its wrongness consists in the fact that the motivation behind it is to do it because it is wrong. By the same token, if it were the just warrior's motive to do what is his duty because it is his duty which makes the act his duty, we would encounter a similar circularity. However virtuous or vicious one's motives, they cannot be what determines the rightness or wrongness of the actions they motivate. Motives are relevant to our judgments of persons. They do not constitute the standard of right and wrong conduct.

7.12   Conclusion

In sum, the preceding account does not succeed in showing that one can consistently maintain: (1) that persons have a basic right to life, (2) that the just warrior and the Nazi inevitably kill innocent persons in war, (3) that in so doing the just warrior, no less than the Nazi, infringes the rights of such persons, and at the same time (4) that nonetheless such infringements on the part of the just warrior are permissible whereas those by the Nazi are reprehensible. If correct, this means that it has not been shown that the killing of innocent persons by those fighting in a just cause is any less wrong than the killing of innocent persons by those fighting in an unjust cause. And if that has not been shown, then it has not been shown that a rights-based interpretation of just cause succeeds in defeating the moral presumption against war. Nor, if the earlier reasoning is correct, does exploiting the distinction between killing and letting die, or between intended and foreseeable consequences, suffice to justify killing innocent persons. In that case, such arguments do not defeat the moral presumption against war.

Part III

The Vietnam War

The French [in Indochina] didn't kill enough . . . If you kill enough you win the war.
—Anonymous US General, 1966

Our mission was not to win terrain or seize positions, but simply to kill: to kill Communists and to kill as many of them as possible.
—Former Marine Lieutenant, Philip Caputo

8.1 Vietnam: A turning point for America

The Vietnam War was pivotal in American history.[1] Even though it ended some sixteen years before the collapse of the Soviet Union, its end marked the beginning of the transition from the clarity and perceived stability of the Cold War to the uncertainty and complexity of the post–Cold War era. More than that, the Vietnam War brought domestic upheaval to the United States of a sort unseen since the Civil War. Faith in the government and the military was shaken. After the war, there was soul searching about the use of American power in the future. Various "lessons" of Vietnam were set forth by critics and supporters of the war alike.

Much of the discussion concerned whether the war was winnable. The predominant view was that it was not. But the assumption—usually unquestioned—behind the view that the war was a mistake was that it was a mistake *because* it was unwinnable. The corollary, also unquestioned, was that it would not have been a mistake if America had won. With the focus having been firmly placed on the issue of winnability, defenders of the war in the years following have argued that, if the United States did not win the war, as some of them seem to think it did,[2] at least it did not lose. In any case, most of them

---

[1] For a detailed account of the influence of the Vietnam War upon US culture and identity, See Christian G. Appy, *American Reckoning: The Vietnam War and Our National Identity* (New York: Viking, 2015).
[2] Phillip Jennings writes: "The biggest myth perpetuated about the Vietnam War is that America lost. However misguided America's leaders might have been in some of their political, strategic, and tactical decisions, we still won the war . . . The United States military lost more than 58,000 men

believe that the United States could have won had it been sufficiently determined and had not the media and critics undermined the effort.[3] The question of the winnability of the war is not, however, the central moral issue, if indeed it is a moral issue at all.[4] The central moral issue is whether the war was morally justifiable. Being winnable is neither necessary nor sufficient for a war's being justified. A just war (were there such a thing) might be lost and an unjust war won. Moreover, the winnability of the Vietnam War, were it established, would not defeat the presumption that the war was wrong.

Standard accounts of the Vietnam War are framed in terms of the concepts that figure prominently in political and international perspectives: national interest, governments, nation states, troop deployments, prestige, casualties, victory, defeat. Contrasted with these are the accounts of individual soldiers who participated. There the central concepts most often are those of killing, fear, fatigue, orders, blood, bravery, women and the like. Somewhere between these two lies a space which emphasizes the centrality of moral concepts, such as right, wrong, justice, injustice, decency, fairness, truthfulness, compassion, integrity, freedom and responsibility. There is overlap, of course, among these three perspectives. Many of the moral concepts appear in the political vocabulary, but mostly as window dressing for decisions that have little to do with morality. Some of them also occur in the soldiers' vocabulary but most often in connection with their immediate experiences, often in relation to comrades. One also finds in standard accounts of the war a perhaps unconscious bias in the language used to describe the combatants. Americans are referred to as US troops, or Marines, or Army. But their Vietnamese opponents are referred to as communists, which of course many of them (or at least their leaders) were but which labels them in ideological terms. Most of the US troops were probably capitalists—and certainly *their* leaders were—in much the same sense as the Vietnamese were communists. Yet one did not read that: "Capitalist troops landed at Da Nang in 1965" or "Capitalist planes bombed North Vietnam in 1964." Similarly, there are accounts which use the language of domestic political rhetoric.[5] Although I shall use the term "Vietcong," a pejorative introduced by South Vietnam's Ngo Dinh Diem to stand for Vietnamese communists, I shall attempt to use relatively neutral terms in characterizing the adversaries.

---

in the Vietnam War. The North Vietnamese military lost more than *1.1 million*. Who would you guess was the victor?" *The Politically Incorrect Guide to the Vietnam War* (Washington, DC: Regnery Publishing, 2010), p. 1.

[3] As Mark Moyar writes: "The war in Vietnam that America's young men were about to fight . . . was not to be a foolish war fought under wise constraints, but a wise war fought under foolish constraints." Mark Moyar, *Triumph Forsaken: the Vietnam War, 1954–1965* (Cambridge: Cambridge University Press, 2006), p. 416.

[4] The JWT, as we have seen, considers probability of success one of the criteria that must be considered in order justifiably to go to war.

[5] Phillip Jennings, for example, begins his book, *The Politically Incorrect Guide to The Vietnam War*, saying, "It was World War II, the 'good war,' that got the United States involved in what liberals would eventually want to paint as the 'bad war' (though liberals were the ones mostly responsible for our fighting it)" (p. 5). Toward the end he puts into the mouth of a fictitious lieutenant, who one presumes represents the author's views, the following: "We fought Communism to a halt in Vietnam but couldn't defeat weaselism in our own back yard. The pink-libs sprouted a feedlot full of bull crap about the morality of the war, and how hard it was to fight" (p. 183).

What follows does not pretend to be a moral history of the Vietnam War, though I think one should be written. My aim is to assess whether the Vietnam War provides a concrete example of a morally justified war in the modern world. I shall begin with a largely factual account, bearing in mind that so much controversy swirls around the Vietnam War that there will be those who contest almost every sentence in the next few sections. Following that I shall attempt to convey some sense of the nature of the war and the atrocities that abounded.

Notice that in speaking of whether the Vietnam War was justified, I am speaking of the partial war, as waged by the United States, and its few allies; that is, war$_1$ in terms of our earlier discussion. But we can also ask, as I want to, whether the whole war—that is war$_2$, as waged principally by the United States and South Vietnam, on the one side, and the Vietcong and North Vietnamese on the other—was justified. In what follows, I shall for the most part leave it to the context to make clear which sense of "war" is being discussed.

8.2 The Indochina War

The Vietnam War was a product of WWII and its resultant realist mentality as much as it was of colonialism. But colonialism stands out as perhaps the most conspicuous cause. The French occupied Vietnam for nearly a century. The first French arrived there in 1858 following earlier Catholic missionaries. They asserted firm control over Vietnam in the early twentieth century, allowing a puppet emperor, Bao Dai, to nominally govern in 1932. The Japanese occupied Vietnam during WWII but allowed the French to continue with administrative responsibilities until 1945, at which point they allowed Bao Dai to proclaim the (nominal) independence of Vietnam within a broader Japanese sphere of influence.[6] They were opposed by the Vietnamese nationalist and Marxist, Ho Chi Minh, who led a guerilla movement, the *Vietminh*, against both the French and the Japanese. "Nationalist" and "Marxist" seem ideologically to be a strange combination, but although Ho became a cofounding member of the French communist party in 1925 during a six-year stay in France, and studied Marxism during a two-year stay in Moscow, he is said later to have become an ardent nationalist.[7] Well-read and intelligent, he had lived in the United States for a time and admired much about America. He even quoted the American Declaration of

---

[6] Bao Dai abdicated in August of 1945 and became a "political advisor" to the government Ho Chi Minh established on September 2, 1945, leaving the country for Hong Kong in 1946. He returned in 1949 to assume the role of emperor under the French. See Neil Sheehan, *A Bright Shining Lie: John Paul Vann and America in Vietnam* (New York: Vintage Books, 1989), pp. 165–171.

[7] This view is challenged by Mark Moyar, who writes: "Ho Chi Minh was a nationalist in the sense that he had a special affection for Vietnam's people and favored Vietnamese unification and independence, but, from his reading of Lenin's Theses onward, he firmly adhered to the Leninist principle that Communist nations should subordinate their interests to those of the international Communist movement ... Further evidence of Ho's commitment to Communism came from his single-minded and unswerving dedication to one objective: the imposition of Communist government on Vietnam and the rest of the world." See his *Triumph Forsaken*, pp. 9, 10. In the same vein, Michael Lind writes: "Ho Chi Minh was not a Vietnamese patriot whose Marxism was a superficial veneer; like North Korea's Kim Il Sung and Cambodia's Pol Pot, Ho was both a nationalist and a doctrinaire

Independence upon the founding of the Democratic Republic of Vietnam (DRV) on September 2, 1945, after the four-year guerilla struggle against the occupying Japanese. This effort was aided by the United States when, in July 1945, seven members of the Office of Strategic Services parachuted into Vietnam on a secret mission to train an elite force of Vietminh, including Ho and Vo Nguyen Giap, who later led the Vietminh in the defeat of the French at Dien Bien Phu, in the use of modern American weapons. They reportedly agreed to rescue downed American pilots.[8] Ho's hopes of seeing Vietnam recognized as an independent state were quickly dashed. President Truman reportedly never replied to a letter given to the Americans to deliver to him requesting US support to the Vietnamese in seeking independence from France. WWII had left Indochina highly unstable, a condition the French exploited to reassert their colonial domination. The British occupied Indo-China up to the 16th parallel at the end of the war. They reached a bilateral agreement with France to allow the French to administer the region below the 16th parallel. The Vietminh, for their part, acquiesced in an Allied agreement to allow the return of 15,000 French troops to the North (above the 16th parallel). The rationale was that the French would enable the Vietnamese to oust the Chinese Nationalists, 200,000 of whose troops occupied the north at the end of the war, and who alienated the Vietnamese with rampant pillaging. Ho Chi Minh may have regarded the Chinese, who had occupied Vietnam for roughly 1,000 years, until AD 938, as a greater long-term threat than he did the French. He expected that the northern and southern regions of the country would soon be reunited. This did not happen. Eventually the French re-established their own puppet government in Saigon under Bao Dai, and by December of 1946 Vietnamese guerillas were again trying to oust them. The conflict dragged on for years, until the French were decisively defeated in May of 1954 in one of history's historic battles at Dien Bien Phu.

Initial US support for the Vietnamese ended quickly after WWII, and the French received increasing financial and military aid from the United States dating from 1950. By the time the French were defeated, the United States was financing 78 percent of the French war effort.[9] The Eisenhower administration had considered intervening militarily in support of the French and had even considered using the atomic bomb to help break the siege of Dien Bien Phu. It decided against direct intervention when it was unable to get allied support, in particular that of Britain.[10] Years later, Gen. William Westmoreland considered the use of tactical nuclear weapons at Khesanh in 1968, which was under siege by the North Vietnamese and looked as though it might develop into America's Dien Bien Phu. The option reportedly was rejected by

---

Marxist-Leninist whose brutal and bankrupt tyranny was modeled on Stalin's Soviet Union and Mao's China." *Vietnam: The Necessary War* (New York: Simon & Schuster, 1999), p. xvi.

[8] *The New York Times*, April 24, 2013. The *Times* account also reports that the mission, though a foot-note in American history, "has been hailed in Vietnam as a golden moment of cooperation with the United States."

[9] As reported by Michael Maclear, *The Ten Thousand Day War: Vietnam 1945–1975* (New York: St. Martin's Press, 1981), p. 33.

[10] Although Eisenhower showed restraint in 1954, by 1967 he was impatient with the pace of the war, saying "What do politicians know about conducting a war? We must use force and get done with it … You should get everything you can, and use it as fast as you can." Jack Bell, reporting for Associated Press. *Ann Arbor News*, August 15, 1967.

Washington because of concern for antiwar sentiment at home.[11] The Vietminh, for their part, had received heavy weapons from Red China following the defeat of Chiang kai-Shek in 1949.[12]

Following the French surrender at Dien Bien Phu, the Geneva Accords of July 20, 1954, ended the first phase of the Indochina War. It provided for the cessation of hostilities, with Vietnamese forces withdrawing to north of the 17th parallel, a provisional military demarcation line, French forces to the South.[13] Upward of a million Vietnamese, mostly Catholics, elected to move to the South, while a smaller number of mostly non-Catholics moved to the North. Free elections to unify the whole country were slated for July of 1956. The United States did not sign the Accord but pledged not to obstruct its implementation. Nonetheless, it took steps to subvert the Accord even before the defeat of the French. Early in 1954 it created The Saigon Military Mission (SMM). "The broad mission for the team," according to the *Pentagon Papers*, "was to undertake paramilitary operations against the enemy and to wage political-psychological warfare. Later, after Geneva, the mission was modified to prepare the means for undertaking paramilitary operations in Communist areas."[14]

8.3 The creation of South Vietnam

The fear of communism that dominated US foreign policies until the collapse of the Soviet Union had taken hold. Vice President Nixon warned in April of 1954, while the siege of Dien bien Phu was still underway:

> [T]he Vietnamese lack the ability to conduct a war by themselves or govern them-selves. If the French withdrew, Indochina would become Communist-dominated within a month. The United States as a leader of the free world cannot afford fur-ther retreat in Asia. It is hoped the United States will not have to send troops there, but if the government cannot avoid it, the Administration must face up to the situation and dispatch forces.[15]

By the time French defeat was imminent it was deemed too late for overt US military action on their behalf. But US troops were already there, principally as advisors, and

[11] As reported by Stanley Karnow, *Vietnam: A History* (New York: Penguin Books, 1984), p. 552. Despite its being widely cited by journalists and others, Karnow calls the analogy between Dien Bien Phu and Khesanh preposterous. Among other things, he points out: "Approximately eight thou-sand Vietminh and two thousand French army soldiers died at Dienbienphu. But the struggle for Khesanh cost the communists at least ten thousand lives in exchange for fewer than five hundred U.S. marines killed in action" (p. 553). The figures for US and Vietcong casualties, of course, were not known until afterward.

[12] As reported by Bernard B. Fall, *Street without Joy: The French Debacle in Indochina* (Mechanicsburg, PA: Stackpole Books, 1961), p. 175.

[13] Fighting continued in the Southern Mountain Plateau, where the armistice did not become fully effective until August 1, 1954. See the account by French journalist Bernard B. Fall, *Street without Joy*, pp. 240f.

[14] *The Pentagon Papers*, p. 54. See also Karnow, *Vietnam: A History*, p. 237.

[15] *The New York Times* (April 17, 1954), quoted in *Vietnam: History, Documents, and Opinions on a Major World Crisis*, ed. Marvin E. Gettleman (New York: Fawcett Publications, 1965), p. 91.

clandestine warfare was underway, with the SMM organizing paramilitary groups that were involved in strikes against the Vietminh in the North. The US Navy and Air Force provided logistical support. A special forces veteran reported later that "when his outfit first went to Vietnam, the men masqueraded as civilians and trained and armed certain ethnic groups for the Central Intelligence Agency, in violation of the Geneva accords." According to the report in the *New York Times*, he "also charged that the Special Forces had trained infiltrators into Laos and North Vietnam . . .Among many other sweeping allegations, he asserted that Special Forces troops were taught torture methods and that they were urged, indirectly, to arrange for the killing of Vietcong prisoners by South Vietnamese troops."[16] It was South Vietnamese commando raids on North Vietnam on August 2, 1964, that led to an attack on nearby US destroyers by North Vietnamese torpedo boats, in which one torpedo boat was sunk and two damaged by US planes. The following night another attack allegedly occurred against two US destroyers. Subsequent accounts produced evidence that the second attack never occurred. Blame for mistakenly believing it had was placed on freakish weather, faulty sonic equipment and perhaps jumpy US sailors. In any event, the view was promoted in the United States that two attacks had occurred, and the United States bombed North Vietnam in reprisal. More importantly, the attack led to the Tonkin Gulf Resolution in Congress, which in its practical effect was as good as a declaration of war.[17] The resolution was repealed in 1971.

Without reference to the JWT, President Lyndon Johnson alleged—among the many rationales the United States gave for the war over the years—that the war was, in effect, a last resort. Last resort, as we have seen, is one of the criteria of JWT justifying recourse to war.

> Only when petition and persuasion failed was the shot fired that was heard around the world. Not until appeals to common sense brought forth the cannon's roar at Fort Sumter did Lincoln, with heavy heart, reply in kind. And not until reason perished in the aggressor's path did we turn—first in 1916, and again in 1941—for force as the ally of freedom . . . Vietnam is different. The aggressor has chosen a different terrain, a different people and a different kind of war to satisfy his appetite. But his goal is the same—someone else's freedom. To defend that freedom . . . is our purpose in South Vietnam. Unchecked aggression against free and helpless people would be a grave threat to our own freedom—and an offense to our own conscience.[18]

The day following the report on President Johnson's speech, the *New York Times* published an interview in Hanoi by British journalist James Cameron with Pham Van Dong, the premier of North Vietnam, and President Ho Chi Minh, in which

---

[16] *The New York Times*, February 10, 1966. The former Green Beret, Donald Duncan, gave this account in an article in the Catholic publication, *Ramparts*, which was forthcoming at the time the *Times* published its account.

[17] It is unclear whether the North Vietnamese knew they were attacking a US naval vessel or believed they were attacking a South Vietnamese boat. It is also unclear whether they actually intended to attack the destroyer, since the destroyer fired first.

[18] *The New York Times*, "Remarks by Johnson and Rusk on War in Vietnam," December 10, 1965.

the premier presented North Vietnam's side of the story. It is an account which, with appropriate modifications, might have been given by the Taliban in Afghanistan before the US attack in 2001:

> Of course, we can't vanquish the United States. That would be fantasy, and we are not talking in terms of fantasy . . . There seems to be some preposterous belief in America that we are threatening them—a poverty-stricken little country like Vietnam threatening the most powerful nation on earth! We are trying to get rid of them. They're on our soil, and we don't want them there. Let them go away and the war is over . . . We are fighting for a perfectly comprehensible and definable thing, which is our independence exactly as set down in the Geneva agreement of 1954 . . . We don't want thousands of American corpses or American prisoners. We want them to go away.[19]

General Giap, who led the Vietminh to victory over the French at Dien Bien Phu, and who commanded the North Vietnamese troops in the war against the United States, wrote—in one of the more trenchant observations of the first phase of the Indochina war, and one which so far as I can tell has been ignored: "The *enemy*, an imperialist power . . . was still strong as compared with us . . . His weak point lay in the unjust character of his war."[20] The point, one may suppose, was that the injustice of a war can offset the military superiority of the side waging it.

The French, beset with growing problems with their colonial position in Algeria, abdicated their responsibilities under the Geneva Accord and withdrew. This paved the way for major US intervention. In lieu of overt military action, the United States at first sought to create a bulwark against communism by creating a democratic, anticommunist regime in the South. Having invested heavily in backing the French militarily and financially in its years of struggle against the Vietminh, the United States supported the creation of a separate state below the 17th parallel. In so doing it backed Ngo Dinh Diem, a Catholic who had lived in the United States for two years and was well-known to leading American political figures (including then senator John F. Kennedy).[21] Initially appointed prime minister by Bao Dai in 1954, Diem became president when he defeated Bao Dai in a referendum which he initiated after Bao Dai had demanded his resignation. Diem won with 98.2 percent of the vote.[22] US advisors

---

[19] *The New York Times*, "From Hanoi: Premier Says, 'Let U.S. Go, and the War Is Over,'" December 11, 1965.

[20] Vo Nguyen Giap, *People's War, People's Army: The Viet Cong Insurrection Manual for Underdeveloped Countries* (New York: Bantam Books, 1968), p. 86.

[21] Diem had met with Ho Chi Minh in 1946, who tried unsuccessfully to persuade him to accept a position in the Vietnamese government (Karnow, *Vietnam: A History*, pp. 232f.). He left Vietnam in 1950, to return in 1954. Sheehan contends that his appointment as prime minister, and later ascendancy to the presidency, was engineered by Colonel Edward Lansdale, who had arrived in Vietnam in 1954 to head the Saigon Military Mission in covert operations (Sheehan, *A Bright Shining Lie*. Book Two, "Antecedents to a Confrontation"). Robert McNamara reports that both Ho Chi Minh and Mao Zedong apparently thought reasonably well of Diem. See Robert McNamara, *In Retrospect: The Tragedy and Lessons of Vietnam* (New York: Times Books, 1995), p. 84.

[22] US Ambassador G. Frederick Reinhardt reportedly said—apparently with a straight face—that no evidence of fraud could be found. As reported by Moyar, *Triumph Forsaken*, p. 55.

had suggested that he keep his victory margin at 60 percent or 70 percent to make it appear more respectable. When Diem later refused to abide by the Geneva Accords and agree to elections to unify the country—which virtually all observers agreed would be won by Ho Chi Minh—the existence of supposedly sovereign Republic of Vietnam (RVN) was announced in October of 1955, heavily backed by the United States. South Vietnam had come into existence. As an analyst for the *Pentagon Papers* put it, "South Vietnam was essentially the creation of the United States."[23] American thinking was that an independent South Vietnam would be a bulwark against communist expansion in South Asia and then the Pacific. If South Vietnam fell, other countries would fall like dominoes, as the metaphor had it.[24] Although Vietnam was 85 percent Buddhist, the United States was confident that a Catholic president with support and guidance from the United States would succeed. The French had lost more than 75,000 lives in Indochina. The United States was to lose more than 58,000, as it repeated the mistakes of the French (and was later to repeat the mistakes of the Soviets in Afghanistan), and gradually itself became involved in conflict with the Vietnamese guerrillas, who were now called "Vietcong."

To provide a veneer of international backing, the United States engineered the creation of a new international organization in September of 1954, the Southeast Asia Treaty Organization (SEATO). A largely ineffectual organization, it was dissolved in 1977. American intervention was presumably the justification for the Treaty, but once created, the Treaty was then used to justify American intervention. A protocol of the treaty expressly included under its collective self-defense provision the "territory under the jurisdiction of the State of Vietnam." Much of the aim was to curb Chinese communist influence in Southeast Asia. Indeed, as the war unfolded, there was a perceived growing risk of war with China. It was even reported that some analysts warned that if escalation of the war by the United States continued, the two nations might be within months of "a direct clash."[25] The concern was not altogether groundless. Minister of Defense of Communist China Lin Piao had indeed issued a new declaration of military doctrine, reportedly saying that China supported revolutionary wars in underdeveloped countries as part of a strategy to encircle the United States and Western Europe, and that the

---

[23] *The Pentagon Papers*, p. 25. Interestingly, Neil Sheehan credits the de facto creation of South Vietnam to US CIA agent, Edward Lansdale, in his role between 1954 and 1955. He writes: "South Vietnam, it can truly be said, was the creation of Edward Lansdale" (*A Bright Shining Lie*, p. 138).

[24] The Domino Theory, though not called such by name, was set forth even earlier in a policy statement by the National Security council in 1952, which wrote: "The loss of any of the countries of Southeast Asia to communist aggression would have critical psychological, political and economic consequences. In the absence of effective and timely counteraction, the loss of any single country would probably lead to relatively swift submission to or an alignment with communism by the remaining countries of this group. Furthermore, an alignment with communism of the rest of Southeast Asia and India, and in the longer term, of the Middle East … would in all probability progressively follow: Such widespread alignment would endanger the stability and security of Europe" (*1952 Policy Statement by U.S. on Goals in Southeast Asia, Pentagon Papers*, p. 27). The Domino Theory arguably originated, though not by name, with the Truman administration in 1946. See Betty Glad and Charles S. Taber, "Images, Learning, and the Decision to Use Force: The Domino Theory of the United States," in Betty Glad (ed.), *Psychological Dimensions of War* (Newbury Park, CA: Sage Publications, 1990), pp. 56–82. Mark Moyar, a defender of the Domino Theory, also sees it originating with the Truman administration. See *Triumph Forsaken*, p. 426, n. 54.

[25] *The New York Times*, "Some U.S. Aides See Risk of Direct Clash with China," December 3, 1965.

focus of the struggle was now Vietnam.[26] The Chinese protested that US planes had intruded on Chinese airspace and shot down a Chinese plane on a training mission.[27] Soon thereafter, Premier Ngyuen Cao Ky of South Vietnam "called for an armed confrontation with communist China now rather than later."[28] Such a confrontation was avoided, and there is evidence neither China nor the United States wanted it. But in the course of trying to establish a showcase of democracy in South Vietnam, we sought to vanquish one of the stronger non-Chinese (if communist) regimes of that area in Hanoi, and in the course of pursuing that end brought about the opposite of what we wanted, increasing dependence upon China for support. Fear of communism led us to overlook both the nationalism of the Vietnamese communists (both in Hanoi and in the South) and a deep-rooted history of antagonism toward China on the part of Vietnamese generally. That antagonism sprang from nearly 1,000 years of Chinese domination of Vietnam (207 BC to AD 929) and the occupation of northern Vietnam by Chinese nationalist troops for a year following WWII.[29] It also overlooked the betrayal of the Vietminh at the time of the Geneva Accords[30] and tensions between the northerners in Vietnam and the indigenous peoples of the South, with whom the action against the Saigon regime began. The tensions were reported as North Vietnamese troops infiltrated to the South and began taking part in the fighting.[31] Even India, which by all odds has a greater stake in Asia than the United States, and just possibly a more realistic perspective on the problems of Asians, was said to welcome a strong communist but neutral Vietnam along the lines of Yugoslavia.[32]

8.4 Beginning of the Vietnam War

What came to be known as the Vietnam War was thus basically a continuation of the Indochina War, as later the Iraq War was to be basically a continuation of the Gulf War. The brief pause following the collapse of French colonial rule was soon followed by gradually escalating guerilla warfare against the US-backed regime in Saigon.[33] There

---

[26] *The New York Times*, "Peking Declares Vietnam Is Focus of Anti-U.S. Fight," September 3, 1965. The declaration may have been meant for Soviet consumption as much as anything else, as it occurred during a growing rift between the Soviets and Red China, with the Soviets adhering to the classical Marxist-Leninist view that revolution must begin with the proletariat and the Chinese revisionists arguing, with Mao, that it must begin with the peasantry. This is the analysis proposed by Seymour Topping in this *New York Times* report.

[27] "Washington Hints at Possibility U.S. Jets Have Been Over China," *The New York Times*, May 27, 1966.

[28] *The New York Times*, July 26, 1966.

[29] Nuon Chea, defendant in a trial on charges of genocide, war crimes and crimes against humanity, in his role as a member of the Khmer Rouge in Cambodia, alleged that the actions the Khmer Rouge took were to prevent a takeover of Cambodia by Vietnamese Communists after the Vietnam War and the extermination of ethnic Cambodians by them. "We didn't kill many," he continued. "We only killed the bad people, not the good" (*The New York Times*, November 23, 2011).

[30] See Karnow, *Vietnam: A History*, pp. 214–221.

[31] *The New York Times*, "Hanoi's Troop Infiltration Said to Trouble Vietcong," May 2, 1966

[32] *Christian Science Monitor*, February 19, 1966.

[33] President Nixon in an October 7, 1970, address spoke of the war as having become an Indochina War, but for different reasons. He cited the North Vietnamese troops in both Laos and Cambodia

had, however, been attempts to unseat the Diem government before guerrilla warfare began. Although he ruled at the sufferance of the United States, Diem was not a puppet and frequently resisted US pressures for reform. Repression by the Diem regime soon sparked armed resistance from both Cao Dai and Hoa Hao, noncommunist religious sects, as well as from the Binh-Xuyen, a nondescript organization of criminal elements, who formed A Unified Front of National Forces.[34] Civil war broke out on March 31, 1955, with an attack on Diem's palace. It concluded on June 30, 1955, with the defeat of the sects, an estimated 2,000 of whom joined the Vietcong in the Mekong.[35] Bernard Fall wrote that with the March 31 attack: "The final battle for the control of South Viet-Nam, and hence, for all of Viet-Nam south of the 17th parallel, had begun."[36]

In addition, South Vietnamese military pilots bombed the Presidential Palace in February of 1962, more than a year and a half prior to Diem's assassination at the hands of other anticommunist South Vietnamese military. Buddhists, led by the monk Tri Quang, also opposed what they perceived as oppression by the Saigon government. The successful plot by South Vietnamese military to remove Diem was well known, and indeed encouraged by some in the US government, though there was strong disagreement among administration officials as to whether it was advisable. Kennedy, who was himself to be assassinated soon after the November 1, 1963, coup against Diem, was reportedly shocked to learn that Diem had been killed in the coup. In any event, it is worth noting that the initial uprisings against the US-backed Diem regime were not from communists, but from Buddhists, military officers and small religious sects.

It is disputed precisely when the Vietcong, as the Vietminh were now called, began armed hostilities against the Diem regime. They likely began in the late 1950s, possibly as early as 1957, in the Mekong Delta where 45 percent of the South Vietnamese population lived.[37] An estimated 8,000 to 10,000 native southerners were reportedly left behind to engage in political organizing when Vietminh troops withdrew to north of the 17th parallel. Others eventually began filtering back to locales in the South from which they came.

The southerners who returned to the South were reportedly at first under strict orders from Hanoi to confine themselves to political organizing and garnering support from the peasants and not to engage in violent hostilities. The expectation was that the

(through which the Ho Chi Minh Trail ran), saying that represented North Vietnamese aggression against those countries as well as against South Vietnam, and belied any suggestion that the Vietnam War was a civil war (*The New York Times* February 26, 1971). Nixon had ordered the secret bombing of Cambodia followed by US-sponsored raids by the South Vietnamese to disrupt sanctuaries the Vietcong and North Vietnamese had developed there.

[34] Bernard B. Fall describes the Cao Dai as a spiritualist blend of Buddhism and Catholicism, the Hoa Hao as a kind of "Buddhist Protestantism," that rejected the extrinsic trappings of religion and extolled a simplicity of faith that disavowed gambling, alcohol and drugs. The Binh Xuyen he describes as having no specific religious or political program, though it came to exert both political and military power in Saigon and the vicinity. See chapter 11, "Religion in Politics," in *Vietnam Witness: 1953–66* (New York: Frederick A. Praeger, 1966) on which I have relied for this account.

[35] Karnow, *Vietnam: A History*, p. 239.

[36] Fall, *Vietnam Witness: 1953–66*, p. 158.

[37] Stanley Karnow contends that in October of 1957 Hanoi instructed the communists in the South to organize armed companies but that until 1959 Ho Chi Minh discouraged them from engaging in armed conflict. *Vietnam: A History*, p. 253f.

country would soon be unified under Ho Chi Minh following the elections mandated by the Geneva Accords. The southerners reportedly became impatient with this restriction in the face of the increasingly repressive Diem regime, and an organization calling itself Veterans of the Resistance issued a declaration in March 1960 calling for taking up arms in self-defense against the Saigon government. Soon thereafter, in December 1960, under Hanoi's direction, The National Liberation Front (NLF) came into existence in what was then Cochin, the Mekong Delta region of the South.[38] According to the Vietcong, that phase of the war began in early 1960 with an attack on a fortress at Tua Hai in Tay Ninh Province. Prior to that, according to a regimental commander in the NLF, a strict "line" had been observed.

> As for the "line," this was set by our leadership the moment the Geneva Ceasefire Agreements were signed for the whole of Vietnam. Absolute strict respect for the Geneva Agreements was spelt out into detailed instructions to observe discipline; not to go beyond the bounds of legal, political struggle. We are revolutionaries. That was an instruction which our sense of revolutionary discipline does not permit us to violate. It cost us the lives of many of the finest of our comrades in the period 1954–59. We are used to having a "line" set for a considerable period. In the first resistance war, it sometimes took a whole year just to get the "line" communicated to all regions . . . And in the conditions under which we worked then, and to a lesser extent now, we were used to working in isolated, autonomous groups, making our own decisions for months, years on end, but always within the framework of the "line." That line was non-violence till towards the end of 1959, and "violence for self-defense" after that.[39]

The issue confronting the Vietcong who attacked Tua Hai in early 1960 was whether the attack could legitimately be called self-defense. With the same ingenuity that heads of government show in stretching the notion of self-defense to fit their purposes, they reportedly decided that "even for self-defense we had to have weapons; that our proposed attack was in fact a 'self-defense' action to get arms and was not a formal violation of the 'line.'"

Some date the start of the war much sooner. Vo Ngyuen Giap, the leader of the North Vietnamese forces, reportedly dates it from December 20, 1946, the time when Ho called for a national resistance war against the French, who had recently bombed and occupied Haiphong.[40] The United States had trained and equipped the South Vietnamese army since 1954. In any event, major escalation of US involvement occurred when President Kennedy sent a secret letter to President Diem in May of

---

[38] These dates are provided by Philippe Devillers, "Ngo Dinh Diem and the Struggle for Reunification In Vietnam," published originally as "The Struggle for Unification of Vietnam," *The China Quarterly* [London], No. 9, January-March, 1962, pp. 2–23, republished in Marvin E. Gettleman, ed., *Vietnam: History, Documents, and Opinions on a Major World Crisis*, pp. 210–235.

[39] As reported by Wilfred G. Burchett, *Vietnam: Inside Story of the Guerilla War* (New York: International Publishers, 1965), pp. 113f. Burchett, an Australian war correspondent sympathetic to the Vietcong, had access to sources US correspondents did not. As Burchett was reportedly a communist, his reporting was largely ignored by the US media.

[40] As reported by Maclear, *The Thousand Day War*, p. 27.

1961, via Vice President Johnson, offering more financial aid and military advisers.[41] President Johnson for his part made a secret decision on February 19, 1965, to commence Operation Thunder, a bombing campaign against North Vietnam. The bombing, in the words of former secretary of defense Robert McNamara, "would continue for three years and drop more bombs on Vietnam than had been dropped on all of Europe in World War II."[42] The stage was set for the American ground war with the landing of Marines at Da Nang on March 8, 1965, supposedly solely to defend the US air base at Da Nang, which was used for bombing attacks on North Vietnam. It was announced by Secretary of State Dean Rusk that the troops were not slated for combat and would fire only in self- defense, but President Johnson shortly thereafter issued a secret advisory that they would engage in combat.[43]

Thus, what was a initially a war for independence from French colonial rule led to a civil war between the Saigon government and relatively small sects, later to a larger civil war against the Vietcong and still later to an even larger war against the Vietcong and North Vietnamese.

8.5 External aggression or civil war?

However one dates the start of the conflict, the US government had a major stake in defining its character. Secretary of State Rusk stated on April 23, 1965, "Were the insurgency in South Vietnam truly indigenous and self-sustained, international law would not be involved." And Undersecretary of State George W. Ball said in a January 1966 address: "[I]f the Viet-Nam war were merely what the Communists say it is—an indigenous rebellion—then the United States would have no business taking sides in the conflict and helping one side to defeat the other by force of arms." However he went on to argue that the "Front [i.e., National Liberation Front] . . . is unmistakably what its name implies—a Communist front organization created to mask the activities of Hanoi and to further the illusion of an indigenous revolt."[44]

Prior to 1965 the Vietcong were largely self-sustained. Although receiving assistance from the north, a major portion of their arms and equipment were of US origin, captured from Saigon troops. The attack on Tua Hai in 1960, referred to above, was reportedly mainly to obtain arms. Indeed—though the story may well have been embellished—the Vietcong in that area possessed only one rifle, an old American rifle which they called Mother Carbine. Through an elaborate set of deceptions they led the defenders of the fortress to believe that they were heavily outnumbered by well-armed insurgents. This led them to surrender and placed in the hands of the Vietcong more weapons than they could carry away.[45] The typical Vietcong, as indicated earlier, had fought against the French, withdrawn to the North in compliance with the Geneva

---

[41] As reported by *Time*, May 19, 1961.
[42] McNamara, *In Retrospect*, p. 174.
[43] I am here following Maclear's account, *The Thousand Day War*. See especially pp. 151, 155.
[44] George W. Ball, "The Issue in Viet-Nam," *Department of State Publication 8043*, Far Eastern Series 141, March 1966, pp. 9f, 14f.
[45] Burchett, *Vietnam: Inside Story of the Guerilla War*, chapter 8.

Accords and returned to his homeland after the Diem regime ignored the Accords. In the Mekong Delta, where the insurrection largely originated, only indigenous South Vietnamese were fighting as late as the end of 1966.[46]

Regular North Vietnamese Army (NVA) troops came to assume a large role in the fighting in the South. Whether their presence constituted morally and legally unwarranted intervention in the affairs of another state depends upon the circumstances of their entry.

Prior to 1964 virtually all of the Vietcong were native southerners.[47] By 1965 a small number of native northerners had also entered the South, though as late as April 27, 1965, the chief evidence of the presence of NVA regulars was the alleged testimony of a single defector.[48] Stanley Karnow reports, however, based on a postwar interview with former North Vietnamese Colonel Bui Tin after the war, that North Vietnamese troops began moving south in mid-1964, and the first complete tactical units began moving South before the end of 1964.[49] Not until October of 1965 did the NVA assume a significant fighting role.[50]

According to a National Security Action Memorandum 328 of April 6, 1965, President Johnson had on April 1, 1965, approved a change of mission for all Marine battalions deployed to Vietnam, permitting a "more active" role. What a more active role meant was not spelled out. But that it was a change of mission was to be kept secret. "The President desires," the memorandum said, "with respect to the actions in paragraphs 5 though 7 [increasing the number of US military troops and authorizing the more active role], premature publicity be avoided by all possible precautions . . .The President's desire is that these movements and changes should be understood as being gradual and wholly consistent with existing policy." When a State Department press officer said on June 8 that US troops would be available for combat along with South Vietnamese forces[51] as necessary, the White House issued a statement on June

---

[46] *Christian Science Monitor*, December 15, 1966.

[47] As reported by George McTurnan Kahin and John W. Lewis, "The United States in Vietnam," *Bulletin of the Atomic Scientists*, June 1965. This article was later expanded into their 1967 book by the same title, published by Delta, by arrangement with Dial Press.

[48] There were reports of a regiment of the North Vietnamese 325th division in February 1965 (*Pentagon Papers*, 409). Robert McNamara reports that on April 6, 1965, the CIA informed President Johnson that North Vietnamese regulars had infiltrated into the Central Highlands and the area near Da Nang (*In Retrospect*, p. 182).

[49] Karnow, *Vietnam: A History*, p. 346. Bernard Fall, however, citing the deceptions used by the Vietcong to create the impression that their numbers were larger than they were, writes: "The 'off-again-on-again' Northern 325th Division may well be an example of such totally unorthodox and highly unfair camouflage tactics. For all anyone knows, only a few small segments of that ten-battalion force may have been 'in country,' as one says in Saigon. As of the time I left [early October 1965] ... no intelligence officer was ready to swear that the 325th as a unit had joined the battle in South Viet-Nam" (*Vietnam Witness*, p. 296). Both accounts could be substantially correct. Northern troops reportedly began moving south in April 1964, but complete tactical units not until near the end of the year. Thus it could be true that some North Vietnamese soldiers were engaging with ARVN (the South Vietnamese army) before the arrival of US Marines in March of 1965, but also true that no major conflict with complete North Vietnamese units occurred until October of 1965. But the marines engaged in battle against the Vietcong on August 18, 1965. See Jennings, *The Politically Incorrect Guide to the Vietnam War*, pp. 72f.

[50] *The New York Times*, October 26, 1966.

[51] Known as the Army of the Republic of Vietnam (ARVN).

9 presuming to clarify matters. It said: "There has been no change in the mission of United States ground combat units in Vietnam." However, it also said: "If help is requested by the appropriate Vietnamese commander, General Westmoreland also has authority within the assigned mission to employ those troops in support of Vietnamese forces faced with aggressive attack when other effective reserves are not available and when, in his judgment, the general military situation urgently requires."[52] The Joint Chiefs of Staff, in response to a recommendation from Westmoreland, ordered the deployment to Vietnam of the 173rd Airborne Brigade from Okinawa, and the Brigade became involved in the first major ground action by the United States from June 27 to June 30. According to the *Pentagon Papers*: "The operation could by no stretch of definition have been described as a reserve reaction. . . It was a search and destroy operation into Vietcong base areas."[53]

For the first seven years of the war, therefore, the fighting on the revolutionary side was by native South Vietnamese.[54] A small minority of northerners participated after 1963, and only in the fall of 1965, long after US troops had entered Vietnam as covert operatives, advisors and combat troops, and some nine months after direct US air attacks upon North Vietnam, was a clearly verifiable fighting role credited to regular North Vietnamese troops.

The question of timing aside, did the entry of northerners into the South even at that late date constitute external aggression? Not if external aggression means violating international boundaries. According to the Geneva Accords there was but one Vietnam, not two. Article 1 of the Accords designates the 17th parallel as a "provisional military demarcation line," and Article 6 of the Final Declaration asserts that this line "should not in any way be interpreted as constituting a political or territorial boundary."[55] If so, the taking up of arms by Vietnamese against Vietnamese—from whatever geographical location within the country and whatever the rights or wrongs of their having done so—cannot have violated international boundaries, because there were no such boundaries within Vietnam itself. The war was a civil war and US involvement was intervention.

[52] *Pentagon Papers*, p. 411. Walt Rostow challenged the coverage of the *Pentagon Papers* by the *New York Times*, charging that it was "as serious a misuse of the power of the press as I've seen in my time." Among alleged factual errors, Rostow said was the claim that the decision to give US troops a combat role was made on April 1, 1965, but kept from the public until announced in July 1965. The decision, Rostow claims, was made just before it was announced on July 28, 1965 (*Chicago Tribune*, July 12, 1971). That claim is at variance with Robert McNamara, however, who writes: "We met at the White House on April 1 [1965]. Dean, Mac, and I questioned the wisdom of the chiefs' proposal … The president accepted our judgment. He deferred the chiefs' proposal but agree to Westy's and Oley's two-battalion request and, much more important, agreed to change the marines' mission from base security to active combat … American ground forces would now directly enter the war." McNamara, *In Retrospect: The Tragedy and Lessons of Vietnam*, p. 179.

[53] *Pentagon Papers*, p. 411.

[54] I am assuming here, with Bernard Fall, that the second phase of the Indochina War began in 1956. Fall writes that within a few months after the deadline had passed in 1956 for elections to reunify the country, "the killing of village chiefs in South Viet-Nam began—by stay-behind guerrillas, not the 'outside aggressors' of 1959–60 cited by the recent State Department white paper. By the time the South Viet–Nam problem had become a military challenge to the United States late in 1961, the Second Indochina War had been under way for almost five years" (*Vietnam Witness 1953–66*, p. 78).

[55] This understanding was reaffirmed by The Paris Peace Accords, Chapter V, Article 15, 1973, ending the US combat role in Vietnam

Various US goals were claimed for the Vietnam War, as they were later for the wars in Afghanistan and Iraq, but among them was to return to the Geneva Accords and to ensure an independent, democratic South Vietnam—goals which obviously were inconsistent, since the Accords made no provision for an independent South Vietnam and expressly stated that the 17th parallel was only a provisional demarcation line. Equally as important, the regime we established in Saigon under Diem was repressive and no match for the Vietcong. Columnist Joseph Alsop wrote in 1954, after visiting Vietnam:

> The thing that impressed me most . . . was not the Communists' extraordinary feat of organizing, maintaining and expanding an independent state in southern Indochina without exterior support, and in the teeth of French power. What impressed me most, alas, was the moral fervor they had inspired among the non-Communist Vietminh cadres and the stout support they had obtained from the peasantry.[56]

The United States supported successive Saigon governments that systematically destroyed organizations capable of exerting counterinfluence to the NLF political organization. In this, the United States, which prided itself on not repeating the military mistakes of the French, repeated the worst of their political mistakes. The French in 1930 destroyed the Vietnamese Nationalist Party and thereby left the Vietnamese communists virtually the whole political field in opposing colonialism. By sustaining a puppet government and destroying the noncommunist Vietnamese National Party, they deprived the southern zone of effective political leadership following their departure after 1954.

After his installation in 1954, Diem, the "Churchill of the decade" as he was called by Vice President Lyndon Johnson,[57] repressed communist and noncommunist opposition alike. The repression continued with succeeding Saigon governments. It not only tried to crush the political power of militant Buddhists, it also attempted to destroy the power of the noncommunist Unified Front for the Struggle of the Oppressed Races, an organization of Montagnard mountain tribesmen, an ethnic minority of 700,000 within South Vietnam which had been seeking independence from the Saigon government since 1957. Despite their disdain for the Saigon government, Montagnards fought alongside US soldiers against the North Vietnamese and led a brief rebellion against Hanoi after the war's end.[58] General Ky, whose candor often embarrassed the United States, conceded that the communists were closer to the people's yearnings for social justice and an independent national life than his own government.[59] David

---

[56] Joseph Alsop, *Herald Tribune*, August 31, 1954.
[57] *Time*, May 19, 1961. Johnson made the remark on the occasion of his delivery to Ngo Dinh Diem of President Kennedy's secret letter of support for his administration. Asked on the plane home by correspondent Stanley Karnow whether he really meant the comparison with Churchill, Johnson reportedly said, "Shit, Diem's the only boy we got out there." See Karnow, *Vietnam: A History*, p. 230.
[58] Montagnards in the United States have protested Vietnamese expansion of coffee plantations into their ancestral lands and, along with members of Cao Dai and Hoa Hao, have protested the lack of religious freedom in their former homeland, *The New York Times*, May 5, 2001.
[59] As reported by columnist James Reston, *The New York Times*, September 1, 1965.

Halberstam, Pulitzer prize–winning reporter for the *New York Times* wrote in 1963 that under Diem

> South Vietnam became, for all intents and purposes, a Communist-type coun-
> try without communism. It had all the controls, all the oppressions and all the
> frustrating, grim aspects of the modern totalitarian state—without the dynamism,
> efficiency and motivation that Communism had brought to the North.[60]

It should not be thought that North Vietnam was not repressive, as well. The regime launched a brutal collectivization campaign, which even the North Vietnamese government leaders came to acknowledge was a "mistake." The precise figures are contested, but it claimed thousands, and perhaps tens of thousands of lives. Opposition to the government was also brutally quashed, through terrorism and execution.[61]

Despite what was happening before their eyes at the hands of the Saigon government, US officials continued in their optimism, typified by Secretary of State Dean Rusk's statement in 1967 that "the South Vietnamese have come through with what really ought to be considered almost a miracle in politics."[62] The United States created a few showplaces to which visiting Americans were carefully guided. The politician who spent two weeks in Vietnam came away, not only an "expert" but an optimistic one as well. Military successes were frequent enough, promises of social reform sufficiently regular, and the turnover of personnel sufficiently rapid to keep alive a misplaced confidence. Even after we lost the war it was claimed we never lost a battle. But what began as ebullient hope for a showcase of democracy under the Churchill of the decade became wishful thinking for a miracle under a succession of self-aggrandizing generals. Eventually, amid rising casualties and domestic opposition at home, the United States, which had Americanized the war in 1965, promoted Vietnamization as a way to ease itself out, and exited Vietnam on March 29, 1973. The South Vietnamese government, now abandoned, and its leaders having fled to the United States,[63] was itself defeated by the Vietcong and North Vietnamese in 1975, bringing the war to an end.

We tried to build a new nation, not from any inherent caring for the Vietnamese people, but because we thought it would help safeguard our own security against the threat of communism. It was basically our own interest, including our prestige in the world, that was thought to be at stake. But by rending the fabric of Vietnamese society in the process we destroyed the conditions under which attainment of our goal was possible. People attached to their land and ancestral burial grounds were forcibly dislocated, creating poorly fed, ill-clothed and largely unemployed refugees by tens of thousands; profiteering and prostitution became the means of survival for increasing

---

[60] David Halberstam, *The Making of a Quagmire* (New York: Random House, 1964), p. 52.
[61] See Karnow, *Vietnam: A History*, pp. 240f. and Moyar, *Triumph Forsaken*, pp. 62f.
[62] Transcript of news conference, *The New York Times*, October 13, 1967.
[63] Referring here to Generals Nguyen Cao Ky, who fled to the United States, and Nguyen Van Thieu who fled to London and eventually settled in the United States. Thieu, in announcing his resig- nation as president, blamed the United States for South Vietnam's defeat, reportedly saying: "The United States has not respected its promises. It is inhumane. It is not trustworthy," as quoted in Appy, *American Reckoning*, p. 224.

numbers; a gentle people with pacifist tendencies were made warlike. Having supposed that because a certain end—a free, independent and anticommunist South Vietnam— was desirable, we thought that virtually any means were justified in the pursuit of that end.

8.6 The nature of the war

The Vietnam War was a savage one.[64] Once it was fully underway, probably not a day passed that did not see the commission of war crimes or crimes against humanity. This no doubt owed in part to the circumstances in which it was conducted. General Maxwell Taylor had said in a cablegram to President Kennedy on November 1, 1961, in which he recommended sending an American military force into Vietnam, that "[a]s an area for the operations of U.S. troops, SVN [South Vietnam] is not an excessively difficult or unpleasant place to operate."[65] This contrasted with the accounts given by soldiers. Much of the fighting consisted of jungle warfare. Bilton and Sim describe: "The patrols meant heat, physical exhaustion, clouds of flies and mosquitoes, a growing sense of rage and frustration, and constant danger." Reportedly, "[d]eaths and injuries from booby traps, mines, and unseen snipers were four to five times higher than they had been in World War II and Korea."[66] Marine officer Philip Caputo, who was with the first combat units to land in Vietnam on March 8, 1965, describes one patrol:

> The trail was narrow and muddy—even in the dry season nothing ever dried in the bush, it only became less wet. A maze of bamboo and elephant grass twice the height of a man grew on one side of the trail, and on the other side there was the sluggish river, and, west of the river, the mountains. The saw-edged grass slashed our skin, sweat made the scratches sting, and the heat pounded against our helmets and wrung the sweat out of us as we might wring water from a sponge. There were moments when I could not think of it as heat—that is, as a condition of weather; rather, it seemed to be a thing malevolent and alive . . . It was the inability to see that vexed us most. In that lies the jungle's power to cause fear; it blinds.[67]

The Vietcong mingled with the civilian peasants, often making it difficult to distinguish combatants from noncombatants. Indeed, many of the Vietcong were peasants—farmers by day, guerrillas by night. This no doubt made some of the killing

---

[64] Whether it was more savage than other recent wars is problematic. Michael Lind, in defending the Vietnam War, contends: "Individual acts of murder, rape, and looting have been committed by U.S. troops in every American war. The claim that the infamous massacre of hundreds of unarmed civilians on March 16, 1968, at My Lai indicated that American soldiers and units were more likely to engage in atrocities in Vietnam than American soldiers in previous wars was an illusion, produced by the relative absence of censorship during the Vietnam War." See Lind, *Vietnam: The Necessary War*, p. 246.

[65] *The Pentagon Papers*, p. 142. Taylor was recommending sending US troops into Vietnam.

[66] Reported in Michael Bilton and Kevin Sim, *Four Hours in My Lai* (New York: Penguin Books, 1993), p. 39.

[67] Philip Caputo, *A Rumor of War* (New York: Picador, 1996), p. 85.

of civilians accidental. But much of the gratuitous killing, whether of prisoners, suspects or civilians, was deliberate. According to numerous accounts, the South Vietnamese regularly killed prisoners. The most notorious of these was caught on film in 1968, when General Nguyen Ngoc Loan, the South Vietnamese police chief, shot a handcuffed Vietcong suspect in the head with his handgun.[68] Many prisoners were tortured. One American advisor made a list in his diary of the methods of torture used by one South Vietnamese Captain Thuong of a Ranger unit:

1. Wrap in barbed wire.
2. Strip skin off back.
3. Rack by use of vehicle or water buffalo.
4. Head in mud—1 1/2 minute.
5. Shoot thru ear.
6. Hook up to EE8. [EE8 was the designation of the American supplied battery-powered field telephone. The common method was to tape the ends of two wires from the phone to the genitals of a man or to a woman's vagina and a breast. Shock was then administered as desired by turning the crank handle on the phone.]
7. Sit on entrenching tool. [The entrenching tool was the folding pack shovel the US Army supplied the ARVN for use in digging foxholes. The shovel blade was thrust firmly into the ground. The prisoner was stripped of his pants and made to sit on top of the end of the shovel handle. He was then forced down on the handle.]
8. Knife strapped to back. [Thuong would tie the prisoner's hands behind his back and lash the Bowie knife to the wrists with the blade pointing inward toward the back. He would have the prisoner hauled up against a tree, place his hand on the victim's chest, and start pressing as he asked questions.]
9. Water treatment. [Water was forced into the mouth until the stomach swelled painfully, when it was beaten to induce more pain, or a wet rag was held over the nostrils while water war poured down the throat to create the sensation of suffocating.]
10. Calves beaten.
11. Knee in back, face down, dislocate shoulders.
12. Beat stomach until it collapses and indiv. Vomits it out.

In a specific incident, witnessed by two American soldiers, Ziegler and Vann:

> Thuong lined up the prisoners, unsheathed his Bowie knife . . . He walked back and forth in front of his captives, speaking quietly to them, telling them that he wanted the truth and that he would not tolerate anyone lying to him, holding the Bowie knife in his hand, flicking the big blade in the air with a snap of his wrist. All of a sudden his dark arm shot forward. He snatched a young farmer by the hair, jerked

---

[68] The execution of the prisoner by Gen. Nguyen Ngoc Loan was clearly a war crime, but charges were never brought against him, and he eventually fled to the United States, where he died in 1998.

the man's head back, and slashed with the bowie knife. Then he resumed walking back and forth, talking softly again about telling the truth and not lying while the guerrilla who had lost to Thuong's whimsy writhed on the ground, clutching at his throat, kicking away the last spasms of his life . . . "That's his way of interrogating," Ziegler replied, shuddering as Thuong cut another throat . . . Thuong quickly slit a third throat to show that he was not intimidated by Vann's screaming.[69]

The Vietcong did their share of gratuitous killing, though they tended to be more selective, for the most part killing village leaders believed to be collaborating with the Saigon government. As far back as the first Indochina War, the French, when besieged at Dien Bien Phu, knew that the Vietminh did not massacre prisoners.[70] And when Australian journalist Wilfred G. Burchett interviewed four American soldiers being held captive by the Vietcong, he quotes them as saying that they had been well-treated and expressing surprise that they had not been killed.[71] This is at variance with the treatment of American pilots shot down over North Vietnam, who report being tortured as POWs. Neil Sheehan reports of an American civilian AID worker taken captive by the Vietcong, who was not only spared, but protected from attack by angry peasants whose village had just been destroyed by the South Vietnamese Army.[72] American prisoners were high value, of course, and South Vietnamese supporters of the Saigon government were not accorded the same treatment. The bodies of nearly 3,000 South Vietnamese executed by the North Vietnamese were excavated near Hué.

The Vietcong killing of noncombatants has been described as "selective terror," the killing of those suspected of collaborating with the Saigon government, often as a public act in front of the other villagers. A South Vietnamese girl who became a Vietcong supporter, reports on the killing of her teacher, a supporter of the Saigon government:

> Without a sound, a half-dozen strangers entered into Manh's house and then shouted "nobody move!" . . . Manh was the last one out, led at gunpoint with his hands atop his head. I could hear this familiar voice arguing with the strangers: "But—I don't know what you're talking about!" and "Why? Who told you that?" . . . Suddenly one of the strangers barked an order in an odd, clipped accent (I found out later this was how everyone talked in the North) and two of his *comrades* prodded Manh to the edge of the road. I could still hear Manh begging for his life when two rifle shots cut

---

[69] Neil Sheehan, *A Bright Shining Lie*, pp. 102–105.

[70] Bernard Fall reports that some of the Foreign Legionnaires cried, "not for fear of their fate, for it was known by then that the Communists did not massacre prisoners, but out of shame that they would have to surrender to the enemy." *Hell in a Very Small Place: The Siege of Dien Bien Phu* (Philadelphia, PA: J.B. Lippincott, 1966), p. 398.

[71] Burchett, *Vietnam: Inside Story of the Guerilla War*, pp. 101–112.

[72] Sheehan writes that "[a] number of the farmers from the hamlet had gathered around and were demanding the right to kill him. The four guerrillas stopped them. They quoted the National Liberation Front's announced policy of 'lenient and humane' treatment for prisoners. Ramsey sensed that they wanted to protect their prize, but they also seemed to be conscientious men who took seriously the preaching of their movement." Sheen, *A Bright Shining Lie*, pp. 561f.

him short. The strangers then ran a Viet Cong flag up the pole that stood outside our schoolhouse and left as quickly as they had come.[73]

The teacher was perhaps fortunate to be shot. Some village leaders were disemboweled. Although most people tend to distinguish between terrorism and warfare, terrorism is an important part of warfare. If the bodies of American casualties could not be retrieved during the day, the Vietcong allegedly would crawl out at night, cut the heads off, then place them on stakes to be seen by American troops during the day. Army veteran, John Ketwig, reports on the case of a Green Beret whose head was found with his genitals in his mouth after he had visited a brothel. The rest of him was missing. Three prostitutes, who were suspected of complicity in his killing, were interrogated at a Green Beret firebase. Ketwig witnessed the first killing:

He [the ARVN officer] nodded to two of the Americans [Green Berets]. They pulled the girl to her feet, tore her silken blouse open, removed her gaudy brassier. Their giant hands closed on her upper arms. The ARVN dragged at his cigarette, stepped forward, and pushed the cherry tip to her nipple. I couldn't believe I was watching this . . . The girl was on her back now, and naked. Her bound wrists were over her head, held by a swarthy GI . . . There was a flurry of activity. I jumped at the sound of the starter as it brought the fire truck to life . . . The girl's legs were held apart. A burly black man stood over her, screaming. "Where Timmy? Where da resta Timmy? Cunt! Whore! You gonna die, oh, you gonna die bad, Mama-san! . . . Everyone gathered round, moving closer to watch the fun. It was obvious the mood was rising toward a crescendo. The girl lay still, impassive . . . The huge hose was brought into the circle . . . She closed her eyes, shuddered a little. The tarnished brass nozzle was force between her legs, forced against the resilient folds of flesh. Her eyes started open. A scream started from her throat, a sound unlike any other! Red and pink and brown and white and green, a torrent of mixed flesh and high pressure steam knocked the intimate circles back. The white flood of water died away, the lifeless hose was discarded.[74]

A US officer who had commented upon the gloomy prospects of success in operations in the delta area was asked what the answer was.

"Terror," he said pleasantly. "The Vietcong have terrorized the peasants to get their cooperation . . .We must terrorize the villagers even more, so they see that their real self-interest lies with us. We've got to start bombing and strafing the villages that aren't friendly to the Government." He then added, "Of course we won't do it. That's not our way of doing things . . . But terror is what it takes."[75]

[73] "A South Vietnamese Peasant Girl Becomes a Vietcong Supporter (ca. 1961), in Robert J. McMahon, ed., *Major Problems in the History of the Vietnam War: Documents and Essays*, 4th ed. (Boston, MA: Wadsworth Cengage Learning, 2008), pp. 284f. It would appear from this account that at least one of the Vietcong was from the North.

[74] John Ketwig, *...and a hard rain fell: A GI's True Story of the War in Vietnam* (Naperville, IL: Sourcebooks, 2008), pp. 86–88.

[75] Jack Langguth, *The New York Times Magazine*, September 19, 1965.

But terror did come to characterize American actions, whether conceptualized as such or not. It was reported soon after:

> U.S. and allied forces are adopting a program of destroying homes and crops in areas which feed and shield the communist forces. For years, Americans have refused to participate in "scorched earth" efforts, leaving them to the Vietnamese. Now Americans are directly involved.[76]

Washington Post correspondent John T. Wheeler reported on one such operation on March 30, 1967:

> The Vietnamese woman ignored the crying baby in her arms. She stared in hatred as the American infantrymen with shotguns blasted away at chickens and ducks. Others shot a water buffalo and the family dog. While her husband, father and young son were led away, the torch was put to the hut that still contained the family belongings. The flames consumed everything—including the shrine to the family ancestors. The GIs didn't have much stomach for the job, but orders were orders . . . " God, my wife would faint if she could see what I'm doing now," an infantryman said. "Killing . . [Vietcong] is one thing, but killing puppies and baby ducks and stuff like that—it's something else, man."

The US commanding general, William C. Westmoreland, said at an Associated Press luncheon, "Every possible precaution is taken to avoid casualties among civilians. Never has a nation employed its military power with such restraint . . . As an individual, this fighting man is a tough, determined professional in battle one day, and the next day, a sensitive, compassionate friend helping the Vietnamese people."[77] This no doubt was true of many, possibly even most, US troops. But it was not true of all. On March 16, 1968, Charlie Company of Task Force Barker, 11th Brigade, massacred an estimated 400–500 Vietnamese men women and children at the hamlet of My Lai in the "village" of Son My. The US soldiers had clear instructions on how to treat civilians and prisoners properly.[78] They were printed on small cards they were expected to carry. Some took this to heart, like one soldier who was quoted as saying, "Just because I was an American soldier, doesn't make them any less than I am as a human being."[79] But many did not. Part of the problem was that it was often difficult to tell who was

---

[76] *Rochester Times-Union,* January 6, 1966.

[77] *The New York Times,* April 25, 1967

[78] General Westmoreland had issued specific orders in late 1965 against the mistreatment of prisoners, which he characterized as a criminal offense. Witnesses had reported the killing of North Vietnamese prisoners by troops the First Cavalry Division, and the International Committee of the Red Cross in Geneva "had complained again that the United States was violating an international accord on the treatment of prisoners by turning them over to the South Vietnamese Army," *The New York Times,* December 1, 1965. Nonetheless, Nick Turse reports that a 1969 survey of US army officers said they "would employ torture or the threat of it to force prisoners to talk during interrogations." Nick Turse, *Kill Anything that Move: The Real American War in Vietnam* (New York: Picador, 2013), p. 31.

[79] Reported in Bilton and Sim, *Four Hours in My Lai,* p. 62. The soldier quoted was from the company involved in the My Lai massacre.

a civilian and who was a Vietcong, as the Vietcong would melt away, often into the villages. But as Bilton and Sim write in their account of the My Lai massacre: "In any case, in the combat zones, it was not just that GIs could not tell the difference between Viet Cong and innocent civilians. In many cases, they had ceased to believe in the existence of innocent civilians at all. . . Under the circumstances, what made many GIs decide to shoot quickly was a dangerous mixture of hatred, fear, revenge, and an infantryman's rule of thumb . . . American operations became laced with a generalized racial fury masked as an anticommunist crusade."[80] To the extent that some soldiers ceased to believe there were any innocent civilians, they were implicitly shifting from the distinction the JWT makes, under the criterion of discrimination for *jus in bello*, between civilians and soldiers, to that between the innocent and noninnocent; and concluding that virtually all Vietnamese, whether Vietcong fighters or civilians were noninnocent. A common view was that "[t]he only good Dink is a dead Dink!"[81] "Dink," of course, was one of the terms (along with "Gook" and "Slope") by which US soldiers commonly referred to Vietnamese. The soldier who said that was being interviewed, along with other soldiers, in the vicinity of Songmy, where the My Lai massacre had taken place earlier. Most of the GIs interviewed later doubted the massacre had taken place. But Bilton and Sim write:

> In fact it was worse than a massacre . . . Several became "double veterans," GI slang for the dubious honor of raping a woman and then murdering her. Many women were raped and sodomized, mutilated, and had their vaginas ripped open with knives or bayonets. One woman was killed when the muzzle of a rifle barrel was inserted into her vagina and the trigger was pulled. Soldiers repeatedly stabbed their victims, cut off limbs, sometimes beheaded them. Some were scalped; others had their tongues cut out or their throats slit or both. Tommy Lee Moss saw Vietnamese place their hands together and bow to greet the Americans, only to be beaten with fists and tortured, clubbed with rifles, and stabbed in the back with bayonets. Martin Fagan saw bodies which had been shot in the head at point blank range. He could tell because the penetration of an M-16 round created a shock wave inside the skull, forcing the brain completely out.[82]

A soldier was quoted as saying, regarding just having killed a woman and her baby upon first entering the village:

> I went to turn her over and there was a little baby with her that I had also killed. The baby's face was half gone. My mind just went. The training came to me and I just started killing. Old men, women, children, water buffaloes, everything. We were told to leave nothing standing. We did what we were told, regardless of whether they were civilians. They was the enemy. Period. Kill . . . I cut their throats,

---

[80] Bilton and Sim, *Four Hours in My Lai*, p. 39f.
[81] As reportedly said by an unidentified twenty-two-year-old soldier. *The New York Times*, December 1, 1969.
[82] Bilton and Sim, *Four Hours in My Lai*, p. 129.

cut off their hands, cut out their tongue, their hair, scalped them. I did it. A lot of people were doing it and I just followed . . . After I killed the child my whole mind just went. And after you start it's very easy to keep on. The hardest is to kill the first time but once you kill, then it becomes easier to kill the next person and the next one and the next one.[83]

One soldier who was accused of participating in the torture and killing of an elderly man later charged that General Westmoreland bore responsibility for whatever casualties were inflicted on civilians. His lawyer cited the precedent set by the US prosecution of General Tomoyuki Yamashita of Japan for crimes his troops committed in the Philippines during WWII, even though Yamashita was not present and was unaware of the crimes.[84] Indeed, one of Yamashita's defense council before the Military Commission (and later the Supreme Court) that convicted him wrote:

General Yamashita personally had nothing to do with any of the atrocities with which he was charged. There was no finding and there was no evidence that he had ordered or condoned them or knew about them. There was not even any charge leveled against him to this effect. The accusation . . . was simply that he commanded all troops . . . in the Philippines Islands during the last ten months of the war . . . It was as though we were now to place on trial for complicity in the My Lai massacre not a lieutenant or captain, but Gen. Creighton W. Abrams or Gen. William C. Westmoreland or perhaps, even the commander in Chief [then President Lyndon Johnson].[85]

Whatever the responsibility of the higher command, there was disagreement among the soldiers as to whether they had received explicit orders to kill and destroy everything in the village. Some claimed they had. Others claimed they had not. Some thought that the orders were not explicit but that it was conveyed implicitly what they were to do. Caputo, in ruthlessly honest account, tells of instructions he gave to several of his unit he sent to apprehend two young Vietcong suspects:

I told them what they were to do, but, in my addled state of mind, I was almost incoherent at times. I laughed frequently and made several bloodthirsty jokes that probably left them with the impression I wouldn't mind if they summarily executed both Viet Cong . . .

"Sir, since we ain't supposed to be in the ville, what do we say if we have to kill 'em?"

"We'll just say they walked into your ambush. Don't sweat that. All the higher-ups want is bodies."

"Yes, sir," Allen said, and I saw the look in his eyes. It was a look of distilled hatred and anger, and when he grinned . . . I knew he was going to kill those men on the slightest pretext. And, knowing that, I still did not repeat my order that the VC were to be captured if at all possible. It was my secret and savage desire that

[83] Bilton and Sim, *Four Hours in My Lai*, p. 130.
[84] *The New York Times*, "Sergeant Accuses Westmoreland in Songmy Case," September 10, 1970.
[85] A. Frank Reel, "Yamashita Precedent," *The New York Times*, March 31, 1971.

the two men die. In my heart, I hoped Allen would find some excuse for killing them, and Allen had read my heart. He smiled and I smiled back, and we both knew in that moment what was going to happen. There was a silent communication between us, an unspoken understanding: blood was to be shed. There is no mystery about such unspoken communication.[86]

The incident Caputo reports was in the early stages of major US combat operations in Vietnam. The events at My Lai took place on March 16, 1968, when those operations were in full swing. In any event, only one person, Lieutenant William Calley, was convicted of a war crime for his actions at My Lai. He was sentenced to life in prison in 1971 but three days later was ordered released by President Nixon pending appeal. His conviction upheld, he returned to prison, only to be pardoned in 1974.[87]

8.7 My Lai unexceptional

My Lai received media attention. But it was thought to be an aberration, a freak episode in which a company of soldiers temporarily lost their sanity. John Kerry (later to become senator and eventually secretary of state), however, detailed such atrocities before the Senate Foreign Relations Committee in April 1971. Evidence of a pattern of similar atrocities surfaced in 2003 in an investigative report by the *Toledo Blade*.[88] The report described the actions of Tiger Force, an elite platoon of the 101st Airborne Division, army unit, from May to November, 1967. "For seven months," the report stated, "Tiger Force soldiers moved across the Central Highlands, killing scores of unarmed civilians—in some cases torturing and mutilating them—in a spate of violence never revealed to the American public."[89] One veteran was quoted as saying that there were hundreds of My Lais in Vietnam.[90]

> Time and again, Tiger Force soldiers talked about the executions of captured soldiers—so many, investigators were hard pressed to place a number on the toll. In June, Pvt. Sam Ybarra slit the throat of a prisoner with a hunting knife before scalping him—placing the scalp on the end of a rifle, soldiers said in

---

[86] Caputo, *A Rumor of War*, pp. 316f.

[87] At his sentencing, Calley made a plea on his behalf that reflected some aspects of a commonly held outlook among Vietnam veterans: "If I have committed a crime, the only crime I've committed is in judgment of my values. Apparently I valued my troops' lives more than I did that of the enemy. When my troops were getting massacred and mauled by an enemy I couldn't see, I couldn't feel, and I couldn't touch—that nobody in the military system ever described them as anything other than communism. They didn't give it a race, they didn't give it a sex, they didn't give it an age … That was my enemy out there. And when it became between me and that enemy, I had to value the lives of my troops," Richard Hammer, *The Court-Martial of Lt. Calley* (New York: Coward, McCann & Geoghegan, 1971), p. 367.

[88] Documentation of extensive atrocities is provided by Nick Turse in *Kill Anything that Moves* (New York: A Metropolitan Book, 2013).

[89] http://www.toledoblade.com/special-tiger-force/2003/10/19/DAY-1-Rogue-GIs.

[90] "Brutal Vietnam Campaign Stirs Memories and Questions," *The New York Times*, December 28, 2003.

sworn statements . . . One Tiger Force soldier, Sgt. Forrest Miller, told investigators the killing of prisoners was an "unwritten law." But platoon members weren't
just executing prisoners: They began to target unarmed civilians . . . During the
Army's investigation of Tiger Force, 27 soldiers said the severing of ears from dead
Vietnamese became an accepted practice ... Platoon members strung the ears on
shoe laces to wear around their necks ... A 13-year-old girl's throat was slashed
after she was sexually assaulted, and a young mother was shot to death after soldiers torched her hut. An unarmed teenager was shot in the back after a platoon
sergeant ordered the youth to leave a village, and a baby was decapitated so that a
soldier could remove a necklace."[91]

The Army reportedly investigated the actions of Tiger Force for four and a half years,
and found that eighteen soldiers committed crimes. But there were no prosecutions.
"To this day," the article said, "the Army's Criminal Investigation Command refuses to
releases thousands of records that could explain what happened and why the case was
dropped." Nicholas Turse, commenting on the *Toledo Blade* article, and relating it to
the more recent war in Iraq, writes:

Underlying attitudes apparently haven't changed either. Captain Todd Brown, a
company commander with the Fourth Infantry Division, told the *Times* late last
year, "You have to understand the Arab mind. The only thing they understand
is force ..." Nearly 40 years earlier, in Vietnam, another U.S. captain told *The
New Yorker's* Jonathan Schell, "Only the fear of force gets results. It's the Asian
mind." That thinking has long been evident in U.S. campaigns against racial and
ethnic "others," from the Indian Wars to the Philippine-American War and occupation: the terrorizing of people in the Dominican Republic, Nicaragua, and Haiti;
on to more conventional wars against the Japanese and Koreans; and perhaps most
spectacularly in Vietnam.[92]

Much has been made of the effect of the war on surviving veterans of combat. This has
been dismissed by some.

For most of us [Vietnam veterans]—the vast majority of us—re-entering civilian life was easy. By every socio-economic measure—income, marriage success,
advanced education, psychological health, lack of drug usage, avoiding prison—
Vietnam Veterans exceed their non-military peers ... The myth that Vietnam
Veterans are racked with guilt and nightmares and angst, disproportionately prone
to violence and drug use, and unable to easily fit into society, tenaciously survives despite the fact that statistics available from hundreds of sources—veterans
groups, the VA, the Department of Defense, studies by scores of universities, and
more—utterly disprove it. So why should this myth—and it is a shameful myth,

---

[91] http://www.toledoblade.com/special-tiger-force/2003/10/19/DAY-1-Rogue-GIs.
[92] http://www.nickturse.com/articles/vietnam_voice2.html. The article was originally published as
    "The Doctrine of Atrocity" in the *Village Voice*, May 4, 2004.

besmirching a generation—survive? Well, I'd say it survives because it makes liberals feel good. If you want to believe that the Vietnam War was an immoral and unnecessary war, it's awfully convenient to say that those who fought the war were traumatized by it.[93]

Jennings speaks of Vietnam Veterans. It is unclear whether he means all veterans who served at the time of the Vietnam War, all veterans who actually served in Vietnam, or all veterans who served in Vietnam in a significant combat role. And he does not detail the evidence by the various agencies and universities to which he alludes. Despite Jennings' claims, there is ample documentation that many who served in Vietnam in a combat role suffered as a result.

Among the costs of the war are the brutalization of many American soldiers, and the legacy of PTSD. Twenty-five years after the war it was estimated that 470,000 of the soldiers who served in Southeast Asia during the war suffered PTSD.[94] The concept of "moral injury" has come to play a role in understanding their situation.[95] The concept of "moral injury" has, in fact, come to be recognized as a cause of PTSD in the wars in Iraq and Afghanistan. The Veterans Affairs found that nearly 200,000 of the veterans they treated suffered from PTSD. A study of 208 marines found that they had suffered moral injury, defined as survivor guilt or guilt at witnessing or participating in the unintentional killing of women or children.[96] This idea of moral injury is introduced by Philip Caputo: "I already regarded myself as a casualty of the war, a moral casualty, and like all serious casualties, I felt detached from everything."[97] A feeling of indifference seems to be an element in what Caputo regards as moral injury. He reports the case of one officer who shot an elderly woman at point blank range after she spit in his face accidentally while chewing betel-nut. What reportedly bothered him most afterward wasn't the fact of the killing so much as the fact that the killing didn't bother him.[98] "We had survived, but in war, a man does not have to be killed or wounded to become a casualty," Caputo writes. "His life, his sight, or limbs are not the only things he stands to lose."[99]

This chapter was headed by a US general's statement that in the Indochina War, the French did not kill enough, and that you win the war if you kill enough. Let us juxtapose this with another statement, one by a judge who overturned Calley's conviction for his role in the My Lai Massacre:

---

[93] Jennings, *The Politically Incorrect Guide to The Vietnam War*, pp. 170–171. In support of this claim, Jennings cites only John Mueller's book, *War, Presidents and Public Opinion*, published in 1973.

[94] Jon Stenzler, Knight Ridder, *Rochester Democrat and Chronicle*, April 30, 2000. The United States Department of Veterans Affairs, in a study written by Jennifer L. Price in January 1, 2007, said: "Overall, the NVVRS [National Vietnam Veterans Readjustment Study] found that at the time of the study approximately 830,000 male and female Vietnam theater Veterans (26%) had symptoms and related functional impairment associated with PTSD [Post-Traumatic Stress Disorder]." Findings From the National Vietnam Veterans Readjustment Study.

[95] On this topic, see Nancy Sherman, *After War: Healing the Moral Wounds of Our Soldiers* (Oxford: Oxford University Press, 2015).

[96] Rochester, *Democrat and Chronicle*, November 27, 2011.

[97] Caputo, *A Rumor of War*, p. 332.

[98] Caputo, *A Rumor of War*, p. 314.

[99] Caputo, *A Rumor of War*, p. 207.

Keep in mind that war is war and it is not at all unusual for innocent civilians to be numbered among its victims. It has been so throughout recorded history. It was so when Joshua took Jericho in ancient biblical times: "And they utterly destroyed all that was in the city, both man and woman, young and old … with the edge of the sword" [Joshua 6:21]. Now Joshua did not have charges brought against him for the slaughter of the civilian population of Jericho.[100]

The statements by the general and the judge are deceptively simple. Both are true. At least the first is true, as Aristotle might have said, for the most part. Its truth or falsity depends on what constitutes "enough" and what counts as winning. In genocidal war, you win if (and only if) you kill every last person you are trying to kill, because the aim is to exterminate a certain group of people. But if your aim is to subjugate a people, to enslave or dominate them, then killing them all will deny you the objective you are pursuing, hence will not count as winning. Dead people cannot be dominated. So, given certain aims of war (war$_1$), too much killing is counterproductive. In fact it guarantees failure. The killing must be calibrated, adjusted to the ends whose attainment constitutes winning. In Vietnam we could have annihilated North Vietnam in a matter of hours with nuclear bombs. It would have brought to a halt North Vietnam's support for the Vietcong. It would not, however, have stopped the infiltration of northerners into the South. Survivors—those among them who were able—would almost certainly have flooded into South Vietnam (and neighboring countries) as refugees. Moreover, depending upon the winds, the radioactive fallout would likely have affected vast areas, maybe the whole of South Vietnam, complicating the creation of the safe and stable democracy we desired. In any event, the Vietcong in the South would have remained. With support gone from the North, their strength in purely military terms would have been much diminished. And although this has to remain speculative, their discipline, political organization and support among the people might well have remained. So, the general's wisdom of war, as we might call it, contains a large measure of truth, but it is simplistic. From a conceptual standpoint—moral considerations aside—simply killing a lot of people rarely ensures winning.

That it is not unusual for innocent civilians to be killed in warfare is also true but an understatement. Insofar as we are talking about warfare in the modern age, it is, as argued in Chapter 7, a virtual certainty that innocents will be killed. Indeed, the statement by the Army regarding its investigation of a reported US massacre of civilians during the Korean War is more accurate. It said that the killings were "inherent" in war. If true, this means that not only must the deliberate killing of soldiers in warfare be morally justified, but also the killing—whether intentional or unintentional—of innocents. Simply dismissing their killings as collateral damage, or repeating over and over that you do not target civilians, is not enough. Those considerations do not constitute arguments—at least not unless they are enthymemes, in which a supposed premise is that it is permissible to kill innocents if you have not specifically targeted them, or if their killing constitutes collateral damage. The Pentagon is correct that the killing of innocents is inherent in warfare. I have said that the killing of soldiers is

---

[100] Bilton and Sim, *Four Hours in My Lai*, p. 356.

intrinsic to warfare, the killing of innocents *inherent* to warfare. It is the very essence of warfare that it kills soldiers, whereas it is only an invariable fact of warfare—meaning standard war between states—that it kills innocents. Many consider that the killing of innocents is intrinsic in this sense to terrorism, but we shall consider that in Chapter 14.

Sometimes the killing of innocents is unintentional (as, no doubt, is at least some of the killing of soldiers). But sometimes it is intentional, as it was at My Lai and before that in the terror bombings of Hiroshima and Nagasaki, and before that still in the fire-bombings of Tokyo and German cities like Dresden and even before that in the German rocket attacks on London in WWII. And it is intentional when it is done on the chance that they are actually combatants in disguise who pose a threat to you. Some of the killings of villagers in Vietnam were of that sort. If you call in a napalm strike against a village from which you think you received fire, you can know for a virtual certainty that you are killing innocents. Even if every last adult villager is a Vietcong supporter, the children are not. When US soldiers in Korea reportedly fired upon civilian refugees, they supposedly were defending themselves because they believed that North Korean soldiers were disguising themselves as civilians to penetrate US lines.[101] Here again, the notion of individual self-defense is imported into the context of war. In the Korean case, South Korea was the collectivity supposedly being defended. In Vietnam, it was South Vietnam.[102] But it was individual soldiers who were in harm's way. And it was their defense of themselves that supposedly prompted the killing they did. Much the same was true of US soldiers in Iraq when they shot and killed civilians in vehicles that failed to stop at checkpoints. The soldiers feared they were insurgents.

The deliberate nonconsensual killing of combatants is, as I have said, intrinsic to warfare. The nonconsensual killing of innocents is inherent to modern warfare. Sometimes that killing is intentional but often not. Either way, it needs moral justification. Pointing out that either type of killing is permissible because it is part of the nature of war is beside the point if the issue is whether war itself is morally justified.

8.8 Does the Vietnam War defeat the moral presumption against war?

Most analysts of the war cling to the macro perspective. Doing so leads one into the discussion of the justice or injustice of the collectivities involved or the pros and cons of US national interest, including global prestige. George Kennan, a preeminent political realist, and head of the Policy Planning Staff of the State Department at the time, gave a good statement of a realist perspective in a hearing of the Senate Foreign Relations Committee on February 10, 1966. He said that were we not already fighting

---

[101] On these issues, see Bruce Cumings, *The Korean War* (New York: The Modern Library, 2011), chap. 7. Regarding recently declassified US military documents, see http://www.bbc.co.uk/history/worldwars/coldwar/korea_usa_01/shtml. US Army investigators concluded that "American soldiers killed a substantial number of Korean refugees … but found no definitive evidence that the soldiers fired under orders," *The New York Times*, December 7, 2000.

[102]

in Vietnam, he would see no reason to become involved, but given that we were there, American prestige required that we not precipitously withdraw:

> Were it not for the considerations of prestige that arise out of our existing involvement, even a situation in which South Vietnam was controlled exclusively by the Vietcong, while regrettable and no doubt morally unwarranted, would not present, in my opinion, dangers great enough to justify our direct military intervention.[103]

By implication, Kennan is rejecting the domino theory, widely held at the time and held even today by some analysts. It is the *prestige* of the United States that is the foremost consideration in Kennan's judgment. And prestige is part of what is considered national interest. He hazards a moral judgment (regarding the Vietcong), as soft realists often do, but national prestige is the governing consideration. A rather similar assessment was given by realist Reinhold Niebuhr in a talk at Union Theological Seminary when he said that we "ought to press for a solution that guarantees an American presence in Southeast Asia, while saving face for the United States and China." He opposed a simple withdrawal, saying: "We are in too deep and what is at stake is imperial prestige."[104] Henry Kissinger, for his part, said "I have never been against the war in Vietnam," though he said that we must end it wisely and "that's very different from stating that we were right to start the war."[105]

W. W. Rostow detailed his view on the morality of the war, in a *New York Times* op-ed piece, responding to an earlier column by James Reston commenting on how seldom anyone in either the Kennedy or Johnson administrations ever questioned the moral basis of the war.[106] Accusing Reston of having unilaterally repealed the domino theory, Rostow details the moral issues in the war. All of them, however, have to do with the pursuit of national interest. The first involves dismissing pacifism, but conceding that all national policy is flawed because it sanctions war. Second, he asks whether defense of American interests is for or against the interests of those most directly affected, and implies that it is for those interests (he does not specify whether he is talking about the South Vietnamese government, the military, or the people). Third, he says it is a moral issue to minimize civilian casualties as much as possible. Fourth, he poses the question of whether "the raw power interests of the nation, in general, are decent and morally defensible in at least relative terms." He concludes that these "objectives demonstrably accord with the interests of the majority of the peoples and nations of Europe, Asia and Latin America." Fifth, he expresses the view that it is immoral for America to walk away from its treaty commitments.

If, as Rostow does, one confines oneself to the macro level, the collectivist ethics of abstract entities like states, it makes sense to ask whether the national interest of any state coincides with the national interest of any other states. But however one answers that question, the answer does not dictate the answer to the question whether one is

---

[103] *The New York Times*, February 11, 1966.
[104] "Niebuhr Calls for an End to the War in Vietnam," *The New York Times*, January 19, 1967.
[105] Interview with Italian journalist Oriana Fallaci, *Rochester Democrat and Chronicle*, December 24, 1972.
[106] W. W. Rostow: "Morality and the War," *The New York Times*, June 22, 1971.

serving the interests of individual human beings, and whether, in particular, it serves to defeat the presumptive wrongness of the nonconsensual, deliberate killing of human beings. In short, the issue is framed from a perspective which enables one to design into it whatever conclusion one wants.

Michael Lind, in *Vietnam: The Necessary War*, to his credit, devotes a chapter to the specific question, "Was the Vietnam War Unjust?" He concludes that it was not and defends his position from a standpoint he calls moral realism:

> If you wish for peace, prepare for war. The only way to achieve peace is to deter potential aggressors. Therefore you must build up your armaments and make it clear that going to war on any particular scale is not necessarily ruled out by your policies. An inescapable part of making *this* clear is being prepared both to fight limited wars and to go not only to, but beyond, the nuclear brink on certain types of occasion. Otherwise you will not avoid war *and* you will be defeated.[107]

Dismissing pacifism, militarism and Marxism, Lind takes the above limited war perspective to be correct, and then applies it to the case of Vietnam. Specifically, he views the Vietnam War as a proxy war, between the United States, on the one side, and the Soviet Union and Red China, on the other, played out in Indochina. The cost of upward of two million Vietnamese lives was worth it, being less than there would have been in a major war among the three powers. Although he questions whether the policy of attrition was morally or practically justifiable in the years 1965–1968, he thinks it would have been more appropriate for the years 1968–1975 when the war evolved into a more nearly conventional war.[108]

Having assumed, without argument, the correctness of the warist position, and assumed the justifiability of the Korean War and US clandestine support of the war against the Soviets in Afghanistan, Lind then concludes that the Vietnam War, though it failed militarily, was justified.

> If the United States was morally justified in going to war in response to the cross-border invasion of South Korea in 1950, then by the same logic the United States had every moral right to defend South Vietnam against a similar cross-border invasion—after 1968, if not earlier.
>
> If the United States is to be condemned for prolonging the Vietnam War by coming to the aid of the South Vietnamese government as well as U.S. allies in Laos and Cambodia, then consistency requires that the United States and its allies be condemned for prolonging the Afghan War by arming and subsidizing the Afghan resistance.[109]

Lind is correct, of course, to raise the question of consistency. But it cuts two ways. *If* the Korean War was morally justified, and if it and the Vietnam War were relevantly

---

[107] Lind, *Vietnam: The Necessary War*, p. 217. Lind quotes this passage, which represents the position he adopts, from Alasdair MacIntyre, *After Virtue*, 2nd ed. (Notre Dame, IN: University of Notre Dame Press, 1984), p. 6. The italics are in the original though not in the passage as quoted by Lind.

[108] Lind, *Vietnam: The Necessary War*, p. 254.

[109] Lind, *Vietnam: The Necessary War*, pp. 231, 228.

similar from a moral standpoint—and *if* the proxy war by the United States against the Soviets in Afghanistan was morally justified, and if that situation was relevantly similar to Vietnam—then, of course, consistency would compel concluding that the Vietnam War was justified as well. But it follows equally that *if* the Vietnam War was morally unjustified, and was relevantly similar to the other two conflicts, then both the Korean War and the US proxy war in Afghanistan were morally unjustified. Instead of assuming the justifiability of problematic wars, and then maintaining their similarity to the Vietnam War, one needs to assess the Vietnam War on its own, with its own unique context, and then draw whatever conclusions are warranted about the other conflicts.[110]

More important than the question of consistency, however, is a moral issue raised by the idea of proxy wars—wars fought in other, usually smaller, countries, at enormous cost in lives and destruction to the peoples of those countries. If one supposes that, suitably qualified, there is truth to the Kantian dictum that people should be treated as ends and not as means only, then the use of other peoples to fight battles between major powers, and the use of their homeland as the battleground, is morally impermissible. Even if some in positions of military or political power in those countries may consent to such use, the people do not. As individual human beings, they arguably are being used as means to the end of a collectivity, the United States of America. Beyond that, still further, to argue for the use of such people as means in no way defeats the presumption against the nonconsensual deliberate killing of persons that such use entails. In that case, the Vietnam War stands as a morally indefensible war, both in its partial aspect, as waged by the United States, and as a whole war waged by the United States and the Vietnamese of North Vietnam and South Vietnam.

8.9 Revisionist and reactionary history

Another revisionist account would have it that the Vietnam War was a noble war, as Ronald Reagan called it, and that Diem was a wise and compassionate leader whose overthrow was a major mistake by the United States. Complicit in his downfall were young, inexperienced, culturally ignorant American correspondents who repeatedly issued false or misleading reports. "Before he left," Mark Moyar writes of Pulitzer prize winner David Halberstam in particular, "he would do more harm to the interests of the United States than any other journalist in American history."[111] Another Pulitzer prize winner, Neil Sheehan, was not far behind Halberstam in Moyar's low estimation, as was a third Pulitzer prize winner, Stanley Karnow. I shall not attempt to defend the journalists in their coverage of the war, but the accuracy of coverage is a relevant issue

---

[110] Lind's conclusion is that Vietnam was a "just, constitutional and necessary proxy war ... that was waged by methods that were often counterproductive and sometimes arguably immoral. The war had to be fought in order to preserve the military and diplomatic credibility of the United States in the Cold War, but when its costs grew excessive the war had to be forfeited in order to preserve the political consensus within the United States in favor of the Cold War," *Vietnam: the Necessary War*, p. 284.

[111] Moyar, *Triumph Forsaken*, p. 170.

in any conflict, provided one backs up one's allegations. It is difficult to be certain of an argument to show that the Vietnam War was a noble war in Moyar's estimation, but much of the reasoning seems to hinge upon the so-called domino theory (or "domino effect"), which Moyar contends was valid. That Vietnam became communist and yet the rest of South Asia, the Philippines and US Pacific interests did not—a fact that would appear to conclusively falsify the domino theory—is dismissed by Moyar. He contends that the theory was valid earlier on, say in 1965, and the fact that the dominoes did not fall in 1975 merely shows that circumstances had changed.[112] It is difficult to find in Moyar an argument to show that the theory was valid at any time. Moreover, he views both South Vietnam and North Vietnam as having been legitimate states. Interestingly, he does not quote the central tenet of the Geneva Accords, that the 17th parallel was merely a provisional military demarcation line and not a territorial or political boundary. Rather, he repeatedly refers to Vietnam as having been "divided" at the 17th parallel, and uses terms like "partition" and "territorial boundaries" to characterize the status quo following the Indochina War. The closest he comes to presenting an argument for the legitimacy of both South Vietnam and North Vietnam as states (hence undercutting the view that the war was essentially a civil war) is the following:

> The leaders of the two Vietnams … had little interest in the debates among Westerners over whether the Geneva agreement, the South's rejection of the all-Vietnam elections, or the absence of democracy within both North Vietnam and South Vietnam determined the "legitimacy" of the two governments. They shared the prevailing Vietnamese belief that whoever had actual military and political power was legitimate. Both North Vietnam and South Vietnam were legitimate states by virtue of their effective armed forces and administrators.[113]

The first two sentences in the above quote contain factual claims. The first is at best problematic. There is compelling evidence that Ho Chi Minh had considerable interest in the terms of the Geneva Accords and the prospect of elections to unify the country, since it was widely believed that he would win any such election and the country would be unified under his direction. The second claim is demonstrably false. Had North Vietnam thought the Diem government was legitimate, they would have had no grounds for challenging that government. To the contrary, they viewed the South Vietnamese government—as did an analyst for the *Pentagon Papers*—as a creation of the United States, and lacking in legitimacy. Even the military generals who overthrew the Diem regime (and the successive generals who overthrew them) did not accept that the government was legitimate. Nor did the religious groups that fought against the Diem regime, including the Buddhists who opposed what they saw as successive government repression of Buddhists. In any event, the final sentence in the quotation above, is a normative judgment. Whatever the attitudes and beliefs of the parties involved as contained in the first two sentences, even the truth of the two factual claims

---

[112] Moyar, *Triumph Forsaken*, pp. 378–391.
[113] Moyar, *Triumph Forsaken*, pp. 58f.

would not entail the normative judgment that the two governments were legitimate. That wielding military and political power alone determines legitimacy is but a thinly disguised version of the view that might makes right. Whatever the merits of that view, it at least needs defense. What passes as revisionist history is more reactionary than revisionist, resurrecting and repeating the rationales given by the US government and military during the war.

8.10 Conclusion

It is difficult to find an argument directed specifically to justifying the killing that took place in Vietnam, hence to defeating the moral presumption that the war was wrong. What we find are assessments at the macro level—in terms of national interest, credibility, prestige, national commitments, treaty obligations and aggression. If one starts at the top, so to speak, with a collectivist macroethics, and then proceeds downward to individual persons at the micro level, it is of course easy to defeat the presumption. You simply maintain the United States was defending South Vietnam in keeping with its treaty commitments under SEATO, and therefore that what it was doing—the killing of individual persons, combatants and noncombatants, innocents and noninnocents alike—was justified. I have argued that this puts the cart before the horse. The basic presumption is that the nonconsensual, deliberate killing of human beings is wrong. When conducted in an organized, systematic way on a large scale it renders warfare presumptively wrong, as well as the partial and whole wars to which it is essential. *This* is the presumption that must be defeated. Only if it is defeated can one proceed upward, so to speak, to justify the acts of governments, states and armies that produce such killing. If that presumption is not defeated, then the whole edifice of organized, systematic violence that constitutes war collapses. In the case of the Vietnam War, I suggest, that is precisely what happens. Both sides tended to view the war in macro terms: the United States as defending a supposedly sovereign, independent state against aggression from another state, the North Vietnamese as trying to unify the country in the face of external US intervention. Only the Vietcong viewed the war much of the time in micro terms. They were, initially at least in their judgment, resisting what they saw as oppression by the Saigon government. Eventually, as the war was Americanized, they came to view their fighting as an attempt to rid their homeland of foreign invaders. These rationales became intertwined as the war wore on and regular North Vietnamese troops became increasingly involved, sometimes in concert with the Vietcong.

The war as a whole—that is, the totality of the warfare by both sides (what I called war$_2$ earlier)—is what needs justifying. That whole war was presumptively wrong. It killed 58,151 American troops and probably more than 3 million Vietnamese, Cambodians and Laotians. The total number of casualties, combatants and noncombatants, is not known with certainty, but forty years after the war the Vietnamese estimated that 3 to 4 million Vietnamese children and adults were still suffering from the effects of 20 million gallons of toxic chemicals used by the United States, particularly dioxin from the defoliant Agent Orange, which had seeped into the soil and well water, as roughly 5.5 million acres of forest and cropland were destroyed.[114] Moreover, violent deaths continue. It was reported in 2011 that in the 36 years since the war ended, 42,132 Vietnamese had been killed by leftover explosives and 62,163 injured, a total of more than 100,000 after the war's end. Cleaning up the explosives, it was said, would take decades.[115] It does not matter that most of those almost certainly were unexploded ordnance dropped or placed by US troops. Both sides fought the war. It was a cooperative undertaking. Unless the product of that cooperative undertaking— the *whole* war—is justified, the presumption that the war was wrong is undefeated.

Nothing in the domino theory justifies the deliberate, nonconsensual killing of human beings. Today, Vietnam is a relatively prosperous country, with a rising demand for luxury cars and moving closer to the United States in its commercial dealings. As it has been written:

> Today's Vietnam is a tourist destination known for sparkling beaches, delicious cuisine, and friendly people. Visitors clamber through old Viet Cong caves, tour onetime battlefields, and enjoy spa treatments at seaside resorts outside Da Nang. There is no Hilton in Hanoi, but the Sheraton boasts "blended décor of local traditional-style and French colonial influence, ensuring a warm and comfortable feeling."[116]

Nothing could more clearly falsify the domino theory than the fact that after Vietnam became communist the dominoes did not fall. Those who still cling to the theory argue that the dominoes would have fallen had the United States abandoned the war effort earlier. That claim, of course, is unverifiable. In the absence of more compelling arguments, the judgment stands that the war was morally, politically and militarily a failure. As such, it did not come remotely close to defeating the moral presumption against war.

---

[114] *The New York Times*, August 10, 2012. The United States has downplayed the number of Vietnamese affected by toxic chemicals and has appropriated $49 million to help restore the environment and $11 million to aid those with chemical-related disabilities. See also *Rochester Democrat and Chronicle*, August 9, 2012. A 2013 study at the Portland Veterans Affairs Medical Center in Oregon found that US veterans who had been exposed to Agent Orange during the Vietnam War were at higher risk for aggressive prostate cancer than those who were not.

[115] *The New York Times*, December 6, 2011.

[116] "With Time, New Views of War's Landscapes," John Yemma, editor, *Christian Science Monitor*, December 12, 2011.

The Gulf and Iraq Wars in Light of the Just War Theory and Western Imperialism

By December 1922, the frustrated Americans were seriously thinking of walking away completely. It was no easy matter to divide up … Iraq, as the British mandate was now called … The participants argued over who would get what share of Iraqi oil.

—Daniel Yergen, *The Prize: The EpicQuest for Oil, Money & Power*

9.1 Continuity between the Gulf War and the Iraq War

The Iraq War and the earlier Gulf War are usually spoken of as though they were two separate wars. In fact, they can more plausibly be considered two phases of a single war.[1] There was, to be sure, a lull in the conventional combat between the two phases of the war. The Iraqi military was overwhelmed swiftly in each phase. But low-level warfare continued almost unnoticed—through sanctions and both the use and threat of military force—between the first phase of the war in 1991 (the "Gulf War") and the beginning of the second phase in 2003 (the "Iraq War").[2]

During this period the United States imposed a no-fly zone above the 36th parallel and below the 33rd parallel to protect the Kurds and Shiites, who had been encouraged to rise up against Saddam Hussein. It also imposed a punishing embargo that between 1991 and 2003 resulted in possibly as many as 500,000 deaths of Iraqi children under the age of five.[3] In addition there was military violence as Iraqi radar units locked onto

---

[1] A similar observation is made by Bassam Romaya, *The Iraq War: A Philosophical Analysis* (New York: Palgrave Macmillan, 2012).

[2] A comprehensive review and analysis of this period, and the legal, moral and political issues it raises is provided by Joy Gordon in *Invisible War: The United States and the Iraq Sanctions* (Cambridge: Harvard University Press, 2010).

[3] The child mortality rate is a controversial issue. After an extensive review of the studies, Joy Gordon writes: "By the most conservative estimate, excess child mortality would be at least 100,000, while the majority of the studies conducted since 1991 have consistently placed the figure for the entire period somewhere between half a million and a million excess child deaths. The latter figures are far more consistent with the other information available concerning food availability and malnutrition,

overflying US aircraft, usually only to be promptly destroyed by missiles from those aircraft.[4] From the beginning of the air assault on Baghdad in January 1991 to the recommencement of the assault in March 2003 there was warfare in progress. Add to this the attack on Afghanistan in October 2001, and the possibility of an Israeli attack on Iran, and the prospects of a major Persian Gulf War loom large in the second decade of the twenty-first century. This fact—and equally as important, the reasons for it—are obscured so long as we think of these as altogether separate wars. Both have to do with oil and power.

The Persian Gulf is essential to the control of a major part of the earth's oil resources. Iran was for years the West's policeman in the Persian Gulf. When the Shah was overthrown in 1979, the United States stepped in itself.

The attempt by America to control the Persian Gulf is but the latest chapter in Western imperialism in the region. I shall begin by sketching the history of that imperialism, then examine the rationales offered by the George H. W. Bush administration to justify the 1991 attack on Iraq, and that offered by George W. Bush to justify the invasion and occupation of Iraq in 2003.

9.2 Western imperialism in the Persian Gulf

Abstracted from the broader historical, cultural and geopolitical context in which it occurred, the first phase of the Persian Gulf War looks like a model of principled and righteous collective action.[5] When Iraq invaded Kuwait on August 2, 1990, one sovereign nation aggressed against another in violation of the norms of civilized international conduct. The international community responded, condemning the aggression and rolling it back through the measured use of force when peaceful means proved unavailing. A new era of international cooperation and responsibility was begun in which the UN was finally empowered to play the role for which it was intended. US will and determination in the service of a just cause made this possible. In the process America exorcised the ghost of Vietnam from its own experience.

Viewed in one light, this all seems so obvious as to make it puzzling why so many in the Islamic world fail to see it that way. It also makes it puzzling why there should be any question whether the war was a just war, as it was proclaimed to be by President George

---

the continual shortages of water fit for human consumption, and the extreme deterioration of medical services ... I will assume that the number of excess child deaths over the course of the sanctions regime in Iraq was at least a half million." See Gordon, *Invisible War*, p. 37, n. 82.

[4] It was reported in August 1999: "It is the year's other war. While the country's attention has focused on Kosovo, American warplanes have methodically and with virtually no public discussion been attacking Iraq. In the last eight months, American and British pilots have fired more than 1,100 missiles against 259 targets in Iraq. That is triple the targets attacked in four furious days of strikes in December that followed Iraq's expulsion of United Nations weapons inspectors" (*The New York Times*, August 13, 1999). The *Washington Post* had earlier referred to the conflict as "a low-grade war, fashioned by the military and the administration without public debate, aimed at salvaging the administration's 'containment' policy toward Hussein and destabilizing his regime" (*The Washington Post National Weekly Edition*, March 15, 1999).

[5] Michael Walzer contends that "in the first Gulf War of 1991, the United States and its allies fought in strict accordance with the classic just war paradigm," in *Just and Unjust Wars,* 4th ed., p. xii.

H. W. Bush and Secretary of State James Baker, and thought to be by the overwhelming majority of people in the West. But viewed in a different light, there emerges a different picture. This light takes in the broader historical context and focuses upon key moral and legal constraints associated with the UN Charter and JWT.

Western interests moved into the Persian Gulf in the early sixteenth century when the Portuguese occupied the island of Hormuz, giving them control of sea traffic in and out of the Gulf. They were followed in the early seventeenth century by the British and Dutch with the formation of their respective East India companies. Trade with Persia required free access to the Gulf, and this soon brought the Portuguese into conflict with the British and the Persians. Backed by ships of the British East India Company, the Persians drove the Portuguese from Hormuz in 1621 and within twenty years Portuguese influence in the Gulf came to an end. Dutch influence gradually waned through the mid-eighteenth century, leaving the British the dominant Western power through the nineteenth and much of the twentieth century, a position which at various times required counteracting French, German, and particularly Russian aspirations in the region. Their Empire at an end, the British finally exited in 1971.

In the meantime, the Turks expanded into the region in the early sixteenth century and in a little over a hundred years came to occupy most of what is today Iraq, which became part of the Ottoman Empire. With the Turks controlling the land areas, and the British enjoying maritime supremacy, foreign interests dominated most of the Persian Gulf region for 400 years. The British consolidated their hold on the Gulf itself with a treaty with the Sultan of Muscat in 1798, denying the French access to the Gulf during the Napoleonic wars. They then signed treaties with the various sheikdoms along the southern Gulf coast—or Trucial Coast as it came to be called—the most important of which was a Treaty of Peace in Perpetuity in 1853. The sheikdoms became virtual protectorates of Britain, as did what was to become Kuwait, when at the end of the nineteenth century the British sought to preempt the extension of German and Russian interests to the Western end of the Gulf. This latter development became of significance in 1990, because the Turks protested the establishment of the British tie with Kuwait, contending that Kuwait was part of its province of Basra. This claim on the part of the Turks provided part of the basis of later Iraqi claims that Kuwait properly belongs to Iraq. However, the British and the Turks enjoyed generally good relations until the early twentieth century, when they fought on opposite sides in WWI. The defeat of the Turks ended the Ottoman Empire and left the British occupying Iraq.

A revolt in 1920 in which 500 British were killed helped dampen British enthusiasm for continuing the occupation, and steps were taken to provide for Iraqi independence upon its admission to the League of Nations. This occurred in 1932, after the British drew the boundary lines for the region's prospective new states and emplaced Faisal I (Faisal bin Hussein) as the first king of Iraq. Faisal died in 1933 and was succeeded by his son Ghazi, who proved a thorn in the side of the British because of his criticism of their influence in Iraqi affairs. He also affirmed Iraq's claim upon Kuwait. Following Ghazi's death in an auto crash in 1939, his son Faisal II, still a child, became the successor-designate to the throne. He was eventually himself killed in a military coup in 1958 that brought to power a General Quasim. Saddam Hussein entered the picture in a 1959 assassination attempt against Quasim. The attempt failed, but Saddam was wounded and fled to Syria, then to Egypt. Quasim was overthrown in 1963. When the government that then came to power was itself overthrown in 1968, Saddam returned to Iraq, eventually becoming president in 1979 and transforming the country into a virtual dictatorship.

The British promised control of its protectorate Kuwait to Sheikh Mubarak al Sabah, of the family that rules Kuwait today, as a reward for mobilizing Bedouins against the Turks at the outset of WWI. Kuwait finally became independent in 1961, whereupon Iraq's Quasim proclaimed it to be part of Iraq. Its 1899 protectorate relationship with Britain having just been terminated, Kuwait immediately requested British protection to forestall possible Iraqi military action against it in support of Iraq's territorial claims. The British sent in some 4,000 troops, a force later replaced by troops of the Arab League, and Iraq backed off. When Quasim was overthrown in 1963, the succeeding government acknowledged Kuwait's independence, but that government itself was overthrown in 1968 and Iraq's claim to Kuwait was reasserted. When small-scale conflict broke out along the Iraqi-Kuwaiti border in 1973, Saudi Arabia sent in close to 20,000 troops in support of Kuwait.[6]

9.3 A Monroe Doctrine for the Persian Gulf

As these events were playing out, superpower maneuvering for influence in the region began, and after WWII the Gulf came to be looked upon as one of the likeliest flash points for conflict. This was an Americanized twentieth-century version of the nineteenth century's so-called Great Game, in which a perceived Russian threat dominated much of Britain's policy in the region. By this time, however, British influence was waning, and the United States sought in earnest to establish its influence in the Gulf. It reached an agreement with the British in 1966 for military use of the Diego Garcia Islands in the Indian Ocean (from which US B-52s would bomb Iraq during the Gulf War); and with Iran in the early 1970s for Iranian safeguarding of US interests in the Gulf in exchange for arms and military training. With the fall of the Shah in 1979, Iran was lost to the United States as a surrogate policeman in the region, and the growing inclination on the part of the United States was to use direct force itself. This stemmed from the time of the 1973 oil embargo and was made explicit in the Carter Doctrine of 1980, which asserted much the same kind of US interest in the Gulf region, and arrogated to the United States the same sorts of rights, as the Monroe Doctrine had done earlier in Latin America. The Carter Doctrine—set forth shortly after the Soviets began their own disastrous misadventure in Afghanistan—reads like a Monroe Doctrine for the Persian Gulf. It says in part: "The region which is now threatened by Soviet troops in Afghanistan is of great strategic importance: it contains more than two-thirds of the world's exportable oil ... An attempt by any outside force

---

[6] It is possible, in light of this, that when Iraq massed troops on the border between Kuwait and Saudi Arabia shortly after the August 2 invasion of Kuwait, the intention was to forestall possible Saudi intervention on Kuwait's behalf rather than to prepare for an invasion of Saudi Arabia itself. To forestall such an invasion was part of the initial US rationale for intervening, as the metaphor of "drawing a line in the sand," and the operational label "Desert Shield" suggested.

to gain control of the Persian Gulf region will be regarded as an assault on the vital interests of the United States of America, and such an assault will be repelled by any means necessary, including military force." The effect was to treat the Persian Gulf as though it were an American lake. The essentials of this commitment, with special reference to oil, were reaffirmed in a secret directive by President Bush in 1989.[7]

The collapse of the Soviet Union made it possible to implement this doctrine with virtual impunity, and the United States did so in the events following August 2, 1990. It emerged from the Gulf War the dominant power of the region, with an intended permanent military presence, and a protectorate relationship with the same sheikdoms (now enjoying the status of Persian Gulf states) as the British had in the nineteenth century. Unlike in the nineteenth century, however, oil is now the paramount commercial interest in the Gulf. Although the United States did not, at the time of the Gulf crisis, import that much oil from the region, many other Western nations did. Moreover, Japan, an economic competitor with the United States on the world scene, and a potential military competitor as well, in light of its gradual re-militarization, depends upon the Persian gulf for much of its oil.[8]

It is against this background that the Bush administration's attempted justification of the war on just-war grounds needs to be assessed.

9.4 The Gulf War and the just war theory

Accounts of the conditions of a just war vary, but as we have seen they commonly require: (1) a just cause, (2) legitimate authority, (3) a right intention, (4) proportionality, (5) probability of success and (6) that the war be a last resort. Even when all of these conditions are met (comprising *jus ad bellum*, or justice in the resort to war), there must be (7) proportionality in the conduct of the war and (8) discrimination among targets, to avoid killing innocents and/or noncombatants (comprising *jus in bello*, or justice in the conduct of war). In order for one to be justified in going to war, each of conditions (1) through (6) must be satisfied; and in order for the conduct of the war to be just, conditions (7) and (8) must be met. In order for the war as a whole to be fully just, all of the conditions must be met.[9] As I have indicated in earlier chapters that one might seriously question whether these are adequate criteria for the moral assessment of war, I shall not repeat those concerns here, and instead shall question only whether the Gulf War satisfies them.

The only condition that is completely unproblematic in the case of the Gulf War is (5) that the war had a probability of success. 700,000 troops led and principally constituted by the forces of a nuclear superpower were arrayed against 183,000

---

[7] See the *New York Times*, May 29, 1992, which quotes the directive as saying in part: "the U.S. remains committed to defend its vital interests in the region."

[8] The perceived US threat to Japanese oil supplies, we should recall, was no small part of the reason for Japan's attack on Pearl Harbor, initiating the Pacific phase of WWII.

[9] By "war as a whole" is meant the entirety of the partial war on one side, not the whole war consisting of all of the partial wars as defined in Chapter 1. Whether the satisfaction of conditions (1) through (6) mean merely that one *may* morally go to war or means that one is obligated to—that is, would be wrong not to do so—is not altogether clear in much of JWT.

poorly trained and (by comparison) poorly equipped troops of an underdeveloped Arab country of 18 million people. It was a mismatch of such proportions as to leave in doubt only how long the war would last, not who would win. Although the American media played up the Iraqi military as one of the largest in the world and gave the impression that it would be a formidable foe, the London-based International Institute for Strategic Studies made the assessment as early as October of 1990 that the conflict would last weeks at most.[10] With regard to just cause, even if one dismisses Iraq's territorial claims on Kuwait and its grievances over alleged Kuwaiti pilfering of Iraqi oil and assumes that Kuwait had just cause to resist the Iraqi invasion by force (which it scarcely did, as its leadership and military quickly fled), that would not by itself confer a just cause upon the United States to go to war against Iraq. One might even question whether President Bush had legitimate authority to involve the United States in war, as is maintained by those who see in his actions a presidential usurpation of powers conferred only upon the Congress. These conditions of just cause and legitimate authority are, after (5), perhaps the least problematic of the eight, but they are problematic nonetheless. Whether there was a good intention as required by (3) depends, of course, upon whether the stated intentions were the same as the actual intentions. If what I have said earlier is correct, the actual intention arguably was one of imperialistic rather than moral design. That, to be sure, is open to question, but furthering perceived US national interest—if that was indeed the intention—at the expense of the Iraqi people would not qualify as a right intention by just war standards.

The condition I want to focus upon is (6), that of last resort. For even if each of the other conditions could be shown to have been satisfied, if this one were not, then the war was not justifiably entered into in the first place, even by just war standards.

9.5 Was the Gulf War a last resort?

The events between August 2, 1990, the date of the Iraqi invasion of Kuwait, and January 15, 1991, the US deadline to initiate hostilities, suggest that practically from the outset Washington sought a military solution to the crisis.[11] By a military solution

---

[10] As reported in the *New York Times*, October 5, 1990.

[11] Still not fully explained, or even verified, is the purported transcript of the meeting held between Saddam Hussein and US Ambassador to Iraq April Glaspie, on July 25, 1990, as Iraqi troops were massed on the border with Kuwait on the eve of the invasion. At that time she reportedly told Saddam: "Mr. President, not only do I want to say that President Bush wanted better and deeper relations with Iraq, but he also wants an Iraqi contribution to peace and prosperity in the Middle East. President Bush is an intelligent man. He is not going to declare an economic war against Iraq … I know you need funds. We understand that and our opinion is that you should have the opportunity to rebuild your country. But we have no opinion on the Arab–Arab conflicts, like your border disagreement with Kuwait. I was in the American embassy in Kuwait during the late '60s. The instruction we had during this period was that we should express no opinion on this issue and that the issue is not associated with America. James Baker has directed our official spokesmen to emphasize this instruction." See "The Glaspie Transcript: Saddam meets the U.S. Ambassador (July 25, 1990)," in *The Gulf War Reader: History, Documents, Opinion*, ed. Micah L. Sifry and Christopher Cerf (New York: Times Books, 1991), pp. 129f. If this is accurate, it would not be unreasonable for Saddam to have taken it to give him a green light for the anticipated invasion of Kuwait or at least assurance that the United States would not intervene.

I mean a solution that relied upon the threat of war to achieve US objectives, and that intended to resort to war itself if those threats did not attain the objectives.[12]

Even before the UN Security Council met on August 6, at which time it passed the resolution calling for an embargo of Iraq and Kuwait, President Bush had decided on a major deployment of US troops to the region and had reportedly set in motion covert plans for the possible overthrow of President Hussein.[13] On August 5 he dispatched a high-level delegation headed by Defense Secretary Richard B. Cheney to Saudi Arabia to persuade King Fahd to accept US troops on Saudi territory. Having given Arab diplomats 72 hours to resolve the crisis, and having convinced King Fahd to allow US troops to be based in Saudi Arabia, he then announced the troop deployment on August 8, characterizing their role as purely defensive. The stage was then set for the use of US military force in the form of a blockade. Secretary of State James Baker said at a NATO meeting in Brussels on August 10 that the Security Council resolution gave the United States the right to use force if it were requested to do so by the deposed Kuwaiti monarch.[14] It was announced two days later, on August 12, that President Bush had received such a request and had, in accordance with Article 51 of the UN Charter, decided that the United States would "do whatever is necessary" to enforce the sanctions.[15]

Thus even before the Security Council had an opportunity to act beyond its August 3 resolution condemning the Iraqi invasion, calling for a withdrawal, and calling for negotiations between Iraq and Kuwait, President Bush initiated military operations. And in less than a week following the August 6 Security Council action imposing an embargo, he unilaterally ordered a blockade (which went into effect on August 16). Thus a nonviolent sanction, as the embargo represented, was given less than one week to work before the use of military force was undertaken in the form of a blockade. The embargo had been undertaken in accordance with chapter 7, Article 41 of the UN Charter, which says that the Security Council "may decide what measures not involving the use of armed force are to be employed to give effect to its decisions."

---

[12] Robert W. Tucker makes an even stronger claim: "Yet it was not so much the ends of the war that thus strained the principle of proportionality to a breaking point as it was the manner in which the nation and its government were determined from the outset to wage war." See "Justice and the War," *The National Interest*, Fall 1991, p. 112.

[13] *Christian Science Monitor*, August 7, 1990. The *New York Times* reported on February 9, 1992, that President Bush had notified Congress—as required before the CIA could proceed—the preceding November, that the administration was stepping up the covert actions, with the possibility that installment of a new and friendly regime in Iraq could be supported by the US military. Iraq had insisted immediately following the invasion that it would begin withdrawing its troops by Sunday, August 5, unless Iraq or Kuwait were threatened. Interestingly, in a retrospective analysis, Michael R. Gordon and Bernard E. Trainor report that Gen. Colin L. Powell, Chairman of the Joint Chiefs of Staff, had argued against intervention. They write: "But General Powell argued that the West had little choice but to accept Saddam Hussein's invasion and should concentrate on defending Saudi Arabia. 'The next few days, Iraq will withdraw,' he said. 'But Saddam Hussein will put his puppet in. Everyone in the Arab world will be happy.'" *New York Times*, October 23, 1994. The article was taken from Gordon and Trainor's then forthcoming book, *The Generals' War* (Little, Brown & Company, 1995).

[14] *The New York Times*, August 11, 1990.

[15] *The New York Times*, August 13, 1990.

A blockade, on the other hand, is an act of war, and the US action was quickly declared to be such by Iraq.

Thus, within ten days of the invasion, military force had been settled upon as virtually the only option for dealing with the crisis. When asked in mid-August whether, amid highly publicized phone calls he was making to world leaders, he had talked with President Hussein, President Bush replied that he had not.

Absent a clear justification for the August 12 unilateral declaration, there were grounds for the Iraqi characterization of the blockade as an act of war. Although the UN Charter does not define aggression, a consensus definition adopted by the General Assembly in 1974 characterizes aggression as "the use of armed force by a State against the sovereignty, territorial integrity or political independence of another State." It then says that regardless of a declaration of war, certain acts—and it specifically includes the "blockade of the ports or coasts of a State by the armed forces of another State"—qualify as aggression. Although the definition is not binding upon the Security Council, it represents the most sustained attempt by the UN—spanning many years—to clarify the concept of aggression.

The Bush administration did offer a rationale for its action. It appealed to Article 51 of the UN Charter, which says that nothing in the Charter "shall impair the inherent right of individual or collective self-defense if an armed attack occurs against a Member of the United Nations, until the Security Council has taken measures necessary to maintain international peace and security."

This, however, was a dubious justification for war. Kuwait was no longer under attack. Its government, its air force and most of its army had fled when Iraq invaded. For better or worse, by August 12 Kuwait had been attacked, occupied and annexed by Iraq. This was a *fait accompli*. It is, in fact, not even possible to defend oneself against an attack that occurred in the past. One can speak intelligibly of anticipatory self-defense (whether preventive or preemptive) to forestall an attack, and for retaliation for an attack that has taken place, but the idea of engaging in self-defense against an attack that is over with is unintelligible. The time for self-defense had come and gone. This may seem a fine point, and many would argue that the Sabah family nonetheless had a right to appeal for military support to try to reverse the outcome of the events of August 2. Even so, the alleged right of the Sabah family to international support to reverse the outcome does not derive from Article 51 of the UN Charter. These considerations aside, self-defense is provided for by Article 51 *only* until such time as the Security Council has acted, which it had already done on August 6, seven days earlier, in authorizing a boycott.[16]

---

[16] The Security Council had on August 3, the day following the Iraqi invasion, passed Resolution 660 demanding an Iraqi withdrawal, and calling for Iraq and Kuwait "to begin immediately intensive negotiations for the resolution of their differences," adding that it supported all efforts in that regard, particularly those of the Arab League. The United States at no time backed this call for negotiations. It ignored a proposal by Yasser Arafat to resolve the crisis and gave short shrift to the efforts by King Hussein of Jordan (which included a trip to the United States to talk directly with President Bush) to achieve a resolution. Reportedly, "U.S. officials believe—and fear—that the King will present President Bush with proposals for diplomatic compromise that could seriously complicate the task of maintaining international unity against Iraq's invasion"(*Watertown [NY]Daily Times*, August 15, 1990). The United States said later that it opposed the king's peacemaking efforts (*The New York Times*, September 21, 1990). President Bush emphasized on October 23: "I am more determined

The rationale was unconvincing to the Security Council, and the Bush administration saw support for its hardline policy eroding rapidly; so much so that on August 19 it undertook a major lobbying effort to get Security Council backing.[17] This it did with the Security Council's passing of a vaguely worded resolution on August 25, which, though it did not mention force, was taken by virtually everyone to authorize the use of force. The Bush administration consistently maintained, however, that it did not need Security Council authorization (or Congressional authorization either, for that matter) for its actions. As an unidentified senior administration official was later quoted as saying: "Our strategy was that we were going to do whatever we had to do on our own, and if we could bring along the UN then fine."[18]

This was a greater victory for Bush administration diplomacy than it was for the integrity of the UN, because it flew in the face of the UN Charter itself. Article 42, which supposedly provided the warrant for the August 25 resolution, says that if the Security Council should "consider that measures provided for in Article 41 would be inadequate or have proved to be inadequate, it may take such action by air, sea, or land forces [including blockade] as may be necessary to maintain or restore international peace and security." There was no finding that the embargo, voted fewer than three weeks earlier, either had or would have proven inadequate. Indeed, evidence was that it was proving overwhelmingly successful.[19] Moreover, quite apart from the question of the justifiability of the use of armed force under Article 42 in those circumstances,[20] for the first time in its history the UN, without clear warrant under its own Charter, gave license to UN members to take military action on their own against a member state without benefit of a UN flag or command.[21] The US understanding of this was made

---

than ever to see that this invading dictator gets out of Kuwait without compromise of any kind whatsoever." (*The New York Times*, October 24, 1990).

[17] The *New York Times* detailed this impending crisis under the heading, "Order for Blockade Largely Isolates U.S. at Security Council," August 14, 1990.

[18] *The New York Times*, August 30, 1990.

[19] A Bush administration official was quoted as saying on August 22 that the embargo was already 90% effective, *The New York Times*, August 23, 1990.

[20] It has been argued that: "Contrary to the view of some opponents of the Gulf War, Article 42 does not require the council to conduct a full-scale study of the likely effects of current or possible non-military measures before it may undertake military action; the council need only conclude that such nonmilitary measures are unlikely to maintain or restore international peace and security." Richard J. Regan, *Just War: Principles and Cases* (Washington, DC: The Catholic University of America Press, 1996), p. 25. True, Article 42 does not require a full-scale study. But neither does it permit the Security Council simply to conclude summarily that nonmilitary means would be to no effect. The word "consider," we may assume, was chosen with some care, encompassing as it does among its meanings: to reflect upon, contemplate and weigh the merits of. Although this raises issues of the interpretation of international law beyond what we can go into here, it would seem on the face of it that a Charter whose aim is to ensure international peace and security would expect substantial reflection and study before authorizing military action.

[21] Quite apart from the question of the legality of the Security Council's action under the UN Charter is the question of UN practice in the past. On this issue, Joy Gordon writes: "Although Iraq had clearly violated international law when it invaded Kuwait, it was not at all obvious that Iraq's actions against Kuwait in 1990 would ordinarily have brought a response from the Security Council. Prior to 1990, the Security Council had rarely invoked Chapter VII measures, even in cases of violations of sovereignty. The Security Council did not use Chapter VII measures to intervene … in 1956, when the Soviet Union invaded Hungary; in 1957, when France and England invaded Egypt to protect their interests in the Suez Canal; in the crisis in the Congo during the early 1960s; in Indonesia's occupation of East Timor, which began in 1975; in the Falklands War in 1982; and in the U.S. invasion of

clear by National Security advisor Brent Scowcroft who reportedly said following the vote that it entitled the United States to act "as it saw fit" to enforce the embargo.[22]

The most rapid and massive buildup of military force in history to that time proceeded at an accelerating pace in the months ahead. President Bush had assured the American public on August 8 that US troops were being sent to the Gulf wholly for defensive purposes.[23] The fear allegedly was that Iraq would invade Saudi Arabia as well as Kuwait. That was the point of drawing a line in the sand. General Schwartzkopf said three weeks later that there would be no war unless Iraq attacked.[24] On that same day, the Saudi Defense Minister insisted that Saudi Arabia could not be used for an attack on Iraq, and that US forces were there for purely defensive reasons.[25] But these professed defensive intentions were quickly forgotten in the face of the increasingly obvious offensive nature of the buildup. Not until November did President Bush acknowledge the offensive character of the forces being assembled. He had all the while been sending in Stealth fighter-bombers and secretly deploying warplanes to other Arab Gulf states. Shortly before the January 16 attack, he reportedly met with his advisors to discuss the possible occupation of Iraq.

Most important for present purposes is that at no time were negotiations undertaken or a diplomatic solution actively pursued. Indeed, negotiations were repeatedly dismissed, most emphatically in President Bush's letter to President Hussein that was presented to, and rejected by, Iraqi Foreign Minister Tariq Aziz on January 9, 1991. Unidentified White House officials had revealed as early as August that a central aim was to give President Hussein no way out short of humiliation. They made clear that "he must not only be defeated, he must also be seen as defeated by everyone in the Arab world and beyond."[26] For good measure, Defense Secretary Cheney said shortly before the attack that the way to peace was for Saddam to go back to Baghdad "with his tail between his legs."

Saddam did go back to Baghdad, but not with his tail between his legs. He continued to defy the United States, and added a dose of humiliation himself when he reportedly observed that President Bush, when he was defeated in a bid for a second term in office, had been consigned to the "dust bin of history." Not only that, he had created a mosaic of Bush's face on the floor to the entrance of the main international hotel in Baghdad, so that all those entering and leaving had to step on his face. He may also have engineered an assassination attempt on Bush when he visited Kuwait, a fact which led Bush's son to say—in what sounded like a hint at revenge—that Saddam had tried to kill "my dad."

Whatever the motivation, the George W. Bush administration finished the job begun by the George H. W. Bush administration, as had been urged by neoconservatives like

Granada in 1983 … Thus the extreme response of comprehensive sanctions followed by massive military action was an abrupt departure from Security Council practice." Gordon, *Invisible War*, p. 41f.

22 *The New York Times*, August 26, 1990.
23 *The New York Times*, August 9, 1990.
24 *The New York Times,* September 1, 1990.
25 *The New York Times*, September 1, 1990.
26 *The New York Times*, August 22, 1990.

Dick Cheney and Paul Wolfowitz. A principal justification was that Iraq had weapons of mass destruction, an allegation that proved false. The invasion and occupation of Iraq began in March 2003. Having failed to engineer a coup behind the scenes, the United States overthrew the government largely by itself—with no warrant for regime change from the UN Charter—and installed a regime to its liking, thereby, the American people were assured, liberating the Iraqi people and establishing democracy.[27]

It did, to be sure, liberate from life the hundreds of thousands who died in the process,[28] and liberated from their homes and way of life the estimated 2 million civilian refugees who fled to Jordan, Syria and Egypt, and the estimated 1.7 million internal refugees, many of them from the 2004 assault on the city of Fallujah.[29] By 2015, between 135,814 and 153,451 Iraqi civilians had died violently since the invasion, 17,000 of them in 2014 alone. The total Iraqi casualties, including combatants, was estimated at 206,000.[30] Saddam, of course, was liberated from life as well, as the United States held him under guard until the new Iraqi government could try and hang him.

It should not surprise us that the survivors are not grateful. A poll taken by the British Ministry of Defense in August 2005 showed that 82 percent of Iraqis strongly opposed the presence of foreign troops, and fewer than 1 percent of them believed that the coalition forces were responsible for improved security. And it should not surprise us that many in the Muslim world did not applaud the conquest of a lesser-developed country of 23 million by a nuclear superpower of 290 million.

Saddam was a dictator and a brutal one. But he was a two-bit dictator (compared, say, to Hitler or Stalin), little different from many we have supported over the years when it suited us—Batista, Trujillo, Pinochet, Mubarak, the Shah and Marcos to name a few. He was also a secular Arab leader, hated by Ayatollah Khomeini and Osama bin Laden, who headed a relatively progressive government (compared with Arab states like Kuwait and Saudi Arabia) with respect to education, medical care and women's rights. The Iraqi invasion of Kuwait in 1991 was a golden opportunity to advance US interests by securing long-sought US bases in the region. Saddam could not have served US ambitions better if he had been on the CIA payroll. Washington's problem with Saddam was not that he was a dictator; it was that he sat on the world's second largest proven oil reserves and would not dance to our tune.[31]

Although considered officially to have ended in December 2011, the Iraq War continues on, having morphed into chaotic sectarian violence compounded by the rise of the Islamic State of Iraq and Syria (ISIS). US troops remaining in Iraq and

---

[27] Interestingly, nearly 30 years earlier, in 1973, the United States backed a military coup against a democratically elected socialist government in Chile and oversaw the installment of a military dictatorship.

[28] Estimates of the number who died in the Iraq War vary, but 500,000 may be a reasonable figure, which includes many who died from health-related consequences of the war.

[29] An estimated 100,000 of these refugees returned to Iraq between 2008 and 2010, only to encounter violence and unemployment so severe as to lead many of them to flee once again. http://www.nytimes.com/201011/27world/middleeast/27refugees.html? Militants believed to be associated with al-Qaeda had seized control of Fallujah by 2014.

[30] https://www.iraqbodycount.org/analysis/numbers/2014.

[31] Saddam's overthrow also served the interests of Israel, America's chief ally in the region, ridding it of one of its main adversaries and one of the main supporters of the Palestinians. The same was true of the overthrow with US support of Quaddafi and the attempted overthrow of Assad in Syria.

Afghanistan will be easy targets for young militants eager to martyr themselves. By confirming in their eyes the picture of the United States painted by terrorists, the US presence will in fact produce more jihadists. Osama bin Laden could not have scripted it better: draw the United States deeper into the Muslim world where it is increasingly feared and hated, then begin drawing blood for as long as it takes. That is how you defeat an empire.

9.6 The just war theory modified

International lawyers who supported the war were quick to argue that the Bush administration's actions complied fully with the UN Charter. Just war theorists who supported the war did the same with just war criteria. The criterion of last resort most obviously failed to be satisfied by the Gulf War. It is not surprising that the criterion has been redefined by the war's supporters. James Turner Johnson, for example, contends:

> It is important to note that the criterion of last resort does not mean that all possible nonmilitary options that may be conceived of must first be tried: rather, a prudential judgment must be made as to whether *only* a rightly authorized use of force can, in the given circumstances, achieve the goods defined by the ideas of just cause, right intention, and the goal of peace, at a proportionate cost, and with reasonable hope of success. Other methods *may* be tried first, if time permits and if they also satisfy these moral criteria; yet this is not mandated by the criterion of last resort—and "last resort" certainly does not mean that other methods must be tried indefinitely.[32]

The first and last claims here are certainly correct (and they are mutually entailing, since to try all *conceivable* alternative means would indeed mean trying indefinitely, and trying indefinitely—unless one were simply trying the same things over again— would mean trying all of the conceivable alternatives). But the claim that to try to find alternatives to war is not mandated, and all that is required is that one *may* try other alternatives if time permits represents an attempt to legislate what the JWT shall mean, not what is has meant for most just war theorists. The JWT does not authorize going to war simply because one *thinks* other alternatives will not work. The whole point is that one must try to find alternatives; it is the trying and failing that provides the warrant for the conclusion, not an a priori determination that nothing other than war will work. Even coauthor George Weigel says later in the same volume from which the above quotation is taken that "what the [just war] tradition means by 'last resort' is that all reasonable efforts at a nonmilitary solution have been tried and have failed."

The above passage confuses the condition of last resort with that of probability of success, as a close reading of the second half of the first sentence suggests. Having said what the criterion supposedly does not mean, Johnson proceeds to state what

---

[32] James Turner Johnson and George Weigel, *The Gulf War and Just War*, (Washington, DC: Ethics and Public Policy Center, 1991), p. 29.

he contends it does mean, namely that "a prudential judgment must be made as to whether *only* a rightly authorized use of force can, in the given circumstances, achieve the goods defined by the ideas of just cause" (etc.). While it is correct that one must make such a judgment in applying the JWT, this does not represent the condition of last resort. That war is a last resort represents a conclusion arrived at by the failure of efforts to find a peaceful solution. It does not say that violent means will be successful (it might sometimes be that neither violent nor nonviolent means would be successful in attaining certain objectives in a given situation). For that one needs an assessment of the likelihood that war would achieve those objectives. And this is the point of the criterion of probability of success. Only when peaceful means have proven fruitless, and there is a probability that violent means would be successful, is one justified in going to war. To say, as Johnson does, that last resort means judging that only the use of force can achieve just war objectives presupposes that the condition of last resort has already been met. It can be true that force would succeed only if peaceful means would not succeed, and one can know that only if peaceful means have been sought.

What obscures this collapsing of last resort and probability of success into one "prudential judgment" is that tacked onto the end of the first sentence is the condition "and with reasonable hope of success." This makes it sound as though the condition of probability of success is being cited there. In fact that condition is already contained in what precedes it. To say that one must judge that only the use of force can achieve just war objectives, and then to add, "with a reasonable hope of success" is redundant. In judging that only the use of force can achieve the objectives one is judging that only the use of force will be successful.

Having reinterpreted last resort so as not to require an attempt to find nonviolent alternatives, Johnson then concludes that the condition was satisfied in the Gulf crisis on the grounds that such alternatives, though untried, would not have worked:

> The decision not to continue with negotiations or economic sanctions after January 15, 1991, did not violate the criterion of "last resort." The failure of the Geneva talks, the continued intransigence of Saddam Hussein, the ongoing process of military buildup by Iraqi forces, the continuing systematic rape of Kuwait, the history of Iraq's relations with its own dissident population and its neighbors, and threats of violence by Iraq against those neighbors all provided ample reasons to conclude that non-military means held little possibility of success, and that the continuing atrocities in Kuwait necessitated action.[33]

It is unclear what negotiations Johnson is referring to here, since at no time did the United States enter into negotiations with Iraq; in fact, it consistently rejected negotiations. In any event, the Geneva talks is the only item in the list which represents an initiative by the United States; the others represent judgments or unexplicated claims ("the history of Iraq's relations with its own dissident population and its neighbors") which would require substantial argument in order to show how they support the intended conclusion. For example, Iraq's military buildup surely is a specious ground

---

[33] Johnson and Weigel, *Just War and the Gulf War*, p. 30.

for concluding that nonviolent means could not have resolved the dispute. Within days of the invasion, Iraqi forces took up defensive positions. This was their posture right up to the time of the US attack.[34] The military buildup took place in response to the massive commitment of US forces and the continuing threat to use those forces if Iraq did not capitulate. Subsequent events show that Iraq had every reason to fear an attack. However one judges the initial Iraqi invasion, the Iraqi response to an attempted military solution to the crisis by the United States does not of itself provide any reason to believe that nonviolent alternatives might not have been better.

The most serious of the allegations concerns the continuing atrocities in Kuwait. There were Iraqi atrocities, and they have been documented. The question is whether they show that nonviolent alternatives would not have worked and that force was necessitated—as the Clinton administration was to argue later with regard to Kosovo. That conclusion does not follow in any obvious way from the fact cited, and we are not provided with the supporting argument by which to draw that conclusion.

The facts surrounding Iraqi brutality, particularly to civilians, have never been made fully clear. But there is at least some evidence that the brutality began when Kuwaiti civilians began attacking Iraqi soldiers. Caryle Murphy, the only American reporter known to have remained in Kuwait following the invasion (and who sent unsigned dispatches to the *Washington Post* before fleeing Kuwait near the end of August) reported on August 11 that the Iraqi soldiers were courteous to civilians and, in general, appeared well-disciplined.[35] Other accounts report some of them as being apologetic for the invasion and critical of Saddam Hussein. At that point opposition to the occupation was essentially nonviolent: daily protest marches by women, the painting-out of street signs, publication of an underground newspaper. The Emir Al-Sabah announced on August 15, however, that armed resistance by underground units and civilians would begin the following week.[36] Shortly thereafter there was an unconfirmed report that US Special Forces in Saudi Arabia were secretly training Kuwaiti resistance fighters to engage in guerrilla warfare within Kuwait. By the end of August it was reported that hundreds of Iraqi soldiers had been killed within Kuwait, mostly ambushed within the city. It was further reported that Iraqi soldiers were being hospitalized at a rate of 75 per day (one Kuwaiti nurse was later quoted as claiming that she had personally killed Iraqi soldiers as they lay wounded in the hospital). In early September it was reported that the United States and Saudi Arabia were helping funnel weapons and intelligence reports to Kuwaiti guerillas.[37] Car bombs and sniper attacks—what would be considered terrorist acts if carried out by an adversary—were reported. US soldiers minus identifying insignia reportedly accompanied Kuwaiti irregulars entering Kuwait City immediately after the war.

Civilians, of course, lose their immunity when they take up arms against an occupying military, so the fact of Kuwaiti civilians dying under the occupation does not of itself establish that Iraq was acting in violation of international norms (though

---

[34] The Pentagon reportedly concluded as early as August 4 that no invasion of Saudi Arabia was imminent (*New York Times,* August 5, 1990).

[35] Caryle Murphy received a 1991 Pulitzer Prize for her reporting.

[36] *The New York Times,* August 16, 1990.

[37] *The New York Times,* September 4, 1990.

the use of torture would clearly show that). Even less does it provide reason to conclude that only military force would have worked to achieve a resolution of the crisis. Indeed, if it should be the case that the brutal Iraqi treatment of civilians began in response to civilian attacks on the Iraqi military, then far from showing that nonviolent alternatives would not have worked, that fact would suggest that the resort to violence by Kuwaiti civilians worsened the situation, much as the US bombing of Yugoslavia arguably worsened the plight of the Kosovar Albanians in 1999. One cannot argue that force is necessitated to counteract a situation itself brought into existence by the use of force.

Weigel, on the other hand, believes that alternatives were tried and failed. But he cites only three events, and only one of those involving a US initiative. He says: "In the face of Iraqi foreign minister Tariq Aziz's behavior at his Geneva meeting with U.S. Secretary of State James Baker on January 9, 1991, and Saddam Hussein's rebuff of the Perez de Cuellar and French initiatives in the last hours before the UN deadline of January 15, it is difficult to argue with President Bush's judgment that all reasonable nonmilitary remedies had been exhausted."[38] Even if one thinks the latter two efforts, particularly that by Perez de Cuellar, were not perfunctory, they were not efforts undertaken by the United States. It is the party proposing to go to war—particularly if it intends to initiate the war—for whom war must be a last resort. But it is puzzling why Weigel should count the failure of the French proposal as supporting the contention that war was a last resort for the United States, since the United States led the opposition to that proposal in the Security Council (on the grounds that it included plans for an international Middle East peace conference which the United States also opposed). One cannot count the failure of a peace initiative as justification for going to war if one of the reasons it failed is because of one's own efforts to ensure its failure.

As for Secretary of State Baker's meeting with Foreign Minister Aziz, which both Johnson and Weigel cite, the administration had made clear that this was not a meeting to engage in negotiations; indeed, when the offer of talks between Baker and Aziz was announced on January 3, White House spokesman Marlin Fitzwater made clear that Baker would not negotiate but would simply reiterate the UN demand. The letter which Baker bore for President Hussein, and which Aziz refused to accept on January 9, specifically stated there would be no negotiations. The function of the meeting was understood in Washington to be to deliver a virtual ultimatum, containing a veiled threat to destroy Iraq itself. The letter reportedly said in part: "What is at issue here is not the future of Kuwait … but rather the future of Iraq" if Iraq did not capitulate. Iraq did not capitulate. Part of the purpose of the meeting, Washington officials acknowledged, was to offset the embarrassment of having offered to have Secretary Baker meet with President Hussein in Baghdad any time up to the January 15 deadline, only to refuse to meet on the January 12 date proposed for that purpose by Iraq.

Thus the single US action which Johnson and Weigel cite as evidence of US efforts to resolve the problem by nonviolent means is the Geneva meeting by Secretary Baker, a meeting which for the United States, by all accounts, never had a negotiated or diplomatic solution as its objective.[39]

---

[38] Johnson and Weigel, *Just War and the Gulf War*, p. 60.
[39] The *New York Times* actually cited three objectives of the meeting in its January 4 account. "By offering to have Mr. Baker meet with Mr. Aziz in Geneva on January 7, 8, or 9, during a trip to the Middle

9.7 Conclusion

None of the preceding justifies Iraq's invasion of Kuwait. Nor does it excuse atrocities against Kuwaitis, or the despoiling of the environment by burning Kuwaiti oil wells, or the attacks against Israeli civilians. Nor does it justify the brutal repression of Shiite and Kurd uprisings following the end of the first phase of the war. It certainly does not excuse the harshness of Iraqi government's dictatorial rule over its own people that continued until the second phase of the war in 2003. All of those deserve condemnation. What it does do is to reflect a different light upon US actions, showing them to be but the latest installment of continuing intervention and attempted domination of the region by Western powers for their own interests. Beyond that, it suggests that far from representing the successful engagement of the UN with an international crisis of the sort it was intended to cope with, the Gulf War is a clear case of a superpower resolved to have its way, with or without UN backing, and then manipulating the Security Council in such a way as to provide an air of legitimacy for what it intended to do anyway. After initial reservations about the apparent course the US was taking following the August 25 vote authorizing the use of force, the Security Council became the virtual lapdog of the United States. It passed a flurry of resolutions in the following weeks, making Iraqi compliance with all of them a near impossibility. This gave the United States virtually a free hand to maintain sanctions in perpetuity, since it could always make a case for noncompliance on some point or the other of some resolution. More importantly still, the Gulf crisis showed a willingness on the part of the Security Council to act in disregard of the clear provisions of the UN's own charter. When the United States unilaterally undertook a military blockade of Iraqi shipping, it acted in clear violation of the UN Charter. And when the Security Council gave in to US pressure to legitimize that action on August 25, it, too, acted in violation of its own charter, the conditions for resort to military action under Article 42 of Chapter VII not having been met. Far from providing a model of effective and responsible collective action to promote and sustain international peace, the Gulf War provided a model of deception and manipulation on the part of the Bush administration, and of weakness of will on the part of the Security Council, of a sort that was subversive of the integrity of the UN itself. Over more than two decades of the Persian Gulf War, tens of thousands of Iraqi civilians—and hundreds of thousands of Iraqi children—paid the cost of the conflict with their lives. That cost is still rising, as the issues between Sunnis and Shiites, and between Kurds and Arabs, remain unresolved, and are boiling over again in 2015 as US troops turn over ostensible control of the country to the Iraqis.

East and Europe that is to start on Sunday, Administration officials said they hoped to extricate Mr. Bush from the diplomatic tangle created by his original offer to send Mr. Baker to Baghdad any time before the January 15 deadline set by the United Nations for Iraq to leave Kuwait or face eviction by force. The proposal for talks was also intended to buy Mr. Bush time in the face of the diplomatic initiatives by other countries and to inject an American presence into those efforts, officials said. Finally, officials said the White House hoped the offered meeting would forestall any Congressional action on the Gulf, which Mr. Bush fears would interfere with his efforts to face down Mr. Hussein," *The New York Times*, January 4, 1991.

Finally, the invocation of the just war tradition to try to justify the war appears intended merely to provide a rationalization. It is possible that just war criteria were seriously discussed and appraised by US administration officials before concluding that the war would be just. But there is no evidence that this was the case. The evidence, I submit, is compelling that, at the very least, the war failed to meet the condition of last resort, and glaringly failed to meet that condition before the beginning of the second phase of the war in 2003. One might argue that the war was justified on the grounds of national interest; or that it was even morally justified on grounds other than those of just-war criteria. I would challenge any such attempts, even though nothing I have said (except for my argument regarding the interpretation of the UN Charter) shows that such arguments might not be successful. But what one cannot do is to argue successfully that the war was a just war, even considered from the limited perspective of the partial war fought by the United States, or that it defeated the presumption against whole war.

10

KOSOVO

Few doubt that if KFOR troops left Kosovo, all the remaining Serbs or Roma would either have to flee or would be killed.

—William G. O'Neill

10.1 The Gulf War and the Kosovo intervention

When Yugoslavia refused to sign the Rambouillet Peace Accord in early 1999, the stage was set for a US-led NATO bombing assault to force compliance. The assault began on March 24 and lasted for seventy-nine days. As a result, Yugoslav President Slobodan Milosovic agreed *inter alia* to cease military operations in Kosovo, withdraw his army, police and paramilitary units, and allow the return of refugees that had fled or been forced out of Kosovo. NATO and Russian troops under UN auspices soon moved into the province. Almost immediately the refugees began returning.

Many hailed this as a model of moral intervention. In this view, nations undertook military action, not to defend themselves but unselfishly to prevent a humanitarian catastrophe from befalling the citizens of another country at the hands of their own government. The words "genocide" and "holocaust" sprinkled liberally throughout press interviews and newscasts underscored the gravity of the crisis. As US Secretary of State Madeleine Albright reportedly saw it, if Hitler had been stopped earlier there would not have been a WWII. NATO intervention would stop criminality in the Balkans before it, too, led to wider conflict.[1]

On the face of it, striking contrasts stand out between the Kosovo intervention and the Gulf War that preceded it and the Iraq War that succeeded it. The Gulf War was heralded as showing the strength and determination of the UN to contain and roll back aggression. It was represented as a model of the legal and just use of force.

---

[1] As reported by the *Washington Post National Weekly Edition*, April 12, 1999.

The Kosovo intervention was undertaken by NATO. And, like the later Iraq War, it was conducted without UN authorization. This seemed a minor detail to many, given the plight of hundreds of thousands of ethnic Albanian refugees and the reports of atrocities against them. But from the standpoint of international law, it was no small point. Some specialists in international law thought there was warrant for the action under the UN Charter. Others did not. But many thought that issue was secondary. What mattered most was that the intervention was right.

So the closing decade of the twentieth century saw two major military actions. One was applauded as a paradigm of the sort of collective action for peace for which the UN was intended. It upheld Kuwaiti sovereignty and seemed to confirm the basic soundness of the global legal order inaugurated at the end of WWII. The other was applauded because it exemplified humanitarian intervention on a hitherto unprecedented scale. It seemed to mark the advent of a new world order in which sovereignty would no longer provide a license for governments to oppress their own people. In both, the use of massive military might was widely applauded.

A moment's reflection reveals the problem with these two actions. The one appeared to uphold the principle of sovereignty in rolling back cross-border aggression from another state. It supposedly reaffirmed the principles of the UN and showed the strength of that organization. The second virtually ignored the UN and supposedly affirmed the right of at least some states (or international organizations) to intervene in the internal affairs of other states for humanitarian reasons.

As argued in the preceding chapter, this conception of the Gulf War is flawed. Far from showing the UN at its best, the war, and the events leading up to it, showed a weak and vacillating Security Council that allowed itself to be used by the United States for its own purposes. The events following it flowed almost seamlessly into the Iraq War, giving rise to the decades-long Persian Gulf War. The purposes of the United States, on the most charitable reading, were those of national interest. Less charitably, they were those of neo-imperialism. Far from fulfilling the promise of the UN, the Gulf War subverted the spirit, and on certain key points, the letter, of the UN Charter.

In any event, I shall argue that the Kosovo intervention represented an even more flagrant disregard of the UN. It set a disturbing precedent for the world in the twenty-first century, a precedent that paved the way for the Iraq War in 2003. Let us begin by recalling some of the key points in the historical context of the Kosovo crisis.

10.2 Historical context

When Constantine Christianized the Roman Empire, he moved its center from Rome to Byzantium (later Constantinople). The emerging division within Christianity between the Roman Church and the Eastern Orthodox Church created a fault-line through the Balkans. The populations of what later emerged as Yugoslavia were predominantly Roman Catholic in the Republics of Slovenia and Croatia, primarily Orthodox in Serbia. With the expansion of Islam into the area in the fourteenth century through the Ottoman Turks, conversions, particularly among peoples in Bosnia-Herzogovina and Albania, added Muslims to the mix. Prior to this, the migration of Slavic peoples into the region created an ethnic division between Slavs and Illyrians, who had long occupied the region, and of whom present-day Albanians consider themselves descendants.

Thus, centered in Yugoslavia were distinctions, first, between Christians and Muslims, second, within Christians between Roman Catholic and Eastern Orthodox, and third, between Slavic and non-Slavic peoples. The term "ethnic cleansing," used in connection with the war in Bosnia was misleading. The conflict among Serbs, Croats and Bosnians was basically a conflict among Slavic peoples, that is, peoples of the same ethnic background. The so-called ethnic cleansing was essentially of Slavs by Slavs. The term was appropriate, however, in the Kosovo crisis, as the Serb routing of ethnic Albanians from Kosovo in the spring of 1999 and the subsequent dispersion of Serbs from Kosovo by the Albanians were indeed cases of ethnically different peoples assaulting one another. It was also a case of a conflict between Christians and Muslims, and could just as easily been represented as such. Both ways of representing the conflict risk being misleading by creating the impression that it was either ethnicity or religion that was at the bottom of the conflict. In fact it was more complicated than that.[2]

Several other particularly relevant points in the historical context warrant mention. The Serbs wrested independence from the Turks in 1878. Backing from Russia—another Slavic nation—helped to establish the bond between the two that factored into the events of 1999. At about that same time the first stirrings of Albanian nationalism were felt, though they were not to result in the formation of an Albanian state until 1913. The Austro-Hungarian Empire sought to extend its influence to the south as the Ottoman Empire crumbled. The Hapsburgs annexed Bosnia-Herzogovina in 1908, creating tensions with Serbia that led directly to WWI. The Serbs claimed a historical entitlement to Bosnia, and in 1914 a group of young Bosnian Serbs assassinated the Archduke Ferdinand of the Hapsburgs in Sarajevo. No one foresaw that the resultant escalation of threats would spiral into WWI. The Balkan Wars of 1912 and 1913 had helped set the stage. Of interest for our purposes is that it was in 1912, when the Serbs, Montenegrins, Bulgarians and Greeks waged war against the Turks that Serbia reclaimed Kosovo, the site of the major defeat of the Serbs by the Turks in 1389. In Serb eyes, a hallowed land of cultural and mythic importance had been reclaimed.

In 1918 the Slavs cobbled together The Kingdom of the Serbs, Croats, and Slovenes. Renamed Yugoslavia in 1929, that state was to be dissolved in 2003, following the wars of the 1990s. WWII brought occupation by the Germans and Italians. The Nazis set up a puppet regime in Croatia, which proceeded to exterminate tens of thousands of Serbs, Roma (Gypsies) and Jews.[3] Serb opposition to the Nazis and Fascists took the form of guerilla warfare by two groups, the Chetniks, who favored a return to the monarchy that had ended just before the outbreak of the war, and the Partisans, communists led by Josip Broz Tito. Ethnic Albanians in Kosovo reportedly fought with the Fascists

---

[2] It may not be unduly cynical to conjecture that one reason the US government chose to represent both the conflict in Bosnia and that in Kosovo as essentially ethnic in character is that in each case it sought backing for its support of Muslims from a predominantly Christian US public, which might have questioned why the United States was supporting Muslims against Christians in the area.

[3] Estimates of the number of Serbs killed in Croatian concentration camps run from 80,000 on the low side, to 800,000 on the high side, with 200,000 being a figure frequently cited.

against the Serbs.[4] The Partisans were the principal force in this struggle, however, and at the close of the war they assumed power under Tito, who ruled until his death in 1980. One could plausibly cite this as the date from which the forces that brought about the dissolution of the former Yugoslavia began to gain strength. Among the six republics that constituted Yugoslavia, first Slovenia and Croatia, then Macedonia and Bosnia, eventually declared independence in the early 1990s.

10.3 Civil conflict

The complexities of the resultant conflicts defy easy summary, but the worst of the bloodshed took place in the fighting between Yugoslav forces and separatists in Croatia and Bosnia. The Serb populations of those two republics threatened to declare their own independence if Croatia and Bosnia broke away from Yugoslavia. They did so, and Serb militias essentially took over the fighting within Croatia and Bosnia when Yugoslav forces withdrew under the weight of sanctions and threats from the international community. The Western nations were quick to recognize the independence of the various Yugoslav republics (though years later they refused to recognize the independence of Crimea or Eastern Ukraine when separatists sought to break away from Ukraine). But they were unwilling to recognize the independence of the Serb minorities within those republics.[5] The West represented Belgrade's military involvement as aggression, and most of the US media followed suit. It was as though Belgrade had marched across international borders to attack neighboring countries. Technically there were grounds for this view, if one assumes that the breakaway republics enjoyed full legal status as nation-states at the time the Yugoslav army sought to hold the country together. In Serb eyes, however, Belgrade was merely trying to put down armed uprisings within their country, Yugoslavia. And whatever one thinks of the hasty recognition given to the independence of the republics by the West, the Serb view was accurate up to the point that recognition was conferred by the West. All that can safely be said is that the peoples of what had been a relatively moderate and neutral communist state turned on one another with extraordinary ferocity. With Slobodan Milosevic, the president of Serbia, and later of Yugoslavia, having largely abandoned the Serb minorities in Croatia and Bosnia, the Croats drove the Serbs out of Croatia[6]— specifically from the Krajina region which Serbs had occupied for hundreds of years— and the West eventually bombed the Bosnian Serbs into submitting to the Dayton Accords in 1995. This ended most of the violence, but left Bosnia in particular in a highly unstable state, in which corruption and the underworld appear to have made greater strides than democracy and liberal principles.

---

[4] See William W. Hagen, "The Balkans' Lethal Nationalism," *Foreign Affairs*, Vol. 78, No. 4, July/August 1999, pp. 52–65.

[5] Only Croatia and Bosnia had significant Serb populations, Croatia about 12% and Bosnia about 32%.

[6] There is evidence that the Croatian offensive, stunning in its swiftness and effectiveness, was planned with the support of some former US generals—at least two of whom were high-up in NATO—through a Virginia based mercenary organization called Military Professionals Resources Incorporated. That

Kosovo, on the other hand, never enjoyed the status of a Yugoslav republic. But it and Vojvodina, the region north of Belgrade, enjoyed substantial autonomy under Yugoslavia's constitution of 1974. Many Serbs had fled Kosovo in the seventeenth century following an abortive rebellion against the Turks, and by the 1980s the predominantly Muslim ethnic Albanians came to constitute 90 percent of the population.[7] They also comprised a large part of the police force in the region. The Albanians in Kosovo had long complained of mistreatment at the hands of the Belgrade government. After Kosovo became autonomous, the Serb minority complained of mistreatment at the hands of the Albanians. Indeed, a large delegation (variously reported as 100 or 200) of Serbs traveled to Belgrade in 1986 specifically to plead for greater protection against the Albanian majority. It was Milosevic's oft-cited vow that no one would ever beat Serbs again—made at a remembrance in Kosovo of the 1389 defeat at the hands of the Turks—that is sometimes said to have ignited Serb nationalism and touched off Yugoslavia's subsequent wars.[8]

The Kosovar Albanians had long agitated for status as a full republic of Yugoslavia. When their autonomy was rescinded by Milosevic in 1989—and as other republics soon gained quick recognition as independent states by the international community— their campaign for greater autonomy evolved into a demand for independence. In the face of repression by Belgrade that removed Albanians from administrative, educational and medical positions throughout Kosovo, the Albanians conducted a nonviolent campaign along Gandhian lines in pursuit of independence. Led by Ibrahim Rugova, they had achieved a large measure of de facto independence through the creation of alternative educational, medical and financial institutions, and had even twice held presidential elections that brought Rugova to the presidency of the self-declared independent Kosovo.[9] A promising 1996 agreement with Milosevic to restore autonomy to Kosovar Albanian schools was never implemented. Stressing the

---

the Croats called their offensive "Operation Storm" could not but help make one think of the Gulf War's "Desert Storm."

[7] There is reason to believe that by 1998 those percentages had changed significantly in favor of the Albanians. The *Christian Science Monitor* of July 3, 1998, reported that thousands of Kosovar Serbs were attempting to sell their homes and flee from Kosovo. It was conjectured that Serb authorities were maintaining silence about the actual numbers, lest it create panic among the remaining Serbs. It had been reported by Reuters in February 1995 that more Serbs were emigrating from Kosovo than were settling there. The Belgrade government, partly, no doubt, to find a place for them, and partly, almost certainly, to help "Serbianize" Kosovo, resettled some 15,000 Serb refugees from the Kraijina region of Croatia in Kosovo.

[8] Serbs had allegedly been beaten by Albanian police. They were again to be victimized following the NATO assault, as detailed by William G. O'Neill, *Kosovo: An Unfinished Peace* (Boulder, CO: Lynne Rienner, 2002; see epigraph at the beginning of this chapter, from p. 54).

[9] Comparing Kosovo's pursuit of independence under Rugova with that of the secessionist republics, Chris Hedges writes: "But after Milosevic revoked Kosovo's autonomy in 1989, Rugova insisted on a very different road to independence, a Gandhi-like plan to withdraw from all state institutions and create a parallel government. His was to be a peaceful revolution and an example of civility and tolerance that would earn the backing of the Western democracies … Under Rugova's leadership, the ethnic Albanians set up their own schools, clinics, and a shadow administration that levied taxes, drawing on the resources of a diaspora of more than 600,000 ethnic Albanians in Europe and some 300,000 in Canada and the United States … But the protest, unsustainable in the long term and a victim of international indifference, collapsed." "Kosovo's Next Masters?" *Foreign Affairs*, Vol. 78, No. 3, May/June 1999, p. 30.

importance of nonviolence, Rugova argued that violence would only give the Serbs a pretext to respond in kind. This they did when the Kosovar Liberation Army (KLA)— a mixture of nationalists, terrorists and suspected drug traffickers—transformed the nonviolent struggle into a violent conflict, targeting Serb police, terrorizing Serb citizens and assassinating suspected collaborators. Confirming Gandhi's conviction that violence begets violence, the Serbs retaliated with increasingly brutal offensives. In shelling and clearing villages suspected of harboring KLA fighters, they created thousands of refugees—much as the United States had done in Vietnam, the Israelis in Lebanon and the Soviets in Afghanistan and Chechnya. It was in the face of this growing humanitarian crisis that the events directly leading to the NATO bombing of Yugoslavia took place.

Having failed to support the nonviolent actions of the Kosovar Albanians, and to initiate creative diplomatic steps to avert the impending disaster, and having failed to make Kosovo a part of the agenda leading to the Dayton Accords, the United States turned, first, to threat, and then to the massive use of force to try to bring about a solution. After all, it had seemed to work against the Bosnian Serbs.

10.4 An attempted military solution

The threat of force to compel Yugoslav compliance with Western demands failed, and the use of force did not proceed as planned. The United States had conducted military maneuvers close to Yugoslavia's border in 1998 to demonstrate that it meant business in demanding that Belgrade end its repression in Kosovo. This did not work. When the United States threatened force in fall 1998, a truce was reached between Belgrade and the KLA. It showed some small signs of leading to a resolution of the crisis, and after October 13, Belgrade withdrew a portion of its forces from the province. Precisely who broke the cease-fire and to what extent is difficult to determine. It was reported on November 11, 1998, that the KLA had killed at least six Serb policemen since the time of the Serb withdrawal. Moreover, the KLA promptly began occupying territory vacated by the Serbs. The Serbs for their part eventually launched a renewed offensive to try to rout the KLA. The first round of the Rambouillet talks that were now underway stalled when the KLA refused to sign on. The second round stalled when the KLA accepted the plan but Belgrade refused to sign on. With Belgrade's offensive against the KLA creating tens of thousands of refugees, an ultimatum was issued by the West: accept the Rambouillet agreement or be bombed.

Indications are that the West thought that the mere threat of bombing would suffice. When this, too, proved mistaken, bombing was commenced on March 24, 1999. Indications are that the United States, the principal architect of the NATO operation, was convinced that after a few days of bombing, Belgrade would capitulate. It did not. Nor did it capitulate after the escalation of the bombing throughout Serbia and to parts of Montenegro and Belgrade itself. It was not until NATO began pounding Serbia's civilian infrastructure seven days a week, twenty-four hours a day, that Belgrade capitulated. Even then it did not agree to a purely NATO presence, as the West had demanded, but insisted that NATO troops enter Kosovo only under UN auspices. This was agreed to. Russia, to the chagrin of the United States and NATO, raced a contingent of its own troops in ahead of NATO to occupy the airport at Pristina. The upshot was that a primarily NATO force, cloaked with a thin veil of UN legitimacy (Kosovo became an international protectorate under UN Resolution 1244), occupied Kosovo. In so doing it also occupied a significant part of Serbia and what remained of Yugoslavia.

Refugees began streaming back, and the KLA moved swiftly to assume administrative control. A young KLA leader, Hashim Thaci, unelected by the Kosovar Albanians, but reportedly a favorite of Madeleine Albright, proclaimed himself prime minister of a provisional government. The Albanians then proceeded to ethnically cleanse most of the minority Serbs and Roma (Gypsies) from Kosovo, attacking religious sites and killing an undetermined number of people. NATO first shrugged off the drive against Serbs as "mischief," then said it was unable to stop it. With the attempted disarmament of the KLA proceeding at a slow pace, and with UN efforts to create a police force and administrative structures proceeding at an even slower pace, the dispersal of Serbs and consolidation of the position of the KLA became *fait accompli.*

NATO found itself in a quagmire. If it continued to coddle the KLA, it would legitimize the KLA's ethnic cleansing of Serbs and Roma and make a mockery of the humanitarian rationale for intervening in the first place; if it did not, it would increasingly find itself in conflict with the KLA, who not only had not seriously disarmed, but also had not given up their fight for independence.

The dilemma NATO created for itself does not, of course, of itself indicate one way or the other whether the action they undertook against Yugoslavia was justified, morally or legally. Let us consider the legal issue first.

10.5 Illegal NATO intervention

The UN Charter is the principal document governing the legal actions of its Member nations. Article 2 of the Charter, paragraph 3, says: "All Members shall settle their international disputes by peaceful means in such a manner that international peace and security, and justice, are not endangered." Immediately following, Paragraph 4 of Article 2 says: "All Members shall refrain in their international relations from the threat or use of force against the territorial integrity or political independence of any state, or in any other manner inconsistent with the Purposes of the United Nations." Paragraph 7 then says: "Nothing contained in the present Charter shall authorize the United Nations to intervene in matters which are essentially within the domestic jurisdiction of any state or shall require the Members to submit such matters to settlement under the present Charter; but this principle shall not prejudice the application of enforcement measures under Chapter VII."

The second document of particular relevance is the NATO Charter, signed April 4, 1949, the preamble to which places NATO squarely under the constraints of the UN. It says in its opening sentence: "The Parties to this Treaty reaffirm their faith in the purposes and principles of the Charter of the United Nations and their desire to live in peace with all peoples and all governments;" and a little later: "They are resolved to unite their efforts for collective defense and for the preservation of peace and security." More specifically, the operative Article 5 of the NATO Charter says in full:

> The parties agree that an armed attack against one or more of them in Europe or North America shall be considered an attack against them all and consequently they agree that, if such an armed attack occurs, each of them, in exercise of the right of individual or collective self-defense recognized by <u>Article 51 of the Charter of the United Nations,</u> will assist the Party or Parties so attacked by taking forthwith, individually and in concert with the other Parties, such action as it deems necessary, including the use of armed force, to restore and maintain the security of the North Atlantic area.
>
> Any such armed attack and all measures taken as a result thereof shall immediately be reported to the Security Council. Such measures shall be terminated when the Security Council has taken the measures necessary to restore and maintain international peace and security.

The Charter clearly authorizes only actions that are in turn legitimized by the UN Charter, with specific reference to Article 51 after which Article 5 of the NATO Charter is patterned. As Article 51 has come in for considerable discussion relating to the issue of intervention, let us have it before us as well:

> Nothing in the present charter shall impair the inherent right of individual or collective self-defense if an armed attack occurs against a Member of the United Nations, until the Security Council has taken measures necessary to maintain international peace and security. Measures taken by Members in the exercise of this right of self-defense shall be immediately reported to the Security Council and shall not in any way affect the authority and responsibility of the Security Council under the present Charter to take at any time such action as it deems necessary in order to maintain or restore international peace and security.

No armed attack occurred against any member of NATO in the events leading up to the March 24, 1999, NATO assault on Yugoslavia. There was, therefore, no warrant under NATO's own Charter for the exercise of the provisions of Article 5 of that Charter as a justification for that assault. Had NATO acted with such warrant under the principal provision of Article 5, it would subsequently have been in violation of that Article's further requirement that the matter immediately be reported to the UN Security Council for its action.

NATO's departure from its own Charter does not in and of itself signify any violation of international law. There are those who would argue that it is up to the NATO nations to define for themselves what their purposes shall be so long as they are consistent with the UN Charter, and that those purposes may be defined by NATO's practice as well as by its treaty commitments. Further, with the end of the Cold War, some would argue that it is the appropriate time for NATO to redefine its role in a changing world order. The events under consideration, moreover, came just on the eve of the celebration of the fiftieth anniversary of NATO's coming into existence, an appropriate time, if any, for such reconsideration of its purposes.

There is some plausibility to this reasoning. For that reason let us look more closely at the legal constraints under which NATO may properly redefine its role in the world. Principally, they are those of the UN Charter, the relevant provisions of which we have just stated. The events involved in the dissolution of the former Yugoslavia were clearly internal events within that country. Whatever one's view of the Yugoslav government of that time, or of its leader, Slobodan Milosevic, from the time of the June 1991 secessions by Slovenia and Croatia to its withdrawal from Kosovo after the 1999 bombing, the Yugoslav government was doing what virtually any government would do in the face of armed insurrections within its own territory. It was trying to put those insurrections down by force. Though the fighting with Slovenia lasted only briefly, the conflicts with Croatia and Bosnia were major, as arguably was the conflict in Kosovo beginning roughly in February 1998. The fundamental issues involved in this breakup of the country were not international issues. They certainly did not constitute international disputes with any NATO countries. Yugoslavia did not attack Hungary, Greece, Turkey or its other Balkan neighbors (though it later made incursions into northern Albania in pursuit of KLA guerillas using that region for attacks against Yugoslavia). It would stretch the meaning of the term to say that the issues behind the ultimatums to Belgrade regarding its role in various Yugoslavian civil conflicts represented an international dispute. To say that it was such a dispute would open the door to any civil conflict within any country being represented as an international issue by other governments taking issue with the first government's role in that conflict. The argument that the conflict became "international" by virtue of the fact that it threatened to destabilize the region is equally suspect. It was the actions of the armed insurgents, the KLA, against an established government that were the threat to stability, not the response of that government to the use of force against it.

Was there, then, warrant under the UN Charter's Article 51 for the NATO assault? There was not. Not only was no NATO nation under attack by Yugoslavia, no member nation of the UN was under attack either. Had it been, moreover, it would have been entitled to engage in armed self-defense only until such time as the Security Council, to which it was obligated to report immediately, had acted to maintain international peace and security. In the events leading up to the NATO assault, President Clinton deliberately bypassed the UN where he faced an almost certain Russian (and possibly Chinese) veto in the Security Council and instead undertook military action through NATO. Indeed, he was quoted as saying the US had the authority to act. Not only was there no pretence of acting through the UN, there was an express resolve *not* to do so. What, then, are we to make of the assault and its subsequent outcome?

In the assault, the United States bombed Yugoslavia for seventy-nine days. Following Yugoslav capitulation, NATO occupied a significant portion of Yugoslav territory. In so doing, it witnessed the expulsion of Serb and Roma peoples—differentiated ethnically from the Albanians—from the occupied territory, along with burning and looting of their homes and what can only be described as terrorist attacks on the persons of many of them. In the process, NATO unintentionally facilitated the breakaway of Kosovo from Yugoslavia. The KLA sought to have Kosovo become, at the least, independent, and at most, part of a Greater Albania that would include parts of Montenegro and

Macedonia. In light of this, let us revisit Paragraph 3 of Article 2 of the UN Charter. It says, once again, that "All Members shall refrain in their international relations from the threat or use of force against the territorial integrity or political independence of any state." And Paragraph 7, which says, "Nothing contained in the present Charter shall authorize the United Nations to intervene in matters which are essentially within the domestic jurisdiction of any state."

These considerations create an overwhelming presumption that the NATO action not only was without warrant by NATO's own Charter, but also was without warrant under the UN Charter, and, even more importantly, was in violation of the UN Charter. In the absence of convincing arguments to defeat that presumption, the NATO action was in violation of international law.

Finally, let us recall Article 6 of the Charter of the International Tribunal at Nuremberg at the close of WWII. Much has been made of the provisions defining war crimes and crimes against humanity. Slobodan Milosevic, and other Baltic individuals, mostly Serb but including Croats, were charged with war crimes in keeping with those provisions.[10] But Nuremberg also defined crimes against peace, specifically: "planning, preparation, initiation, or waging of a war of aggression, or a war in violation of international treaties, agreements, or assurances, or participation in a common plan or conspiracy for the accomplishment of any of the foregoing." Whether or not one considers the NATO attack a war of aggression, it indisputably was in violation of an international treaty, specifically the Charter of the UN. Just as there is a prima facie case that Milosevic and others within Yugoslavia were guilty of war crimes (and perhaps crimes against humanity as well) by the terms of the Nuremberg Charter, there is strong evidence that the leaders of the NATO nations were guilty of crimes against peace by the provisions of the same Charter. It is indisputable that atrocities took place in Kosovo at the hands of Serbs, but it is as yet unclear what measure of legal responsibility any particular individual had for those crimes. NATO leaders, on the other hand, openly undertook actions that constitute prima facie evidence of international crimes against peace. If the twenty-first century is to learn anything from the violence of the twentieth century, it is that it must apply even-handedly the precedents of the twentieth century established in the interests of peace.

10.6 The killing of civilians

There is no space here to take up the arguments of those who think that there is warrant within the UN Charter for humanitarian intervention. While I do not find those arguments persuasive, they do merit consideration in any thorough analysis of the legal dimensions of the intervention. If they should be sound, then, of course, the question would be whether the conditions thought to warrant such intervention were met in the case of Kosovo. If they were, then there was no violation of the Charter and no violation of the Nuremberg principles, insofar as they proscribe war in violation of international treaties. But even if that could be established, it would not settle the issue

---

[10] Slobodan Milosevic died before his trial was completed.

of the moral justifiability of the intervention. By the same token, my analysis in the foregoing does not settle the moral issues one way or the other either, except insofar as there may be moral reasons for compliance with international law. Many, however, might feel that even if the preceding analysis is granted, moral considerations outweigh those of law when it comes to humanitarian catastrophes, and the crisis in Kosovo was on the verge of turning into just such a catastrophe. So some of the more important moral issues involved in the assessment of the intervention remain to be examined.

It is at least relevant to ask at the outset whether there is convincing reason to believe that the governing motivation was humanitarian at all. There was, to be sure, no lack of statements that appealed to high moral purpose, as when Britain's Tony Blair said: "This is the first time that my generation has had to come to terms with the fact that it is necessary to use force on certain occasions to do what is right."[11] And a succinct statement of the humanitarian issue was made by Polish Foreign Minister Bronislaw Geremek, who characterized Kosovo as a new kind of war. In the coming century, he said, "relations between nations can no longer be founded on respect for sovereignty—they must be founded on respect for human rights."[12] Interestingly, in the light of such pronouncements, NATO looked the other way at the Russian onslaught in Chechnya, which created tens of thousands of refugees and took thousands of lives, and at the Israeli conflict with Hezbollah that produced approximately the same number of Lebanese refugees as the Kosovo crisis had Albanian refugees. On the other hand, it has been said that in early 1999 Clinton thought of Kosovo as "a conventional foreign policy problem: he wanted it quickly solved and moved off his agenda."[13] As events unfolded, and pressure grew from some within his own government, particularly from Secretary of State Madeleine Albright, Clinton reportedly soon found himself deeply committed to resolving the Kosovo crisis, and doing so in a way that would reflect favorably on his presidency. It became, in the words of Washington Post staff writer, John F. Harris, a "defining moment" for the Clinton presidency, and he came to represent the issue in terms of vast, historical significance.[14] Other anonymous American officials reportedly held that humanitarianism was not the sole reason the United States was prepared to intervene in Kosovo. Some apparently suggested that it was not even the prime reason.[15] The United States had for years cultivated ties with the militaries of newly independent states arising from the collapse of the Soviet Empire. This gave the United States growing influence in an arc extending from the Baltic, through Slovenia and Croatia, to Azerbaijan and the former Asian republics of

---

[11] Quoted by Jim Hoagland, *The Washington Post National Weekly Edition*, April 26, 1999.

[12] Quoted by Barton Gellman, Washington Post staff writer, *The Washington Post Weekly Edition*, May 3, 1999.

[13] John F. Harris, "Kosovo: Clinton's Defining Moment," *The Washington Post National Weekly Edition*, April 26, 1999.

[14] As John F. Harris puts it: "Standing up to Milosevic's 'organized ethnic hatred,' as Clinton described it to newspaper editors, would make a historic statement that NATO has learned the lessons of a blood-stained century, Clinton asserted, and provide a potent example of the benign purposes for which American power can be applied in the post–Cold War world. A victory, he said, would advance a 'vision of the 21st century world with the triumph of peace and prosperity and personal freedom.'" *The Washington Post*, April 26, 1999. Clinton is considered a hero in Kosovo and a statue of him stands there.

[15] See *Christian Science Monitor*, October 15, 1998.

the Soviet Union; an arc, moreover, that encompassed most of the border of Russia. Albania, moreover, is a pivotal country in the Balkan region, with its placement on the Adriatic.[16] With the fiftieth anniversary of NATO's founding approaching at the time, NATO credibility and prestige were also considered to be on the line. The alliance was seeking a new role for itself following the end of the Cold War. The humanitarian instincts that led the United States and NATO, with a standing army thirty-seven times greater than Yugoslavia's, and with 696 times its wealth, to pound a small country into submission may not have been unalloyed and may not have run very deep.[17]

The central moral point is that the US-NATO attack killed innocent persons. And it was certainly known in advance that it would do so. One cannot target the infrastructure of an entire country in the way in which NATO did without inflicting widespread suffering on the civilian population. The aim, as was oft-repeated, was to "break the will" of Milosevic. The war was personalized around a demonized Milosovic (much in the way the Persian Gulf War was personalized around Saddam Hussein and the crisis over Ukraine around Vladimir Putin), and the bombing was calculated to bring him to his knees. And while the killing of innocent persons almost certainly was not the intention of the assault, it was a clearly foreseeable outcome, being inextricably linked to the means that were used. The words of an anonymous Serbian student are apt here. After detailing long-standing opposition to Milosevic, he wrote: "Now we condemn a NATO that uses the very same arguments, proposals, and threats it has condemned. It may seem that we've joined Milosevic's club. But it's the West that has done so by accepting Milosevic's rules of the game."[18]

But was not the bombing worth it to save the lives of the ethnic Albanians being killed and routed by the Serbs? First, by all accounts, the US-NATO bombing provoked the worst of the onslaught against the Albanians. One cannot justify an action on the grounds that it was necessary to stop wrongs precipitated by the action itself. Not only did it bring on the onslaught, NATO allowed the onslaught to continue for weeks rather than undertake actions that would have risked US and NATO lives. The bombing was conducted from 15,000 feet to render US planes impervious to Yugoslav air defenses, but at considerable cost in accuracy and effectiveness. And Apache helicopters, which were dispatched with much fanfare to Albania, were never used at all, almost certainly because so doing would have entailed US casualties. What we might call the "Hiroshima Principle" was at work here. Better to risk the lives of an adversary's civilian population than those of your own military personnel.[19] More important, we must ask by what

---

[16] Albania was brought into existence as a country in 1913 under pressure from Italy and Austria, both of which wanted to deny Serbia access to the sea. The long-term effects of manipulation by outside powers is evident from the fact that, in drawing the borders of Kuwait, the British likewise tried to deny Iraq full access to the Persian Gulf.

[17] The figures are quoted from *The Washington Post National Weekly Edition,* May 3, 1999.

[18] *Christian Science Monitor,* April 2, 1999.

[19] A similar point is made rather bluntly by Edward N. Luttwak: "In the calculus of the NATO democracies, the immediate possibility of saving thousands of Albanians from massacre and hundreds of thousands from deportation was obviously not worth the lives of a few pilots. That may reflect unavoidable political reality, but it demonstrates how even a large-scale disinterested intervention can fail to achieve its ostensibly humanitarian aim. It is worth wondering whether the Kosovars would have been better off had NATO simply done nothing." See his "Give War a Chance," *Foreign Affairs,* Vol. 78, No. 4, July/August 1999, p. 41.

right one group of people—US and NATO leaders, in this case—decide to kill one set of innocent people in order to save another set of innocent people? More important still, we must ask by what right one group of people decide to kill innocent people in order to ensure NATO's prestige or US credibility? An estimated 1,200 civilians were killed by the US and NATO. Place those bodies in a mass grave and the world would call it an atrocity.

10.7 Conclusion

Oppressive and brutal treatment of citizens by their own governments should not be excused on the grounds of sovereignty. But it is not new, and as such abominations go, the oppression of the Kosovar Albanians by the Belgrade government was not exceptionally severe. The worst of it came only after the KLA resorted to violence and NATO bombing began. Had the West taken more than passing notice of Kosovo as the problems there were developing, there might well have been possible a peaceful resolution to the problem. In particular, some creative diplomacy could have supported the nonviolent resistance of the Kosovar Albanians to the Belgrade government and thereby possibly defused the violence of the KLA. But when the chosen means to counteract a government's repression are the very means one condemns when used in the hands of that government—violence, killing, destruction—the outcome is destined to be tainted and to contain within it the seeds of future violence. Such violence has continued since the occupation of Kosovo by NATO. It is just that the primary victims are now Serbs and Roma. And the resultant instability has allowed Kosovo to become a breeding ground for crime, particularly drug trafficking and human trafficking. Predictably, the day will eventually come when some nationalistic Serbs, or perhaps a Serbian government, will undertake to reclaim Kosovo for Serbia. Having been largely ignored by the rest of the world as it sought a transformation of its political status by nonviolent means, Kosovo is again being largely ignored. Meanwhile, the oppression of Serbs within Kosovo continues and the conditions ripen for an eventual resurgence of violence that could dwarf that witnessed at the end of the twentieth century. The US-NATO action was not a war, but it was warfare, and presumptively wrong, a presumption that was not defeated by the rationales given for the conflict.

Part IV

11

The Metaethics of Pacifism

*and they shall beat their swords into plowshares,and their spears into pruning
hooks: nation shall not lift up sword against nation, neither shall they learn war
any more.*

—Isaiah 2.4

*But in whichever way you interpret the [above] prophecy, no inference can be drawn
from it against the justice of wars, so long as there are men who do not suffer those
that love peace to enjoy peace, but do violence to them.*

—Hugo Grotius

*Sure [the critics say] pragmatic pacifism would be wonderful if everyone was a prag-
matic pacifist, but not everyone is. Those who are not will take advantage of those
who are. Only a fool or a coward practices pragmatic pacifism.*

—Richard Werner

11.1 The argument continued

I have argued in Part I that war$_2$ is presumptively wrong. In Part II I have argued that
the presumption against war$_2$ has not been defeated, on the theoretical side, by either
war realism or the JWT. In Part III I have contended the presumption is not defeated,
on the practical side, by the examples of Vietnam, the Kosovo intervention or the Gulf
War. Vietnam is chosen because of its central importance in American history and the
fact that revisionist histories now defend the war as a just war. The second and third
are chosen because they are widely regarded as models, respectively, of just collective
action under the UN and just humanitarian intervention by NATO. Although I have
argued that the JWT has not been shown to be an adequate moral theory from which
to assess war, the three conflicts in question fail to be just even by standard JWT.
None of the conflicts, in fact, stands up to the tenets of international law. All three are
representative of warfare in the modern world.

I now want to explain the conception of pacifism I believe these conclusions support. To this end, let me summarize the argument to this point:

A1. The deliberate nonconsensual killing of persons is prima facie wrong.
  2. If the deliberate nonconsensual killing of persons is prima facie wrong and tends to be actually wrong, then such killing is presumptively wrong.
  3. The deliberate nonconsensual killing of persons tends to be actually wrong.
  4. Therefore: The deliberate nonconsensual killing of persons is presumptively wrong.
B1. Warfare by its nature is the deliberate, organized and systematic nonconsensual killing of persons.
  2. Therefore: Warfare by its nature is the deliberate, organized and systematic performance of presumptive wrongs.
  3. If warfare by its nature is the deliberate, organized and systematic performance of presumptive wrongs, then warfare by its nature is presumptively wrong.
  4. Therefore: Warfare by its nature is presumptively wrong.
C1. War_1 (partial war) consists of warfare by a collectivity against one or more other collectivities engaged in warfare against it.
  2. If warfare by its nature is presumptively wrong, then war_1 by its nature is presumptively wrong.
  3. Therefore: War_1 by its nature is presumptively wrong.
D1. War_2 (whole war) consists of two or more $wars_1$.
  2. If war_1 by its nature is presumptively wrong, and war_2 consists of two or more $wars_1$, then war_2 by its nature is presumptively wrong.
  3. Therefore: War_2 by its nature is presumptively wrong.
E1. To defeat the presumption that war_2 by its nature is wrong requires showing that the deliberate, organized and systematic nonconsensual killing of persons by all sides that is intrinsic to war_2 is justified.
  2. Rape, torture, the killing of innocents, mistreatment of women, orphaning of children, destruction of property, creation of refugees, and the causing of economic dislocation, medical crises, PTSD, moral injury, unwanted pregnancies and harm to animals and the environment are inherent in war_2 in the modern world.[1]
  3. It is presumptively wrong to rape, torture, kill innocents, mistreat women, orphan children, destroy property, create refugees and cause economic dislocation, medical crises, PTSD, moral injury, unwanted pregnancies and harm to animals and the environment.
  4. Therefore: To defeat the presumption that war_2 by its nature is wrong in the modern world also requires justifying these practices in war_2.

---

[1] Rape, as noted in Chapter 2, is often used as a weapon in war in the contemporary world. Nick Turse writes of US actions in Vietnam: "Rape was a way of asserting dominance, and sometimes a weapon of war, employed in field interrogations of women captives to gain information about enemy troops." Turse, *Kill Anything that Moves*, p. 167. In the 1990s rape was rampant in the civil conflicts in the former Yugoslavia. In the twenty-first century tens of thousands of rapes, mostly against women

5. It has not been shown that the totality of the deliberate, organized, and systematic nonconsensual killing of persons by all sides that is intrinsic to war$_2$, and the rape, torture, killing of innocents, etc. that are inherent in war$_2$ in the modern world, are justified.
6. Therefore: the presumption that war$_2$ by its nature is wrong in the modern world has not been defeated.

To complete the argument, let us return to some earlier distinctions and introduce a concept essential to understanding pacifism of the sort I defend.

11.2 Actionable wrongness

I earlier distinguished prima facie, presumptive and actual wrongness. An act is presumptively wrong if, and only if, there are no evident moral considerations offsetting and overriding its prima facie wrongness, and an act is actually wrong if, and only if, there are in fact no other moral considerations offsetting and overriding its prima facie wrongness. These distinctions are framed in terms of acts, or kinds of acts, as though wrongness were an objective property of acts or kinds. But to speak of a presumption being defeated or not introduces agents into the picture. To defeat a presumption is to do something. It signifies an achievement, the successful outcome of a practical activity. One can succeed or fail at defeating a presumption. If a presumption has not been defeated, that does not mean that it is undefeatable, though the failure of repeated efforts to defeat it provides good reason for concluding that it is undefeatable. But f a presumption has not been defeated, one has no moral warrant to perform the act in question. That is the upshot of calling an act actionably wrong, which we may now characterize as follows:

> An individual act is *actionably wrong* if, and only if, it is presumptively wrong and that presumption has not been defeated.

Accordingly, we may say also:

> A kind of act is *actionably wrong* if, and only if, the individual acts constitutive of that kind are actionably wrong.

To justify a presumptively wrong act is to defeat the presumption against it. Justification, unlike validity, is not an objective relation among propositions. It is, as I have said, the outcome of a practical activity. Most acts that have not been justified are perfectly permissible. As noted in Chapter 2, many acts come heavily weighted on the side of rightness, and there is normally no need to justify them. It is acts that come heavily

but many against men, were used in warfare, particularly in Congo. See "Congo Confronts Rape," *Christian Science Monitor*, August 2, 2009, and "Latest Tragic Symbol of an Unhealed Congo: Male Rape Victims," *The New York Times*, August 5, 2009.

weighted on the side of wrongness—that is, acts that are presumptively wrong—that need justification and are actionably wrong if they fail to receive that justification. To say that an act is actionably wrong does not entail that it is actually wrong. It is to say that we are not morally entitled to perform it, notwithstanding the possibility that it might at some future time in fact be justified or even be shown to be actually permissible. If an act should at some future time be justified, then the act, though now unjustified, would be justifiable, and the presumption of wrongness, though undefeated, would be defeatable. As it relates to the above argument, to say that war$_2$ is actionably wrong is to say that there is no moral warrant to engage in it. This does not entail that it is actually wrong. Even less does it imply that it is absolutely wrong. Actual wrongness I take, on the face of it, to be a character of the act itself.[2] To say that it an act is actionably wrong is to characterize the act in relation to the practice of justification.

That the presumption against war has not been defeated by the reasoning in support of war realism and the JWT does not mean that it cannot be defeated by any conceivable argument. It means only that such an argument has not been produced. While I do not believe that such an argument can be produced, I do not claim to be able to prove that. And that the presumption has not been defeated by the examples of the three conflicts discussed in Part III (Vietnam, the Gulf War and Kosovo) does not show that it has not been defeated in long past wars (e.g., the Revolutionary War, the Franco-Prussian War, the Thirty Years War, The Peloponnesian War, etc.) or could not be defeated with regard to hypothetical future wars. As indicated, my concern is war in the modern world. For this purpose, and specifically to avoid a discussion of WWII—which is a special case and a complex one—I mean war from the time of WWII and extending into the foreseeable future. By saying that war is actionably wrong, I mean that it may not permissibly be engaged in unless the presumption against it is defeated. We may now return to the argument, the fifth stage of which is as follows:

F1. If war$_2$ by its nature is presumptively wrong in the modern world and that pre-
    sumption has not been defeated, then war$_2$ by its nature is actionably wrong in
    the modern world.
 2. Therefore war$_2$ by its nature is actionably wrong in the modern world.
 3. If war$_2$ by its nature is actionably wrong in the modern world, then it is mor-
    ally impermissible in the modern world.
 4. Therefore: war$_2$ by its nature is morally impermissible in the modern

The assertion that war is morally impermissible in the modern world defines what I mean by *pragmatic pacifism*.[3] Since warfare that does not rise to the level of war (either

---

[2] I say "on the face of it" so as not to prejudge the question of whether there are objective moral properties.

[3] In an entry on "Pacifism" in the *Cambridge Dictionary of Philosophy*, 2nd ed. (Cambridge: Cambridge University Press, 1999), I characterize pragmatic pacifism as pacifism held on practical as opposed to moral grounds. I now think of it as a practical but moral position. In so doing, I am following Richard Werner in "Pragmatism for Pacifists," *Contemporary Pragmatism*, Vol. 4, No. 2 (December 2007), pp. 93–115. Werner, however, defines pragmatic pacifism more narrowly, writing "I consider the pragmatic pacifist to be someone who holds, first, that knowingly killing innocent people (such

because only one side is engaging in it or it takes place in limited circumstances, such as in the humanitarian military interventions in Kosovo and Libya) is also presumptively wrong, it also will be wrong in the modern world unless that presumption is defeated.

11.3 Pragmatic pacifism

Pragmatic pacifism, so understood, is not absolute. It does not pretend to knowledge that outstrips what can be established by a practical engagement with the world's problems. It does not mean, as we shall consider shortly, that all logically conceivable wars are wrong, or all possible wars fought by whatever means by whatever agents, human, electronic or robotic, throughout an indefinite future. Other than by persuasively defining war in such a way that wrongness is part of its very meaning, there is no way to rule out the possibility that some logically conceivable wars—and even some possible wars in a remote future—might be justified. To do that would be to make pacifism absolute. It is mostly critics of pacifism who represent it as absolute, by which they seem to mean that it is opposition to all wars in some vague and undefined sense.[4] I have argued that war by its nature is presumptively wrong but have not made it part of the definition of war that it is either presumptively or actionably wrong, much less that it is actually wrong.

Let us locate pragmatic pacifism in the scheme of moral positions with regard to war. I have argued that the central moral issue with regard to war is whether war$_2$ in the modern world is morally permissible, where that hinges upon whether warfare is permissible. I shall discuss that question further in Chapter 12, in connection with the issue of whether pacifism and the JWT converge. While I believe this is the most important issue, there is a broader question. It is whether war can be justified at all, morally or otherwise. One answer to this question is that it can. That view I take to define *militarism*. Militarism has two dimensions, depending upon whether the contention is that war can be morally justified or that it can only be nonmorally justified. That war can be morally justified I take to define warism. That war can be justified, if at all, only on nonmoral grounds (such as national interest) I take to be a realist view and part of militarism. The other answer to the question whether war can be justified at all, morally or otherwise, is that it cannot. I take this view (properly qualified) to represent pacifism. Militarism thus stands on one side of the most important question with regard to war, pacifism on the other. On the side of militarism stand war realism, with its contention that war cannot be justified morally but can be justified nonmorally, namely on grounds of national interest, and the JWT, which contends that war can be morally justified. I have also identified a further category here, the moral war theory, for any approach to the moral justification of war that is not part of the JWT. As we shall see in Chapter 12,

---

as children) against their will is strongly presumptively wrong and, second, that since modern wars involve knowingly killing innocent people against their will, the burden of proof is on the one who wants to wage war to show why we are allowed to knowingly kill innocents in the war" (pp. 94–95).

[4] Interestingly, warists also sometimes claim that war is always wrong. Thus Peter Temes writes: "Yet today the idea that war is always wrong but sometimes necessary makes sense." Peter S. Temes, *The Just War* (Chicago, IL: Ivan R. Dee, 2003), p. 21.

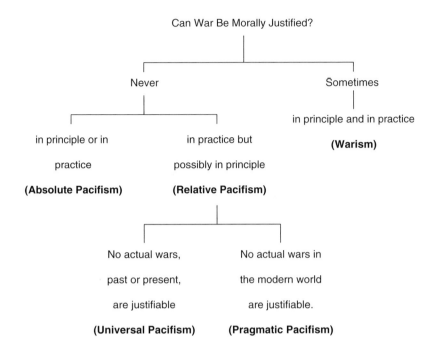

the view that war is justified if commanded by God would be a moral war theory that is not a JWT.[5]

I shall in what follows focus upon pacifism and warism. We may represent these above as answers to the question whether war can be morally justified.

War is justifiable in principle if, and only if, there are hypothetical wars (i.e., wars under conceivable circumstances) that could be morally justified. War is justifiable in practice if, and only if, there are actual wars (present or past) that are, have been or could be morally justified. We may accordingly define warism more specifically than in Chapter 1 and define pacifism in contrast to it as follows:

> *Warism*: There are (a) some hypothetical wars and (b) some actual wars that are morally justifiable.
>
> *Absolute Pacifism*: There are (a) no hypothetical wars and (b) no actual wars that are morally justifiable.
>
> *Relative Pacifism*: There may be hypothetical wars that are morally justifiable but there are either (a) no actual wars (past or present) that are morally justifiable (*Universal Pacifism*) or (b) no actual wars *in the modern world* that are morally justifiable (*Pragmatic Pacifism*).[6]

---

[5] I say this bearing in mind that for Augustine any war commanded by God is just, and some might want to include this claim within the JWT, even though it is not a standard element in the JWT.

[6] Pragmatic pacifism does not attempt to answer the question whether any past wars were morally justified. For an analysis of pacifism understood as grounded in opposition to killing, see Cheney

The various dimensions of pacifism can then be represented as follows:

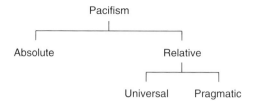

11.4 Pacifism and pacificism

The term *pacifism* appears to have been used for the first time in 1901 by a Russian author, Ivan Novikoff (a.k.a. Jacques Novicow).[7] The term *pacificism* is said to have been coined by A. J. P. Taylor in 1957[8] but was in fact used in 1910 by William James in his classic essay, "The Moral Equivalent of War," in which he called himself a "pacificist" and spoke of Tolstoy's "pacificism."[9] The term is also used at least once by Richard Wasserstrom in a 1969 article.[10]

The first uses of the terms are of historical interest but of limited interest for our purposes here. Of greater interest is whether the two mark out significantly different positions. Sometimes they are used synonymously. At other times different meanings are attached to them. Sometimes those different meanings are thought to render pacifism and pacificism mutually exclusive; at other times, they are understood in a way that makes them mutually supportive. Taylor's position is understood to use

C. Ryan, "Self-Defense, Pacifism, and the Possibility of Killing," *Ethics*, Vol. 93, No. 3, April 1983, pp. 508–525. For an influential expansion of the notion of nonkilling to a worldwide setting, see Glenn D. Paige, *Nonkilling Global Political Science* (Philadelphia, PA: Xlibris Corporation, 2002). For a good account of the array of different conceptions of pacifism, particularly of a religious sort, see Alexander F. C. Webster, *The Pacifist Option: The Moral Argument against War in Eastern Orthodox Theology* (San Francisco: International Scholars Publications, 1998), particularly chapter 4, "Pacifism in Western Ethics."

[7] See Jacques Novicow, selection from "A Sense of Direction for the Peace Movement" (1901), in Chatfield and Ruzanna Ilukhina, *Peace/Mir: An Anthology of Historic Alternatives to War* (Syracuse, NY: Syracuse University Press, 1994), pp. 102–103. Unlike some other peace advocates of his time, Novicow claims that social issues such as poverty are central to the agenda of pacifists. He writes: "Precisely because pacifists … alone can solve the problem of poverty, they will be proudly and justly called the true tribunes of the peoples and the future redeemers of humanity." This idea is also central to the views of Alfred Fried in *The Basis of Pacifism*, 1909, who argues that what he calls *revolutionary pacifism* "turns its energies against the causes of war" (also quoted in *Peace/Mir*, pp. 104–106).

[8] See Teichman, *Pacifism and the Just War*, p. 3.

[9] "The Moral Equivalent of War" is reprinted in Richard A. Wasserstrom (ed.), *War and Morality* (Belmont, CA: Wadsworth, 1970), pp. 4–15. The terms "pacificist" and "pacificism" occur on pages 7 and 10.

[10] Richard A. Wasserstrom, "On the Morality of War: A Preliminary Inquiry," *Stanford Law Review*, Vol. 21, No. 6, June 1969, pp. 1627–1656; an abridged version appears in Wasserstrom, *War and Morality*. The occurrence of "pacificism" is on p. 93, n. 19 of the abridged version.

pacificism to cover "all attempted made (for any reason) to abolish war." Modifying this a bit, I shall understand pacificism as follows:

> *Pacificism*: the view that war can and should be abolished, whether for moral, religious, political, economic or other reasons.[11]

Pacificism implies that war is not inevitable. It can be eliminated and people should work toward that end. Probably most people, if they reflected on the issue, are pacificists in this sense. Pacifism, in most general terms, is different:

> *Pacifism*: Principled opposition to war.

Principled opposition to war might be on moral or nonmoral (including religious) grounds. It is distinguished from mere opposition to one's own participation in war, which we discussed in connection with private pacifism in Chapter 4. One need not repudiate war in general to be against personally participating in war. Ethical pacifism, of which pragmatic pacifism is a subspecies, is defined by the moral judgment that war is morally wrong. Pacifists in this sense will almost certainly be pacificists, but not all pacificists will be pacifists.[12] If one has no principled moral objection to the killing and destruction of war, but thinks war is harmful to the economy, and should be done away with for that reason, one might well be a pacificist but not a pacifist. Pacificism, as defined, is consistent with the belief that states should retain their military forces. It is even consistent with the view that sometimes waging war is morally justifiable.[13] There are, however, many different permutations of pacifism over and above those distinguished in the preceding section. These emerge when one refines the judgment that war is morally wrong, as I shall do in the next chapter. To anticipate that discussion, war can be clarified not only according to whether one means whole or partial war, but also according to whether by *war* one means all conceivable wars or some subset of

---

[11] Sometimes pacificism is defined more narrowly as the view that war ought to be eliminated for moral reasons. See Nigel Dower, *The Ethics of War and Peace: Cosmopolitan and Other Perspectives* (Cambridge, UK: Polity Press, 2009), particularly chapters 5 and 6. "Pacificism," he writes, "may be characterized thus: a belief in the possibility of making peace a more durable and robust feature in human relationships, both locally and globally, and in its ethical desirability as something that ought—morally—to be the object of human endeavour … We should note that not all pacifists are pacificists. It is perfectly possible … that someone's pacifism in respect to his or her belief in the wrongness of killing … goes along with a pessimism about peace becoming more likely, and with no interest in or even with skepticism about there being a general obligation to create the conditions of peace." See *The Ethics of War and Peace*, pp. 144, 147.

[12] As is pointed out by Teichman, *Pacifism and the Just War*, p. 3.

[13] This is how Michael Allen Fox understands pacificism when he writes: "a pacificist usually accepts the necessity of maintaining armed forces and their possible use in the short term to prevent aggression," *Understanding Peace*, p. 272. Richard Norman, following (and quoting) Martin Ceadel (*Thinking about Peace and War* [Oxford, 1987], pp. 4–5), says pacificism "rules out all aggressive wars and even some defensive ones (those which would hinder the political reform for which it is working), but accepts the need for military force to defend its political achievements against aggression." Richard Norman, *Ethics, Killing & War* (Cambridge: Cambridge University Press, 1995), p. 238. Although reasoning along lines that are similar to the argument of this book, Norman in the end rejects pacifism but appears to endorse pacificism

such wars, such as possible wars or war in the modern world. The notion of wrongness admits of elaboration according to the distinctions already made among prima facie, presumptive, actionable, actual and absolute wrongness.[14] The vision of a nonviolent world order cited in the Introduction is clearly pacificistic. This book argues specifically for pacifism but defends pacificism as well.[15]

11.5 An objection to pacifism

To characterize war as a collaborative undertaking invites an objection, of course. The objection is that it might be all well and good if everyone were to refrain from warfare, but the fact is that not everyone will; and if some refrain while others do not, the consequences will be calamitous for those who do.

On the face of it, the argument is compelling. What such critics seem to have in mind is that unless their nation engages in war_1, the consequences will be worse for their nation than if they do. But in light of our argument, this is not the central moral issue. Even if we suppose for the sake of argument that refraining from war_1 would have worse consequences for a particular state than going to war—and assume furthermore that the appeal to consequences is the decisive consideration—that would show at most only that the war_1 was called for by national interest, which is perfectly consistent with its being the case that the resultant war_2 would be unjustified from a moral standpoint. What must be shown is that unless a state collaborates in the production of a war_2, the consequences will be worse overall. One rarely finds an argument to support such a view. The focus almost invariably is upon the consequences of war for one's own nation. Thus those who believe that America's war_1 in Vietnam was justified believe that the deaths of Americans whose names are inscribed on the Vietnam Memorial were justified. The consequences would have been even worse if they had not been killed.[16] But one might envisage another Vietnam Memorial that inscribes not only the names of the Americans who died but also those of all the Vietnamese, Cambodians and Laotians who died as well. Those are the casualties of the whole war brought into existence by America's war_1. It is those casualties that must be justified as well in order for the whole of the Vietnam War to have been justified.

---

[14] For an insightful extended discussion of the distinction, see Andrew Alexandra, "On the Distinction between Pacifism and Pacificism," in Barbara Bleisch and Jean-Daniel Strub (eds), *Pazifismus: Ideengeschichte, Theorie und Praxis* (Bern: Haumpt Verlag, 2006), pp. 107–125.

[15] Alexandra in his discussion of what he calls political pacifism, writes: "war as a political institution consists not simply of episodes of armed conflict between states and the rules and norms governing such conflicts, but also the whole complex of activities and organizations that lead up to and make possible such episodes. It is the institution of war in this comprehensive sense to which the pacifist is opposed: it follows that the peace that the pacifist desires is not simply the absence of fighting, but rather the dissolution of the institution of war." Andrew Alexandra, "Political Pacifism," *Social Theory and Practice*, Vol. 29, No. 4, October 2003, pp. 594–595.

[16] One might, of course, ask exactly the same questions of the Vietnamese regarding the war. One suspects that when they reckon the costs of the war and conclude that it was justified, they do not tally the costs in American casualties.

Some critics might bite this particular bullet and claim that the world is better for the whole wars that nations produce when they engage in wars$_1$ than it would be if they did not. Few, other than Treitschke, actually argue this, though one finds elements of this way of thinking in those who extol the virtues of bravery and self-sacrifice that warfare fosters. But as Sanytayana wrote of this way of thinking, "[t]o call war the soil of courage and virtue is like calling debauchery the soil of love."[17] It is as though one revered the heroism that 9/11 brought out in countless people and then argued for crashing planes into buildings in order to foster heroism.[18]

Pushed a little further, though, this line of reasoning becomes of philosophical interest, for there are the makings of a paradox here. The point of pacifism is to improve the world. It would do this preeminently if universally adopted.[19] But if to adopt it in the actual world (in which there is no universal adoption) were to make things worse than they now are, there would be something wrong with pacifism; something more interestingly wrong than if it were simply mistaken about what would make for a better world. Pacifism would then be self-defeating,[20] just in case there were any who did not accept it. Since there are many who do not accept it, this means that there is no possible state of affairs that does not count against pacifism save the one in which all nations already act as it prescribes; in which case its advocacy would be pointless. Pacifism therefore is either self-defeating or otiose.

Let us now look more closely at the objection and what it entails. Consider the following passage from R. A. Wasserstrom:

> This argument is something of a paradox. If everyone were to accept and consistently to act upon the principle that force ought never to be used, even in cases of self-defense, then there would be nothing to worry about. No one would ever use force at all, and we really would not have to worry about misapplication of the principle of self-defense.
>
>   But ... [the] appeal is to persons to give up the principle of self-defense even if others have not renounced even the aggressive resort to force. In other words ... [the] argument is one for unilateral rather than bilateral pacifism, and that is precisely what makes it so hard to accept.[21]

As framed, this objection applies more accurately to nonviolence than to pacifism, since it appears to have to do with the personal resort to force in self-defense. But, by

---

[17] George Santayana, *Reason in Society* (New York: Collier Books, 1962), p. 68.

[18] As A. A. Milne argued regarding the sinking of the Titanic, in *Peace with Honour* (New York: E.P. Dutton, 1934), p. 66.

[19] Except, of course, in the view of Hitler, Tretischke, Hegel and others who think that war is a good thing.

[20] Meaning that it would be morally self-defeating, not necessarily self-defeating from other points of view, such as national interest. A pacifist can readily concede that on the usual interpretations of self-interest a commitment to pacifism may involve sometimes having to sacrifice that interest. This means only that for the pacifist there is the possibility of a conflict between self-interest and morality—a problem, to be sure, but no more of a problem for pacifism than for any other nonegoistic moral position.

[21] "On the Morality of War: A Preliminary Inquiry," in R. A. Wasserstrom (ed.), *War and Morality* (Belmont, CA: Wadsworth, 1970), pp. 92f. Wasserstrom is here assessing the claim that the

extrapolation, it may be taken to apply to the conduct of states as well, and I shall so take it in what follows. A similar point made specifically with regard to pacifism as an antiwar position is the following:

> The trouble with pacifism in general is that it sends … the wrong set of signals to the people we need to be concerned about, namely those who are ready to achieve their various ends by the use of violence against others … And surely the same thing applies in the case of states. The rationality of laying down one's arms is contingent on the reciprocal laying-down of arms by the rest. If only some of us do, unconditionally, then we simply put ourselves into the power of, or at any rate lay ourselves open to the evils ready to be imposed by whose who did not … Pacifism, then, is a mistake. Starting with the reasonable premise that violence is evil, it arrives at a conclusion that paves the way for more evil rather than less. That, indeed, is self-refutation.[22]

A similar, though distinguishable, point is made explicitly with regard to states in the following passage:

> Although all decent states prefer a situation in which all are unarmed to a situation in which all keep their military forces, since each decent state is interested, first and foremost, in protecting the legitimate interests of its own citizens, each most prefers for all others to disarm, while it alone retains its military capacity.[23]

This passage is plausible as a representation of the probable outlook of most states. It tends to confirm descriptive realism, as described in Chapter 3. The moral issue that interests me concerns the value of the overall consequences of these various states of affairs and how that reflects upon pacifism.

On first consideration, it is an unusual condition to attach to the acceptance of a moral position that others accept it as well. It might suggest that we should refrain from lying, stealing, murder and rape only on condition that others do, too. But the critic who advances this sort of objection against pacifism has two replies available. The first is to point out that what is at issue is whether pacifism is sound, not whether *if* it is sound, one should allow considerations of self-interest to override it. The second is to concede that with regard to conduct like lying, cheating and thieving, the fact that

---

consequences of renouncing the use of force even for purposes of self-defense would have been (or would be) better than those which have in fact resulted from the use of force. This is a more specific issue than the one concerning pacifism in the objection. It is not entirely clear that Wasserstrom himself subscribes to the objection we are considering; he may be simply posing the problem. Notice that, convenient as they are, the terms "Bilateral" and "Unilateral" pacifism are misleading if taken to represent types of moral positions. They simply indicate the extent to which pacifism is held and are more accurately descriptive of alternative states of affairs than of moral positions.

[22] Jan Narveson, "Is Pacifism Self-Refuting?" in Barbara Bleisch and Jean-Daniel Strub (eds), *Pazifismus*, pp. 143–144. It has also been argued by Narveson, in his influential "Pacifism: A Philosophical Analysis," *Ethics*, Vol. 75, 1965, pp. 259–71, that pacifism is self-contradictory. His argument there, however, runs along different lines from the one we are considering and has been so widely analyzed by others that I will not consider it beyond what I have said in Chapter 7.

[23] Benbaji, "The Moral Power of Soldiers to undertake the Duty of Obedience," p. 51.

not everyone will accept the injunctions against them is not a good reason for my not doing so, but then to maintain that there is an important dissimilarity between these cases and the issue over pacifism. For, it might be argued, I can normally refrain from these other practices without disadvantaging myself in vis-à-vis other persons so long as I retain the right of self-defense; so long, that is, as I draw the line against possible depredations against me at the point at which they threaten violence. When and only when that line is crossed may I resort to conduct I otherwise deem reprehensible. The same, it might be claimed, is true of nations.[24]

This second reply is open to several interpretations. It might be taken to mean that in cases of self-defense self-interest overrides moral considerations; or it might be taken to mean that self-defense overrides considerations of overall value produced or, third, that utility always falls on the side of self-defense.[25] On the first interpretation the issue would hinge on the question of the relationship between prudence and morality and would involve pacifism only incidentally. The point of the objection is not simply that to act pacifistically is to risk having to yield self-interest to morality; it is that pacifism is *morally* self-defeating. On the second interpretation the pacifist has an immediate reply in the form of a denial that self-defense is an overriding consideration morally. The door to such a reply is opened by a further comment of Wasserstrom's:

> Still another argument against unilateral pacificism [*sic*] is, of course, that there are evils other than the destruction of lives. Suppose, for example, that unilateral pacifism would result in fewer deaths but in substantially greater human slavery. It is by no means clear that such would be a morally preferable state of affairs.[26]

The point here is a fair one but it cuts two ways. For the pacifist may maintain, with Tolstoy, Gandhi and King that morally speaking there are more important things than saving one's own skin, one of them being to refrain from killing other persons. It is the person who claims an imprescriptible right to self-defense who is as likely as not to deny the claim referred to in the first sentence of this quotation. Either pacifism does not entail the overwhelming risk of personal sacrifice that is often alleged, or it cannot be charged with placing nothing above the value of human life. In any event, if in taking this line the pacifist and his critic are appealing to considerations other than value produced (as Wasserstrom may be doing in the allusion to justice), they would have departed from the consequentialist orientation which is our present concern.[27] On the third interpretation, finally, this reply collapses into the first one by throwing the issue back upon the question of whether or not pacifism is sound on consequentialist grounds.

---

[24] In international law governing reprisals, states may engage in specific acts, otherwise prohibited, in response to such acts by other states.

[25] By self-defense I shall here assume is meant violent self-defense; pacifists can—and most do— support nonviolent national defense.

[26] *War and Morality*, p. 93, n. 19.

[27] My concern is not to adjudicate between consequentialist and nonconsequentialist theories, though some of what I say will bear on that dispute, but to see whether or not, within a consequentialist framework, pacifism is peculiarly self-defeating.

The first reply, I suggest, more nearly captures the spirit of the original objection. What is at issue is whether pacifism is refuted by virtue of universal pacifism's being shown to have less than optimal consequences. So let us look further at the critic's position.

11.6 A pacifist reply

Note that the objection implicitly distinguishes among the following states of affairs:

a. everyone acts pacifistically;
b. no one acts pacifistically;
c. some act pacifistically and some do not;

The objection claims that the progression from (a) to (c) is from best to worst.[28] Bilateral pacifism obtains if (a) is the case, unilateral pacifism if (c) is the case. The critic then rejects the pacifist principle:

P: Everyone ought to act pacifistically.[29]

even though he concedes that full compliance with (P) (and only full compliance with it) would yield the best state of affairs. He maintains that because not everyone will act pacifistically, unilateral pacifism is the best we could hope for, and as it is untenable, pacifism is untenable. Notice, however, that if, as we are assuming, the critic is also a consequentialist, then of the two negations of (P), namely

NP1: It is not the case that everyone ought to act pacifistically,

and

NP2: No one ought to act pacifistically,

he is committed to (NP2), since his objective is to maximize value in the given circumstance, and (NP1) would be compatible with its being the case that some persons act pacifistically, which is alleged to be the worst state of affairs.

---

28 The question "Worse for whom?" is pertinent here. It makes a difference whether acting pacifistically has worse consequences only for pacifists or for others as well. Its having worst consequences only for pacifists would be compatible with its having better consequences overall than would full compliance with warism, since the benefits to those who would try to take advantage of pacifists might substantially outweigh the harms they cause. To interpret "worse for whom?" as meaning worse for everyone would, however, conflict with the spirit of the original objection, because it says in effect that no one, not even aggressors, profits from the fact that some nations act pacifistically. Between these two extremes there is an indefinite number of ways of both quantifying the persons who are alleged to suffer from the conduct of pacifists and of specifying their identity. Which of these one concentrates upon makes a difference to how the objection is to be understood and assessed. I shall take the objection to mean that the consequences would be worst overall and on balance if pacifism were adopted by only some nations.

29 I shall at this point introduce only as much specificity into the characterization of pacifism as is necessary for our present purposes. As we have seen, there are many different forms of pacifism, as well as different grounds upon which it might be held.

But note that by parity of reasoning the same kind of argument can be used against the warist. For if, as seems to be the case, some people will persist in refusing to use violence, that is, will persist in acting pacifistically, then no less than in the case of (P) when some people refuse to refrain from violence, the consequences of following (NP2) will be worse than as though either everyone or no one followed it. For then circumstance (c) will obtain no less than as if (P) were adopted, and violent conduct will similarly prove to be self-defeating. Thus the pacifist may say that while it might be nice if everyone could be counted upon to be violent, it is unrealistic to suppose that they will, and that so long as there are some who will not, a warist principle like (NP2) cannot be consequentially justified.

By this analysis, the critic's line of reasoning would be self-defeating, in the sense that it could succeed against the pacifist only by succeeding equally against his own position. This would mean that neither argument prevails and that there is a standoff between the pacifist and the warist on this point. But although this argument is just as good as the original one, it is also just as bad, and bad for the same reasons; which means that although it is effective as an *ad hominem* it leaves unresolved the basic issues in the dispute. To see what these issues are, and why, if I am correct, the original argument is wrongheaded, let us allow this dialectical interplay between the pacifist and the warist to unfold further.

11.7 A second pacifist reply

Suppose the warist modifies his position so that state of affairs (c) no longer exposes warism to the same objection brought against the pacifist. Suppose that rather than maintaining that it is both necessary and sufficient that everyone follow (NP2) in order to achieve the favorable balance of value, he maintains only that it is sufficient, and that all that is necessary is that there be *general* acceptance of (NP2). Then the claim on behalf of (NP2) would be compatible with the existence of a small minority of unregenerate pacifists, and following (NP2) would not, by their recalcitrance, be rendered self-defeating.

If, however, the warist takes this line of defense, then his original objection to pacifism no longer holds. For that objection derives its force from showing that unilateral pacifism commits one to a state of affairs (c) which allegedly is the worst of the three, and from assuming that (NP2) is preferable by virtue of committing one only to (b) (which, while less desirable than (a), is more desirable than (c)). And now that tack is no longer possible. The modification of (NP2) has the effect that, if the claim made on its behalf is true, then a state of affairs (c) does obtain, in which case it cannot be the worst state of affairs. That is, it cannot be the case both that the claim advanced in the modified warist position is true and that pacifism is refuted simply by virtue of entailing (c). If so, to show that this state of affairs is worst cannot refute either pacifism or warism without refuting the other also.

Moreover, if the warist takes this line he must be prepared to entertain a similar modification of bilateral pacifism, to the effect that the general acceptance of (P) would have the best consequences. Such a modification would mean that one could no longer refute pacifism by arguing that the nonuniversal acceptance of it is self-defeating, since the claim contained in the modified version is compatible with nonuniversal acceptance.[30]

To proceed in a fashion analogous to the original objection, one would have to argue that although general acceptance of (P) would have the best consequences, following (P) in circumstances in which there is not general acceptance of it would have worst consequences.[31] But if one argues this then he must deal with a question that has been pertinent almost from the outset: How is it that, if the pacifist's claim is that *general acceptance* of (P) would have best consequences, it is at all relevant to point out that following (P) under conditions of *non-general acceptance* would have bad consequences.[32] This latter claim not only is not denied by pacifism, it is in fact asserted by it. Indeed, it is entailed by the pacifist position. If it were not the case the nongeneral acceptance of (P) would have bad (i.e., less than optimal) consequences, the original claims—acknowledged by both sides—that general acceptance (and only general acceptance, as we are understanding this) would have best consequences would not be true. Thus the pacifist may say that if one's basic moral principle calls for the maximization of value, and if it is agreed that this can be achieved only if everyone (or, on the modified version, people generally) acts pacifistically, then it is no argument against the soundness of this principle to insist that some people will not do as it prescribes. It is precisely *because* not everyone acts pacifistically—and more to the point, nations do not act pacifistically—that there is some point to the judgment that they ought so to act.[33]

11.8 Consequentialist considerations

Let us look, therefore, at specific arguments the warist might marshal against this pacifist rejoinder. These derive from the debate over utilitarianism. For (P) is what has come to be called an ideal rule (roughly, a rule whose general following would have best consequences), and the justification of (P) presupposed by the foregoing discussion is

[30] If by "general acceptance" is meant "accepted by most but not all persons," then the claim entails that value may be maximized even if not everyone accepts (P).

[31] Meaning that it would have worse consequences relative to both general acceptance of (P) and general nonacceptance of (P).

[32] Or, in the original form, if the claim is that everyone's following (P) would have best consequences, how is it relevant to say that not everyone's following (P) would have less than optimal consequences?

[33] There is an altogether different line of attack open to the warist. It is to challenge the pacifist to detail how one gets from the truth of the claim that everyone's following (P) (or that general acceptance of (P)) would have best consequences to the conclusion that everyone should follow (P). This, in effect, is the question of how one justifies the particular version of rule-consequentialism represented by the defense of pacifism under consideration. And it is a fair question. But the warist who takes the original line discussed above has the same type of problem. The warist has to show how one gets from the claim that no one's following (P) would have better consequences than some persons (only) following it, to the conclusion that no one ought to follow (P). Since there is in fact neither total compliance nor total noncompliance with (P), in each case a judgment about what everyone in fact ought or ought not to do is derived from a value judgment about a hypothetical state of affairs. The warist fares somewhat better on the modified version of his theory. The modified version claims only that the consequences of general acceptance of (P) would be better than the consequences of partial

a form of ideal rule-utilitarianism (IRU) (roughtly, the view that one ought always to follow ideal rules). One of the clearer statements supportive of the theoretical position represented by the objection we are considering is the following:

> The general point here is that if one person were to act in accordance with a rule the general following of which would have best consequences, this might, if there is *not* general following of this rule, be of considerable disutility, and clearly wrong according to common-sense standards.[34]

The point is that following ideal rules under the conditions described would in effect be anti-consequentialist, hence, as the objection against pacifism puts it, self-defeating. How is this argued?

There are two closely related points to be considered here. The first is that following such rules would sometimes prevent us from minimizing the bad consequences of the conduct of others. The second alleges a serious defect in the framing and imaginative "testing" of such rules consequentially.[35] We shall discuss the first of these points later, but as its formulation is necessary to understanding the second, let us introduce it now:

> Suppose that there is a general practice of cutting across the lawn, sufficient to keep the grass in a bad state irrespective of what any one agent does. Suppose further that if there were instead a general practice of walking around the lawn except in cases of urgency, the situation would be very much better: the lawn could be made and kept attractive, and so give much pleasure; no really urgent appointments would be missed; and the time lost and energy expended in going around the lawn would make little difference in other cases … It seems likely … that rule F [forbidding the taking of the shortcut except in cases of urgency] would be the relevant ideal

acceptance, and that therefore (given that there is no general acceptance) no one ought to follow (P). If this modified claim is said to describe the existing state of affairs in the world, then it is hard to see what basis has been provided for prescribing a change in that state of affairs (so that no one should act pacifistically); or why, if that state of affairs is to be changed, it is better changed in the direction of no one's acting pacifistically than in the direction of everyone's acting pacifistically. If the modified version does not describe the existing state of affairs, then once again the warist is basing a prescriptive judgment on a value judgment about a hypothetical state of affairs, in which case the warist stands no better than the pacifist.

[34] D. H. Hodgson, *Consequences of Utilitarianism: A Study in Normative Ethics and Legal Theory* (Oxford: Oxford University Press, 1967), p. 166. If only one person is following a rule and everyone else is not, somewhat different issues arise than in the problem we are considering. It is one thing to claim that an individual is under no obligation to do *x* if *no one* else recognizes that obligation; it is another to claim that one is under no obligation to do *x* if *not everyone* recognizes that obligation. It might plausibly be argued, in the manner of Hobbes or Hume, that some version of the former claim is correct (at least with respect to certain obligations, such as those connected with justice) without the latter claim's being correct. I take Hodgson to be making the latter claim (appropriately qualified to cover the "general following" of rules rather than full compliance), and shall so interpret him in what follows.

[35] David Lyons, in his classic *Forms and Limits of Utilitarianism* (Oxford: Oxford University Press, 1965), presents a similar argument, but one which focuses directly upon (IRU) itself rather than upon the rules whose following it prescribes. Formulating (IRU) as follows: (IRU): An act is right if, and only if, it conforms to a set of rules general acceptance of which would maximize utility, he reasons:

rule; and in this case, it would be right for an agent to act in accordance with F, and wrong for him not to do so. This is quite irrespective of whether or not there would be a change in the existing practice of cutting across the lawn, and so quite irrespective of whether or not complying with rule F would have any real point.[36]

Such allegedly is the reasoning behind (IRU). What is the hitch here? It is that

in order to arrive at a rational decision as to whether or not to take the shortcut, an agent would need to weigh the time and energy he would save by taking it, against the possibility of a change in the practice which would result in an improvement in the state of the lawn. If there would in fact be no change in the practice, no matter what the agent did, it would be pointless for him to walk around the lawn; and it would surely not be wrong for him to cut across it. Indeed, the bad consequences of the practice would be *minimized* by his saving time and energy by cutting across the lawn.[37]

In short, it would appear that acting on an ideal rule like F would prevent us from minimizing the bad consequences of certain practices, hence would prevent us from maximizing value.

Even if one were to grant the major portion of this analysis, the claim advanced in the final sentence quoted is a curious one. If my fellow townspeople are looting and will continue to loot irrespective of what I do, then whether or not it would be pointless for me to refrain, it would seem self-deceptive to convince myself that I am minimizing the bad consequences of their conduct by joining them. Whether or not looting is ever morally permissible (and there are easily imaginable circumstances in which it would be), such reasoning would be a suspect justification.

Perhaps it will be urged that we should distinguish between bad practices which are negatively value-saturated, in the sense that their constituent acts individually have bad consequences, and those which are not so saturated (and whose constituent acts do not individually have bad consequences), and that the point about minimizing bad consequences applies only to the latter.[38] We would then have a relevant dissimilarity

---

"(1) The point of (IRU) is to maximize utility. (2) But there are some cases in which applying and acting upon (IRU) will not yield the best possible consequences, that is, when (IRU) is not generally accepted. (3) Thus (IRU) cannot be an acceptable moral principle, since in some cases (that is, when it is not generally accepted—which is the normal state of affairs) applying and acting upon (IRU) would be self-defeating" (p. 142).
It is unclear whether this is Lyons's own view or simply an argument he presents for consideration. In any event, the issues are similar whether we are discussing IRU or particular ideal rules, since to show that (P) or any other ideal rule is self-defeating would suffice to show that IRU is also self-defeating. For it would mean that consistent application of IRU would sometimes fail to maximize value. Whether the reverse is also true, and one could show that any given ideal rule is self-defeating by showing that IRU is self-defeating, would depend upon precisely what was shown regarding IRU; specifically, whether it was shown that following IRU is always self-defeating, or only that it is sometimes self-defeating, and if so, whether it is self-defeating in the type of situation governed by the rule in question.

[36] *Consequences of Utilitarianism*, p. 167f.

[37] *Consequences of Utilitarianism*, p. 167.

[38] This would be part of a broader distinction between what we might call *value-saturated* and *value-unsaturated* practices. Value-saturated practices would be those whose constituent acts, considered

between lawn-crossing and looting and could apply the minimization of disvalue argument in the one case (lawn-crossing) but not in the other.

As useful as this distinction may be, it will not do the service expected of it here. The issues involved in pacifism are more akin to those in the looting example than to those in the lawn-crossing example. If we think of the acts of warfare (inflicting violence, killing and destruction) that are the concern of pacifism as constituting a practice, it is clear that, unlike the practice of taking a shortcut across a lawn, it is a negatively saturated practice. Pacifism is concerned with acts of violence. And it is part of the very meaning of an act of violence that its successful performance causes harm, destruction or death.[39] Such acts are not only bad they are presumptively wrong as well. That an act of violence causes harm or death does not normally depend upon the performance of similar acts by anyone else, either at the same time or at other times. Walking across a healthy lawn, on the other hand, causes harm only if done by a large number of people over a short period of time.[40] If, therefore, application of the minimization of disvalue argument were limited in the way proposed, it would miss the mark against pacifism.

There is more to be said about this objection, however, and we shall return to it later. For the moment let us proceed to the second objection, which alleges a defect in the procedure for testing ideal rules.

> This result [in favor of F] is reached because in testing rule F, the existing practice sufficient to keep the grass in a bad state had (logically) to be ignored. To postulate general following of rule F (in accordance with the ideal-rule-utilitarian principle) is to postulate a situation where there is no such practice. That is, in testing rule F,

---

individually, all have either good or bad consequences, or both. The practices would then be respectively positively, negatively or both positively and negatively saturated. Unsaturated practices would be those which are not value-saturated in this sense. Some of the more vexing problems in ethics arise over the fact that positively saturated practices can have bad consequences overall and negatively saturated practices can have good consequences overall. We have seen in Chapter 6 a closely related issue (framed in deontic rather than value terms) for warists who hold that there is moral equality among soldiers. If all soldiers may permissibly kill one another in war, some wars could be unjust virtually all of whose particular acts were permissible.

[39] This is compatible, nonetheless, with its being the case that the concept of an act of violence is normatively (though not evaluatively) neutral, since it does not entail that to call something an act of violence is to be committed to a final moral judgment about its rightness or wrongness.

[40] Thus making its bad consequences dependent upon threshold-related effects; that is, effects pertaining to the performance of a certain type of act with a certain frequency, or by a certain number of persons at the same time or in the same place, and so forth. David Lyons stresses the importance of threshold-related effects for minimization of disvalue arguments, saying: "Minimizing-conditions allow for circumstances in which there is in fact a general practice of A (and thus A's bad threshold effects are produced): acts A would be allowed under such circumstances. That is, in so far as the bad effects of acts A are threshold-related, if the threshold is already passed, then further acts A would not be considered wrong" (*Forms and Limits of Utilitarianism*, p. 137). Hodgson implies much the same in saying that the problem arises "especially in regard to circumstances where desirable or undesirable effects would be produced by a general practice of acting in a certain way, but would not be produced if only a few persons acted in that way" (*Consequences of Utilitarianism*, p. 167). Both may therefore intend that the minimization of disvalue argument not apply to what we are calling negatively saturated practices.

before any consequences were calculated, a circumstance which would in fact have important consequences was postulated out of existence.[41]

The point here is that what is supposedly wrong with (IRU) is that it systematically ignores a relevant circumstance in calculating the consequences of the general following of the rules it proposes, namely the existence of precisely the bad practice whose elimination is its aim. To rectify this, the argument continues, we need an exclusionary condition disqualifying from an (IRU) justification any rule whose general following *"would have best consequences by reason of its involving the following of that rule by some person or persons (other than the agent) who were not in fact following it and/or would not in fact do so."*[42]

According to this modified version of (IRU), the existence of the practice producing bad consequences is specified as one of the circumstances of the application of the rule. This means, as Hodgson observes, that the rule then applies "only to those (not necessarily determinate) persons whose participation was not (logically) necessary for the existence of such a practice."[43] Such a condition would clearly rule out a defense of pacifism on the grounds we are considering, since when it is claimed that pacifism would have best consequences if either fully or generally complied with, the ground of that estimate is surely meant to include the following of (P) by some who are not now in fact following it, and it is almost certainly meant to include the following of (P) by some who will not do so.

What are we to make of this argument? First notice that once again a parallel argument can be advanced against the non-pacifist position (NP2), by pointing out that it ignores the "practice" of pacifism and only by so doing comes out with the conclusion that following (NP2) would have better consequences than following (P). This means that if the argument in question were sound it could be turned with equal effectiveness against the non-pacifist. Not only that, but if the continuation of the practice is specified as one of the conditions of the application of the rule, then, as in the above case, we have the untoward consequence that the rule would not apply to any who were not already acting as it prescribes or could not be expected to act as it prescribes. And as it is normally one of the functions of normative rules to redirect the conduct of those whose conduct does not accord with it, to deny the application of such rules to persons falling under this description would be to deprive normative rules of one of their characteristic functions.

These considerations aside, what I wish to focus upon is the fourth sentence of the last long quotation: "That is, in testing rule F, before any consequences were calculated, a circumstance which would in fact have important consequences was postulated out of existence." This claim is central to the argument against (IRU). Now if, as Hodgson may intend, this claim is meant merely to explain what exposes (IRU) to the first objection,

---

[41] *Consequences of Utilitarianism*, p. 168. Hodgson appears at one point to take this to be definitive of ideal rules, saying that "rule F is an ideal rule because, when testing it, one has to ignore a circumstance which in fact has important consequences, and which (one would think) an agent would need to take into account in order to arrive at a rational decision on the matter" (p. 169).

[42] *Consequences of Utilitarianism*, p. 172.

[43] *Consequences of Utilitarianism*, p. 168.

then its assessment will hinge upon our disposition of that objection. If, however, there is a separate point here, what is it? It cannot simply be that what is ruled out in the testing of F is the continuation of the bad practice in question, since that, after all, is what is hypothesized in the testing of F in the first place. To hypothesize the general following of F *is* to hypothesize a state of affairs in which there is no bad practice in question, and one cannot without question-begging require that its continuation be considered a relevant circumstance in the projection and estimation of the consequences of the general following of F. It sounds, rather, as though the point is that built into (IRU) is a procedure for testing rules which systematically omits a relevant consideration and thereby rigs the outcome in favor of the rules whose following it prescribes. And indeed it would be a serious objection to (IRU) if, say, it logically precluded consideration of consequences relevant to the testing of its rules. But does it do this? It seems clear that it does not. The good state of affairs associated with the hypothesized following of an ideal rule is not postulated before any consequences are calculated but precisely *as a result* of the calculation of consequences; specifically those of the rule's being followed by the appropriately quantified number of persons. Bad consequences are not logically ruled out of the hypothesized situation, since they are merely a causal and not a logical consequence of the practice in question. All that is ruled out is the continuation of the practice (since, once again, that is what is being hypothesized). Once the general following of the rule is hypothesized, it is the judgment that *in consequence* of such general following a desirable state of affairs will eventuate, which constitutes the so-called testing of the rule.

11.9 Act utilitarianism

But does this really help the pacifist? If (IRU) is not restricted in the manner just considered, does it not fall prey to counterexamples of the lawn-crossing type? And do not such examples suffice to establish the soundness of the original objection that (P) is self-defeating?

This requires taking a closer look at the first objection. It maintains, we recall, that following ideal rules is self-defeating because it would sometimes prevent us from performing specific action that would minimize the bad consequences of the conduct of others. To be pertinent, however, alleged counterexamples must themselves be justifiable by reference to the consequentialist principle, (C), that one should maximize value in the consequences of conduct; otherwise their certification could not show that following (P) is self-defeating. And that justification will have to be one that requires that we judge individual acts according to whether or not they maximize value *in the particular circumstances* in which they are performed (or at least that we so judge all cases of the kind at issue over pacifism). If the alleged rightness of my taking the shortcut across the lawn is based on the claim that by so doing I can maximize value (read: minimize the disvalue of the practice I am joining), then *my particular act in those circumstances* must be held to be justified directly by reference to (C), rather than by reference to rules whose general following is held to be justified by (C) (if, *ex hypothesi*, F is the ideal rule in that circumstance, then any rule that is incompatible with it—as a rule would have to be which sanctioned violating F—could not also be an ideal rule). But this would mean that the justification for the act in question will be an act utilitarian (or act consequentialist) justification, and if so, to advance such cases as counterexamples to (IRU) will be question-begging, since it is no objection to an ideal rule-utilitarian justification that it is not act utilitarian. If (IRU) and act utilitarianism (AU) are in fact competing theories, we should expect that they would sometimes yield different moral judgments. Indeed, one of the motivating forces behind rule-utilitarianism of any sort is precisely to show that certain types of action called for by (AU) (such as breaking promises to achieve a gain in utility) are not mandatory and may even be prohibited on consequentialist grounds. The objection therefore merely highlights the differences between (IRU) and (AU) and does not constitute a refutation of the former.[44] Much less does it constitute a refutation of (P).

It will not do, notice, to counter this by arguing that, if properly understood and correctly applied, (IRU) and (AU) are in fact extensionally equivalent and cannot yield different moral judgments. For this would undercut the original argument that pacifism is self-defeating, since that argument turns upon the claim that following (P) will sometimes fail to have the best consequences, and that can be the case only if the (IRU) basis for (P) *can* yield conclusions different from (AU). Either, therefore, (IRU) and (AU) are not extensionally equivalent or the argument that (P) is self-defeating fails (or, of course, both). One cannot have it both ways. More importantly, if the two were extensionally equivalent, the correct assessment of the value of the consequences of particular acts would always yield precisely the judgments which a correct application of (P) would dictate, namely that one ought to act pacifistically; in which case the pacifist, whose aim after all is to show that pacifistic conduct is morally justified, and not to insist upon one and only one philosophical account of that justification, could concede the preceding little skirmish but claim to have won the war.

11.10 Some implications

The preceding does not mean that pacifism—or, for that matter, consequentialist theories in general or (IRU) in particular—is justified, though it does have an important bearing upon the question of its justification. What it does mean, if correct, is that the pacifist's second reply has not been met, and it has not been shown to be relevant to the assessment of the consequences of everyone's following (P) to point out that the

---

[44] This does not mean, of course, that (IRU) is the most plausible moral theory or even the most plausible consequentialist theory. It means simply that it is not refuted by citing the conclusions of a different theory and noting that it does not yield those conclusions. To adjudicate between (IRU) and (AU) would require assessing their respective claims to an ultimate justification by reference to the principle of teleology. (IRU) requires for that justification a premise on the order of: The one and only way to maximize value overall is always to follow ideal rules; (AU) requires a premise like: The one and only way to maximize value overall is always to maximize value in individual acts. These propositions, if understood in a way which distinguishes between the maximization of value overall and the maximization of value in any particular situation, cannot both be true (though they might both be false), and their assessment would provide the key to identifying the most plausible form of consequentialism.

consequences of nongeneral-acceptance of (P) would be bad. If (P) or any other rule simply asserted that "I" or "you" or "group X" but no one else should act as it prescribes—that is, if it were advanced as part of a "limited" consequentialist theory—then it would be relevant to assessing the consequences of the following of that rule to consider what others would be doing in that circumstance, since, depending upon the nature of the rule, the hypothesized consequences in question might well be conditioned by the conduct of those others. But if, as is the point of (IRU), it is the consequences of the following of (P) by *everyone* (or, on the modified version, by people generally) that is relevant. We cannot require that in the estimation of those consequences one postulate the continuation of the bad practice contravening (P). That would be tantamount to requiring that to assess the consequences of everyone's following a rule we must assess the consequences of not everyone's following it, a requirement that would be incoherent. I suspect that this is also the flaw in the reasoning of those some who claim that pacifism has bad consequences.[45]

We can now see that were such a procedure of counting the consequences of the *violation* of a rule by one set of persons among the consequences of the *acceptance* of that rule by others to be credited, it could be used to show that any consequentialist rule is self-defeating, including the principle of teleology itself. Suppose, for example, that not everyone follows (C) and, moreover, that those who do not have it in for those who do, whom they regard as officious do-gooders whose acts of beneficence are to be punished. Suppose, however, that but for this particular quirk the nonfollowers of (C) are not otherwise particularly bad people; if, like most people in the world as we know it, they do not do very much good, they do not do very much harm either. Given this situation, it would be worse overall if only some people followed (C) than if no one did, for although in the latter case value would not be maximized, no great harm would be done either, whereas in the former case great harm would be done (specifically to those who do good) and this would make the "consequences" of following (C) self-defeating.[46]

11.11 Mediated and unmediated consequences

Whether to count the consequences of the rejection of a rule by some people among the consequences of its acceptance by others is part of a larger issue. That is the question of whether to count the conduct—and/or consequences thereof—of some people among

---

[45] See Elizabeth Anscombe, "War and Murder," in Richard A. Wasserstrom (ed.), *War and Morality* (Belmont, CA: Wadsworth Publishing Company, 1970). Anscombe writes, "I now want to consider the very remarkable effects [pacifism] ... has had: for I believe its influence to have been enormous, far exceeding its influence on its own adherents ... pacifism teaches people to make no distinction between the shedding of innocent blood and the shedding of any human blood. And in this way pacifism has corrupted enormous numbers of people who will not act according to its tenets. They become convinced that a number of things are wicked which are not; hence, seeing no way of avoiding 'wickedness,' they set no limits to it. How endlessly pacifists argue that ... those who wage war must go as far as technological advance permits in the destruction of the enemy's people ... Pacifism and the respect for pacifism is not the only thing that has led to a universal forgetfulness of the law against killing the innocent; but it has had a great share in it." Quotation excerpted from p. 46 and pp. 49–50.

[46] The same could be argued with respect to (AU), and has in fact been argued, though along lines which differ both from the above and from one another, by Hodgson, *Consequences of Utilitarianism*, chap. II and Gerald Barnes in "Utilitarianisms," *Ethics*, Vol. 82, No. 1, October 1971, pp. 56–64.

the consequences of the conduct of others. This is an important question even where rule-acceptance or rejection is not at issue. *The problem is at the heart of almost every major problem in social and international affairs, as well as at the heart of the dispute between consequentialist and deontological theories of obligation.* The issue arises both in cases where the conduct of others is in response to the initial acts and in cases where it is not. Consequences which depend upon some cognitive response (choice, decision, judgment, etc.) on the part of others we may call *mediated consequences*. Those which do not we may call *unmediated consequences*. Unmediated consequences are always relevant to moral assessment (except for extreme deontologists). Their value—the comparative good and bad they bring about—may be called circumstantial. Mediated consequences are problematic. It is important to see why. Their value may be called agential. But agential value includes not only that of mediated consequences. It includes the value of the acts of others even if they are not in response to the initial act. Sometimes the acts of others, even if they are not in response to the initial act, would not have happened but for the initial act. A person who buys an old house would not (and could not) have done so but for the actions of the person who built it 100 years before. An example of the second sort occurs in voting, when it is argued that support of a good candidate with little chance of winning will take votes away from a mediocre but potentially winning second candidate and thereby help elect a third but inferior candidate. It is agential disutility that raises difficult issues for the assessment of moral problems. It is often assumed that agential disutility is to be included in our assessment of the consequences of actions. An example where the agential disutility consists of mediated consequences would be when reform groups are admonished that their efforts will lead to more harm than good by generating a backlash among reactionaries. In such circumstances it is often acknowledged that but for the anticipated response of others the demands would be justified.

One of the implications of giving an unqualified affirmative answer to the question of whether to count negatively valued mediated consequences in the moral assessment of acts is that it would commit us to an extreme moral conservatism, giving enormous moral power to persons willing and able, either directly or through institutional devices at their command, to inflict harm upon others. Specifically it would give political authorities the power to render opposition to them not only imprudent, as they have almost always been able to do, but also immoral, simply by ensuring, through the swift and ruthless application of sanctions, that the "consequences" of such opposition are always worse than those of acquiescence. States often warn that there will be "consequences" if another state engages in acts of which it disapproves. What they mean is that there will be such consequences because they will bring them about.

Although he did not detail its implications, G. E. Moore opened the door to such conservatism in his contention:

[O]ne of the chief reasons why an action should not be done in any particular state of society is that it will be punished; since the punishment is in general itself a greater evil than would have been caused by the omission of the action punished. Thus the existence of a punishment may be an adequate reason for regarding an action as generally wrong, even though it has no other bad effects but even slightly good ones. The fact that an action will be punished is a condition of exactly the same kind as others of more or less permanence, which must be taken into account in discussing the general utility or disutility of an action in a particular state of society.[47]

Generalized to cover cases other than those strictly involving legal punishment, this position would enable political authorities to render the actions of other persons immoral after the fact of their performance, even if they would not otherwise have been immoral (and might even have been obligatory), and even if the purpose of such rendering were to maintain personal, political, racial, gender or class advantage.[48] It would not matter that the exercise of such power itself is immoral. That would merely be to say that it has worse consequences than would other available alternatives and would be consistent with its having the indicated consequence. Such thinking, moreover, would make it possible to invalidate moral rules simply by violating them, provided that enough people do so and that the "consequences" of such violation are sufficiently bad.[49] Because the bad consequences will always weigh on the side of the following of the rules by those who do follow them, it will always turn out that following those rules is self-defeating. In fact, the worse the consequences of violating those rules (hence, one would have thought, the stronger the case for *not* violating them) the worse the consequences of following them (hence the stronger the case *for* violating them). Thus the greater the obliquity of one's fellow citizens, the more one would be compelled morally to behave like them. The upshot is to perpetuate the worst features of a morally retrograde society.

11.12 Conclusion

I submit, then, that if it would be best if everyone acted pacifistically but comparatively bad if only some do, then the badness of the latter is a consequence, not of the following by the "some" of the pacifist principle, but of the *violation* of that principle by others. And once the malefactions of nonpacifists are distilled out of the consequences of following (P), any appearance of paradox disappears. That being so, it is no objection to pacifism as a moral position to say that, while the world might be a better place if everyone were a pacifist, one cannot be a pacifist so long as there are others who are not. Applied to collectivities, it is no argument against pacifism to say that a state cannot adopt pacifism so long as there are other states that do not.

The preceding represents perhaps the most common theoretical objection to pacifism. There are two relatively recent practical objections. One arises from the concerns that motivate humanitarian intervention, the other from those governing the response to terrorism. I shall consider them in Chapters 13 and 14. Before that, we need to consider a central question for the philosophy of war, which is whether pacifism and JWT converge.

---

[47] G. E. Moore, *Principia Ethica* (Cambridge: Cambridge University Press, 1903), p. 159.

[48] Those who puzzle over whether one can now act in the past may note that, in this view, one can by one's present actions render past actions of persons or groups morally right or wrong.

[49] On the unmodified form of (IRU), it would be enough if the consequences of anyone's violating such rules were sufficiently bad; on the modified form, it would be necessary that such consequences result from the violation of the rule by enough persons to establish that the rule was not generally followed.

Do Pacifism and Just War Theory Converge?

[O]ne must strain to find examples of justified applications of just war theory in recent history ... What this shows is that ... both views [pacifism and just war theory] can be reconciled ... We can call the view that emerges from this reconciliation, "just war pacifism."

—James P. Sterba

12.1 The issue

A central question for the philosophy of war is whether pacifism and JWT converge. They converge if they yield the same judgment about the morality of war, which they might do whether they are both defensible, both indefensible or it is indeterminate which (if either) is defensible.[1] I have argued that pacifism is the correct position on the morality of war and shall assume that they converge only if JWT leads to pacifism. The question, in any event, is a metaethical one, the answer to which depends largely upon how one understands pacifism and JWT, as well as upon what one means by war. For that reason, in what follows I shall draw upon, and refine where necessary, the analyses of Parts I and II and Chapter 11.

The basic issue of the morality of war arises only if war is not inevitable. If war is inevitable, there may be moral issues about how to prepare for it, how to conduct it and how to conclude it, but the elimination of war will not be a realistic option. Only if war is not inevitable does the basic moral question of war arise. The basic moral question of war (BMQW) I take to be whether war is ever morally permissible.[2]

---

[1] Pacifism and JWT could both be defensible if pacifism were the correct position on the morality of war but JWT is the correct theory by which to establish the pacifist position (as it is for some so-called just war pacifists). They could both be indefensible if they agreed that war is impermissible but were mistaken in that judgment. Their defensibility would be indeterminate if they agreed that war is impermissible but it was unclear whether that position was correct and/or whether JWT was the correct theory by which to make that determination. If they fail to converge, which is the standard view of the matter, it could be indeterminate which is mistaken and which (if either) is correct.

[2] I take this to be the BMQW rather than the question whether war is ever obligatory, since the permissibility of war is a condition of its being obligatory but not vice-versa. As indicated in Chapter 2, the

12.2 The basic moral question of war

Pacifism in most general terms, as we have seen in the preceding chapter, is opposition to war. Such opposition might be based on either moral or nonmoral grounds, and if moral, on religious or secular grounds. Pragmatic pacifism answers the BMQW by saying that war, properly understood, and as qualified in the preceding chapter, is never morally permissible. One might oppose war because one believes it is uneconomical or counterproductive or even irrational. While these grounds would yield forms of pacifism, they would not—at least without elaboration—represent an ethical opposition to war *per se*. One might also oppose war on religious grounds, such as by appeal to divine authority, but do so without anything in the way of moral argument. Pragmatic pacifism answers the BMQW at the conclusion of a moral inquiry, a rational exploration of the morality of war. It is part of a moral philosophy of war. As such, it is a form of philosophical pacifism, as distinguished from religious pacifism and pacifism held on secular but nonmoral grounds.

12.3 Standard just war theory

Standard just war theory (StanJWT), as we have analyzed it in Chapter 5, is a moral theory, basically a deontological one with consequentialist elements.[3] Unlike pacifism it does not expressly answer the BMQW. It does not answer the BMQW because it does not ask it.[4] In fact, StanJWT represents the answer to a different question from the one answered by pacifism. It assumes that some wars are just and some wars unjust[5] and asks how we determine which is which. For this purpose it proposes the criteria of *jus ad bellum* (JAB), governing recourse to war, and *jus in bello* (JIB), governing the conduct of war.[6] Wars are justly resorted to, as we have seen, if, and only if, the conditions of JAB are satisfied and justly conducted if, and only if, the conditions of

permissibility of war is dependent on the permissibility of warfare—the actual killing and destruction that war entails. Biblically, wars were believed to be obligatory when commanded by God, but JWT, even in its religious versions, has come to hold that there may be just wars other than those in response to divine command. In any event, theoretically there might be wars that are permissible, in the sense that it would not be wrong to engage in them, but none that are obligatory in the sense that it would be wrong not to engage in them.

[3] I take deontological theories to be those which hold either that goodness is irrelevant to the determination of moral rightness or relevant but not decisive, and consequentialist theories to be those which hold that moral rightness is determined solely by the consequences of actions.

[4] As Michael Walzer writes: "just war theory, even when it demands a strong critique of particular acts of war, is the doctrine of people who do expect to exercise power and use force … they also insist … that fighting itself cannot be morally impermissible. A just war is meant to be … a war that it is possible to fight." Walzer, *Arguing bout War*, p. 14.

[5] To quote Brian Orend: "The core proposition of just war theory, uniting all its theorists, is this: *sometimes it is permissible for a political community to go to war.*" Brian Orend, *The Morality of War* (Toronto: Broadview Press, 2006), p. 31; See also Douglas Lackey: "The theory of just war asserts that some wars are just and some wars are unjust." Douglas Lackey, *Moral Principles and Nuclear Weapons* (Totowa, NJ: Rowman & Allanhead, 1984), p. 9; and Jenny Teichman: "it follows from the doctrine [JWT] itself that some wars are just and others unjust." Teichmann, *Pacifism and Just War*, p. 46 (brackets added).

[6] The conditions of JAB, once again, are typically: legitimate authority, just cause, right intention, comparative justice, proportionality and last resort; those of JIB: proportionality and discrimination.

JIB are satisfied.[7] A nonpacifist answer to the question whether war is ever morally permissible is thus presupposed at the outset. Warism, the view that some wars are morally permissible in principle and in fact, is the starting point of StanJWT.[8]

There may, however, we may now note, be strong and weak forms of warism. I have taken the BMQW to be whether war is ever permissible. An affirmative answer to that question defines warism in general. But if one means only that war is *merely* permissible the answer defines weak warism. To say that an act is merely permissible (and not obligatory as well) means that one may perform it or not as one pleases. Either choice will do. Just as one might refrain from doing something one has a right to do, so one might refrain from doing something it is permissible to do. If one consistently refrained from going to war even though it was sometimes permissible to do so, one would be a *de jure* warist but at the same time a *de facto* pacifist. There could then be a convergence between StanJWT and *de facto* pacifism, even though there would not be a convergence between StanJWT and ethical pacifism.

The view that war is sometimes morally obligatory, on the other hand, defines strong warism. According to strong warism, there will be times when it will not only be permissible to go to war but wrong *not* to do so. Strong warism fails to converge with either ethical pacifism or *de facto* pacifism. As the tenor of much StanJWT suggests the stronger view, and I know of no clear cases enunciating the weaker view, I shall take StanJWT to exemplify strong warism.

Are the criteria of JWT distilled from an examination of what are taken to be examples of actual just wars or fashioned independently? If the former, then the differentiation of just from unjust wars would be antecedent to construction of the JWT.[9] In that case, JWT would not be necessary to identify just wars. One could—by whatever criteria—identify some wars as just and, having done that, then look to see, so to speak, what exactly it was about those wars (e.g., that they were waged by legitimate authorities with a just cause, etc.) that made them just.[10] JWT, in other words, would be then derivative from judgments about the justice of particular wars. Although JWT would in that sense be founded on a descriptive ethics, it could still serve a normative function, since criteria initially providing explanatory reasons for the justice of certain past wars could serve as justifying reasons for some future wars. If the latter—that is, if the JWT is created independently and then used to distinguish just from unjust wars in the first place—then the JWT would be fully action-guiding.

I shall deal with these further only insofar as they are relevant to the issue at hand, which is the possible convergence of pacifism and JWT.

[7] Just war criteria are often extended to humanitarian intervention and asymmetric warfare (such as the campaign against terrorism), but I shall in this discussion take StanJWT to deal only with interstate war. I will discuss humanitarian intervention in Chapter 13.

[8] By "some wars" I shall take StanJWT to mean some actual wars, past or present, and not merely some possible, imaginable or conceivable wars, which would render JWT indistinguishable in its practical import from some forms of contingent pacifism.

[9] It is reasonable to assume that this is true of the judgments of most warists, since most people who think some wars are just have scarcely heard of JWT much less have any familiarity with its particulars.

[10] By rough analogy, just as it has sometimes been held that one can know the truth of a proposition without knowing its analysis, it might be claimed that one can know that a war is just without knowing precisely why it is just. I shall not undertake to evaluate either of these claims here.

12.4 Revisionist just war theory

But here the plot thickens. There may be departures from StanJWT. Rather than starting from the assumption that some wars are just and examining them to see what makes them just, one might start from the criteria of JAB and JIB, however arrived at, and look to see which, if any, wars satisfy them. One could, so to speak, examine actual (as opposed to merely hypothetical) wars armed in advance with the JWT and with an open mind about whether any of them are indeed just. I shall call this approach revisionist just war theory (RevJWT). To mark a difference between StanJWT and Rev JWT we might formulate them as follows:

> *StanJWT*: There are (actual) just wars, and what makes them just is that they are (1) resorted to in accordance with JAB, and (2) conducted in accordance with JIB.

> *RevJWT*: There may or may not be any (actual) just wars, but if there are, what makes them just is that they are (1) resorted to in accordance with JAB, and (2) conducted in accordance with JIB.

But there may be two versions of RevJWT, depending upon where it ends up on the question of whether there are any actual just wars:

> *RevJWT$_1$*: There are few (actual) just wars, and what makes them just is that they have been (1) resorted to in accordance with JAB and (2) conducted in accordance with JIB.

> *RevJWT$_2$*: There are no (actual) just wars, because no actual wars have been (1) resorted to in accordance with JAB and (2) conducted in accordance with JIB.

In these formulations I am ignoring the possibility that justice in JAB might offset injustice in JIB, and vice-versa, an issue on which there is no clear consensus among just war theorists. RevJWT$_1$ presumably would allow that there may be occasional just wars in the future, whereas RevJWT$_2$ presumably would deny that (at least if the absence of any such wars in the past is to be a reliable indication). There may, finally, as we saw in Chapter 5, be ramified versions of both StanJWT and RevJWT in either of its forms, depending upon how extensively the relevant criteria are reinterpreted or modified. The criteria most subject to modification are last resort, proportionality, right intention, legitimate authority and just cause.

StanJWT implies that there are in fact some just wars. RevJWT—with qualifications for RevJWT$_1$—does not. It would take a study of actual wars, of the sort undertaken in Part III, to resolve the issue between them. If one found that at least a fair number of wars have been just, that would support StanJWT. If one found that few if any wars have been just, that would support RevJWT. In that case, RevJWT would approximate what some just war theorists call *just war pacifism*,[11] and there would to that extent be

---

[11] I say "approximate," because at least some of those who call their position one of just war pacifism do not quite say that no wars are permissible, as ethical pacifism does; only that nearly all wars are unjust. See, e.g., James P. Sterba, *Justice for Here and Now*, pp. 162–163. Andrew Fiala says that the just war theory "should be used as a critical tool with which we can examine the morality of actual wars.

a convergence between pacifism and JWT.[12] If just war pacifism is taken to be a form of JWT, then JWT is vindicated whether or not there are in fact any just wars.[13]

It might seem that with the preceding clarification the answer to the question whether pacifism and JWT converge is at least in principle within easy reach, and that one need only apply just war criteria to actual wars (or the relevantly specified subset of such wars and to realistically possible future wars) to see whether some of them are just. If some are, then pacifism is wrong, in which case pacifism and JWT do not converge. If none are, then pacifism is correct—and can be shown to be so on grounds of JWT itself—and pacifism and JWT converge.

12.5 Justice and morality in war

But matters are not this simple. Refashioned along the above lines, JWT (whether in standard or revisionist forms) answers only the question whether any wars are *just*, not whether any wars are morally permissible. As we have seen in Chapter 5, these are different questions. Justice is but one dimension of morality, and considerations of justice—certainly of distributive and retributive justice—may conflict with other kinds of moral considerations, such as utility and rights. There is no consensus among ethicists that one type of moral consideration invariably supersedes all others. Considerations of justice, for example, may sometimes be taken to override utility, and considerations of utility may sometimes be taken to override justice. The same is true with regard to utility and rights. What is right or wrong or obligatory, as a final judgment in particular cases, depends upon how one resolves this issue. For this reason, even if a particular war were shown to be just according to JWT, it could still be morally wrong, all things considered. In that event, JWT, even if taken to be the correct theory for evaluating the *justice* of war, would not be the correct theory by which to answer the BMQW. It would not, in other words, represent an adequate moral theory of war.

By parity of reasoning, there is the possibility—theoretically at least—that a war might fail to be just according to JWT and yet, on balance, be morally permissible. If it might sometimes be right to perform an act that is unjust (if, e.g., the injustice is offset by a greater good), then it might sometimes be right to wage a war that is unjust. Perhaps some such thinking, if only at a subconscious level, is at work among those just war theorists who scuttle the criterion of last resort or revise such criteria as just cause, right intention, proportionality and discrimination when applying them does not establish the justness of particular wars which they are convinced are right (such

There is no reason to believe that any real war is actually just." See Fiala, *The Just War Myth*, p. 11. But Fiala also says, somewhat more guardedly, that we need a military and that "[r]easonable individuals should take the just war ideal seriously as describing circumstances in which war would be just. But reason will also show us that in reality, very few if any actual wars live up to this ideal" (p. 27).

[12] I have said that pacifism and JWT might theoretically converge if both lead to the conclusion that war is never permissible but are mistaken in that judgment. For practical purposes we may assume that pacifism and JWT converge only if they agree that war is never permissible and are correct in that judgment.

[13] If there are just wars, then either StanJWT or $RevJWT_1$ is vindicated, depending upon whether there are many or few such wars. If there are no just wars—which one might have supposed falsified JWT—then $RevJWT_2$ is correct, but in that case, because $RevJW_2$ is a version of JWT, JWT is again

as the Gulf War or the Iraq War). The risk, of course, is that by proceeding in this way one goes down the path of proliferation, with as many JWTs sprouting up as there are revisions of the theory. To evaluate whether a given war could fail to meet just war criteria and still be morally permissible would require scrutiny of the reasons allegedly offsetting the injustice of a war in favor of its permissibility or necessity. I am unaware of a sustained effort to do that with any war.[14]

12.6 Just war theory and moral war theory

Apart from the fact that it approaches the moral assessment of war from one dimension of morality only, JWT, as we have noted in Part II, cannot, without supporting argument, be taken to be the privileged theory from which to assess war. It is but one possible theory among many. Virtually every basic moral theory can be framed in such a way as to yield a moral theory of war (MTW), by which I mean a theory that provides a basis for the moral assessment of war. To elaborate the argument of Chapter 5, the following are possible MTWs grounded, respectively, in consequentialism, the divine command theory and Kantianism—three traditional kinds of moral theory. For the sake of simplicity, I shall not deal with forms of virtue ethics, though one might do so.

> MTW_1: A war would be permissible if, and only if, it had better consequences on balance than any other alternative.

> MTW_2: A war would be permissible if, and only if, commanded by God.

> MTW_3: A war would be permissible if, and only if, the maxim on which one acted in going to war could at the same time be willed to be a universal law.

As framed, these principles identify conditions under which a war *would* be permissible.[15] They do not answer the question whether any actual wars are permissible. To determine that, one would have to examine actual wars to see whether any of them meet the specified conditions. If some do, then warism would be the indicated conclusion. If none does, then pacifism would be the indicated conclusion.

One could, as I say, refashion JWT to be a MTW as part of a moral philosophy of war. One could state it as follows:

> MTW_4: A war would be permissible if, and only if, it satisfied the criteria of JWT.

If one accepted MTW_4, JWT would be the means by which one would evaluate the permissibility of war. But in the absence of a showing that moral permissibility with

---

vindicated. These considerations suggest that it might avoid confusion if just war pacifism, at least of a sort identified with RevJWT$_2$, is thought of as a form of pacifism rather than as a form of JWT.

[14] Michael Walzer's analysis of supreme emergencies comes close to doing this, insofar as it implies that some wars, or at least some actions in war, might be morally indefensible but still necessary. See his *Just and Unjust Wars*, pp. 251–284.

[15] To keep them in line with our earlier discussion, I have framed the formulations of MTW in terms of permissibility, even though with slight modification they might plausibly be thought to express obligatoriness.

regard to war is reducible to justice, and a showing that MTW_4—which is but one theory among others—is the correct MTW, MTW_4 cannot by default be taken to be the favored theory from which to assess war. If it were, however, and if no actual wars satisfied the just war criteria, then there would be a convergence, not between JWT and pacifism *per se*, but between MTW_4 and pacifism.

12.7 Modalities of pacifism

Even this is not quite correct, though. To see why requires closer examination of pacifism. I said at the outset, that the question of the possible convergence of pacifism and JWT depends upon what one means by pacifism and JWT. It also depends in part upon what one means by war. Let us recall that pragmatic pacifism holds that no wars are morally permissible. So as to leave no hairs unsplit, we should note that this can mean different things, depending upon the modalities involved. We can refine our account in Chapter 11 by defining different possible versions of pacifism according to which is intended[16]:

P_1: No logically conceivable wars are morally permissible
P_2: No probable or possible wars are morally permissible.
P_3: No actual, probable or possible wars are morally permissible.
P_4: No actual, probable or possible wars in the modern world are morally
    permissible.[17]

P_1 represents absolute pacifism. The others represent relative or contingent pacifism. Contingent pacifism has come to stand for many different things. Sometimes it is used to stand for just war pacifism, in which case it is a form of JWT, identifiable with either $RevJWT_1$ or $RevJWT_2$. At other times it is taken to be a view in which "the possibility of a just war is conceded but not under present conditions."[18] I use the term to stand for any nonabsolute form of pacifism. P_4 represents pragmatic pacifism. It is a form of contingent pacifism, grounded in the practical world. It makes no claim about the wars of the distant past or about logically conceivable hypothetical wars that are wildly improbable or even causally impossible. It involves a judgment about wars in the world today and likely in the foreseeable future. It does not require that one renounce all violence. One can, if one chooses, be a pragmatic pacifist and still support the use of violence in personal self-defense. Americans need not even give up their Second Amendment right to possess firearms. Pacifism is not nonviolence. To be a pragmatic

---

[16] For a broader understanding of pacifism, namely as opposition to killing, and a subtle exploration of the relationship of pacifism to self-defense, see the aforementioned: Cheney C. Ryan, "Self-Defense, Pacifism, and the Possibility of Killing," *Ethics* Vol. 93, No. 3 (1983), pp. 508–525.

[17] WWII was an actual war, a large Middle Eastern War is a possible war, a war between Australia and Costa Rica is a possible but improbable war (considering, among other things, that Costa Rica does not have an army); and a war between humankind and the walking dead is logically possible but neither a probable nor possible war, given presently known laws of nature.

[18] John Rawls, *Theory of Justice* (Cambridge: Harvard University Press, 1971), pp. 381–382.

pacifist one need only hold that the large-scale, organized and systematic violence of war is impermissible in today's world.

12.8 Ambiguity in the notion of war again

One final qualification regarding the ontology of war. We saw in Chapter 1 that a systematic ambiguity runs through the discussions of war. Often by "war" people have in mind not the whole of a war but the warfare conducted by one side only. When Americans say that the Revolutionary War was a just war, what they mean is that the part of the war consisting of the fighting by the colonists was just, not the whole of the war, including the fighting by Great Britain. On the other hand, when it is said that the US Civil War resulted in more American casualties than any other war, what is meant is that the whole of the war as waged by both sides had such casualties. When the Korean War is referred to as the "forgotten war," what is meant is that the whole of the war, by both sides, has largely been disregarded in subsequent discussions.

Now JWT, as I have said, deals (directly) only with the warfare by one side in war.[19] Its aim is to identify when one side fights justly, which, according to JWT, is when it satisfies the conditions of JAB and JIB. And the conditions of JAB and JIB can both be satisfied by one side only. Thus a "just war" is but one aspect of a whole war—what I have called a partial war—that can at most be waged by one side. A whole war consists of two or more partial wars (depending on the number of belligerents) and cannot be just in its entirety, though it can be unjust in its entirety.[20] When nation A goes to war with nation B, together they produce a whole war. It does not matter that this is not their express intention, any more than it matters in Adam Smith's invisible hand that it is not the express intention of the countless persons pursuing self-interest to produce a common good. It is foreseeable that they will do so. Nor does it matter which side, if either, has a just cause. If either side refuses to engage in the violence of warfare, there cannot be a war. As we saw in Chapter 1, in order for aggression to constitute war, the nation aggressed against must fight back. The aggressor and the state aggressed against

---

[19] It deals indirectly with both sides to the extent that one side's having a just cause presupposes wrong-doing by the other side, and that determination needs to be made to establish that the first side is justified in resorting to war. But the aim is still to establish that one side is fighting a just war. It is arguable that the requirement of proportionality in JAB requires some consideration of the whole war that would be the outcome of one's going to war (as opposed to the consequences of one's specific act of going to war, the justice of which it is the aim of JAB to determine), but that is far from clear, and the treatment of proportionality is among the most obscure and tangled topics in JWT. The occasional JAB requirement of comparative justice requires some consideration of whether there is a measure of justice on the opposing side in a projected war. But that requires only looking at the possible partial war on the other side and stops short of requiring consideration of the morality of the whole war that would result if one went to war.

[20] By saying that a whole war can be unjust in its entirety, I mean that each of its constituent partial wars may be unjust. Those sensitive to the fallacy of composition might question whether a property (unjustness) of the parts of a war necessarily characterizes the whole of the war itself. I believe the inference is sound in this case but will not argue that here.

together produce the war. The resultant whole war is the outcome of their joint effort. It is as though they tacitly agree to resolve their differences by warfare. This has the paradoxical consequence that, even if one side meets all the criteria of JWT, once it goes to war it brings into existence an unjust war on the other side. This follows from the fact that one side can have a just cause only if the other side has committed (or threatened) a wrong that deprives it of a just cause, hence makes its war "unjust." Even if warists deny that the resultant war as a whole can be either right or wrong (which would make them realists about whole war), the fact that the resort to war transforms aggression (or the commission of some other wrong) into an unjust war must be reckoned among the outcomes of the resort to war, hence factored into judgments of proportionality.

Commonsense would say that when a war results from aggression, it is the aggressor that starts the war. This is true, but only if one counts as a consequence of the aggression the response of the state that is attacked. That response is a mediated consequence of the attack. It involves a choice. On the other hand, the resort to organized military violence by the state under attack transforms the aggression into war as an unmediated consequence.[21] The resort to violence changes the event immediately, both conceptually and morally, without need of any other cognitive intervention. In that sense—also paradoxically—it is the state that is aggressed against that "starts" the war. Once it is attacked, it is fully within its control whether or not a war will occur. War commences the moment it chooses to fight back militarily and not otherwise. As it is a normative, and often a moral, question what to count as mediated consequences of an action, the judgments regarding responsibility for starting a war cannot be settled by a completely neutral observation of the facts. The alleged "facts" themselves reflect normative judgments.[22]

JWT does not ask about the justice of a whole war, much less about the permissibility of a whole war.[23] Pacifism does. This means that our formulation of pragmatic pacifism should be revised to state:

P_5: No actual, probable or possible whole wars in the modern world are morally permissible.

---

[21] See Chapter 11 for a discussion of mediated and unmediated consequences. For a further analysis of the distinction, see my "Consequentialism and Its Consequences" in *The Ethics of Nonviolence: Essays by Robert L. Holmes*, ed. P. Cicovacki (New York: Bloomsbury Press, 2013), pp. 33–47.

[22] Thus when ISIS militants in 2014 claimed that the beheading of Americans was in retaliation for US air strikes against them, they were saying, in effect, that the beheading was a consequence of the air strikes. And they were correct, insofar as it was a mediated consequence. It was a consequence because they made it a consequence. The United States, on the other hand, downplayed the fact that the beheading was in retaliation for US action, which might have implied some US responsibility for the killing, and instead emphasized other depredations by ISIS which were not responses to US actions and which could be condemned on other grounds. Each side thus interpreted the "facts" in a manner best suited to justify its position. Any adequate analysis of the morality of war must take account of the distinction between mediated and unmediated consequences.

[23] To the extent that just war theorists deny that whole wars can be just or unjust, they become realists about whole war at the same time that they make moral judgments about partial wars. The examples of possible MTWs that I gave earlier also do not expressly deal with the morality of whole war, though they could be amended to do so.

It says that what both sides do in a war is wrong, and the whole war, which is the joint product of what they do, is wrong. Pacifism and JWT, in addition to asking different moral questions, operate with different assumptions about the ontology of war and the relevant historical frame of reference regarding the scope of war. This makes it highly improbable that they will converge. But they could. If just war criteria are never met in actual wars, then no partial war will be just. If no partial war is just, then no whole war will be just, because every whole war will consist of two or more unjust partial wars. Leaving aside for the moment the issue of the place of justice within morality, and assuming, for the sake of argument, that justice supersedes other moral considerations (such as utility and rights) in the assessment of war, pacifism and JWT could then converge. No whole war would be permissible for either pacifism or JWT, but this would be for different reasons in each case. For JWT it would be because just war criteria are never met in the case of actual (partial) wars, hence *a fortiori* are never met in the case of whole wars. For pacifism it would be because no whole wars (properly qualified according to modality) are permissible, which would be for reasons grounded in the actionable wrongness of war, as discussed in Chapter 11. In the absence of a showing that no partial wars are just, however, and that justice plays the problematic role indicated, pacifism and JWT will not converge.

12.9 Conclusion

In summary, pacifism is opposition to war. Pragmatic pacifism is opposition to war on moral grounds. It asks whether war, understood as whole war, is ever morally permissible in the modern world and answers that it is not. Although pragmatic pacifism is not a theory, it presupposes a moral theory. What that is lies beyond the scope of the present discussion. StanJWT, on the other hand, as the name implies, is a theory. This establishes an incongruence between pacifism and JWT at the outset. But StanJWT presupposes a moral judgment, namely that some wars are just and some wars unjust, and asks how to differentiate the two, a question it answers by proposing the criteria of JAB and JIB which, when satisfied, suffice to render a war just. It therefore makes two assumptions: first, that there are some just wars, and second, that JWT is the correct theory from which to evaluate war. The first assumption bypasses the BMQW by assuming an answer to it in advance. In so doing it also assumes in advance that pacifism is mistaken. The second assumption privileges JWT over other possible theories by which to evaluate war. RevJWT does not make the first assumption. It considers it an open question whether some wars are just. It does, however, make the second assumption. It holds that if applying JWT showed that no wars are just, that would suffice to establish pacifism on just war grounds. But we have seen that it would not quite suffice. Justice is but one dimension of morality. What is right or permissible, all things considered, requires taking account of justice (as it requires taking account of consequences and rights) but is not settled by appeal to justice alone, at least not without convincing supporting argument to that effect. The questions (1) Are any wars just? and (2) Are any wars permissible? are different. Stan JWT answers (1) by saying yes, RevJWT by saying no.[24] Advocates of each seem to think that in answering (1) they are at the same time answering (2), but they are not. To answer (2) requires further argument.

Pragmatic pacifism and StanJWT are therefore fundamentally incongruent and cannot converge. Pragmatic pacifism consists of a moral judgment, Stan JWT of a theory that presupposes a contrary judgment. If StanJWT is correct, then pacifism does not get out of the gate; it is mistaken at the outset. If pacifism is correct, then StanJWT does not get out of the gate; it is mistaken at the outset. Because RevJWT does not presuppose a judgment that conflicts with pacifism, it could converge with pacifism. The conclusions to which it leads in the judgment of actual wars (assuming, once again, that showing that a war is just suffices to show that it is morally permissible) could be the same as the judgment that represents pacifism.

It should be said that to show that war is never permissible, as pacifism maintains, requires taking account of whatever role justice may have in war, and JWT, even if it is not an adequate MTW, might be a plausible theory by which to make that determination. In that event, pacifism would be obliged to take account of JWT, even though JWT would be incapable by itself of answering the BMQW. Just war considerations would then be part of the MTW that establishes pacifism.

In any event, one can formulate another MTW which sets necessary conditions for war to be permissible. It is:

> MTW_5: A collective action producing a whole war in the modern world would be permissible, all things considered, including the role of justice, if, and only if, it actualized in itself and its consequences, mediated and unmediated, a greater balance of good over bad (morally and nonmorally),[25] than if it were not undertaken.

If no whole war meets the conditions specified in MTW_5, and *if* MTW_5 is the proper moral perspective from which to evaluate war, then no war in the modern world is permissible, and pacifism is the correct moral stance toward war. I take MTW_5 to be the proper moral perspective from which to evaluate war and know of no whole war in the modern world that meets its conditions.

---

[24] Subject to qualification for $RevJWT_1$ above.

[25] I am assuming that some things, such as pleasure, are good intrinsically, apart from moral considerations, and that other things, such as justice and respect for rights, are good on moral grounds. MTW_5 requires taking account of both moral and nonmoral values so understood. As I am uncertain whether even these conditions would suffice to justify war, I am stating them only as necessary conditions of war's permissibility.

Part V

13

Pacifism and Humanitarian Military Intervention

If I am right that unilateral humanitarian intervention can be morally permissible, it follows that aggression can be permissible.

—Jeff McMahan

[T]he argument that one must protect the innocent may well be one of the greatest contributing factors … to the deaths of innocents themselves.

—Barry Gan

13.1 The plight of individuals worldwide

Calls for humanitarian intervention appeal to some of the finest human instincts. These include a desire to relieve suffering and protect the weak. With worldwide media coverage, the plight of victims in all corners of the earth can now be known almost instantaneously. Our capacity to feel sympathy for the suffering of people we once might never have known about, or known about only after the chance had passed to be of any help, has grown accordingly.

When suffering is the result of oppression and injustice, passions are doubly engaged. People feel compassion for the victims and outrage toward their victimizers. The tendency is to respond to moral abominations with force, as though to do less is to betray a moral failing, an unwillingness to do all that one can on behalf of the oppressed. Thus Kosovo is held up as a model of successful humanitarian intervention, Rwanda as an abject failure. As one commentator writes: "One of the central moral questions for our time is when to intervene militarily on humanitarian grounds."[1] Notice, the question is not seen as *whether* to intervene but *when* to intervene.

My concern is not with whether these instincts are reducible in the end to some form of egoism. That is a question for moral psychology. I shall assume, as the evidence overwhelmingly supports, that there is a genuine regard for other human beings

---

[1] Nicholas D. Kristof, *The New York Times*, June 27, 2003.

capable of generating sufficient motivational force to lead to action on behalf of others for their own sake. My most immediate concern is also not with many of the forms this action may take, from writing a check to Oxfam to joining the Peace Corps. My concern is with humanitarian military intervention, understood as utilizing a state's military power within another state for humanitarian reasons.[2]

We have examined the specific case of the intervention in Kosovo. My concern now is with the challenge of such intervention to pacifism. Secondarily, I shall consider its implications for the JWT as well. Humanitarian intervention does not necessarily mean going to war, but it does mean using war-fighting capabilities in ways that risk war. It pursues its ends through the use or threat of violence. If pacifism is correct, humanitarian military intervention is wrong in the modern world. As such intervention is at least sometimes permissible in the eyes of most people, pacifism would seem to be false. By the same token, if as JWT is sometimes taken to hold, defense against aggression is the only just cause for going to war, then humanitarian intervention (inasmuch as it is not a case of self-defense) would again appear to be impermissible. In short, the permissibility of humanitarian intervention would seem to be a problem for both pacifism and at least some versions of JWT, though for different reasons.

13.2 What is humanitarian intervention?

As applied to foreign relations, intervention is interference in the affairs of a state. The interveners can be individuals or groups.[3] My concern is with intervention by other states. Intervention is usually thought of as intervention in a state's internal affairs, but there can be intervention in a state's external affairs as well. The US blockade of Iraq following its 1990 invasion of Kuwait was interference in the affairs of Iraq. But it was interference in its external affairs, not internal.

Our concern, however, is with state interference in the internal affairs of another state. Such intervention can be covert, as was the CIA-sponsored overthrow of the government of Iran in 1953 and its support of the 1973 coup in Chile, or overt, like the invasion of Lebanon in 1958 and the economic embargo of Cuba in 1963. The encouragement of Kurds and Shiites to overthrow Saddam Hussein following the Gulf War, and the encouragement of Iranian protests against their government were also overt, though they fell short of direct physical involvement. And intervention can be nonmilitary, as the preceding examples largely were, and if nonmilitary it can be, *inter*

---

[2] There is a complicating conceptual question of whether a country that has no effective government, as was the case with Somalia in 1993, can properly be called a state, but I shall not take that up here.

[3] Although they are affiliated with a group, the International Solidarity Movement, the foreigners acting on behalf of Palestinian rights in the West Bank and Gaza Strip are acting principally as individuals. The most notable example is that of Rachel Corrie, an American killed by an Israeli bulldozer on March 16, 2003; a death for which Israel's Supreme Court ruled in 2015 that Israel could not be held liable, since it took place in a "war zone." Their actions, moreover—whether justifiable or not—represent interference in the affairs of Israel. Whether they represent interference in the internal or external affairs is unclear, considering the problematic status of those territories.

alia, economic, political or judicial.[4] But it can also be overtly military, as was the 1999 bombing of Yugoslavia in the crisis over Kosovo.

Narrowed further, my concern will be with nonconsensual military intervention in the internal affairs of another state for humanitarian reasons.[5] To call this "humanitarian intervention" is controversial. The International Commission on Intervention and State Sovereignty (ICISS) explains why. It writes: "We have responded in this respect to the very strong opposition expressed by humanitarian agencies, humanitarian organizations and humanitarian workers towards any militarization of the word 'humanitarian': whatever the motives of those engaging in the intervention, it is anathema for the humanitarian relief and assistance sector to have this word appropriated to describe any kind of military action."[6] Some, however, simply define humanitarian intervention in an evaluative way. Fernando Tesón, for example, defines it as "the *proportionate transboundary help, including forcible help, provided by governments to individuals in another state who are being denied basic human rights and who themselves would be rationally willing to revolt against their oppressive government*."[7] A normative definition of humanitarian intervention begs the moral issue. It tacitly says that humanitarian intervention by its very nature is justified; the rationale for military intervention—that there is a violation of human rights—is built into its very meaning. The only moral issue then is whether or not a particular intervention is a case of humanitarian intervention, not whether humanitarian intervention is morally justified. Since the issue I shall discuss is whether military intervention of the sort in question is morally justified, it is important not to foreclose that question by definition.

Humanitarian intervention per se is any unauthorized interference in a state's internal affairs on behalf of human rights. As typically conceived it involves the use of a state's military power. Unless indicated otherwise I shall use the term in this sense. Accordingly, I shall define *putative* humanitarian military intervention as the nonconsensual use of a state's military power to try to prevent, or bring to an end, the alleged mistreatment of persons within another state. By "nonconsensual," I mean without the consent of the government (if any) of the state in which the intervention takes place. This will cover the case of failed states that do not have a functioning government. I shall take such intervention to be either *motivated* by the desire to help threatened or mistreated individuals or having at least the *intention* to help them, whatever the motivation. Incidentally helping such persons is insufficient, even if it

---

[4] There were allegations of covert US political intervention in the events leading up to the military overthrow of the democratically elected government of Egypt in 2013.

[5] I shall understand "humanitarian reasons" broadly, to cover not only violation of rights but any form of significantly wrongful treatment. David Rodin defines humanitarian intervention more specifically as "unauthorized military intervention in a state for the purposes of alleviating suffering or preventing the abuse of human rights." *War and Self-Defense*, p. 106.

[6] Established by the Canadian government, in conjunction with a group of foundations, the ICISS issued its report, entitled *The Responsibility to Protect*, in December, 2001. The quote is from p. 21.

[7] Fernando R. Tesón, *Humanitarian Intervention: An Inquiry into Law and Morality* (Dobbs Ferry, NY: Transnational Publishers, 1988), p. 5. Tesón has more recently expressly defined *permissible* humanitarian intervention as the "*proportionate international use or threat of military force, undertaken in principle by a liberal government or alliance, aimed at ending tyranny or anarchy, welcomed by the victims, and consistent with the doctrine of double effect.*" Fernando R. Tesón, "The Liberal Case for Humanitarian Intervention," in J. L. Holzgrefe and Robert O. Keohane (eds), *Humanitarian*

is expected or foreseen that the intervention will provide such help. "Mistreatment" (about which we shall say more later) includes harming, killing and violating human rights. It is intended to signify that the treatment is morally wrong. It can cover everything from oppression and ethnic cleansing to torture, massacre and genocide. In typical cases the mistreatment must be *severe* and the numbers affected *large*. But these are among the supposedly justifying conditions of humanitarian intervention. As I want to leave it open whether humanitarian intervention is morally justified, I shall for that reason not include them in the definition.[8]

This does give the notion of humanitarian military intervention a normative character, but it locates that character where it properly belongs, in the intentions or motives of those undertaking the intervention. It does not foreclose the moral question of whether the intention is in fact justified.

13.3 Why is humanitarian military intervention problematic?

Humanitarian intervention is problematic even for many who have no objection to war. To understand why requires looking at the constellation of ideas that provides the background for the discussion of humanitarian intervention.

Autonomy is the freedom to live your life as you choose. Moral autonomy holds that, all other things being equal, it is morally permissible to exercise that freedom. The corollary, again *ceteris paribus*, is that it is wrong of others to interfere with your living your life as you choose, provided you do not use your freedom to impede the exercise of a like freedom by others.

Implicit within the state system emerging after the Treaty of Westphalia in 1648 is the idea of state equality, which soon became explicit in the works of Hobbes and Pufendorf.[9] Just as equality among individuals requires that they enjoy the same rights and freedoms regardless of their size, strength, wealth, religion, sex or race, so equality among nations holds that states have the same rights and freedoms regardless of size, power, form of government, racial and ethnic composition and the like.[10] Such normative equality is to be distinguished from physical equality. To affirm the equality of all persons is not to say that they all have the same intelligence, strength, talent and initiative. It is to say that, whatever their attributes, they should be treated similarly (not necessarily identically) with regard to rights and freedoms. Likewise, to say that all nations are equal is not to say that they are all of the same size, strength and stage of

---

Intervention: Ethical, Legal, and Political Dilemmas (Cambridge: Cambridge University Press, 2003), p. 94

[8] President George H. W. Bush, though he did not use the term "humanitarian intervention," initially cited the death of a single US serviceman as grounds for military intervention in Panama. Had the motive or intention been in fact to safeguard US citizens within Panama, and had the other conditions cited above been met, the US invasion would have constituted a case of humanitarian intervention.

[9] See Edwin DeWitt Dickinson, *The Equality of States in International Law* (Cambridge: Harvard University Press, 1920), p. 82.

[10] These notions are at the heart of the Westphalian System, as Kissinger calls it, that he sees as being under threat in the evolving world order. See Kissinger, *World Order*, passim.

civilization, which obviously they are not. It is to say that—again, all other things being equal—they should be treated similarly with regard to rights and freedoms.

Such reasoning extends autonomy to states as well as individuals. Autonomy applied to states is "sovereignty." If states have a right to choose their own government, set their own policies and devise their own economic systems, then their internal affairs must be respected by other states. Thus a norm of nonintervention is a corollary of state sovereignty. Indeed, it has been called the "fundamental principle of international law."[11] The ICISS says, "The starting point, here as elsewhere, should be the principle of nonintervention. This is the norm from which any departure has to be justified."[12]

The nonintervention principle is entailed by Article 2(4) of the UN Charter. It mandates that "[a]ll Members shall refrain in their international relations from the threat or use of force against the territorial integrity or political independence of any state, or in any other manner inconsistent with the Purposes of the United Nations." Article 2(7) also prohibits the UN's own intervention: "Nothing contained in the present Charter shall authorize the United Nations to intervene in matters which are essentially within the domestic jurisdiction of any state or shall require the Members to submit such matters to settlement under the present Charter."

If international law contains a bedrock prohibition against intervention, then violations of that prohibition arguably constitute aggression. Indeed, aggression has been characterized as "legally impermissible intervention."[13] Although it does not define aggression, the UN Charter makes clear in Article 2 Paragraph (3) the responsibility imposed on member nations to "settle their international disputes by peaceful means in such a manner that international peace and security, and justice, are not endangered." This, combined with paragraphs (4) and (7) of Article 2, makes the Charter strongly anti-interventionist. The sense of the sovereignty and equality of nations is paramount.

If each state fully respects the sovereignty of other states there will be no interstate war. States will then be free to steer their individual courses as they choose, without interference from others.

Matters are not this simple, of course. Nothing of what has been said prevents individual persons from rising up against their government. Governments typically respond by using force. The result can be civil war—a mode of war not prohibited by the UN Charter. What, then, if the state fighting a civil war within its border seeks

---

[11] R.J. Vincent, *Human Rights and International Relations* (Cambridge: Cambridge University Press, 1986), p. 113. As Vincent puts it, the logic is simple: "if the members of international society are taken to be sovereign states acknowledging each other's rights to rule in their own domains, then it follows that intervention—the attempt to subject another state to one's will—is illegitimate as an infraction of sovereignty: if sovereignty, then non-intervention." With regard to the notion of equality, Dickinson points out that "[t]he conception of natural equality was introduced into the law of nations by drawing an analogy between natural persons and separate states or international persons." Writing at the end of WWI, he maintains that "it is generally agreed that intervention and equality are irreconcilable." Edwin DeWitt Dickinson, *The Equality of States in International Law* (Cambridge: Harvard University Press, 1920), pp. 29, 261.

[12] The ICISS, as noted in n. 6 *supra*, sought to avoid the term "Humanitarian Intervention," speaking instead of "intervention" or "military intervention" for human protection purposes (p. 21).

[13] Christopher C. Joyner, "International Law," in Peter J. Schraeder (ed.) *Intervention into the 1990s: U.S. Foreign Policy in the Third World* (Boulder, CO: Lynne Rienner Publishers, 1992), p. 237.

assistance from another state? If it is sovereign, can it not do this? And cannot the other state, if it is sovereign, assist the first state? To do so is intervention. But in these circumstances, it is consensual intervention. Suppose a third state, viewing with suspicion the intervention of the second state, and not much liking the government of the first state, receives an "invitation" from rebels in the civil war, who have formed their own government which they maintain is the legitimate government of the state in question; and suppose the third state intervenes in support of the rebels. We then have a counterintervention. This pits the second and third states against one another as they support opposing sides in a civil war. If the interventionists and counterinterventionists in turn seek assistance from their respective allies, a full-fledged war may emerge from the initial civil conflict that was not precluded by international law.[14]

Or suppose the government of the first state has collapsed and the civil war is a contest to see who will form the government. What happens to sovereignty then? Is there even a state in existence if there is no government? There is a country to be sure, but if there is no state, there is no sovereignty. It is still intervention in a commonsense meaning of the term if a state enters the conflict on one side or the other, but is it intervention in a sense proscribed by the foregoing principles?

Still further, what if the UN itself enters the conflict militarily? Here we have to reckon with the Charter's requirement that members handle disputes peacefully and not intervene in one another's domestic affairs. There is also Chapter VII's allowance for UN military responses to threats to international peace. The UN would be toothless if it simply shook its finger at breaches of the peace. It must be prepared to act. And indeed Article 39 says:

> 39.   The Security Council shall determine the existence of any threat to the peace, breach of the peace, or act of aggression and shall make recommendations, or decide what measures shall be taken in accordance with Articles 41 and 42, to maintain or restore international peace and security.

Article 41 says that the Security Council "may decide what measures not involving the use of armed force are to be employed to give effect to its decisions, and it may call upon the Members of the United Nations to apply such measures." As we have already seen in connection with the Gulf War, Article 42 then says:

> 42.   Should the Security Council consider that measures provided for in Article 41 would be inadequate or have proved to be inadequate, it may take such

---

[14] There are many possible permutations to this scenario. The rebels may only intend to form a new government and seek assistance in doing so, as insurgents in Crimea and Eastern Ukraine are thought to have done with Moscow. It may also happen that an outside state is responsible for the creation of the government that then asks for that state's assistance in combating an insurgency, as happened in Vietnam, when the US-installed government of Diem enlisted the aid of the US in fighting the Vietcong. In that case, the very state that called for assistance, South Vietnam, was brought into existence by the outside state whose assistance it then sought. The Soviets, for their part, initially justified their intervention in Afghanistan in 1979 on the grounds that it was requested by a new government. The makings of a potential confrontation also exist in 2015 as US warships prevent Iranian ships from supplying rebels in the civil war in Yemen.

action by air, sea, or land forces as may be necessary to maintain or restore international peace and security. Such action may include demonstrations, blockade, and other operations by air, sea, or land forces of Members of the United Nations.

Imagine that the three states in the first example do not respond to finger-shaking from the UN and persist in their escalating conflict. If the UN then tries to restore peace by itself using force, it takes only a little imagination to suppose that a large-scale war could emerge.[15]

So, on the face of it, the UN Charter would appear to rule out military intervention by states in the affairs of other states but allows the possibility of UN intervention under special circumstances. Those circumstances, however, have a different rationale from that typically appealed to by advocates of humanitarian intervention. The rationale appeals to the preservation of international peace and security, not to the prevention of mistreatment of individuals within the state in question.

In light of these considerations, it is not hard to see why military intervention per se is of concern to many. If nonintervention is a cornerstone of international law, then interventionist policies threaten the foundations of international law. And if international institutions built around a system of law are the best safeguard against war—as the world order existing from the end of WWI until the present has assumed—then interventionist policies threaten world peace as well. The growing acceptance of interventionist practices in the twenty-first century threatens to undermine the very foundations of the international order. This was the implied message of then UN Secretary General Kofi Annan when he reportedly called for "a rethinking of the international institutions that were largely sidelined during the Iraq war." He asked: "Did what happened in Iraq constitute an exception? A precedent others can exploit? What are the rules?"[16]

Because humanitarian intervention is a form of military intervention—a point to which we shall return—the concerns surrounding military intervention will likewise surround humanitarian intervention.

13.4 Rights versus sovereignty

Beginning roughly in the fourteenth century rights began to play an important role in the thinking about the moral guidance of conduct. Through Hobbes, and more particularly Locke, rights made their way into the conceptual framework underlying the US Declaration of Independence. The notion of "unalienable rights" provides the basis for people to overthrow oppressive rule. Locke had written that "*All men by nature are equal... equality* being that *equal right* that every man hath *to his natural freedom*, without being subjected to the will or authority of any other man."[17] He was, of course,

---

[15] The Korean War was, technically, not a war but police action by the UN.

[16] As reported in the *New York Times*, July 31, 2003. Russia's Vladimir Putin even more explicitly condemned the US attack on Iraq, claiming that only the UN has the right to use force. As reported in the *Jordan Times*, internet edition, Friday-Saturday, December 19–20, 2003.

[17] John Locke, *Second Treatise on Civil Government*, ed. Richard Cox (Arlington Heights, IL: Harland Davidson, 1982), p. 33.

speaking of the equality of individuals, not states. It was the rights of individuals that were preeminent. The authority of states supposedly derived from those individuals who, in the standard Hobbesian version, were thought to transfer certain rights to the state in exchange for security. State legitimacy thus derived from the rights of individuals. There being no higher authority over states themselves, however, they were held to exist in a kind of state of nature, equally free and autonomous save for depredations against them by other states.

Thus at the same time that the nation-state system was taking form around the notions of equality, sovereignty and nonintervention—a Westphalian System, as Kissinger calls it—a conception of the rights of individual persons was being forged that provided the foundation for that system. With the notions of sovereignty and nonintervention in the forefront, the understanding was that safeguarding the rights of individuals was understood to be the affair of governments, a matter of their internal affairs. If a state is sovereign, other states should not intervene in its dealing with its own citizens.

But in an act of momentous moral significance, much of the international community declared in 1948 that states do not have *carte blanche* in their treatment of persons. The UN, the same institution that framed its Charter around the notion of state sovereignty, set forth that year a landmark (though nonbinding) Universal Declaration of Human Rights. It specified the bedrock standards that all states should follow in their treatment of persons within their borders. Indeed, the final article, Article 30, states explicitly: "Nothing in this Declaration may be interpreted as implying for any State, group or person any right to engage in any activity or to perform any act aimed at the destruction of any of the rights and freedoms set forth herein." By implication, nothing in the notion of sovereignty entitles states to violate these human rights.[18]

It was one thing for governments to acknowledge individual human rights, another for them to pay such rights more than lip service. Not until the Carter Administration were human rights issues made a central concern of the US government and used as a tool in foreign policy.[19] With the Cold War in full swing, human rights issues were placed at the forefront of relations with the Soviet Union. The focus was Soviet treatment of dissidents, particularly Soviet Jews who sought to emigrate. Sovereignty came up against human rights. Predictably, the Soviets protested that American support for the rights of Soviet citizens was interference in their internal affairs. Since the Universal Declaration was not binding, the issue was in one sense a moral one: whether, in deference to state sovereignty and the principle of nonintervention, states ought to look the other way at human rights abuses within other countries. But it had practical political implications as well, particularly when a state's record on human rights was made a factor in trade and the setting of a tone for diplomatic relations.

States have used one or the other of three different tacks to counter interference in their internal affairs on human rights issues. The first is to compartmentalize rights.

---

[18] By analogy, no one would maintain that the notion of privacy of a home entitles one to engage in domestic violence or child abuse or commit other crimes there with impunity.

[19] For an excellent account of how this came about, see Edward Hodgman, "Détente and the Dissidents: Human Rights in U.S. Foreign Policy, 1968–1980," Unpublished PhD dissertation, History, University of Rochester, 2003.

When the United States challenged the Soviet Union on civil rights, such as freedom of speech, the Soviets replied by challenging the United States on social rights, such as healthcare, pensions and education.[20] The second is to speak of collective rights, which are supposedly set apart from individual rights and capable of clashing with them. When group rights (say to economic development on the part of society) came up against standard individual rights at the UN World Conference on Human Rights in 1993, the claim was that group rights superceded individual rights.[21] In this way, a collectivist (macro) ethics was given priority over an individualist (micro) ethics. The third is to claim that human rights, rather than being universal, are culturally relative, so that what is right in the treatment of persons in one society may not be right in another. Thus, the distinction between universal (or even absolute) rights versus culturally relative rights entered the debate.[22]

All of these approaches acknowledge that there are human rights. They simply represent ways to combine that acknowledgment with a continuation of policies the governments in question see fit. Left unresolved is the question of how human rights, however conceived, are to be squared with the traditional ideas of sovereignty and nonintervention.

13.5 The responsibility to protect

It is important to note that humanitarian intervention is sometimes contrasted with a so-called Responsibility to Protect. That responsibility is understood in a way that attempts to resolve some of the preceding problems. The term Responsibility to Protect was used by the aforementioned Commission established by the Canadian government that issued its lengthy publication, "The Responsibility to Protect," in 2001. There, as noted earlier, it was argued that the use of the term "humanitarian intervention" is misleading because it tends to confuse humanitarian intervention with humanitarian

---

[20] China in 2013 responded to allegations of human rights abuses in China by detailing alleged human rights abuses in the United States.

[21] At the 1993 UN World Conference on Human Rights in Vienna it was argued by some governments that "Democracies in the developing world … must give more weight to the rights of the collective society than to individuals who may threaten its stability. 'Human rights are vital and important,' says Indonesian Foreign Minister Ali Alatas, but 'so are efforts at accelerated national development.' When the two conflict, he says, development must take priority." As reported in the *New York Times*, June 18, 1993.

[22] This argument had entered into the aforementioned UN conference. As reported by the *New York Times*: "From United States delegates to the Dalai Lama, most everyone in Vienna for the United Nations World Conference on Human Rights is condemning suggestions by several Asian, Middle Eastern, and Northern African governments that human rights are culturally relative" (ibid.). The American position on this was set forth later by President Bill Clinton at Beijing University in 1998, when he said: "We do not seek to impose our vision on others. But we are convinced that certain rights are universal, that, as one of the heroes of our independence Thomas Jefferson wrote in his last letter 172 years ago: 'All eyes are opened, or opening, to the rights of man.' I believe that everywhere, people aspire to be treated with dignity, to give voice to their opinions to choose their own leaders, to associate with whom they wish, to worship how, when and where they want. These are not American rights or European rights or developed world rights. They are the birthrights of people everywhere," *The New York Times*, June 20, 1998. For a critique of the attempt to ground a principle of nonintervention on ethical relativism, see Rodin, *War and Self-Defense*, ch. 7.

aid. Officials connected with humanitarian aid have objected to the term humanitarian intervention for precisely that reason. In 2005 the UN World Summit Outcome[23] unanimously affirmed in paragraphs 138 and 139:

> 138. Each individual State has the responsibility to protect its populations from genocide, war crimes, ethnic cleansing and crimes against humanity. This responsibility entails the prevention of such crimes, including their incitement, through appropriate and necessary means. We accept that responsibility and will act in accordance with it. The international community should, as appropriate, encourage and help States to exercise this responsibility and support the United Nations in establishing an early warning capability. 139. The international community, through the United Nations, also has the responsibility to use appropriate diplomatic, humanitarian and other peaceful means in accordance with Chapter VI and VIII of the Charter, to help to protect populations from genocide, war crimes, ethnic cleansing and crimes against humanity. In this context, we are prepared to take collective action, in a timely and decisive manner, through the Security Council, in accordance with the Charter, including Chapter VII, on a case-by-case basis and in cooperation with relevant regional organizations as appropriate, should peaceful means be inadequate and national authorities are manifestly failing to protect their populations from genocide, war crimes, ethnic cleansing and crimes against humanity.

A 2009 Report of the secretary-general on the implementation of the Responsibility to Protect[24] makes clear the intention to distinguish this principle from humanitarian intervention. That report states:

> Two distinct approaches emerged during the final years of the twentieth century. Humanitarian intervention posed a false choice between two extremes: either standing by in the face of mounting civilian deaths or deploying coercive military force to protect the vulnerable and threatened populations. Member States have been understandably reluctant to choose between those unpalatable alternatives. Meanwhile, Francis Deng, at that time the Representative of the Secretary-General on internally displaced persons, and his colleagues had been refining a conceptually distinct approach centered on the notion of "sovereignty as responsibility."[25] They underscored that sovereignty entailed enduring obligations towards one's people, as well as certain international privileges. The State, by fulfilling fundamental protection obligations and respecting core human rights, would have far less reason to be concerned about unwelcome intervention from abroad.

[23] A/RES/60/1, pars. 138–140.
[24] "Implementing the Responsibility to Protect: Report of the Secretary-General, January 12, 2009. A/63/677
[25] Francis M. Deng et al., *Sovereignty as Responsibility: Conflict Management in Africa* (Washington, DC: Brookings Institution Press, 1996).

States have often undertaken to protect other states, often in the interests of the state doing the protecting. According to the principle enunciated above, states under some circumstances have a responsibility to protect individuals within other states as well. The principle of the responsibility to protect (commonly referred to as R2P) seeks to avoid any conflict between sovereignty and human rights by defining sovereignty to include a respect for core human rights. Indeed, interpreters of R2P take sovereignty to include a responsibility to protect populations within a sovereign state's borders. Specifically, the plight of victims of genocide, ethnic cleansing, war crimes and crimes against humanity is no longer a matter exclusively of the internal domestic affairs of a state. The international community has not only the right, but the responsibility, to concern itself with the well-being of those individuals and to intervene on their behalf if necessary. Whether this means that the international community merely has the right to intervene or has an obligation to do so (as is implied by the term "responsibility") is unclear. In any event, unlike with humanitarian intervention, as often understood, such intervention is to be undertaken only through the UN Security Council and in keeping with the UN Charter. Unilateral intervention by states is not countenanced. It is often emphasized that R2P is intended to strengthen sovereignty not to impair it.[26]

Just as Kosovo is seen as a model for humanitarian intervention, Libya is seen as a model for implementation of R2P. The intervention in Kosovo was undertaken without UN authorization, and supposedly for humanitarian reasons, whereas the intervention in Libya had UN backing, in which the Security Council specifically referred to the responsibility to protect. The projected US intervention in Syria in 2013, as initially conceived, would have been without UN backing. Russian efforts to derail that intervention seemed intended to move the issue into the UN.

Thus three different conceptions have emerged in the latter years of the twentieth and early years of the twenty-first centuries. The first holds that any state may intervene in another state where that state has lost its legitimacy—and with it, its claim to sovereignty—because of significant mistreatment of persons among its population. The second holds that groups of states, whether ad hoc or represented by organizations like NATO, may intervene in other states for similarly humanitarian reasons. The third, as represented by R2P, holds that states acting with authorization from the UN Security Council may intervene in other states when those states are either committing, or unwilling or incapable of preventing, the specific offenses of genocide, war crimes, ethnic cleansing or crimes against humanity.

Since military intervention is what is ultimately at issue in all of these cases, and as humanitarian concerns are presupposed in all of them, I shall speak of humanitarian

---

[26] "To avoid misunderstandings, several aspects of R2P are worth underlining. The concept is designed to reinforce, not undermine, national sovereignty ... though R2P is based on a long tradition of international law, it does not impose any new legal obligations on governments. There is no duty to engage in military intervention. R2P's overriding goal is to encourage and, when necessary, help states protect their own people. When that does not happen, the first recourse will ordinarily be to diplomatic, economic, and other measures. Collective military action to enforce R2P will be rare." See Madeleine K. Albright and Richard S. Williamson, "The United States and R2P: From Words to Action" (The United States Institute of Peace, the United States Holocaust Memorial Museum, and the Brookings Institution, 2013), p. 10.

military intervention in what follows, bearing in mind that the conceptual thinking on these issues is still evolving.

13.6 The problem for pacifism

The challenge of humanitarian intervention to pacifism can be framed in terms of a simple argument.

A1. If pacifism is correct, humanitarian military intervention is impermissible.
  2. Humanitarian military intervention is permissible.
  3. Therefore, pacifism is incorrect.

The permissibility here is moral, not legal. It should also be noted that premise (2) is not meant to preclude the possibility that humanitarian intervention is morally obligatory. Since humanitarian military intervention will arguably be permissible if it is obligatory, that issue is left open.

The argument has initial plausibility. Humanitarian military intervention involves sending a state's uninvited military forces into another country to achieve its objectives. While this may not result in war, it risks war. And it clearly involves a commitment to warfare. One could scarcely condone this and still adhere to pacifism. Surely, the reasoning continues, there are *some* circumstances in which such intervention is permissible.[27] Hence pacifism is mistaken.

Two possible objections should be disposed of right away. As a moral position, pacifism is principled opposition to war, not necessarily to all violence. So unless pacifists are also nonviolentists, as we may call advocates of nonviolence, they need not oppose humanitarian intervention (which, though it might lead to war, is conceptually distinguished from it). A principled opposition to war is related to, but distinct from, a principled commitment to nonviolence. As applied to pacifism of a sort that countenances some use of violence, say in self-defense or defense of others, premise (1) would be false.

While this is correct, it is a fine point. Although I have defined pragmatic pacifism as holding that war in the modern world is wrong, it would also hold that warfare that does not rise to the level of war is also wrong unless the presumption against it is defeated. I construe pragmatic pacifism broadly enough (though without identifying

---

[27] Some maintain that humanitarian intervention is not only permissible but a moral duty. See Kok-Chor Tan, "Military Intervention as a Moral Duty," *Public Affairs Quarterly*, Vol. 9, No. 1, January 1995, pp. 29–47. Tan is concerned with "purely altruistic" interventions, and believes that a duty to engage in such intervention conflicts not only with the sovereignty of the state intervened against, but also with the sovereignty of the state in a position to intervene as well: "To say that a state has a duty to intervene is to deny it its sovereign right to remain neutral. Can this aspect of sovereignty also be subject to higher moral considerations? In other words, can human rights concerns not only override the sovereignty of the target state, but also the sovereignty of neutral states?" (p. 31). Answering these questions in the affirmative, Tan's position envisions an encroachment upon state sovereignty from two directions in the debate over humanitarian intervention. Since humanitarian intervention can be obligatory only if it is permissible, we shall focus upon the issue of permissibility.

it with nonviolence) to oppose the use of force represented by humanitarian military intervention. So I consider the objection a fair one.

Second, as indicated in Chapter 11, it might also be argued that pacifism, unless it is absolute, need not oppose all conceivable wars (or, if you like, war in all possible worlds), or even all conceivable forms of military intervention; in which case it is at least unclear that (1) is true. This claim also is correct, but it, too, is a relatively fine point. Pragmatic pacifism holds that war (and interventionary military violence) is wrong in the world as it is and as it is likely to be in the foreseeable future, not necessarily as it might be conceived to be in imaginative scenarios. I shall assume in what follows that (1) is true, and that pacifism, broadened and appropriately qualified, rules out humanitarian military intervention. What I shall question is premise (2).

Much of our discussion in Chapters 5 and 7 is relevant here, and I shall not repeat those arguments. They have to do with the foreseeable killing of innocents in military intervention, the distinction between killing and letting die, and the question of the violations of a right to life when innocents are killed. Suffice it to say that what is needed to justify humanitarian military intervention is an argument to show by what right an army may kill some innocent people to save others. If saving others is thought to constitute a just cause, then much of the argument of Chapter 7 in particular is relevant here. If it has not been shown that killing innocent persons in the service of a just cause in general is justified, then it has not been shown that killing innocent persons in order to save other innocent persons is justified in particular.

13.7 Epistemic problems with humanitarian military intervention

An initial concern from a pacifist perspective will be shared by anyone who is skeptical of the case for humanitarian military intervention: It may be difficult or impossible ever to know that a particular military intervention is humanitarian.

Often humanitarian intervention is defined with regard to motive. In this view, in order to constitute an instance of military humanitarian intervention, the motive (or the governing motive, if there is more than one) must be benevolence in general or concern, caring or compassion in particular for the persons suffering or under threat. But it is difficult to be confident of motives, not only of others, but of one's own as well. And when dealing with governments, which are given to secrecy, dissimulation, prevarication and often outright mendacity, one often can have little confidence about what motivates the large-scale deployment of troops to another country. Some realists are sufficiently skeptical that humanitarian motives will be strong enough to lead states to initiate or sustain humanitarian action that they argue that national self-interest must be involved as well. At other times, intention is appealed to.[28] Intentions are less difficult to know than motives. One can infer intentions somewhat more reliably

---

[28] Intentions and motives are often used interchangeably, but I shall distinguish them. One's intention I take to be that which is one's purpose to bring about by an action; motive to be that which explains *why* one intends what one does.

from actual conduct and its context than one can motives. But one and the same act or policy may have a primary intention and a variety of subsidiary intentions, and it may be difficult in practice to be confident which is which. When it attacked Iraq in 2003, the United States pretty clearly intended to establish a democracy in Iraq (defined, at the minimum, as a government that holds elections).[29] But this may have been subordinate to, or correlative with, other possible intentions, such as to combat terrorism, prevent Iraq from developing nuclear weapons or ensure US control over Persian Gulf oil resources.

The point is that to define humanitarian military intervention by reference to motives and intentions means that in any actual case one may not know whether the intervention is humanitarian or not.

If correct, this means that it cannot be known with any certainty whether the long list of candidates for humanitarian intervention—from the Great Powers in Turkey on behalf of Greece in 1827, France in Syria in 1860, Russia in Turkey on behalf of Bulgarian nationalists in 1877, the United States in Cuba in 1989, the Great Powers plus Japan in China in 1900 to the US-led NATO in Kosovo in 1999 and in Libya in 2011—are in fact instances of humanitarian intervention.[30] At best, we can know only that the stated intentions in these cases were to secure the well-being of innocents, and even that may be difficult to know with confidence.

In addition to knowing the motives and/or intentions of interveners, one needs to know that persons are being mistreated and on a sufficiently large scale (how large is left vague by advocates of military intervention), which often is difficult to know, at least in the short term. The notion of "mistreatment" implies three kinds of knowledge: first, that persons are being threatened, harmed or killed; second, that this treatment is unjustified; and third, that even if unjustified, the treatment is of such magnitude and severity as to make it a candidate for intervention. It is often apparent that persons are being threatened, harmed or killed in some country. That happens regularly. But little of it shocks the "conscience of mankind" in the way advocates of humanitarian intervention think justifies military action. Without knowledge of the second sort, that the treatment is unjustified (a pertinent question for violentists but not for nonviolentists and most pacifists), the treatment cannot be assumed to be *mis*treatment. To those, for example, for whom capital punishment is a violation of human rights, Singapore and China are among the most flagrant in their mistreatment of persons: Singapore because it has the highest per capita execution rate in the world, China because it executes the largest number of persons per year. These facts are known. But to the extent that there is disagreement over the morality of the death penalty, there is disagreement over whether such punishments are justified. If they are justified, they presumably do not constitute mistreatment (so long as the manner of killing is not

---

[29] Interestingly, the New York–based Human Rights Watch has argued that neither the United States nor Britain can retroactively justify the Iraq War as a case of humanitarian intervention. Kenneth Roth, speaking for the group, is quoted as saying "The Iraq war and the effort to justify it even in part in humanitarian terms risk giving humanitarian intervention a bad name ... It could be devastating for people in need of future rescue." *The Jordan Times*, internet edition, January 27, 2004.

[30] For a discussion of these examples (other than Libya), see Gerhard van Glahn, *Law Among Nations*, 2nd ed. (London: The Macmillan Company, 1970), p. 168.

unnecessarily cruel). No one argues for humanitarian intervention in these countries to save the lives of the thousands now being killed by their governments, or in the United States to rescue the thousands on death row. Similarly, some countries are notorious for torture or for denying rights to suspects. But there are no calls for humanitarian intervention to stop these practices. Indeed, the practices have been made use of by the United States in the so-called "rendition" of suspects secretly to such countries.

Regarding the third kind of knowledge, even if the threats, harms and killing of persons are assumed not to be morally justified, that by itself is insufficient to warrant humanitarian intervention (or, alternatively, to qualify an intervention as humanitarian). Thousands and often millions of persons are killed in wars. But the deaths of soldiers, and even of civilians so long as they are not intentionally targeted, are not thought to warrant humanitarian intervention. If they were, countries that are not at war would intervene against both sides in a war to stop the killing. Even the deaths that occur on the side that is supposedly justified in fighting the war (hence whose losses may be thought to be unjustified killings by the other side) are not thought to warrant humanitarian intervention. Estimates of civilian deaths in the US war and occupation of Iraq run into the thousands. But the US military insists that they do not intentionally target civilians,[31] and there are no calls for humanitarian military intervention against the United States. The killings or harms must be horrendous to a certain unspecified degree, arousing the "conscience of humanity." Atrocities, massacres and attempted genocide qualify, even if the harm and death caused by them pales in comparison with those inflicted in wartime. One of the problems with the situation in Rwanda (one of the few recent cases to which the much abused term "genocide" accurately applied) was, first, that the extent of the killing was unknown until well into the killings, and second, that much of the killing that took place was presumed to be in connection with the ongoing civil war, hence not to be genocide.[32]

13.8 Military intervention

The epistemic problems surrounding humanitarian intervention do not apply to military intervention. We can know for certain when military intervention occurs.

---

[31] Although there is no evidence the US soldiers (as opposed to private contractors) intentionally targeted civilians in Iraq, there is ample evidence that they knowingly killed civilians. As one sergeant reportedly said, "If someone runs into a house, we're going to light it up. If civilians get killed in there, that's a tragedy, but we're going to keep doing it and people are going to get the message that they should do whatever they can to keep these people out of their neighborhoods." "In Tough Iraqi Conflict, Civilians Pay High Price," *The Christian Science Monitor*, January 21, 2004.

[32] In his excellent analysis of the Rwanda case, Alan J. Kuperman points out that "because of five trends in the reporting during the first two weeks, the president of the United States could not have determined that a nationwide genocide was under way in Rwanda until about April 20, 1994. First, violence was initially depicted in the context of a two-sided civil war—one that the Tutsi were winning—rather than a one-sided, ethnic genocide against the Tutsi. Second, after a few days, violence was reported to be on the wane when in reality it was accelerating. Third, most early death counts were gross underestimates, sometimes by a factor of ten, and did not reach genocidal proportions. Fourth, the initial focus was almost exclusively on Kigali, a relatively small city, and failed to indicate the scope of violence. Fifth, no credible and knowledgeable observers, including human rights groups, raised the prospect that a genocide was under way until the end of the second week." *The Limits of Human Intervention: Genocide in Rwanda* (Washington, DC: Brookings Institution Press, 2001), p. 24.

It is verifiable empirically, without regard to subjective factors such as motive and intention. Both sides of the issue of humanitarian intervention can agree on this.

Because humanitarian military intervention is obviously a form of military intervention, it can be justified only if military intervention can be justified. Conversely, if military intervention *cannot* be justified, then humanitarian military intervention cannot be justified. Moreover, if, as the ICISS says, nonintervention is "the norm from which any departure has to be justified," then there is a strong presumption against military intervention of any sort. It must be defeated if humanitarian intervention is to be justified.[33]

But the permissibility of military intervention implies the permissibility of war. As war is actionably wrong (assuming the soundness of my earlier argument), then military intervention is actionably wrong unless relevant dissimilarities can be shown between it and war. To assess this possibility requires looking more closely at military intervention and the conditions it presupposes. Again, my concern is not with hypothetical interventions in an idealized world. It is with actual interventions of the sort one finds in this world and may expect to find in the future if such interventions are considered permissible. If the notion of military intervention is not contextualized, it has no immediate and obvious connection with the realities of the twenty-first century.

It seems clear, in light of this, that military intervention of the sort in question is undertaken by a state. This means that it presupposes a military establishment, with armies and weapons of modern warfare. It will usually include a system of conscription and will almost always do so in times of war of any magnitude. Accordingly, it will include an economy in which significant portions of the country's wealth are devoted to creating and maintaining its armies. It will, in other words, have a war system. One has to look at the war systems pervading the states that conduct such interventions. These are necessary conditions, not of idealized interventions in hypothetical cases but of actual interventions in the real world. Such interventions are by states prepared for war.

As measured by the historical evidence, few states can maintain war systems of that sort for long without using them. And if war is largely the work of men, and if men can be expected to predominate in positions of power in the world for the foreseeable future, then wars (or forms of state violence that approximate war) may be expected to continue.[34] It is this which is of concern to pacifists.

The rationale for humanitarian military intervention grounds the whole war system in ways that can be expected to contribute to that system's perpetuation and expansion. George R. Lucas, Jr. maintains:

> Military forces have been used sporadically for centuries for the decidedly second-
> ary purpose of peacekeeping and nation-building in their own nation's political or

---

[33] It is unclear whether the ICISS means only that departures from nonintervention must be legally justified or that they must be morally justified, or both. If the above claims—that international law is founded on nonintervention and is the best safeguard against war—are correct, then arguably there is a moral presumption in addition to the legal. I shall not argue for either of those claims here.

[34] For a good review of feminist thinking on this issue, see Carol Cohn and Sara Ruddick, "A Feminist Perspective on Weapons of Mass Destruction," in Sohail Hashmi and Steven Lee (eds), *Ethics and Weapons of Mass Destruction* (Cambridge: Cambridge Universiry Press), pp. 405–436.

economic interest. *It is extraordinary and utterly without historical precedent, however, to appeal to humanitarian exercises in behalf of this interventionist imperative, rather than to national self-defense or the defense of vital national interests, as the primary justification for the use of military force.*[35] [Italics added]

The historical accuracy of this claim will be questioned by some, who believe they can document cases of humanitarian intervention back at least to the early nineteenth century. And it will be questioned by those political realists who argue that US policy, at least through much of the twentieth century, was governed—unwisely, in their judgment—by moral considerations rather than national self-interest. But few will question that national self-defense has been the bedrock justification for going to war since the formation of the nation-state system.

Further, just war and humanitarian intervention theories have been feeding on each other. JWT has gradually been adopting a humanitarian rationale for war, and the justification for humanitarian military intervention has been increasingly patterned after the JWT.[36] These developments may in part be byproducts of the growing emphasis upon human rights.

13.9 War, just war theory, and humanitarian military intervention

For some, however, humanitarian intervention might seem to pose as great a problem for traditional JWT as for pacifism. As I have noted, many take the JWT to legitimize war only for national defense. That is taken to be the only just cause.[37] Some, like C. A. J. Coady, maintain that "any argument for humanitarian intervention has to overcome the presumptive case against aggressive war, and has to discharge the other requirements of just war theory."[38]

The structure of this reasoning can be framed in an argument similar to the one considered above in connection with pacifism.

B1. If the JWT is correct, humanitarian intervention is impermissible (because it constitutes aggression).

[35] George R. Lucas, Jr., "From *jus ad bellum* to *jus ad pacem*: Re-Thinking Just-War Criteria for the Use of Military Force for Humanitarian Ends," in Chatterjee and Scheid, *Ethics and Foreign Intervention*, p. 75.

[36] Two of the principals involved in the ICISS report detail the adaptation of just war criteria to the justification of humanitarian military intervention. See Gareth Evans and Mohammed Sahnoun, "The Responsibility to Protect," *Foreign Affairs*, Vol. 81, No. 6, November/December 2002, pp. 99–111.

[37] Where it is not taken to be the only just cause, national defense is taken to be the paradigmatic just cause. As Bernard Williams writes, "One of the few moral ideas about warfare that is generally agreed upon is that the use of armed force can be justified in the cause of national self-defense. This aspect of traditional 'Just War' doctrine is widely accepted by public opinion and is enshrined in international law." Foreword to Rodin, *War and Self-Defense*.

[38] C. A. J. Coady, "Challenging the Paradigm: The Case for Intervention," in Chatterjee and Scheid, *Ethics and Foreign Intervention*, p. 283. He also maintains that "the moral presumption against unsought military intervention in the affairs of other nations is broadly defensible in just-war terms, and should still carry considerable weight even when the primary motive for intervention is humanitarian" (p. 291).

2. Humanitarian intervention is permissible.
3. Therefore, the JWT is incorrect.

Others see JWT as simply inadequate to dealing with humanitarian intervention or largely irrelevant to it. As George R. Lucas, Jr. puts it, "the attempt simply to assimilate or subsume humanitarian uses of military force under traditional just war criteria fails because the use of military force in humanitarian cases is far closer to the use of force in domestic law enforcement and peacekeeping."[39] Even more strongly, he says "[t]here is a straightforward, almost pedestrian, sense in which *jus ad bellum* does not apply to humanitarian operations: they are not, nor are they intended to be, acts of war on the part of the intervening forces."[40] Others see no problem in reconciling JWT with humanitarian intervention. They readily adapt just war criteria to the justification of humanitarian intervention.[41]

Through the twentieth century the moral and legal grounds to justify war narrowed largely to national defense. If understood in a straightforward way, namely as a response to aggression, national defense was too narrowly defined for many who wanted to justify war. Two things happened. First, the notion of self-defense became elasticized to cover the use of military force in circumstances other than a response to aggression, and, indeed, to cover virtually any international use of military force a government wanted to undertake. Second, those who were uncomfortable with such a freewheeling way with the language of self-defense sought a higher moral ground, often couched in the language of human rights. Thus the American Catholic Bishops in formulating the condition of just cause assert: "War is permissible only ... to protect innocent life, to preserve conditions necessary for decent human existence, and to secure basic human rights."[42] National defense—with its underlying rationale of national interest—serves the collective egoism of the state. The protection of the innocent, preservation of conditions for decent human existence and the securing of basic human rights are loftier. Just cause now involves doing something for others, not first and foremost for oneself, or even for the collective self of the state. The kinds of considerations traditionally appealed to by pacifists are now appropriated by warists to justify war. People with little patience for the rationales often given for war reluctantly concede that you have to make exceptions in these cases. They appeal to Somalia, Bosnia, Rwanda, Kosovo, Darfur—and some of them even to Iraq, Syria, Libya and the challenge posed by ISIS.

Once high moral sentiments become enlisted on behalf of warfare, those who oppose war, and who are often grudgingly thought to be well-intentioned if misguided,

---

[39] Lucas, "From *jus ad bellum* to *jus ad pacem* p. 73.

[40] Lucas, Jr., "From *jus ad bellum* to *jus ad pacem*," p. 77. The paradigm cases of humanitarian intervention are clearly acts of war according to international law whether or not they are intended to be. Lucas's point perhaps is that they are not intended to represent the initiation of war on the part of the intervener.

[41] For an account that locates a just cause for war in the same concern for human rights that justifies humanitarian intervention, see Fernando Tesón, *Humanitarian Intervention: An Inquiry into Law and Morality*.

[42] *The Challenge of Peace: God's Promise and Our Response: A Pastoral Letter on War and Peace*, May 3, 1983, National Conference of Catholic Bishops (Washington, DC: United States Catholic Conference, 1983), p. 28.

come to be viewed as reprehensible. Gone from view is the bloodletting of warfare that pacifists oppose. In its place is the plight of the innocent that warfare is alleged to alleviate. References to atrocities, massacres and genocide then dominate the discussion. To be against war is to be, if not *for* these abominations, at least not against them. The moral considerations at the forefront of the arguments for humanitarian intervention are, in effect, arguments for war. It is this fact that presents the challenge, not only to pacifists, but to advocates of humanitarian intervention as well.

These developments are interesting on a number of counts. At the outset, JWT allowed for the initiation of war. The issue was whether by doing so one avenged a wrong, the principal ground of a just cause.[43] Who began the war was of itself of little consequence. As the theory developed, and particularly as something resembling a legal version of it became enshrined in international law in the twentieth century, the principal just cause for war came to be seen to be self-defense. Article 51 of the UN Charter epitomizes this. Now, however, JWT, insofar as it has assimilated the humanitarian interventionist rationale, has reverted to justifying the initiation of war. If one's own country is attacked, then, by this rationale, innocent persons within one's borders are at risk and one then has a just cause. If one's country is not attacked, but persons within the borders of other countries are at risk, then one has a just cause to rescue or protect them. Militarily intervening in another state without authorization of that state's government is an act of war. Throughout much of the twentieth, only one *type* of war was allowable, a war of self-defense. Now, what throughout most of the twentieth century were regarded as wars of aggression are permitted, provided they are for humanitarian purposes. Indeed, Pope John Paul II says that humanitarian intervention is "obligatory where the survival of populations and entire ethnic groups is seriously compromised. This is a duty for nations and the international community." Even more explicitly related to our present concerns, he says: "The principle of the sovereignty of states and of non-interference in their internal affairs—which retain all their value—cannot constitute a screen behind which torture and murder may be carried out."[44] Add to this the elasticity introduced into the notion of self-defense by the Bush doctrine of preemption[45] (according to which the United States may take

---

[43] As John Finnis writes of Aquinas, "[c]learly, Aquinas' discussion of just war is focused upon the decision to initiate war. ...His discussion, therefore, is seeking to explain when actions which today would often (sometimes questionably) be called 'aggression' can be justified." See *Aquinas: Moral, Political, and Legal Theory* (Oxford: Oxford University Press, 1998), IX.3. With regard to both the initiation of war, and the grounding of just war in rights, the Catholic Encyclopedia (1908), s.v., says under War: "The right of war is the right of a sovereign state to wage a contention at arms against another, and is in its analysis an instance of the general moral power of coercion, i.e., to make use of physical force to conserve its rights inviolable. Every perfect right, i.e., every right involving in others an obligation in justice a deference thereto, to be efficacious, and consequently a real and not an illusory power, carries with it at the last appeal the subsidiary right of coercion....Catholic philosophy, therefore, concedes to the State the full natural right of war, whether defensive, as in case of another's attack in force upon it; offensive (more properly, coercive), where it finds it necessary to take the initiative in the application of force; or punitive, in the infliction of punishment for evil done against itself, or in some determined cases, against others."

[44] Quoted in the *Harvest of Justice Is Sown in Peace*, National Conference of Catholic Bishops, November 17, 1993.

[45] The Bush doctrine, although billed as justifying preemption, actually justifies *prevention*, which does not require the imminence of an attack.

preemptive action against states that are perceived to be threats) and the floodgates are open. Practically no kind of war is prohibited, provided it can be represented as being either in self-defense, as expanded into preemption (or, more accurately, prevention), or for humanitarian purposes.

There is a certain irony in the way in which this thinking is playing out. The growing concern for human rights has led to calls for humanitarian intervention. But when one looks at the way in which such action is carried out, say, in Iraq (one of whose innumerable "justifications" has been humanitarian, to free the Iraqi people from Saddam Hussein's brutality), it is evident that the action carries a terrible price. An estimated 5,000–8,000 persons were killed during the invasion itself and more almost weekly by US troops.[46] Priority clearly was given to safeguarding the lives of the invaders over the lives of those they supposedly were protecting. The very concern that supposedly was part of the justification of the intervention was largely displaced in the carrying out of the policy.

These considerations, I suggest, provide grounds for concluding that if military intervention is permissible, war is permissible. Logically, one could maintain that military intervention is permissible without conceding that war is permissible. But if the preceding is correct, not only will military intervention *in fact* sometimes lead to war, the rationale for humanitarian intervention will provide a justification for war. The forcible violation of sovereignty entailed by humanitarian intervention, as I have said, has traditionally been considered an act of war. Humanitarian intervention is a Trojan Horse that has been wheeled into the moral debate between pacifists and warists. Concealed within it is a rationale for war itself. If humanitarian intervention is permissible, then military intervention is permissible, and if military intervention is permissible, then war is permissible.

It is, then, on these grounds that the pacifist will challenge premise (2) in the original argument, because that premise camouflages the host of issues that divide pacifists and warists in the first place.

In trendier terms, one might say that there is a slippery slope from humanitarian intervention to military intervention to war. While the first phase of the slope (from humanitarian intervention to military intervention) proceeds by a conceptual entailment, the concluding phase (from military intervention to war) proceeds by social, psychological, and historical predispositions that can be gathered under the heading of the "logic" of war. It is arguable that, in addition to providing a rationale for war, acceptance of the moral permissibility of humanitarian intervention in fact makes war more likely. It places in the hands of the scrupulous and the unscrupulous alike the means to justify pretty much whatever they want to do. There will always be some innocent, weak or vulnerable people in almost any country whose protection can be used to justify violence. Some examples illustrate this.

---

[46] In addition, civilians have regularly been killed by insurgents and by Iraqi troops. For an argument to try to justify the killing of innocents in such interventions, see Erin Kelly, "The Burdens of Collective Liability," in Chatterjee and Scheid, *Ethics and Foreign Intervention*, pp. 118–139.

13.10 "Humanitarian" military intervention in the real world

The Spanish-American war, a prominent example of imperialism in US history, was billed as a humanitarian defense of rights. Former senator John J. Ingalls wrote in 1898, "[a]ll have known that the misrule of Spain was the denial of the inalienable rights of man, and its continuance an affront to civilization, a reproach to the conscience of mankind, and an insult to the ruler of the moral universe … We draw the sword to avenge the wrongs of the helpless. Our cannon speak for those who are voiceless."[47] The Senate resolution of April 16, 1898, not only said "the people of the island of Cuba are, and of right ought to be, free and independent," but also "it is the duty of the United States to demand … that the government of Spain at once relinquish its authority and government in the island of Cuba, and withdraw its land and naval forces from Cuba and Cuban waters."[48]

A second example is Hitler's exploitation of the plight of the Sudeten Germans in the 1930s. It, too, was billed as humanitarian. When Czechoslovakia was carved out of the Austro-Hungarian Empire at the end of WWI, 3.5 million Germans (along with Hungarians, Poles, and others) found themselves minorities within the Czech state. The Sudetenland in which the Germans largely resided was contiguous with Germany. A movement grew up among the Sudeten Germans (instigated by Hitler according to some) for greater autonomy within Czechoslovakia or actual incorporation into Germany. Though he did not call it humanitarian intervention, Hitler intervened in Czechoslovakia supposedly on behalf of the Sudeten Germans.[49] Without the benefit of the more recent term "ethnic cleansing," Hitler said in a Berlin speech on September 26, 1938:

> So in the end … these Czechs annexed Slovakia. Since this State did not seem fitted to live, out of hand three and a half million Germans were taken in violation of their right to self-determination and their wish for self-determination … At the time Mr. Benes [then Czech President] lied this State into being, he gave a solemn pledge to divide it on the model of the Swiss system into cantons … We all know how Mr. Benes has redeemed his pledge to introduce this cantonal system. He began his reign of terror. Even at that time the Germans already attempted to protest against this arbitrary violence. They were shot down. After that a war of extermination began. In these years of the "peaceful" development of Czechoslovakia nearly 600,000 Germans had to leave Czechoslovakia. This happened for a very simple reason: otherwise they would have had to starve! The whole development

---

[47] John J. Ingalls, *America's War for Humanity: Cuba's Struggle for Liberty* (New York: N.D. Thompson Publishing Company, 1898), pp. 16, 20.

[48] Cited in Ingalls, *America's War for Humanity, I* p. 19.

[49] I say that Hitler intervened in Czechoslovakia "supposedly" on behalf of the Sudeten Germans in deference to those, like Shirer, who maintain that this was just a pretext for aggression. See William L. Shirer, *The Rise and Fall of the Third Reich* (Greenwich, Conn.: Fawcett Publications, Inc., 1960), p. 488. Pretext or not, such action was consistent with the pervasive theme throughout *Mein Kampf* and Hitler's speeches on the urgency of promoting and safe-guarding the well-being of the German people. This, I want to stress emphatically, does not justify German actions. But it underscores the uses of force that lend themselves to justification by appeal to humanitarian considerations.

from the year 1918 up to 1938 showed one thing clearly: Mr. Benes was determined slowly to exterminate the German element ... He has hurled countless people into the profoundest misery. He has managed to make millions of people fearful and anxious. Through the continuous employment of his methods of terrorism he has succeeded in reducing to silence these millions.[50]

This was not simply groundless railing. Woodrow Wilson had appealed repeatedly for the self-determination of peoples,[51] and Hitler used that plea to advantage. This helped create sympathy for the German cause, particularly in Britain. Historian B. H. Liddell Hart maintains that Britain quietly gave Hitler a green light for expansion into Eastern Europe, a position on which it later reversed itself.[52] At the conclusion of the war, Benes stripped the ethnic Germans of property and citizenship. Fifteen million of them were expelled from Czechoslovakia and Poland. The decrees depriving them of Czech property and citizenship remained in effect nearly sixty years later.[53]

That the desire to acquire *Lebensraum* for the German nation was a major element in Hitler's thinking does not alter the fact that considerations appealed to today under the heading of "humanitarian intervention" are there as well. A concern for the German people (the *Volk*) was central to Hitler's overall philosophy.

The radical realignment of national boundaries is most conspicuously associated with the outcomes of major wars, as in the case of WWI. But it can occur also with the collapse of regimes, as in the case of the Soviet Union and Yugoslavia. In each case, a people who are part of a majority in one state suddenly find themselves a minority in a new state formed out of the wreckage of the old. Thus, for example, ethnic Russians suddenly found themselves a minority in Lithuania when it declared its independence from the Soviet Union. And Serbs suddenly found themselves a minority in Croatia when it broke free from Yugoslavia and later in Kosovo when it became independent of Serbia. With both the Soviet Union and Yugoslavia having ceased to exist as states, new fears of oppression surface as newly formed states replicate the same systems of governmental control and coercion (though not, of course, always with the same degree of harshness) that preexisted in the collapsed state. This opens the way to the same rationale for humanitarian intervention that Hitler exploited in the case of the Sudeten Germans. It is worth noting that Russian Defense Minister Sergei B. Ivanov

---

[50] Adolf Hitler, speech of September 26, 1938, Berlin. Adolf Hitler, *My New Order*, edited with commentary by Raoul de Roussey de Sales (New York: Rynal & Hitchcock, 1941), pp. 524f.

[51] Woodrow Wilson said, for example, in an Address to Congress on February 11, 1918: "National aspirations must be respected; peoples may now be dominated and governed only by their own consent. 'Self-determination' is not a mere phrase. It is an imperative principle of action, which statesmen will henceforth ignore at their peril." *The Messages and Papers of Woodrow Wilson* (New York: The Review of Reviews Corporation, 1924), Vol. I, p. 475.

[52] B. H. Liddell Hart, *History of the Second World War* (New York: G.P. Putnam's Sons, 1971), p. 8. It is interesting to compare this claim with the allegation, cited in Chapter 9, that the United States through its ambassador to Iraq, April Glaspie, similarly gave a green light to Saddam Hussein before his invasion of Kuwait in 1990. For a purported transcript of this interview, see *The Gulf War Reader* (New York: Random House, 1991), pp. 122–133.

[53] Regarding the current situation of the Germans expelled from Czechoslovakia and Poland, see "World War II's Latest 'Victims,'" *The Christian Science Monitor*, September 23, 2003.

made clear that Russia reserved "the right to intervene militarily in former Soviet states if the human rights of ethnic Russians were violated."[54]

The third example of putative humanitarian intervention is the March 17, 2011, Resolution 1973 by the UN Security Council authorizing imposition of a no-fly zone over Libya. The stated aim was to protect civilians in the ongoing civil war. But Secretary of State Hillary Clinton had stated before the UN Human Rights Council that "Qaddafi has lost the legitimacy to govern, and it is time for him to go without further violence or delay."[55] The following day, the Libyan government announced that it would cease all military operations in light of the UN call for a cease-fire. Whether the announcement was meant seriously or simply to forestall military action against the Libyan government is unclear, but British, French and American aircraft commenced attacking. Command was later taken over by NATO. By March 24, in the words of Secretary of State Hillary Clinton, "the coalition is in control of the skies of Libya."[56] French Foreign Minister Alain Juppé was quoted at the same time as saying: "The destruction of Ghadaffi's military capacity is a matter of days or weeks, certainly not months." It was clear that the aim was far more than to enforce a no-fly zone. It was to defeat Qaddafi's ground forces. And it was clear that it was to bring about the downfall of Qaddafi.[57] Qaddafi himself was killed in October when NATO intercepted a satellite phone call of his that enabled NATO to attack a convoy of seventy-five vehicles in which he was traveling. Escaping the attack, Qaddafi was apprehended by Libyan rebels. TV footage showed him being brutalized before being loaded onto a vehicle. He was soon thereafter executed, by whom remains unclear. The Security Council voted to end NATO's mandate on October 31, 2011.

Whether the NATO intervention saved any civilian lives, or if so, how many, is unclear. What is clear is that following the overthrow of Qaddafi, Libya spiraled into a chaos of disorder and violence. While Americans were fixated on the death of its ambassador in a militia attack on Benghazi on September 11, 2012, there was little attention to the suffering of Libyan civilians. The humanitarian concern evaporated quickly once regime change was achieved.

Translated into terms applicable to the actual world, the right of states to intervene militarily in other states for humanitarian reasons means, in effect, the right of states to intervene when they *believe* that humanitarian grounds warrant it. It also opens the door to states intervening militarily in other states when they can *represent* the intervention as motivated by humanitarian considerations. Among the flurry of justifications given (after the fact) for the US attack on Iraq in 2003 was the need to free the Iraqi people from an oppressive dictatorship. The idealistic notion of dedicated

---

[54] The statement, made to a meeting of NATO ministers, was reported in the *New York Times* on October 10, 2003. If one attaches credence to this statement, it suggests that the rationale for Moscow's support of ethnic Russian insurgents in Crimea and Ukraine had a basis in much earlier pronouncements.

[55] http://www.nytimes.com/2011/03/01world/africa/01military.html?hpw=&pagewanted=print.

[56] As reported by *Jane's Defense Weekly*, Vol. 48, no. 13, March 30, 2011, p. 5.

[57] "The strategy for White House officials … is to hit Libyan forces hard enough to force them to oust Colonel Qaddafi, a result that Mr. Obama has openly encouraged." http://www.nytimes.com/2011/03/29/us/29military.html?_r=l&hp=&pagewanted/. The murder of Qaddafi after his apprehension appears to have been of little concern to the United States.

saviors riding in, figuratively, on white horses to save oppressed peoples bears little relation to the actual world, in which force is wielded by governments with enormous military power, at the cost of many innocent lives, and more often than not in the service of their own interests.

Added to these considerations are the concerns of those involved in humanitarian aid programs who contend that to characterize military intervention as humanitarian is to appropriate a term that characterizes their programs, which stand for something that is radically different. Some of them find those values of neutrality and objectivity essential to effective humanitarian aid simply lacking in most military ventures of the sort that would purport to be humanitarian. Neutrality, for these purposes, means that organizations do not take sides in conflicts; impartiality means that the only criterion for providing aid is need, not politics or ethnicity.[58] If these values are important for nonviolent aid to be effective, they would seem absolutely essential for military intervention to be effective. When we look at the past, governments can be seen to be duplicitous, conniving and sometimes engaging in outright lying to promote interests of importance to them, whether those interests be those of the state, the nation or of the individual leaders themselves. They are the ones who become credentialed in the effort to legitimize humanitarian intervention.

As we saw in Chapter 10, the case of Kosovo has been held up as a model of humanitarian intervention. When the Belgrade government tried to suppress the armed uprising by Albanian Kosovars, NATO, led by the United States, launched a seventy-eight-day bombing campaign until the Serb army withdrew. It is now clear, if it was not at the time, that the campaign violated one of the key tenets of humanitarian aid: neutrality. Much of the action was undertaken on behalf of, and coordinated with, the KLA (Kosovo Liberation Army). Kosovo has now become independent of Serbia. And the Serb minority within it was subject to escalating violence and terrorism of a sort the UN administration was unable to control. Human rights abuses were possibly as great as before the US-NATO attack on Serbia. They were simply redirected from one group (Albanians, then a minority within Serbia) to another (Serbs, now a minority within Kosovo). Moreover, the region—largely forgotten about in the wake of 9/11 and the wars in Afghanistan and Iraq—has become a breeding ground for criminals and extremists.[59] Whatever the humanitarian component, the deteriorating situation in Kosovo—and more recently Libya—needs to be added to Somalia and Iraq when assessing the outcomes of promoting humanitarianism out of the barrel of a gun.

[58] Sarah Kenyon Lischer, "Humanitarian Aid Is not a Military Business," *Christian Science Monitor*, April 15, 2003. In a similar vein, see Jan Egeland, "Humanitarianism Under Fire," *Christian Science Monitor*, August 5, 2004, and Gil Loescher, "An Idea Lost in the Rubble," *The New York Times*, August 20, 2004. When Doctors Without Borders announced in July 2004 that it was withdrawing from Afghanistan after twenty-four years of service there, it criticized the United States for linking aid to support for US military and political policies, thereby increasing the risk to supposedly neutral aid workers. The principal reason given for the withdrawal, however, was the failure of the Afghan government to apprehend those responsible for the killing of five aid workers by the Taliban. See *The New York Times*, July 29, 2004.

[59] In the words of one American security official, "Some countries have a mafia, but in Kosovo, the mafia has a country. Especially with the increased activity of Islamic extremists and Al Qaeda groups in and around Kosovo, this situation could pose a real security threat to Europe." Quoted in *The Christian Science Monitor*, September 26, 2003. The security official remained anonymous.

The other dimension of the Kosovo crisis that is interesting is that the bombing campaign did not bring down Serbian strongman, Slobodan Milosevic. If anything, it strengthened his position as Serbs became defiant in the face of US bombing. It was not until fall 2000 that he was forced from power. And then it was not by military force but by the concerted nonviolent action of the Serbian people, particular youth associated with the organization *Otpor*. Trained in the techniques of nonviolent action, and well-funded by US organizations, they undertook a sustained campaign of nonviolent action that culminated in Milosevic's downfall in October of 2000. This was intervention, to be sure.[60] But it was nonviolent intervention. And it was successful beyond anything attained by the military campaign, and at far lesser cost. And it was successful beyond anything that could have been attained without enormous bloodshed had US troops invaded Serbia to depose Milosevic. It has been argued by Peter Ackerman and Jack DuVall that similar nonviolent campaigns might have brought down Saddam Hussein in Iraq and could bring down the repressive regime in Iran.[61]

The point is that pacifists need not reject humanitarian intervention, if it is plausibly construed. Most will not do so if it is nonviolent intervention. In that case, pacifists will, in the end, not reject premise (2) in the original argument. They will reject premise (1), which holds that if pacifism is correct, then humanitarian intervention is impermissible.

One further dimension of the problem deserves mention. If, as interventionary theory holds, it does not matter *where* human rights violations occur, it is arguable that it should not matter *who* undertakes to combat those violations—whether it be states or groups or individuals. We are talking here about the use of violence. If violence is thought to be warranted to put an end to human rights violations by states, there is no obvious moral reason why the use of violence for that end should be limited to states. If states are not immunized against action to prevent human rights violations, they should not be privileged to be the sole initiators of such preventive action either. What is of paramount importance is that the harm and suffering be ended.

This, of course, opens the door to guerrilla and possibly terrorist actions on the world scene. Recall the Fatwa issued by Osama bin Laden and others in 1998. In calling for violent action against Americans anywhere, it detailed grievances

---

[60] The intervention, however, was funded by nongovernmental organizations such as the National Endowment for Democracy and the International Republican Institute, as well as the United States Agency for International Development. It is possible that there was covert funding as well. The funding for the campaign, including the training of nonviolent activists in Hungary, ran into millions of dollars. On this, see Gan, *Violence and Nonviolence*, p. 98.

[61] See Peter Ackerman and Jack DuVall, "The Nonviolent Script for Iran," in the *Christian Science Monitor*, July 22, 2003. The US government, as represented by Secretary of State Colin Powell had already arguably intervened in the internal affairs of Iran by openly encouraging protests against its government at a special meeting of the World Economic Forum. Indeed, he said the US had a duty to do so, and cited the protests as confirmation that the US was "on the right track" in its policies in the region, including in Iraq. *The Jordan Times, electronic edition, June 23*, 2003. Others have questioned the humanitarian rationale for the war on Iraq. As Michael Ignatieff writes: "[T]he Bush administration did not invade Iraq just to establish human rights. Nor, ultimately, was this intervention about establishing a democracy or saving lives as such. … The Iraq intervention was the work of conservative radicals, who believed that the status quo in the Middle East was untenable….They wanted intervention to bring about a revolution in American power in the entire region." Michael Ignatieff, "Why Are We in Iraq?" *The New York Times Magazine,* September 7, 2003. p. 71.

against the United States.[62] Notable among them was the alleged harm and suffering inflicted by the United States against the Iraqi people. If one takes this at face value (as, of course, many will not), it signifies a humanitarian dimension to this particular terrorist concern. President Bush offered a humanitarian rationale (among others) for the invasion and occupation of Iraq. Osama bin Laden has offered a humanitarian rationale (among others) for targeting the United States and its citizens. The point is that once the justifiability of the use of violence in the pursuit of one's moral, religious, or political ends is conceded, only lack of imagination and ineptness in logic limit one's extension of that use to whatever areas one chooses.

13.11 Conclusion

It should be stressed that in the preceding I have been discussing putative humanitarian intervention. I would now maintain that "humanitarian intervention" is a misnomer. I agree with those who argue that the term "humanitarian" not be used for this purpose. To do so misleadingly appropriates a term that is already well established for neutral, impartial and nonviolent assistance. If it is used, then it should be specifically designated as violent or military humanitarian intervention.

So far as violent intervention may have humanitarian ground, there is no insurmountable problem here for JWT. Just war theorists need simply, as many of them have already, to expand or revise the notion of just cause to admit humanitarian considerations. The same considerations that justify war will then justify violent humanitarian intervention and, *mutatis mutandis*, vice-versa.

For pacifism, the problem is partly conceptual. The basic distinction should be between violent intervention and nonviolent intervention. If nonviolent intervention is recognized as a dimension of humanitarian intervention, then pacifism is not incompatible with humanitarian intervention per se and premise (1) of the earlier argument is not true. Pacifists can then accept the permissibility of nonviolent humanitarian intervention, and with it the truth of premise (2). What forms such nonviolent intervention might take there is not space to explore here, but they include financial aid, relocation and support of refugees, talks with perpetrators and a personal presence in support of victims. The preceding considerations would not, of course, settle the many issues dividing pacifists and warists. But it would help to focus them. The question would then be, not whether humanitarian intervention in general is ever justified, but whether violent humanitarian intervention is ever justified; and if it is, why the use of such violence should be the privilege of states to the exclusion of individuals and groups. That would require assessment of the earlier pacifist argument against military humanitarian intervention.

---

[62] For the full text of the Fatwa, see Bernard Lewis, "License to Kill: Usama bin Ladin's Declaration of Jihad," *Foreign Affairs*, Vol.77, No. 6, pp. 14–19. In Chapter 14, I shall quote a portion of the article.

Terrorism, Violence and Nonviolence

What is so deeply painful about terrorism is that our enemies, whom we see as evil, view themselves as saints and martyrs. As such, religious terrorism ... is psychological and spiritual warfare, requiring a psychologically and spiritually informed response.

—Jessica Stern, *Terrorism in the Name of God: Why Religious Militants Kill.*

14.1 What is terrorism?

The September 11, 2001 attack on the World Trade Center and the Pentagon is widely regarded as having changed America forever, inaugurating a new era in which the United States is threatened as never before. The threat, in this view, can be met only by an open-ended war against terrorism.[1] President Bush said that 9/11 was "a day of decision for our country. As a united and resolute people, America declared, 'We'll start the war from here.'"[2] It is also seen as having brought the country together.

There is a measure of truth to these claims. But that measure is less easy to assess than media commentary and government pronouncements would suggest. What is surprising is that people were surprised at the targeting of the United States in the way symbolized by 9/11. That targeting was predictable in the broader context of the US role in the world after the Gulf War and the collapse of the Soviet Union. US actions in Somalia, the former Yugoslavia, Kosovo, Afghanistan, Iraq, Libya and Syria strike many, particularly in the Muslim world, as part of an assault on Islam.[3] Others view them as counterproductive even from the standpoint of national interest. They see

---

[1] In these respects, 9/11 arguably had much the same effect that many experts believed would follow only from a terrorist attack using weapons of mass destruction. See Ashton Carter, John Deutch and Philip Zelikow, "Catastrophic Terrorism: Tackling the New Danger," *Foreign Affairs*, November/December 1998, Vol. 77, No. 6, pp. 80–94.

[2] From an August 26, 2003, speech to the American Legion Convention in St Louis, Missouri. http://nytimes.com/2003/08/26/politics/26TEXT-BUSH.

[3] Some of those actions, as in the case of Bosnia and Kosovo, were actually on behalf of Muslims against Christians.

these US actions as representing a superpower run amuck, a rampaging giant with a brain the size of a pea. There is no simple response to the growing global crisis unfolding in the twenty-first century. But a constructive response must begin by trying to understand terrorism itself.

Maurice Merleau-Ponty once wrote that history itself is terror, and that the common assumption of all revolutionaries is that "the contingency of the future and the role of human decisions in history make political divergences irreducible and cunning, deceit and violence inevitable."[4] This association of terror with cunning, deceit and violence is overly broad, of course. But it highlights the fact that violence is at the heart of terrorism. And by implication it suggests that violence in human affairs is widespread and widely accepted.

This latter claim is not altered by the fact that most of us do not use violence ourselves. That is done for us by others. Nor is it altered by the fact that we deplore violence at some level of our thinking. Our social life has so institutionalized violence that, despite ourselves, we support and sustain its use through government, taxation, the economy and even the educational system, which at many top universities trains officers for the military through ROTC and profits from military-related research. Internationally, we deplore the threat of nuclear war but support preparations for conventional war as though it were a respectable compromise. Talk of "regime change"—a euphemism for the overthrow of the governments of other countries—flows freely from the mouths of politicians and government leaders, with scarcely a murmur of concern from the general public.

Violence that maintains the status quo tends to be approved by those who are its beneficiaries; that which threatens the status quo is condemned. But the mode of violence that is almost universally condemned is terrorism. Although it is at the other end of the scale of destructiveness from nuclear war, it rivals nuclear war in the dread it inspires. When the fear of nuclear war and the fear of terrorism are brought together, they are an explosive mix. When these fears are focused on one country—and more specifically, on one person, as happened in the case of Saddam Hussein—they generate powerful motives to turn to violence to remove those threats.

More and more the term *terrorism* is used emotively to stand for virtually any use of political violence of which we disapprove. One and the same person becomes a terrorist or a freedom fighter, depending upon whether we approve or disapprove of his or her cause.

But terrorism has an underlying descriptive meaning. To terrorize is to instill extreme fear. This can, of course, have a pathological and sadistic motivation and be undertaken for its own sake. But it can also be rationally directed, and then it becomes of moral interest. Terrorism is the calculated creation and manipulation of such fear. It can be defined as:

Terrorism: Instilling fear to achieve one's ends, typically by the use or threat of violence, often against innocent persons.

---

[4] Maurice Merleau-Ponty, *Humanism and Terror* (Boston, MA: Beacon Press, 1969), p. 96.

Who does the terrorizing does not matter. What counts is what is done and for what reasons. Individuals acting alone can terrorize. But so can governments or armies. And *what* the ends are does not matter. They may be social, political, religious or moral. What makes one a terrorist are the means by which ends are pursued, not the ends themselves. One can terrorize in the service of just as well as unjust causes.

Terrorism presents the greatest challenge when undertaken for a cause. For then it often represents a rationally chosen means to an end. However much we deplore terrorism, it is not necessarily a less rational choice—purely in the sense of being a perceived means to an end—than many conventionally accepted modes of violence.[5] Trotsky perceived this when writing of the Russian revolution. A victorious war, he observed, usually "destroys only an insignificant part of the conquered army, intimidating the remainder and breaking their will. The revolution works n the same way: it kills individuals, and intimidates thousands."[6] Although he was describing the terror of the revolutionary class, what he said applies to terrorism of any sort. Terrorism typically kills few people by comparison with warfare. That remains true, despite 9/11. But it will change as terrorists eventually come into the possession of nuclear and/ or chemical-biological weapons.[7] Terrorism seeks to achieve its ends by breaking the will of the thousands who learn of it. That is why publicity is normally important to its success, as is well understood by ISIS in its beheadings. Whereas conventional war intimidates by inflicting losses, terrorism intimidates by instilling fear.

Conventional war, however, *may* be terroristic. Its rationale then is usually military necessity. This was phrased with remarkable honesty by the Kaiser during WWI. He said:

My soul is torn, but everything must be put to fire and sword; men, women, and children and old men must be slaughtered and not a tree or house be left standing. With these methods of terrorism, which are alone capable of affecting a people as degenerate as the French, the war will be over in two months, whereas if I admit considerations of humanity it will be prolonged for years.[8]

Much the same rationale, though never stated as bluntly, underlay the fire bombings of Tokyo and Dresden and the atomic bombings of Hiroshima and Nagasaki during

---

[5] Not that terrorism has a good track record at achieving its ends. As Walter Laqueur writes, "the decision to use terrorist violence is not always a rational one; if it were, there would be much less terrorism, since terrorist activity seldom achieves its aims." "Post Modern Terrorism," *Foreign Affairs*, September/October 1996, Vol. 75, No. 5, p. 31

[6] Leon Trotsky, *Terrorism and Communism* (Ann Arbor, MI: the University of Michigan Press, 1963), p. 58.

[7] Daniel Benjamin and Steven Simon observe in this regard that the "combination of terrorists and weapons of mass destruction is the stuff of countless movies and television shows. The reality is otherwise: very, very few groups have ever seriously tried to acquire such weapons. Almost all of those that have—the Japanese cult Aum Shinrikyo is the most notable exception—have sought them primarily for purposes of blackmail ... Its forays into procuring unconventional arms are an unmistakable sign that al-Qaeda is prepared to cross a threshold never before approached and kill in a way unlike that of any earlier terrorists." See their *The Age of Sacred Terror* (New York: Random House, 2002), p. 129

[8] Quoted in Richard A. Falk, Gabriel Kolka and Robert Jay Lifton (eds), *Crimes of War* (New York: Vintage books, 1971), p. 135.

WWII. Those, too, were acts of terrorism. They employed massive, indiscriminate violence against mostly innocent persons. The aim, in each case, was to destroy the morale of the whole country.

Because of the resources at a government's command, state terror is often the most systematic kind. Some believe that governments lie behind most of international terrorism. When governments terrorize openly, they have a propaganda apparatus to justify what they do. When they terrorize surreptitiously, they can recruit, train, equip, and finance operatives beyond the reach of public and international scrutiny. And they can direct terror against their own people. Stalin did this in the 1930s, as did South Africa and many Latin American governments in the past. Governments like those in Columbia, Indonesia and Uzbekistan do so today. But whereas many governments operate through torture and death squads, some enlist the country's legal system in the service of terrorism. Stalin worked though the Soviet Union's legal institutions. Through trial, conviction and execution, perceived enemies were eliminated as effectively as though they had been gunned down.[9] In the process, countless others were terrified into submission.

14.2 Stereotyping

Terrorism is commonly represented as primarily Arab and Muslim. When a toy manufacturer produced a doll representing a terrorist, the doll was named Nomad, dressed in Arab garb and, according to the company's description, engaged in "terrorist assaults on innocent villages."[10] Political cartoonists often depict terrorists as grizzled and wearing keffiyehs. Some of the most dramatic acts of terrorism, from the Munich Olympics in 1972 to the 9/11 attacks were indeed by Arabs. But it is misleading to represent even Middle East terrorism as exclusively the work of Arabs. The Jewish underground used terrorism against the British in Palestine. Both Yitzhak Shamir and Menachem Begin, who eventually became Israeli prime ministers, led such groups.[11] Iran, which is high on the US list of terrorist governments, is not even an Arab country. Nor is Arab terrorism all the work of Muslims. The Phalangists who massacred Palestinians in the Sabra and Shatila refugee camps of Lebanon in 1982 were

---

[9] Thousands were executed by Stalin's regime, of course, but emerging evidence is that they were executed in secret and buried far from Moscow.

[10] *The Christian Science Monitor*, December 10, 1986.

[11] Begin's Irgun was responsible for the 1946 bombing of the King David Hotel in Jerusalem. Shamir was one of the leaders of the Lehi (Fighters for the Freedom of Israel) responsible for the assassinations in 1944 of Lord Moyne, Britain's minister of state for the Middle East, and in 1948 of Sweden's Count Folke Benadotte, the UN representative to the Middle East. Although Shamir claims to have had no direct knowledge of the Bernadotte assassination, Israeli scholars disagree. Interestingly, Geula Cohen, former Knesset member who worked with Lehi at the time, reportedly says the assassination "was no less moral than other wartime actions." *Jerusalem Post International Edition*, October 10, 1998. James Bennet says that after ignoring a British plea to him and other prisoners to renounce their terrorist activities, Yitzhak Shamir "later escaped and returned to the underground, to a campaign of assassination, bombing and arms smuggling, with bank robbery thrown in to finance the effort." "How Ben-Gurion Did It: Is Everyone Listening?" *The New York Times*, August 13, 2003.

Christian. Ariel Sharon, the Israeli commander whose troops oversaw the massacre was, of course, Jewish and later became Prime Minister of Israel. Also Christian are the founders of the two principal PLO factions after Fatah: George Habash[12] of the Popular Front for the Liberation of Palestine and Nawef Hawatmeh of the Democratic Front for the Liberation of Palestine. Nor was terrorism (before 9/11) by any means confined to the Middle East or those acting in Middle Eastern interests. The Pol Pot regime undertook a campaign of genocidal terror in Cambodia, exceeded in recent history only by the Nazis' extermination in the Holocaust. Terror was used by the IRA in Northern Ireland, the Basques in Spain and the African National Congress in South Africa.[13]

The point is that it is simplistic to represent terrorism as a struggle between good and evil. Any people desperate enough are capable of engaging in it, any government unscrupulous enough capable of using it.

14.3 Terrorism and the killing of innocents

Terrorism is not clearly worse than many conventionally accepted forms of violence. True, it is probably intentionally directed against civilians more often than is standard warfare. But, as the preceding quotation from the Kaiser attests, warfare can and does target civilians. The terror bombings of Dresden, Hiroshima and Nagasaki probably killed more civilians than have been killed by terrorists throughout the world in all the years before or since.[14] Many of the fifty million or so killed in WWII were civilians, as most likely would be those killed in any sizable war in the future. And while most of them were not targeted as civilians, many of their deaths were foreseeable from the military actions that caused them. US fighter pilots reportedly were ordered to shoot down Flight 93 if necessary to prevent it from reaching Washington on 9/11. They were prepared to kill the innocent people on board to prevent the plane from reaching its objective. The hijackers were prepared to kill those very same people in the course of achieving *their* objective.[15] This says nothing of the broader context of the two actions or their intended objectives or of the justifiability of either. It is meant only to say that the deliberate killing of innocents does not suffice to distinguish terrorism from much of conventionally accepted military violence.

---

[12] George Habash, trained as a pediatrician, retired as head of the PFLP in 2000. He had been living in Syria. His successor, Ali Mustafa, who was living in the West Bank city of Ramallah, was assassinated soon after by the Israelis.

[13] "Necklacing," burning to death by a gasoline-filled tire around the neck, was a particularly ghastly form of terrorism used by black South Africans against other black South Africans.

[14] This excludes the genocidal slaughters of the Pol Pot regime in Cambodia and of Tutsis in Rwanda. Genocide is meant to eradicate a people, not to terrorize them into submission. The case of Cambodia was complex, of course. It arguably was the elimination of a particular class (the educated and well-to-do) that was intended to terrorize others into submission. Thus it combined terrorism and genocide.

[15] The terrorists did, of course, kill those innocent persons on board in the course of trying, but failing, to achieve their objective. It is reported that two mid-level generals are authorized to order the destruction of US and other passenger planes in the future if it is believed that they constitute a comparable threat to the United States.

As we have seen in Chapter 7, it would take a casuist of exceeding skill to make much of the moral difference between killing innocents intentionally and killing them foreseeably. Is it that the fighter pilots on 9/11, had they felt compelled to shoot down Flight 93, would not have intended to kill the civilians, even though they knew that they would do so? The Pentagon routinely maintains, after killing civilians in Afghanistan or Iraq, that it is not its policy intentionally to target civilians. In so doing, it made use of the same reasoning that underlies the so-called principle of double-effect, discussed in Chapter 5. That principle holds that, *ceteris paribus*, it is permissible to perform an act foreseen to have bad consequences so long as one's intention in performing it is good. But such reasoning is available to terrorists as well. The hijackers of Flight 93 might not have intended to kill those particular civilians either. But they were willing to do so in pursuit of their objective (believed to be to hit a target in Washington). In fact, all of the hijackers of the four planes on 9/11 probably would have preferred to fly empty planes that day, if only because it would have simplified their task (rebellious passengers, after all, are believed to have caused the premature crash of Flight 43). Moreover, with a dash of the same ingenuity with which some warists manipulate the principle of double effect, they might have argued that their objective was not to kill civilians at all but rather to destroy symbols of US military and economic power. Had those nearly 3,000 innocents been assembled in an open field and the hijackers had the choice to kill them or attack an empty World Trade Center, Pentagon and White House (if that was indeed a target), they might well have chosen to destroy the buildings, which symbolized America far more than the few thousand citizens who had the misfortune to be in them or on the planes.

In the case of the hijackers, most people would be quick to say that such reasoning is not good enough; that if the hijackers could foresee that they would kill innocents, they are culpable. But if we say that, then we must say the same when military power is used in ways that foreseeably will kill innocents—as, for example, in the July 23, 2002, Israeli dropping of a 2,000-pound bomb in a Gaza neighborhood that killed not only the targeted Hamas leader but fifteen others as well, including nine children.[16] It is unclear why the same logic thought to justify the killing of civilians in wartime— namely that so doing is believed useful, necessary or unavoidable in the pursuit of chosen objectives—does not equally justify killing them in terroristic warfare.

It is also unclear why terrorists as persons are necessarily any worse than soldiers in uniform. If terrorists use unconventional means to kill, that is because they have only these at their disposal. Are we to say that if terrorists had an army and an air force at their disposal, it would be all right to use them; but since they do not, they may not use the homemade bombs or boxcutters they do have? The terrorist, in fact, may more often be a person of deep conviction than the ordinary soldier. Rank and file soldiers do what they do because told to. Often as not, they have little understanding of the issues for which they are required to kill. Terrorists often do what they do knowledgeably and

---

[16] When US forces bombed Afghan villages in July 2002, killing 48 civilians and wounding 117, mostly women and children (according to Afghan government figures; the Pentagon claims they killed only 34 and wounded 50), they denied targeting them, and blamed the Taliban for "placing women and children near valid military targets." *The New York Times*, September 7, 2002.

with conviction of the rightness of their cause. They often think of themselves engaged in a legitimate military struggle. When Palestinian Georges Abdalla was convicted of terrorist activities in France, he claimed that he was a "Palestinian fighter," not a terrorist.[17] When former Jewish terrorists gathered to reminisce about their bombing of the King David Hotel that left 91 dead, one said, "I am very proud of the operation militarily. I felt myself like a soldier of these Jewish forces." As Algerian-born suspected terrorist Kamel Daoudi awaited trial in Paris, he wrote: "I accept the name of terrorist if it is used to mean that I terrorize a one-sided system of iniquitous power and a perversity that comes in many forms. I have never terrorized innocent individuals and I will never do so. But I will fight any form of injustice and those who support it."[18] Aimal Khan Kasi, in a death row interview before his execution for killing two CIA employees, said, "What I did was in retaliation against the U.S. government" for its Middle Eastern policy and support of Israel. "It had nothing to do with terrorism," he said, adding that he opposed the killing of American citizens in the 9/11 attack.[19] To all appearances, these are people who freely commit themselves to a cause and pursue it with conviction. It is precisely because their conviction is stronger than that of the average person—at least as measured by their willingness to sacrifice and kill—that they are willing to do things ordinary persons consider abhorrent.[20]

Men the world over readily become killers if compelled to do so by their governments or, as with terrorists, if they believe strongly enough in their cause. And there is not that much difference among them. Americans, Russians, Afghans, Israelis, Palestinians, Iraqis, Indonesians, Columbians and so on do or have done comparable things in varying degrees according to the means at their disposal. There may be, as psychologist David Grossman argues, an inborn reluctance to kill one's fellow humans.[21] But the techniques have been nearly perfected by which to overcome that reluctance in most people, whether by governments, armies or terrorist leaders.

14.4 Militarization of the campaign against terrorism

FBI Director William H. Webster announced in 1986 that the agency had achieved "extraordinary success" in combating terrorism in the preceding six years by lawful techniques. He said those same principles could be applied internationally as well.[22]

---

[17] *The New York Times*, September 26, 1981.
[18] *The New York Times*, September 22, 2002. Notice that, unlike the Palestinian and Jewish terrorists quoted, Daoudi accepts the label "terrorist" if (and presumably only if) it represents a struggle against iniquity. By implication—at least as it applies to himself—it precludes attacks upon innocents. Most who discuss terrorism accept the emotively pejorative force the term has, and then apply the term only to those of whom they strongly disapprove. Daoudi, on the other hand, tacitly redefines the term in such a way that it acquires a descriptive meaning that most people would find unobjectionable, provided they do not object in principle to the use of violence.
[19] *The New York Times*, November 8, 2002.
[20] There are, of course, sadistic terrorists just as there are sadistic combatants. According to some reports, this appears to be true of the British spokesperson for ISIS featured prominently in some of that group's beheadings.
[21] Grossman, *On Killing*.
[22] *The New York Times*, August 12, 1986.

He added that "[t]he more we increase our ability to deal with terrorism as a criminal activity, the more successful we will be." Others at the same American Bar Association convention at which Webster spoke—including then attorney general Edwin Meese—applauded the American attack on Libya in April of that year following the bombing of a discotheque in Germany as a deterrent to terrorism.[23] Implied was the thought that tough military retaliation was the answer to terrorism.[24]

Though not seen as such at the time, two perspectives on how to deal with terrorism were represented there. The first was to treat it as a form of criminal activity and to respond by refining and expanding the lawful investigative techniques to locate, apprehend and bring to justice those responsible for such acts. This approach implied intelligence sharing, international cooperation and compliance with domestic and international law. The second was to militarize the campaign against terrorism by visiting swift retribution on offenders with a view to deterring future such acts. This approach implied reliance upon military power, unilateralism, torture and little more than lip-service to law. The declaration of "war" on terrorism and the October 7, 2001, attack on Afghanistan symbolized the final stage in the installment of this second perspective as the dominant approach to terrorism by the United States.[25]

This militarization of the campaign against terrorism has been a gradual process. And it has been two-pronged. One prong has been highly secretive. The details are sketchy. Arguably it began when the US Defense Department created secret elite units to combat terrorism and engage in covert operations in Central America, Africa and Asia.[26] As reported by the *New York Times*, the units were established in 1980 following the abortive attempt to rescue the US hostages in Iran. As distinguished from the traditional Special Forces, these units are so secret they are not even officially acknowledged by the government. Referred to as Delta Force and Seal Team 6, many of them wear beards, do not have identifying insignia and, in Afghanistan, dress like Afghans. They identify themselves only by first name and on more than one occasion have turned journalists back at gunpoint from covering controversial stories. Then defense secretary Donald H. Rumsfeld reportedly favored sending them anywhere in

---

[23] Fifteen years later, when convictions for the disco bombing were handed down in a German court, it was still far from clear precisely what connection the attack had with Libya beyond its connection with a few persons in the East Berlin Libyan embassy. *Christian Science Monitor*, November 2, 2001.

[24] A thoughtful article that same year argues that "[t]he law has a poor record in dealing with international terrorism ... What good is the law in fighting international terrorism? Why has it failed?" See Abraham D. Sofaer, "Terrorism and the Law," *Foreign Affairs*, Vol. 64, Summer 1986, pp. 901–922.

[25] It is arguable that, at least where Libya was concerned, the United States retreated to legal rather than military methods. "After the Libyan role in the bombing [Pan Am Flight 103 in 1988] was confirmed ... the Bush administration decided that the existing strategy of military retaliation was futile. 'We thought that we weren't likely to get anywhere with another bombing raid and that you couldn't rule out that indeed the Pan Am 103 shoot-down was a consequence of the last bombing raid,' Brent Scowcroft, Bush's national security adviser, recalled. Weary of the cycle of killing, President Bush decided to seek a legal solution. The White House redirected its energies into backing UN sanctions against Tripoli in the conviction that the United States did not have an interest in waging an all-out war against Libya and that concerted international pressure provided a better way to change its behavior." Benjamin and Simon, *The Age of Sacred Terror*, p. 223. The quotation from Scowcroft is from John Lancaster, "Compromising Positions," *Washington Post Magazine*, July 9, 2000, p. 10

[26] *The New York Times*, "The U.S. Military Creates Secret Units for Use in Sensitive Tasks Abroad," June 8, 1984.

the world, with or without the knowledge of local governments, to capture or kill al-Qaeda,[27] as they did successfully in the killing of Osama bin Laden. Operations of this sort have brought the United States into tension with European countries. In February 2003, for example, the United States reportedly abducted a suspect in Italy without the knowledge or permission of the Italian government, and transferred him to Egypt for interrogation, a process known as "rendition." The Italians, in response, sought the arrest of thirteen suspected CIA agents involved in the abduction.[28] Whereas the United States has militarized the campaign against terrorism, the Europeans tend to regard it as a problem for criminal justice.

The other prong has been high profile, including the bombing of Libya in April 1986 and the cruise missile attacks on Sudan and Afghanistan on August 20, 1998, in retaliation for the US embassy bombings in East Africa. The culmination of the process came in the 2001 attack on Afghanistan following 9/11, in which both massive military power and elite secret units combined to devastate the Taliban as a conventional fighting force.

Whether by initial design, or through later realization of its potential in this regard, the militarization of the campaign against terrorism has now dovetailed with a radical transformation of US military policy. Whereas containment and deterrence characterized the years of the Cold War, the Bush administration seized upon preemption as the keystone of policy.[29] It appears that this new policy will involve a willingness on the part of the United States to act unilaterally in virtually any place in the world that it believes there are serious threats. Both the aforementioned elite units and the massive use of conventional and perhaps nuclear power presumably will be the chosen means. The so-called war on terrorism[30] needs only to have tacked onto it "and tyrants" to expand its scope. This conjunctive escalation of policy lends itself to tacking on virtually any other descriptive term (such as "and threats to American interests") to give it limitless scope. After the collapse of the Soviet Union, theorists speculated about whether the end to the Cold War would bring a unipolar world, with the United States as the dominant figure, or a multipolar world, with power distributed among various units, or something altogether different. In 2002 the Bush administration appears to have decided the issue conclusively. The United States will reign as the sole superpower and supreme state, determined to nip in the bud attempts by any other power to rival it militarily.

---

[27] *The New York Times*, August 12, 2002.

[28] As reported in *The Christian Science Monitor*, June 29, 2005.

[29] Although speaking about conventional war and not terrorism, Franklin Roosevelt had set the stage for such thinking. He said in May 1941: "Some people seem to think that we are not attacked until bombs actually drop on New York or San Francisco or New Orleans or Chicago ... The attack on the United States can begin with the domination of any base which menaces our security—north or south ... Old-fashioned common sense calls for the use of a strategy which will prevent such an enemy from gaining a foothold in the first place." Funk, *Roosevelt's Foreign Policy, 1933–1941*, p. 399f. Quoted from Charles A. Beard, " 'In Case of Attack' in the Atlantic," in Robert A. Divine (ed.), *Causes and Consequences of World War II* (Chicago, IL: Quadrangle Books, 1969), p. 101.

[30] Americans accustomed to "war" on drugs, "war" on poverty, "war on crime" and so on, have scarcely noticed that what is a war only in a metaphorical sense is being treated by the administration, when it serves its purposes, as a literal war. As Susan Sontag writes, "When a president of the United States declares war on cancer or poverty or drugs, we know that 'war' is a metaphor. Does anyone think that this war—the war that America has declared on terrorism—is a metaphor? But it is, and one with powerful consequences." Op Ed, *The New York Times*, September 10, 2002.

There is one final step before this logic has run its course. This is the extension of this supposed right to virtually unrestricted use of force in the domestic scene. This implies the gradual militarization of the government's control over its own citizens as well. Congress obligingly facilitated the move in this direction with the Patriot Act. The administration is incrementally arrogating more and more power to itself with readiness to put religious and other groups under surveillance, encouraging of Americans to become informers on one another, and a readiness to remove any person from virtually all protection of any laws by attaching to them the label "enemy combatant." The militarization of local police forces, often by supplying them with military equipment, is part of this trend.

Appropriating the term "war" for the campaign on terrorism serves this purpose well. It readies people for extreme measures; and it makes available to the government all of the language of war to keep emotions running high. With the enemy ill-defined, all the boundaries are down. Those associated with so-called al-Qaeda reportedly do not call themselves by that name, and it is difficult to find more than passing reference to al-Qaeda prior to 9/11. Still, five thousand of them and their sympathizers are alleged to be in the Unites States, with multiples of that number conspiring abroad. Add to this the thousands flocking to join ISIS from foreign countries, and this "war" can be carried on at the discretion of the administration anywhere of its choosing and against virtually anyone of its choosing.

The language of war has been superimposed upon the effort to combat one type of criminal activity and exploited to expand governmental powers almost without limit.[31] Evidence becomes secondary. Ronald Reagan took 10 days to attack Libya after the La Belle disco bombing in 1986. It was not until 15 years later that sufficient evidence was gathered to convict four persons (two Palestinians, a German and a Libyan) of the crime in a German court; and even then, though the Libyan and one of the Palestinians worked in the East Berlin Libyan embassy, it had not yet been shown conclusively that Qaddafi and the higher levels of the Libyan government were involved. Bill Clinton took 13 days to launch retaliatory cruise missile strikes against Sudan and Afghanistan after the August 7, 1998, attacks on US embassies in Kenya and Tanzania, even though Osama bin Laden had not been shown to be behind the attacks, and neither he nor anyone else was under indictment for the crime in any US court.[32] George W. Bush dismissed requests from the Taliban to produce evidence of Osama bin Laden's role

---

[31] Author Bob Woodward writes that the Bush administration discussed "whether to issue a white paper, designed to prove that bin Laden and Al Qaeda were behind the September 11 attacks," an idea that was rejected. "The danger of issuing a white paper that presented evidence," Woodward writes, "was that it could condition people to view the war on terror as a law enforcement operation, within the model of the judicial system with its evidentiary standards, burden of proof on the government and proof beyond a reasonable doubt—things that could not possibly be met." Bob Woodward, *Bush at War* (New York: Simon & Schuster, 2002), pp. 135f.

[32] Osama bin Laden was subsequently indicted in a US court for the attack. On September 17, 2003, a Spanish judge specifically charged him, along with nine others, of committing the 9/11 attack. *The New York Times*, September 18, 2003. Polls showed that a majority of Americans believed that Saddam Hussein was involved in the 9/11 attack. "I think it's not surprising that people make that connection," Vice President Cheney said on NBC-TV's "Meet the Press." Although the administration repeatedly affirmed that Saddam Hussein had al-Qaeda ties, it had not asserted that he was responsible for 9/11, and President Bush, following the Cheney statement, reportedly said that

in 9/11 attacks before turning him over[33] and began bombing on October 7, less than four weeks after the attack. The logic of this spiraling government power risks treating lack of evidence as itself evidence. If an adversary is highly secretive, then you expect there to be little evidence of his activity before he strikes. So the fact that a there is little evidence connecting a given suspect with terrorism is what one would expect. In this way of thinking, the estimate of a person's cunning and deceit begins to vary inversely with the evidence against him. With the 1996 antiterrorism legislation being so broad as to implicate anyone who so much as lends support to terrorists, the net is cast so wide as to dampen dissent and criticism of government. An antiwar speech, an op-ed piece or a book on pacifism could be considered suspect.

14.5 The violence of war and terrorism

If the violence of terrorism is arguably no worse morally than that of much of warfare, the violence of warfare is arguably no less terrible than that of terrorism. We have compartmentalized our thinking so as to think of the one as respectable, the other vile. Common to the violence of the terrorist and the soldier alike is the treatment of human beings as objects to be destroyed when seen as obstacles to the attainment of one's ends. Once people accept the idea that violence is a permissible means by which to pursue ends,[34] then you need only overcome their natural revulsion to killing to turn them to your purposes. The techniques are there. The armies of the world specialize in them.

It is this feature of violence that highlights the central fact in its moral assessment. Kant captured the idea in his second formulation of the categorical imperative: "Act so that you treat humanity, whether in your own person or in that of another, always as an end and never as a means only." To allow oneself to be used by others to do their killing is to allow yourself to become a means. This is as true of the soldier as of the suicide bomber. To kill others to promote your own ends is to use the others as means. The alternative is simple to state. Rediscover the humanity of all persons, friends and adversaries alike. Accord them the respect owed all persons. But what that means in the concrete is less easy to state. What are people to do who suffer persecution and injustice? What should European Jews have done who fled the Holocaust and sought a homeland in Palestine only to be turned back by the British? What are Palestinians to do who seek recovery of their homeland only to be turned back by the Israelis? Should European Jews have folded their hands and waited for the world to offer them security?

he had seen no evidence of such involvement. *The New York Times*, September 18, 2003. Yet the President repeatedly encouraged people to make a connection between Saddam and terrorists, such as in his statement, the month before, that "Al Qaeda and the other global terror networks recognize that the defeat of Saddam Hussein's regime is a defeat for them." http://nytimes.com/2003/08/26/politics/26TEXT-BUSH.
[33] Some experts in the area believed the Taliban were willing to hand over bin Laden, or have him expelled to another country, if only because he was believed to have become a liability in their quest for international recognition.
[34] President Bush asked Congress for authority to use "all means he determines to be appropriate" to overthrow Saddam Hussein. *The New York Times*, September 20, 2002.

Should Palestinians resign themselves to refugee camps until the Israelis invite them back? And what should American have done in the wake of 9/11? There are no easy answers to these questions.

A beginning would be to open communication with terrorists rather than, as now, refusing to deal with them at all, or worse yet, expanding their putative ranks by labeling—for political reasons—as terrorists those who may simply be involved in rebellion against what they see as a repressive state. Terrorism does not exist in a vacuum. People do not just decide to become terrorists and then conspire with others to go about their deadly business. "We are people," one of the women said at the aforementioned gathering at the King David Hotel. "We know how to love, we know how to hate. We know how to kiss. We have all the emotions of everybody else."[35] We need to recognize terrorists as, for the most part, persons like ourselves, who take into their own hands the violence most of us leave to others. They are not subhuman monsters, to be fought with all the righteous fury that civilized people can muster. Part of our responsibility is to try to understand what leads them to perform such acts and what measure of justice their cause may embody.[36]

In 1985 when the hijackers of a TWA airliner reportedly shouted the words "New Jersey" in the aisles of the plane, most Americans, if they learned of it at all, would not have realized that the reference was to the battleship New Jersey, which had in 1983 turned its 16-inch guns upon Shiite Muslim villages in Lebanon following a suicide bombing of a Marine barracks. The guns hurtled 2,000 pound shells into the homes of those who could not possibly have been responsible for the bombing.[37] Nor were the more than eighty people killed when a US organized covert Lebanese unit acted on its own to try to assassinate Hezbollah leader Mohammad Fedlallah. It is decent, well-dressed men in Washington—family men, churchgoers, no doubt good neighbors and friends—who ultimately bear responsibility for such actions. With the unprecedented military power at their command, they need only issue a command, and a sequence of events is set in motion that results in bombs exploding thousands of miles away in Afghanistan or Iraq. Those who burn to avenge such actions, or to redress what they perceive as wrongs wrought by the policies of such men, have only guns or explosives and their own strength and wit with which to work. When they commandeer a plane, or plant a bomb, they are terrorists. But what they do is no different in kind from what others do or have done. By no means are any, much less most, of the acts they perform

---

[35] *The New York Times*, September 26, 1981.

[36] We need also to see the humanity in those who do their killing "legitimately," as part of an established military unit. A journalist reported in an interview with a teenage Israeli soldier on duty in Bethlehem: "'I know I look like a monster in all this,' he said, tapping his helmet, then his vest, then his rifle. 'I'm not a monster,' he said. 'I don't like this. I'm a human being just like you.'" *The New York Times*, May 10, 2002.

[37] As Neil C. Livingstone writes, "the 1983 shelling of the Chouf Mountains in Lebanon by the U.S. battleship *New Jersey* ... could not reasonably have been expected to punish those specifically responsible for the incidents. Although enemy command and forward observation positions were hit ... the naval bombardment also inflicted casualties on the civilian population of the region without having a real impact on those who actually carried out the attacks on the marines. Using the *New Jersey* to fight terrorists is rather like employing a sledge hammer to kill a bothersome flea." In Neil C. Livingstone and Terrell E. Arnold, *Fighting Back: Winning the War against Terrorism* (Lexington, MA: Lexington Books, 1986), p. 122.

to be presumed justified. Often it is not even known fully what the justification is alleged to be. But sometimes a rationale is set forth. And sometimes it is one that needs to be taken seriously. Such, arguably, is the 1998 document by Osama bin Laden and other leaders of militant Islamist groups, entitled "Declaration of the World Islamic Front for Jihad against the Jews and the Crusaders." Writing in *Foreign Affairs*, Bernard Lewis says: "The statement—a magnificent piece of eloquent, at times even poetic Arabic prose—reveals a version of history that most Westerners will find unfamiliar. Bin Ladin's grievances are not quite what many would expect." The document reads in part:

> First—For more than seven years the United States is occupying the lands of Islam in the holiest of its territories, Arabia, plundering its riches, overwhelming its rulers, humiliating its people, threatening its neighbors, and using its bases in the peninsula as a spearhead to fight against the neighboring Islamic peoples …
>
> Second—Despite the immense destruction inflicted on the Iraqi people at the hands of the Crusader-Jewish alliance … the Americans nevertheless … are trying once more to repeat this dreadful slaughter … So they come again today to destroy what remains of this people and to humiliate their Muslim neighbors.
>
> Third—While the purposes of the Americans in these wars are religious and economic, they also serve … to divert attention from [Jewish] occupation of Jerusalem and their killing of Muslims in it.[38]

If the challenge is to understand better and appreciate the position of the terrorist, or the revolutionary, or the advocate of violent change, the imperative is to find nonviolent ways of dealing with the problems of injustice, poverty and oppression that are typically at the root of their actions. As former deputy secretary of state Strobe Talbott has written:

> Disease, overcrowding, undernourishment, political repression, and alienation breed despair, anger, and hatred. These are the raw materials of what we're up against, and they constitute a check on the willingness of Arab and other regimes to take effective action against networks of conspirators … [T]here will be a temptation to squeeze down the very programs that will allow us to move from reactive, defensive warfare against the terrorists to a proactive, prolonged offensive against the ugly, intractable realities that terrorists exploit and from which they derive popular support, foot soldiers, and political cover. That's why another phrase from America's political past needs to be dusted off, put back in service, and internationalized: the war on poverty. Only if the long struggle ahead is also fought on that front will it be winnable.[39]

To undertake such a commitment seriously requires that *others*, who are not desperate in the way in which the oppressed or aggrieved are, and who have the means, power,

---

[38] Quoted from Bernard Lewis, "License to Kill: Usama bin Ladin's Declaration of Jihad," *Foreign Affairs*, Vol. 77, No. 6, November/December 1998, pp. 14–19.

[39] Strobe Talbott, "The Other Evil: The War on Terrorism Won't Succeed without a War on Poverty," *Foreign Policy*, November/December 2001, pp. 75f.

and influence to redirect the course of events, involve themselves cooperatively with all sides in the controversies that lead to violence in an attempt to find creative solutions to them.

Nonviolence, so conceived, must be active, not passive. In a sense, violence—meaning reliance upon violence as the ultimate recourse for resolving problems—is more passive than nonviolence. Violence often waits until situations have deteriorated to the point of no return, doing nothing, or worse yet, doing the wrong things, then flaring up and engulfing those it would help as well as those it opposes. Reliance upon the institutionalized violence of modern war systems did not prevent Hitler from coming to power. While it eventually vanquished him at a horrendous cost, it left in its wake a situation arguably as bad as that which, following WWI, eventually led to WWII, with the world divided between communists and noncommunists; a world that has thus far been lucky to avoid the calamity of nuclear war. The Vietnam War was ostensibly begun to secure the freedom of the South Vietnamese people. But today the whole of Vietnam is communist. Arab states went to war in 1948 to liberate Palestine, but today Palestinians live by the millions in diaspora, almost certainly never to return to their homeland. Israel relies on military might to preserve itself, yet its security gradually erodes as its margin of superiority over its Arab neighbors diminishes and there remains always the possibility of further Palestinian intifadas. The United States shelled Lebanon in 1983, bombed Libya in 1986, waged war on Iraq in 1991, and bombed the Sudan and Afghanistan in 1998 and Serbia in 1999 in part to deter terrorism. But it did not deter the 9/11 attack and has enflamed more terrorists.

Nonviolence goes beyond pacifism. It requires vigilance and active engagement with the problems of peace and justice, not ignoring them so long as things remain orderly and then sending in troops when bloodshed finally becomes inevitable. This is what nonviolence meant for leaders like Gandhi and Martin Luther King, Jr.

But can nonviolence "work?" Can it resolve the problems of injustice and oppression? We know that resort to war and violence for all of recorded history has not worked. It has not secured either peace or justice to the world. The most it has brought are brief interludes in which the nations of the world regroup, catch their breath and prepare for the next war. We know that nonviolence worked in India with Gandhi, in the United States with King and in Scandinavia against the Nazis in WWII. It worked in the Philippines in the mid-1980s when nonviolent "People Power" averted what might have been a bloody civil war by sitting in front of the government's tanks as the Marcos regime sought to confront rebel commanders in their headquarters. It brought dignity and respect to the Solidarity movement in Poland throughout the 1980s when violence would almost certainly have brought a crushing Soviet response. It worked in the early 1990s when Lithuanians rallied nonviolently in support of independence in the face the overwhelming military superiority of the Soviet Union. No one can foresee what the results might be if a country like the United States were to spend $300 billion a year in research on techniques of nonviolent resistance and on educating and training people in their use.

14.6 Conclusion

What is needed is a new perspective which, in Kantian terms, respects persons as ends in themselves. We need a willingness to cultivate and put into practice an awareness of the humanity in our adversaries, even when they are terrorists; a perspective that approaches conflict in a spirit of seeking the truth in the issues that divide us from our adversaries rather than assuming our own righteousness and trying only to work out the means to our ends. This spirit is captured in a remarkable statement by Mariane Pearl, widow of the American journalist Daniel Pearl, just after confirmation of his beheading in Pakistan at the hands of terrorists:

> Revenge would be easy, but it is far more valuable in my opinion to address this problem of terrorism with enough honesty to question our own responsibility as nations and as individuals for the rise of terrorism. My ... hope now—in my seventh month of pregnancy is that I will be able to tell our son that his father carried the flag to end terrorism, raising an unprecedented demand among people from all countries not for revenge but for the values we all share: love, compassion, friendship and citizenship far transcending the so-called clash of civilizations.[40]

Violence is for the morally infallible. Nonviolence is for those who recognize their own limitations and the possibility that others with whom they disagree may have hold of part of the truth, and are willing to put forth the effort to uncover and cultivate that truth in the interests of nonviolent conciliation.

---

[40] Quoted from the Rochester *Democrat & Chronicle*, February 23, 2002.

15

Existential Pacifism

My conscience won't let me shoot my brother or some darker people, or some poor hungry people in the mud, for big powerful America.

—Muhammad Ali

It is curious … that physical courage should be so common in the world, and moral courage so rare.

—Mark Twain

15.1 Pragmatic contextualism

If the reasoning of the preceding chapters is sound, warfare in the modern world is morally wrong. This does not mean, as I have said, that warfare is wrong in all logically conceivable worlds. One can readily contrive examples of hypothetical wars whose justifiability it would be pointless to deny. To falsify pragmatic pacifism one must not only show that the preceding reasoning is flawed. One must also produce examples of actual wars that are morally permissible. It is for this reason that I have examined conflicts in the modern world and argued that they fail to defeat the presumption that war is wrong.

I have pointed out that the JWT is but one possible approach to the evaluation of war and cannot simply be assumed to be the privileged theory in the absence of supporting argument. The burden is likewise upon me to show that the perspective from which I have reasoned is the way to assess war or at the very least a preferable way to the JWT. I have tried to do this by beginning with the prima facie wrongness of the nonconsensual killing of human beings, which I take to be part of the bedrock foundation of morality and as likely to provide a common ground between warists and pacifists as one can hope for.

In the end, however, I believe our actual moral reasoning (as opposed to the theoretical constructs we create after we have settled on what we believe) is not as linear and structured as my argument might suggest. It is, rather, contextualistic and pragmatic. This is a metaethical and psychological claim for which there is not enough space here to argue. Its basic idea is that we formulate rules and principles as guidelines for the future, but conformity to them is not what makes actions right or wrong. It is the other way around. It is the soundness of our particular judgments of right and wrong that justifies the rules and principles, and justifies them only as guidelines, or as Dewey puts it, hypotheses, which are always subject to revision. The moral world is flexible and progressive, not rigidly structured. Justification, if you like, proceeds upward from contextually grounded judgments to rules and principles, not downward from rules and principles to particular judgments.[1]

For this reason I have argued that in assessing war we must begin with the persons it affects directly, the soldiers and civilians, the innocent and the noninnocent, the human beings who are killed in war and those who suffer physically and mentally in its aftermath, often for a lifetime.

Most of us at times cling to what we want to believe in the face of countervailing evidence. If the JWT shows a particular war to be unjust that you believe is just, you need only tweak the theory in enough places to get it to conform to what you antecedently believed. Troublesome criteria, such as last resort, discrimination, proportionality and just cause can readily be revised, the result being as many revisionist JWTs as there are modifications to the standard theory. The JWT then becomes the theoretical scaffolding that supports what has been decided in advance.

15.2 Support of troops

It is odd that people applaud an enterprise like war that is redolent with blood, death and destruction and deplore the pacifism that opposes it. But it is understandable. Centuries of custom lie on the side of war and its glorification. War, in this view, is fought by heroes who sacrifice for others, who by the thousands give to their country that "last full measure of devotion." Custom deems this as among the most noble of human enterprises, and to question what soldiers do is thought unpatriotic.

But this way of thinking leaves out those who are truly responsible for the killing and dying soldiers do. Bumper stickers exhort people to support the troops. They do not exhort them to support the government. But it is the government that determines their mission, the relatively few men and women who control that government who design it. And supporting the troops readily translates into supporting their mission, whomever and wherever they are fighting and for whatever reason.[2]

It matters not that many wars have been fought for conquest, territory, material gain, the glory of rulers and for the punishment and even extermination of whole peoples, sometimes at the alleged direction of God, and only occasionally for the high

[1] Even the judgment of the prima facie wrongness of killing persons does not represent a particular judgment in a particular context, but it invites us to reflect on those contexts for confirmation of the judgment.

[2] As former secretary of defense Robert M. Gates puts it when he cites approvingly what he takes to be the view of soldiers: "The frequently used line 'We support our troops' coupled with 'We totally disagree with their mission' cut no ice with people in uniform. Our kids on the front line were savvy; they would ask me why the politicians didn't understand that, in the eyes of the troops, support for them and support for their mission were tied together." Robert M. Gates, *Duty: Memoirs of a Secretary at War* (New York: Alfred K. Knopf, 2014), p. 60.

and selfless values custom imagines. Yet it is the cultural mindset that glorifies war and helps to perpetuate it that must be dealt with, even though it is a mixture of fact, fiction and fantasy. There lurks within it an appeal to patriotism and a suspicion of dissent in times of war. In this view, politics ends at the water's edge and with it any attempt at critical moral scrutiny. The dismissal of pacifism does not rest solely upon the view that it is unpatriotic, but that is an important part of it.

15.3 Soldiers and their mission

Consider the idea that to support our troops is to support their mission. First and foremost, the troops are human beings: brothers, sisters, parents, sons and daughters, friends or simply fellow countrymen. They deserve sympathy and compassion for their sacrifices and the best in medical care for the harms they suffer. Caring for them as persons means caring for their psychological and moral well-being as well as for their physical well-being. In the prime of their lives they risk not only death and maiming but also the societal dysfunction, alcoholism, drug addiction, suicide and moral harm many of them suffer. To support them meaningfully is not to support them *as troops*, that is, as specialists in inflicting death and destruction at the command of others, but as fellow human beings who have had extraordinary demands placed on them. If those demands require of them what they ought not to be asked to do, then support for them means addressing the issues involved in their being placed in that position in the first place. The risks of doing so are great, given that it involves challenging the thinking of those who wield power. As the Secretary of Defense during the Iraq War writes:

> the comments that most angered me were those full of defeatism—sending the message to the troops that they couldn't win and, by implication, were putting their lives on the line for nothing. The worst of these comments came from the Senate majority leader … who said in a press conference, "This war is lost" and "The surge is not accomplishing anything." I was furious and shared privately with some of my staff a quote from Abraham Lincoln I had written down long before: "Congressmen who willfully take actions during wartime that damage morale and undermine the military are saboteurs and should be arrested, exiled, or hanged." Needless to say, I never hinted at any such feelings publicly, but I had them nonetheless.[3]

Public criticism might well adversely affect troop morale, but sometimes it should. If it is a war they should not be fighting, then they are killing people they should not be killing, and responsible criticism might lead them to reflect upon that fact.[4] No one among the Allies would have objected if the morale of German and Japanese troops

---

[3] Gates, *Duty*, p. 60.

[4] A VFW Post commander, who had served as a Marine in Vietnam, is reported to have said that "media coverage and protests at home hurt service members' morale." David Riley, "Vietnam Vets Mark Peace Accords Date," *Rochester Democrat & Chronicle*, January 28, 2014. An appeal to morale was reportedly made by the Justice Department, in arguing that the former warden of Guantanamo should not have to testify in court regarding the force-feeding of prisoners because doing so could adversely affect the morale of troops under his command. http://america.aljazeera.com/articles/2014/7/8/guantanamo-wardenmorale.html.

had been adversely affected by criticism (had such criticism been possible) during WWII. What is relevant is whether the killing that soldiers do is justified, not whether the flag they salute is the one we fly. It is one thing, however, to criticize a policy because it is morally wrong, another to criticize it because it is not working. The above passage focuses on whether a policy is working; that is, whether it is achieving its objectives. That is a factual matter, not a matter of value judgment, even if value judgments of various sorts may have led to the setting of those objectives in the first place. If a mission is failing, then troops are in fact risking their lives in vain by pursuing it. To try to convince them otherwise is to perpetuate an illusion[5] and in the process to contribute to their victimization. If the mission is not morally justified, they are doubly victimized. Not only are they failing to achieve the policy's objectives, those objectives are ones they should not even be asked to pursue.

15.4 Patriotism

The implication of the Lincoln quote in the above passage by Gates raises the issue of patriotism. If to point out the obvious failure of a policy is defeatism, and defeatism is by implication unpatriotic, then dissent to government policies is at best unpatriotic and at worst treasonous.[6]

But patriotism is love of one's country. It is not love of one's government. It is not even—except perhaps in fascist philosophy—love of the nation state which the government and country comprise. A country is more than a body of land and a collection of people. It is certainly more than the individuals who govern it at a given time. It has a character or national spirit, and a history of growth and development.[7] To love one's country is to love the best of what it stands for and to envision what it could become. It is to want to see its people flourish. It cannot be equated with serving those who happen to be in power at a given time. The German soldiers of WW II, many of whom also gave that "last full measure of devotion" to their country, doubtless were generally brave men individually and followed scrupulously the orders of their

---

[5] Efforts to raise morale are often the mirror image of propaganda to undermine morale. As an example, during WWI, a British newspaper published a widely applauded letter by "A Little Mother" responding to an earlier letter by a soldier. Her letter read in part: "To the man who pathetically calls himself a 'common soldier,' may I say that we women ... will tolerate no such cry as 'Peace! Peace!' where there is no peace. The corn that will wave over land watered by the blood of our brave lads shall testify to the future that their blood was not spilt in vain ... We women pass on the human ammunition of 'only sons' to fill up the gaps, so that when the 'common soldier' looks back before going 'over the top' he may see the women of the British race at his heels, reliable, dependent, uncomplaining ... Women are created for the purpose of giving life, and men to take it." Quoted in Robert Graves, *Goodbye to All That* (London: The Folio Society, 1981), pp. 200–201. Attempts to undermine the morale of adversaries are commonplace in war; they range from the propaganda broadcasts of "Tokyo Rose" to the fire bombing of German cities and the atomic bombing of Japan in WWII.

[6] On the perceived dangers of dissent in the United States, with particular reference to the Vietnam War, see Appy, *American Reckoning*, part 3.

[7] I say this without intending to personify it in a way that gives it an ontological reality I do not believe it has, and certainly without supporting everything that goes into a country's founding and history, which often is centered around war.

superiors. Who could fault Adolf Eichmann when it came to following orders? But in serving those who governed them they did not serve their country. Indeed, they were the instruments of its betrayal.[8]

Genuine patriotism must be informed, intelligent, insightful and critical. At times, as we learned from Thoreau, it may have to be disobedient. To measure devotion to one's country by blind obedience and ostentatious show of colors is to confuse patriotism with the incandescence of the patrioteer.

15.5 Conscience and killing

In the preceding I have attempted to present the strongest argument I can for pragmatic pacifism. I now want to endorse another form of pacifism, one that may, though need not, underpin pragmatic pacifism. I call this existential pacifism. It is a highly personal pacifism, rooted in conscience. But it is distinguished from the pacifism discussed earlier in connection with Augustine, which is opposition to personal participation in war and not to participation by others, much less to violence in general. Augustine's stance is sometimes called private pacifism rather than personal pacifism, which I think is a more appropriate term.[9] It will be useful to distinguish among the three following positions:

Private Pacifism: Violence, including self-defense, is wrong, not only for oneself, but also for anyone not acting in the public realm as an agent of established political authority.
Personal Pacifism: Violence, including self-defense, is wrong for oneself but not necessarily for others, whether in the public or private realms.
Existential Pacifism: Killing other human beings in warfare is wrong for oneself and others.

Personal and private pacifism deal with violence, existential pacifism with killing in warfare.[10] For this reason, a private pacifist might fail to be either a personal or

---

[8] The British poet, Siegfried Sassoon, a decorated officer wounded in WW I, was led to indict those responsible for the war in a declaration entitled: "Finished With the War": *I am making this statement as an act of willful defiance of military authority, because I believe that the War is being deliberately prolonged by those who have the power to end it. I am a soldier, convinced that I am acting on behalf of soldiers ... I have seen and endured the sufferings of the troops, and I can no longer be a party to prolong these sufferings for ends which I believe to be evil and unjust. I am not protesting against the conduct of the War, but against the political errors and insincerities for which the fighting men are being sacrificed. On behalf of those who are suffering now I make this protest against the deception which is being practiced on them; also I believe that I may help to destroy the callous complacency with which the majority of those at home regard the continuance of agonies which they do not share, and which they have not sufficient imagination to realize."* Siegfried Sassoon's, *Memoirs of an Infantry Officer* (London: Folio Society, 1974), p. 226. Sassoon's experience in the war and his flirtation with pacifism are documented in his books, *Memoirs of an Infantry Officer* and *Sherston's Progress*.

[9] As noted in Chapter 4, the term private pacifism is used in connection with Augustine by both Frederick H. Russell, *The Just War in the Middle Ages*, p. 18, and by Douglas Lackey, *The Ethics of War and Peace*, pp. 16–18.

[10] Both private and personal pacifism might, however, be understood more narrowly, as applying only to one's position with regard to war. Such positions are sometimes considered forms of *vocational pacifism*. See Dower, *The Ethics of War and Peace*, p.118.

existential pacifist. This was true of Augustine. To amplify our discussion in Chapter 4, we might now say that Augustine was a private pacifist but neither a personal nor an existential pacifist. For him, private pacifism was fully consistent with the conviction that war is justifiable. A personal pacifist might likewise fail to be a private or existential pacifist and an existential pacifist fail to be either a private or a personal pacifist.[11] Personal pacifism leaves it open whether others may use violence, either in self-defense or in warfare. It may be that the personal pacifist simply chooses to suspend judgment in these areas, thinking perhaps that it would be presumptuous to judge such matters for other people.[12] It might also be that he simply finds it undecidable what others should do in those circumstances. All three are distinguishable from pragmatic pacifism, which is a moral position toward war. Existential pacifism entails pragmatic pacifism, since if killing in war is wrong, then war in the modern world is wrong. Pragmatic pacifism might not entail existential pacifism. Whether it does would depend upon whether existential pacifism affirms the wrongness of wartime killing for all wars and not just wars in the modern world. In any event, the emphasis of existential pacifism is upon personal conviction. It is by extrapolation from the conviction that it would be wrong for oneself to kill in war that one concludes that such killing is wrong for others as well, hence that war as practiced by collectivities is wrong. It is with the wrongness of one's own (actual or possible) killing in war that one begins. An existential pacifist might or might not be a nonviolentist, in the sense of holding a principled commitment to nonviolence in general. Whether a consistent existential pacifist would be committed to that broader position would depend upon whether there are morally relevant dissimilarities between the killing and violence of warfare and that in other areas, such as self-defense and police work. It would also depend upon whether one's commitment to nonviolence is as a form of conflict resolution that comes into play only in situations of conflict, or as a way of life intended to govern all aspects of one's life, including one's relation to animals and the environment.

I call this view existential pacifism in deference to that aspect of existentialism that stresses personal responsibility for our choices and the lives we make for ourselves. This responsibility is nowhere greater than in the matter of killing. Conscience in this regard often breaks through in time of war. Citing evidence that in the Battle of Gettysburg the majority of soldiers did not try to kill their adversaries, psychologist Dave Grossman writes: "Secretly, quietly, at the moment of decision, just like the 80 to 85 percent of World War II soldiers ... these soldiers found themselves to be conscientious objectors who were unable to kill their fellow man."[13] Such stirrings of conscience are the seeds of existential pacifism. They are often found even before one becomes part of the system that would compel one to kill. Muhammad Ali, who refused

---

[11] It is with some reluctance that I use *pacifism* in connection with views about nonviolence, since I think that in the interests of clarity they should be kept separate, but I do so here to be in keeping with the way the terms are used by others in this connection.

[12] Some conscientious objectors during WWII were willing to serve in the military but were unwilling to carry guns. Others would not serve but were willing to do alternative service. Some nonviolentists, like Gandhi, were willing to serve in an ambulance corps during war. There is probably no single category of pacifism that is appropriate to all of those individuals who refuse to engage in wartime killing.

[13] Grossman, *On Killing*, p. 25.

to serve in Vietnam and was subsequently stripped of his title and banned from boxing for three years at the peak of his career, summed it up simply in the quotation at the beginning of this chapter.[14] Still others experience the maturation of conscience only after they have killed and experienced the effects of war. An ace Japanese fighter pilot in WW II often flew close enough to the nineteen Allied planes he shot down to see the terror on the faces of their crew before they went down. "They were fathers and sons, too," he has said. "I didn't hate them or even know them." He suffered nightmares for years afterward, leading him to devote his life to speaking out on behalf of pacifism, and in particular to teaching children the value of peace. "I realized the war had turned me into a killer of men, and that was not the kind of person I wanted to be."[15]

The root of existential pacifism, as I say, is a sense of personal responsibility for the kind of person you are. Taking this seriously may lead one to a de facto pacifism that is grounded in repudiation of the coercive apparatus of social systems that in varying degrees tries to take control of one's life. Such de facto pacifism is not yet existential pacifism. If an eighteen-year-old boy so much as registers for the draft, he lets those who frame and implement the law take control of some of the potentially most important aspects of his life. The same holds true of those who volunteer for military service. A free and responsible moral agent refuses to concede to others (whether they be government officials, tribal elders, religious leaders or military commanders) the right to force him to kill other human beings at the time and place of their choosing, for reasons he may be unaware of or not understand or find repellent. To refuse to concede that right does not mean that one thinks the presumption against killing can never be overridden. One may think that, or not. One need not think that self-defense is wrong, though one may think that. One need not even think that all wars are wrong, though one may think that as well. One need only reject the idea that a free and open society is compatible with a coercive system which empowers some people to command others to kill, and requires those others, on pain of severe punishment for refusal, to obey those commands.[16] Such a view, we might say, represents pacifism for nonpacifists. It is grounded in faith in the institutions of a free and open society. Democratic processes are the antithesis of violent processes. At its best, democracy is a system of nonviolent conflict resolution.

But if one cannot defeat the presumption against the systematic organized killing of other human beings represented by warfare, then one is an existential pacifist. Existential pacifism is an extension and deepening of the conviction in the de facto pacifism I have just described. A person might refuse to concede to others the right to compel him to kill but still believe that he may permissibly kill when cleared by his

---

[14] The epigraph is from the *New York Times*, June 21, 2013, from a June 20, 1967 radio interview. Quoted by Wm. C. Rhoden, "Voice From the Past and a Stand for the Ages." "Muhammad Ali is a great man. What he did 46 years [ago] was a heroic deed for the ages."

[15] *The New York Times International*, April 4, 2015.

[16] There is some evidence that in the ancient world this was the view of the Essenes, who required for a person's membership into their community an oath that, among other things (notably showing piety toward God), "he will observe justice towards men, and that he will do no harm to any one, either of his own accord, or by the command of others." See Josephus, *Wars of the Jews*, Bk. II, in *The Works of Flavius Josephus*, trans. William Whiston (Hartford, CT: The S.S. Scranton Col, 1902), p. 674.

conscience. It is when one's conscience does not allow a person to kill as part of the collective violence of war that he or she is an existential pacifist.

Existential pacifism differs from the pacifism of those who accept antiwar counsels handed down from on high by religious leaders or who by cold calculation conclude that war is counterproductive. Such pacifism takes courage, more so than to march lockstep into battle as part of an army. This is not to denigrate physical bravery, only to see it for what it is. Men (and increasingly women as well) by the millions can be drilled and trained to kill and risk death on command. That fact perhaps attests to what Nietzsche called a herd instinct more than to bravery. As a Marine captain who served in Afghanistan and Iraq puts it, "*The primary factors that affect an individual's ability to kill are the demands of authority, group absolution, the predisposition of the killer, the distance from the victim and the target attractiveness of the victim.*"[17] Knowingly risking death is often sheer recklessness. But it may be bravery. Even when it is bravery, it is not valor, a virtue that only a few display, and usually in the spontaneous performance of high-risk acts on behalf of others that go well beyond what is expected of them. And neither bravery nor valor is moral courage. Moral courage represents inner strength that stands against the pressures of peers and authorities, sometimes at great cost to oneself. Muhammad Ali displayed no bravery for refusing to serve in Vietnam. But he showed moral courage. Although his stand did not involve a commitment to nonviolence, it represents the seed of existential pacifism. Gandhi and King observed that nonviolence requires greater courage than violence. The same is true of existential pacifism. It renders one vulnerable to condemnation and sometimes imprisonment or death. Criminals risk condemnation, imprisonment and sometimes death for what they do, but their risks are for personal gain and they go to lengths to avoid the negative consequences. Moral courage involves taking the risks as a matter of principle, in which there is only the prospect of personal loss in conventional terms.

15.6 Training young people to kill

Established institutions and attitudes of society work against those who think killing in war is wrong. Although most Americans think war is sometimes justified, they do not glorify war *per se*. But they strongly support those whose lives are directly at risk in warfare—"our kids on the front line" they call them.[18] During the Iraq and Afghan wars they were routinely referred to as "heroes." Their sacrifices were often extraordinary and heartrending. Thousands gave their lives. Tens of thousands lost the wholeness of their physical bodies and the stability of their emotional lives. For this they deserve support and compassion.

But there is another side to their situation. It is a side that is true of all combat soldiers, whatever the army and whatever the justice of the causes for which they fight. Not only do they risk harm and death to themselves, they inflict it upon others. They train to kill other human beings. And they yield to others the power to decide

---

[17] Timothy Kudo, Op-ed, *The New York Times*, February 27, 2015.
[18] Gates, *Duty*, p. 60.

whom they will kill and when and where. They become obedient trained killers. Where they do not personally do the killing, they support those who do. In the case of commanders, they give the orders that produce the killing. The killing soldiers do often goes unspoken. Yet killing is at the heart of warfare, and killing is what soldiers do. Simply risking one's life accomplishes nothing. Nor does being killed or maimed. It is the killing one does that advances the objectives for which one is fighting. Handing out candy to children or helping build schools is ancillary. To refuse to confront squarely what soldiers do does them a disservice. Only if young people receive the necessary moral and intellectual preparation to make a thoughtful choice about whether to kill other human beings does society fully support them. Meaningful consent requires nothing less. To profess support for them while backing the decisions that have placed them in harm's way is sham support. Worse yet, to praise them on the grounds that such praise is necessary to maintain their morale helps perpetuate their victimization. It is more suited to salving one's conscience for shared responsibility for their plight than to showing compassion for them.

Robert M. Gates, secretary of defense under both the Bush and Obama administrations, unquestioningly had a heartfelt affection for the troops in the Iraq and Afghan wars. Still he believed in full support of their missions, lest their morale be adversely affected. As he writes:

> When soldiers put their lives on the line, they need to know that the commander in chief who sent them into harm's way believes in their mission. They need him to talk often to them and to the country, not just to express gratitude for their service and sacrifice but also to explain and affirm why that sacrifice is necessary, why their fight is noble, why their cause is just, and why they must prevail.[19]

It is one thing to know that the president believes in the mission to which he has committed troops. It is another to know that he is correct in that belief. Morale that is propped up by propaganda, manipulation and misguided judgments will not—and should not—long survive a confrontation with the truth.

15.7 The logic of war

We saw in Chapter 6 one influential argument for war based on self-defense. Governments field armies, then hurl them against one another and justify the killing they do on the grounds that they all are acting in self-defense. Here the argument is different. The focus is upon the sacrifices soldiers make and the importance of maintaining their morale. Governments can order them into combat for whatever reasons, but once the killing begins, it is important to maintain their morale lest they question why they are there. The call to support the troops plays into this. And as we

---

[19] Gates, *Duty*, pp. 298–299. In fairness, Gates never says that Barack Obama, about whom he is speaking in the passage, did not fully believe all of these things, only that he lacked passion for the war in not saying them.

have seen, this readily translates into supporting their mission. Their mission consists of objectives set for them by their commanders and government leaders, objectives that may be just or unjust, legal or illegal. The mission is theirs only in the sense that they carry it out. It has been chosen by others and assigned to them. It thus happens that there is a subtle shift from supporting the men and women who are in harm's way to supporting the objectives of those who put them in harm's way. And those persons share few of their risks. Not only do they not personally share the risks, their children rarely do either. President George H. W. Bush had served, and at serious risk, in WW II, but he was comfortably ensconced in the White House during the Gulf War, as were presidents Bill Clinton, George W. Bush and Barack Obama during the conflicts they initiated. Although George W. Bush had served in the National Guard during the Vietnam War, he was not deployed and did not see combat. None of the children of Clinton or George W. Bush entered the military when they became of age, despite ongoing conflicts at the time.[20] There is little reason to believe that the children of Barack Obama will do so either.

Once soldiers enter combat, the fact that they are in harm's way produces the justification for keeping them in harm's way, otherwise their morale may suffer. Whatever their morale, some of them will be killed, and as casualties mount a further justification emerges. It then becomes important that those who have died not have died in vain: the objectives for which they fought must not be abandoned. Thus more troops must be sent so that the objectives for which their predecessors died can be achieved, which means continuing the policies that led to soldiers being sent into harm's way in the first place. *Go to war, and the justification for the war materializes in the process.* The argument works no matter what the objectives are. Any objectives will do, so long as men and women are killed or wounded in the course of fighting.[21]

---

[20] A. A. Milne wrote that "just as the war-makers, who condemn millions to death, are the very people who will not themselves be facing death, so are they just the people to whom war is not an interruption of their ordinary life. Who are the men responsible for war? Obviously not poets, and painters, and butchers and bakers, and farmers and doctors and candlestick makers. However we divide the credit, we can say that those responsible for it will necessarily be found among politicians, soldiers and sailors of high rank, financiers, armament kings, and newspaper proprietors, editors and lead-writers. And what happens when war breaks out? All these people merely intensify their previous activities. Not one of them interrupts his work at his country's call. Indeed, to nearly all of them an outbreak of war is just an opportunity of greater fame, greater self-expression and greater rewards." A. A. Milne, *Peace with Honour* (New York: E.P. Dutton & Company, 1934), pp. 132f. Milne was reflecting upon WWI and its legacy of militarism. For a devastating critique of those who promote war but do not themselves sacrifice for it, particularly with reference to the wars in Iraq and Afghanistan, see Cheyney Ryan, *The Chickenhawk Syndrome: War, Sacrifice, and Personal Responsibility* (New York: Rowman & Littlefield Publishers, 2009).

[21] McMahan contends that it would be wrong for a government to compel soldiers to fight to redeem the deaths of those who go before them, and he would restrict the relevant harms to those who are fighting with a just cause, that is, whose objectives are just. Nonetheless, he asserts that the good represented by ensuring that just combatants have not died in vain can become an element in a just cause, and may provide "a new reason for continuing the war." That "new reason" may, however, in the minds of those responsible for the war, eclipse whatever reason one had for going to war initially and become the governing consideration in continuing the war. Given that both sides in modern war typically think they are in the right, redemption of losses incurred in the pursuit of objectives— whether in the abstract those objectives are just or not—can provide the rationale for the war itself. See Jeff McMahan, "Proportionality and Time," *Ethics*, Vol. 125, No. 3, April 2015, especially pages 710–720.

The point is that the reality of war in the modern world bears little resemblance to just war in the rationales of warists. The wars they extol are reluctantly entered into by peace-loving democratic leaders. They are necessary wars, fought with determination by brave warriors making heroic sacrifices to defend the innocent, whether our own or those of other countries. Precautions are taken to protect civilians. Air strikes are surgical, targets carefully selected. Some civilians die, but those deaths are accidental. These are good wars, judiciously chosen. They preserve democracy and free enterprise. So runs the mythology of war.

15.8 Bringing good out of evil

The cultural mindset we have inherited that accepts unquestioningly the war system that has evolved over centuries drains the best moral energies from us. It cannot be transformed overnight, but it can be transformed, and a future can begin to be envisaged in which we are unwilling to kill thousands or even millions of our fellow human beings to attain national objectives. Fully recognizing the role of mediated consequences in human history provides grounds for optimism. Just as it takes light from the heavens thousands or even millions of years to reach earth, so it takes the consequences of behavior from the distant past hundreds of years to reach us. In studying the heavens we are looking into the universe's past, and in studying today's world we are looking into humankind's past. We see now the effects of what humankind has done in its history. This enables us to evaluate the broad social consequences of certain kinds of actions, of values and practices that may have outlived whatever usefulness they once may have had. It gives us the opportunity now to begin to change direction. This means that we can view humankind's course as a kind of experiment. It cannot be a controlled experiment in a narrow scientific sense; we cannot live one way for a few thousand years, then another way for a few thousand years, and then compare the results and decide which is better. But we can learn what the consequences are of certain *kinds* of actions, practices, customs and conventions. They are the world we see before us, which includes not only the awesome advances in science and technology, but also the threat of nuclear annihilation, the degradation of the environment, the decimation of animal species and the gross inequalities in wealth and power. Is this cause for despair? It is not. We can, by how we act now, change all this. As the Stoic Seneca wrote, it is "a masterpiece to draw good out of evil."[22] Augustine saw the work of God as turning the evil that men do to his purposes. He said that those who work evil in the world do not and cannot control the outcomes of that evil. If there is a God, God can turn those outcomes to good purposes. But whether there is a God or not, we can do so as well. For, our responses to past acts are among those acts' consequences. They are mediated consequences. So are most of the created objects and practices and institutions of advanced civilization. By our efforts we can make the consequences of past actions good when otherwise they would be bad. In so doing we can, by our

---

[22] *Seneca's Morals of a Happy Life, Benefits, Anger and Clemency*, trans. Sir Roger L'Estrange (Chicago, IL: W.B.Conkey Company, n.d.), p. 296.

present actions, affect the past. If consequences are considered properties of acts and practices, we can today alter some of the properties of past practices. We cannot alter acts' intrinsic properties. Those are not within our control. But we can alter their mediated consequences, and in that way transform what may have been harmful and misguided actions (as judged by their consequences to date) into good. The challenge of our time is to find creative ways to do this.

15.9 Conclusion

My hope is that reflection on the thoughts of the foregoing chapters will contribute, if only in a small way, to the movement toward a nonviolent world order. America is uniquely positioned to play a role in helping transform the world in that direction. Nonviolence can be most effective when practiced from a standpoint of strength, and militarily America remains the most powerful nation in the world. But military power will not save the world. It will not even sustain America indefinitely in its reliance upon force to achieve its ends. Gibbon once wrote that historically the Davids of the world have always defeated the Goliaths. In the modern world, it was the Minutemen who prevailed against the British, Mao's guerilla warfare that succeeded in China, Castro's guerilla warfare that won out in Cuba, and the Vietcong's guerilla warfare[23] that ousted the United States from Vietnam. More recently, the Mujahadeen defeated the Soviets in Afghanistan and their successors stymied the United States in that country. In each of these cases the use of force by the militarily weaker party was in addition to the social, psychological and political efforts undertaken at the same time. The effectiveness of massive military force—vast armies, tanks, planes, battleships—has been challenged by decentralized, mobile, smaller forces that can harass and demoralize larger forces and undermine their support base through psychological and political action.

The need now is to take the next step and transition to nonviolent action, utilizing some of the same principles as guerilla warfare but adapted to nonviolent action. Essential to such a change is to recognize the effectiveness of essentially nonviolent action in the modern world. These include not only the well-known actions of Gandhi in India and Martin Luther King Jr. in the United States, but also the largely nonviolent revolutions that swept Eastern Europe following the collapse of the USSR and that took place in Tunisia and Egypt in the twenty-first century.[24] The time has come for people to explore the implications of such actions for the social defense of a nation like the United States. Such an exploration would require the efforts and resources of countless people. It would require hypothesizing possible objectives of an aggressor and the design of nonviolent tactics to prevent those objectives from being achieved. Importantly, this would require far deeper understanding of the world's peoples than we now have.

The repeated complaint of terrorists—from Osama bin Laden to the home-grown terrorists like Timothy McVeigh—has been against the policies of the United States, and often in particular its treatment of Muslims. We have launched wars in Afghanistan

---

[23] Later augmented, as we have seen, by the largely conventional forces of North Vietnam.

[24] For a comprehensive empirical study of the effectiveness of nonviolent action in the twentieth century, see Erica Chenoweth and Maria J. Stephan, *Why Civil Resistance Works: The Strategic Logic of Nonviolent Conflict* (New York: Columbia University Press, 2011).

and Iraq, resorted to torture, drone strikes and assassination. The one thing we have not done is to change our policies. We have not even seriously reconsidered them. Republicans and Democrats debate. But they are like people quarreling over the arrangement of the deck chairs on the Titanic. They do not question the course of the ship. If one intends to be realistic about the long-term well-being of the United States, much less about creating a nonviolent world order, one must make the effort to understand the nature of the problems we face. This requires understanding those we now see as adversaries. It requires truly learning their beliefs, problems and fears. It requires communicating with them.

To move toward a nonviolent order we cannot remain wedded to an essentially collectivist perspective. That perspective conceptualizes the issues almost exclusively in terms of collectivities and their interactions. We think in terms of nation states and their conduct.[25] That defines the international scene. And it defines the standard approach to war. The JWT emphasizes just causes and legitimate authority, and it is states that have (or fail to have) just causes and legitimate authority.

When it comes to terrorism and asymmetric warfare, both sides use whichever perspective, macro or micro, most suits their purposes. We view terrorists and those involved in asymmetric warfare as attacking innocent civilians, thus seeing what they do from a micro perspective. But they see their attacks as directed against a collectivity—the United States (or its allies)—often in retaliation for the deaths of people they consider innocent civilians. In so doing, they often think of themselves in the same way soldiers think of themselves. They are attacking the enemy. The enemy is not the particular human beings they may kill by means of their violence. Those persons are simply a part of the collectivity. Enemy combatants are not personally your enemy. They are simply the ones before you, the designated agents of the collectivity licensed to kill you and whom you are licensed to kill. Terrorists simply do the licensing themselves, or think it is provided by their religion or ideology. Many of them do not think of themselves as terrorists. As we saw in the preceding chapter, they think of themselves as soldiers. Thought of in this way, terrorism is, as has sometimes been pointed out, irrational, because soldiers typically try to achieve their objectives by the quantity of death and destruction they can inflict, but terrorism accomplishes comparatively little of that. Terrorism, properly understood, tries to achieve objectives by instilling and manipulating fear, not only in those immediately targeted, but in the thousands, hundreds of thousands or millions who learn about what they do.

It is interesting that warists should approve the attainment of ends by causing harm, death and destruction but deplore the attainment of ends by causing fear. In this there is a fine line between warism and terrorism. Both embrace violentism, that is, the use of violence in a systematic and organized way to achieve social, political, religious or moral ends. But violence causes death and destruction. It also causes fear. Warists utilize the death and destruction. Terrorists mostly utilize the fear. Warists use armies, tanks, planes, drones and missiles because they have them. Their success, accordingly, is measured mainly by the quantity of violence they use. Terrorists use knives, improvised

---

[25] As William V. O'Brien expresses it, "this task of evaluating the substance of just cause leads inescapably to a comparative analysis of the characteristics of the polities or political-social systems posed in warlike confrontation." *The Conduct of Just and Limited War* (New York: Praeger, 1981), p. 20.

explosives and whatever other weapons they can buy or steal because that is all they have. They cannot normally cause that much death and destruction by those means, but what they do cause, and the manner in which they cause it, is capable of terrorizing countless persons far removed from the acts themselves.[26] It is, if you like, the quality of the violence they use rather than the quantity that they count on.

If America as an entity is the enemy and violence the chosen weapon, it makes sense to attack America. How does one do that? By attacking the individuals, territory or property that make up the United States, those that have symbolic value and that help define the collectivity: members of government, the military, the CIA and certain buildings and institutions. The 9/11 hijackers targeted symbols of America's military, economic and political power. The aim is to target the heart of the collectivity, but if one cannot do that, then one attacks individuals who are part of the collectivity. They are the easiest targets, as in the Boston Marathon bombings of 2013. They may be innocent, but the collectivity is not, and it is the collectivity that is targeted. If the whole of the collectivity is the enemy, then it makes sense to attack whatever aspects of that entity are most accessible. Attacking American citizens wherever they are is attacking America.

The same logic applies to much of the violence in the Israeli-Palestinian conflict. If you are a Gazan and view Israel as the enemy, then you are attacking the enemy by firing rockets across the border. Never mind if many of them are homemade and land harmlessly in fields. Some of them kill or cause injury. Even those that do not still strike Israel. Such attacks make no sense from a micro perspective, since the number of casualties caused is so small. But they make sense if one clings to a macro perspective. The enemy is the collectivity, and you attack whatever aspects of the collectivity are vulnerable. Similarly, if you think of al-Qaeda or ISIS—or more broadly, terrorists in general—as the enemy, it makes sense to attack them wherever they are. If some of them happen to be American citizens as well, so be it. A nation-state cannot wage war in any standard sense against individual persons. At most, it can declare them criminals and seek to bring them to justice. But if you think of those individuals as part of a collectivity, you can, at least in your own mind, make sense of war against them. Conceptualize the conflict as war, and there come into play all of the conventions and legalities of a state of war that do not apply when dealing with scattered individuals with minimal cohesion engaged in criminal activity.

Even if one continues to view the world primarily from a collectivist perspective, one can develop a nonviolent repertoire of responses to violence, aggression and injustice. Nonviolent strategies of social defense seek ways to deny aggressors the capacity to achieve their objectives. Warists often speak as if we would promptly be taken over by an aggressor the moment we let down our military guard. But by whom? And why? Suppose they hope to take command of our industrial capacity—say, our production of automobiles and armaments. Unless one seriously thinks that Canada or Mexico (or some Latin American country) would march across the border for that purpose, an

---

[26] Not that simple weapons, used by enough people, cannot kill large numbers. The attempted genocide in Rwanda between April and July 1994 killed roughly 800,000 people, many through the use of machetes. Genocide, strictly speaking, is not terrorism. The objective of genocide is the extermination of a people, not the changing of their policies or the subordination of them by instilling fear, though fear is often used to cleanse a region of a people. Killing and instilling fear are often intermingled as objectives in the use of violence, and warists and terrorists alike often do not carefully distinguish the two.

aggressor with those objectives would have to cross an ocean. It would take hundreds of thousands—perhaps millions—of persons to take over and run with even minimal efficiency a country like the United States. And they presumably would need to be able to speak or at least read English. How would they get here? They would have to cross an ocean by air or sea. We would see them coming, indeed know well in advance as they assembled the thousands needed for the occupation. If they are coming by air—and at present no country has sufficient air power to transport that many people virtually at once across an ocean—we need only blockade or tear up the airstrips needed for landing. If they come by sea, we blockade the ports needed for landing. If they succeeded in landing other than at established ports, how would they get from there to widespread centers of the military-industrial complex. By rail? Tear up the railway tracks or (with advance planning) change the gauge on the tracks, so that even if they bring their own railway cars, those cars would be useless on the American rail system. By truck? How many trucks would they need to bring to transport the hundreds of thousands of persons they would need to govern the United States? If the highways have been blocked or torn up, they would need repair to be usable.

Assuming invaders surmounted all of these problems, how would they govern without the cooperation of citizens? Noncooperation is the hallmark of a nonviolent collective action. Who would direct traffic, collect trash, fight fires, transmit communications? Who would replace all of the street signs that could have been removed? No invading army could possibly do all of these things without cooperation from the citizenry. And if they could, how would they make use of the industrial capacity (which we are supposing, according to this scenario, is their objective) if workers have dismantled the plants and machinery, hiding or destroying vital components, destroying operating instructions. The industrial capacity which (by hypothesis) it is the aggressor's aim to exploit could be crippled even before they set foot on American territory. All of this could be known in advance. If deterrence means anything, it means leading a potential aggressor to refrain from doing what he otherwise would do by knowledge of how you will respond if he does it. The concerted efforts to deny invaders the capacity to attain their objectives would be among the mediated consequences of their actions. If even a modicum of rationality prevails–and the idea of military deterrence likewise fails if one does not assume this—the futility of such an attempted conquest would be evident. America could, by concerted effort of millions of Americans, become virtually unconquerable. It would occasion hardship. But that must be compared with the hardship of a war on our homeland. A ruthless invader could kill lots of people. But so could a ruthless adversary in war. Even a non-ruthless adversary in a major war could inflict enormous casualties.

I have only scratched the surface of the policy of nonviolent national defense given one particular set of possible objectives of an invader. The same would need to be done for the range of reasonably realistic objectives an adversary might entertain in attacking America. And the same would have to be done for possible objectives an adversary might have to adversely affect American interests short of an attack on the American homeland, which is the likeliest scenario. This would in some ways be more difficult, and begins to approximate the situation in the world today, in which nations jockey for positions of advantage and influence throughout the world. But this is what must be done to move toward a nonviolent world order.

My point is that even if one maintains the collectivist perspective, and its associated macroethics, there are promising avenues to explore in the interest of nonviolent national defense and the safeguarding of American interests. This represents the practical aspect of pragmatic pacifism.

Existential pacifism represents a commitment to a micro perspective. An existential pacifist refuses, as a matter of conscience, to kill other human beings on the order of others or in the service of causes defined by them. A country as a whole can be committed to pragmatic pacifism, but it cannot be committed to existential pacifism. At most, it can consist of individual persons who are existential pacifists, who associate freely and respectfully with the minimum of pressure and coercion. Ideally, they would live in small communities. Such communities would not concentrate military, political and economic power in the hands of a few people. Their relations among one another would be the product of education that stresses from the earliest age the values of nonviolence. It is first through education and nonviolent parenting that a transformation of society can come about. The particulars of how such a transformation might be brought about would require more extensive exploration than there is space to undertake here. But it is a program for the future, and indeed a program that must be undertaken if humankind is to survive indefinitely.

The appearance of human beings in the universe—whether by the design of a God or by chance—can be thought of as a grand experiment, one whose beauty and complexity inspires awe and whose outcome is yet to be determined. That outcome will be determined in considerable measure by whether we take command of those aspects of our lives that are within our control and transform them according to our highest ideals. It is not the lead of military and political figures that we should be following, but of those of the likes of LaoTzu, Socrates, Jesus, Henry David Thoreau, Leo Tolstoy, Jane Addams, Dorothy Day, Albert Schweitzer, Albert Einstein, Mahatma Gandhi and Martin Luther King, Jr. They have shown, in their various ways, the vision and inspiration within the human spirit. We can pay them lip service and continue down a destructive path, or we can commit ourselves to pursuing the kind of world they envisioned. There is no guarantee that we will succeed. But our resolve would guarantee that we would strive with courage and dignity to transform our world in keeping with the potential for goodness that lies within it.

I am not worried lest America may not be able to assert a leadership of force and power; I am worried lest she may. I am concerned to see America assume a moral leadership of humility, so that the world may pay her glad homage and uphold her forever. Like the great river that nourishes life along its valley, she shall be the exuberance and richness of her life be a blessing upon the peoples of the earth … This is my Dream America. Will it come true?

—Lin Yutang, *Between Tears and Laughter*

Select Bibliography

Ackerman, Peter and Duvall, Jack. *A Force More Powerful: A Century of Nonviolent Conflict*. New York: St. Martin's Press, 2000.

Alexandra, Andrew. "Political Pacifism." *Social Theory and Practice*, Vol. 29, No. 4 (October 2003), pp. 589–606.

Appy, Christian G. *American Reckoning: The Vietnam War and Our National Identity*. New York: Viking, 2015.

Bacevich, Andrew J. *Washington Rules: America's Path to Permanent War*. New York: Metropolitan Books, 2010.

Bainton, Roland. *Christian Attitudes toward War and Peace*. New York: Abingdon Press, 1960.

Baker, Deane-Peter. "Epistemic Uncertainty and Excusable Wars." *The Philosophical Forum*, Vol. 46, No. 1 (Spring 2015).

Bellamy, Alex J. *Just Wars: From Cicero to Iraq*. Cambridge: Polity, 2006.

Benjamin, Daniel and Simon, Steven (eds). *The Age of Sacred Terror*. New York: Random House, 2002.

Biggar, Nigel. *In Defense of War*. Oxford: University Press, 2013.

Bilton, Michael and Sim, Kevin. *Four Hours in My Lai*. New York: Penguin Books, 1993.

Bleisch, Barbara and Strub, Jean-Daniel (eds), *Pazifismus: Ideengeschichte, Theorie und Praxis*. Berne: Haupt, 2006.

Bondurant, Joan V. *Conquest of Violence: The Gandhian Philosophy of Conflict*, rev. ed. Princeton: Princeton University Press, 1988.

Bove, Laurence F. and Kaplan, Laura Duhan (eds). *From the Eye of the Storm: Regional Conflicts and the Philosophy of Peace*. Amsterdam: Rodopi, 1995.

Brimlow, Robert W. *What about Hitler? Wrestling with Jesus's Call to Nonviolence in an Evil World*. Grand Rapids, MI: Brazos Press, 2006.

Brock, Peter. *Pacifism in the United States: From the Colonial Era to the First World War*. Princeton: Princeton University Press, 1968.

Brock, Peter. *Twentieth-Century Pacifism*. New York: Van Nostrand Reinhold, 1970.

Brock, Peter. *Freedom from Violence: Sectarian Nonresistance from the Middle Ages to the Great War*. Toronto: University of Toronto Press, 1991.

Brock, Peter. *Freedom from War: Nonsectarian Pacifism 1814–1914*. Toronto: University of Toronto Press, 1991.

Burchett, Wilfred G. *Vietnam: Inside Story of the Guerilla War*. New York: International Publishers, 1965.

Burrowes, Robert J. *The Strategy of Nonviolent Defense: A Gandhian Approach*. Albany, NY: State University of New York Press, 1996.

Cady, Duane L. *From Warism to Pacifism: A Moral Continuum*, 2nd ed. Philadelphia, PA: Temple University Press, 2010.

Cady, Duane L. and Werner, Richard (eds). *Just War, Nonviolence, and Nuclear Deterrence*. Wakefield, NH: Longwood Academic, 1991.

Caputo, Philip. *A Rumor of War*. New York: Henry Holt and Company, 1996.

Charles, J. Daryl. *Between Pacifism and Jihad: Just War and Christian Tradition*. Downers Grove, IL: InterVarsity Press, 2005.

Chatfield, Charles and Ilukhina, Ruzanna (eds). *Peace/Mir: An Anthology of Historic Alternatives to War*. Syracuse, NY: Syracuse University Press, 1994.

Chatterjee, Deen K. and Scheid, Don E. (eds). *Ethics and Foreign Intervention*. Cambridge: University Press, 2003.

Chenoweth, Erica and Stephan, Maria J. *Why Civil Resistance Works: The Strategic Logic of Nonviolent Conflict*. New York: Columbia University Press, 2011.

Clausewitz, Carl von, Howard, Michael and Paret, Peter (ed. and trans.). *On War*. Princeton: Princeton University Press, 1976.

Coady, C. A. J. *Morality and Political Violence*. Cambridge: University Press, 2008.

Coker, Christopher. *Can War Be Eliminated?* Cambridge: Polity Press, 2014.

Cortright, David. *Gandhi and Beyond: Nonviolence for an Age of Terrorism*. London: Paradigm Publishers, 2006.

Cortright, David. *Peace: A History of Movements and Ideas*. Cambridge: University Press, 2008.

Cox, Gray. *The Ways of Peace: A Philosophy of Peace as Action*. Mahwah, NJ: Paulist Press, 1986.

Dobos, Ned (special ed.). "The Ethics of War and Peace: New Problems for Just War Theory." *The Philosophical Forum: A Quarterly*, Vol. XLVI, No. 1 (Spring 2015).

Dombrowski, Daniel A. *Christian Pacifism*. Philadelphia, PA: Temple University Press, 1991.

Dower, John W. *Cultures of War*. New York: W.W. Norton, 2010.

Dower, Nigel. *The Ethics of War and Peace: Cosmopolitanism and Other Perspectives*. Cambridge: Polity, 2009.

Doyle, Michael W. "Kant, Liberal Legacies, and Foreign Affairs," Part I. *Philosophy & Public Affairs*, Vol. 12, No. 2 (Summer 1983).

Elshtain, Jean Bethke (ed.). *Just War Theory*. New York: New York University Press, 1992.

Elshtain, Jean Bethke. *Just War against Terror*. New York: Basic Books, 2003.

Emerson, Ralph Waldo. *Miscellanies*. Boston, MA: Houghton, Mifflin and Company, 1885.

Fall, Bernard B. *Viet-Nam Witness 1953–66*. New York: Frederick A. Praeger, 1966.

Fall, Bernard B. *Street without Joy: The French Debacle in Indochina*. Mechanicsburg, PA: Stackpole Books, 2005.

Fiala, Andrew. *The Just War Myth: The Moral Illusion of War*. Lanham, MD: Rowman & Littlefield, 2008.

Fotion, Nicholas. *War and Ethics: A New Just War Theory*. New York: Continuum, 2007.

Fox, Michael Allen. *Understanding Peace: A Comprehensive Introduction*. New York: Routledge, 2014.

Frankena, W. K. "The Concept of Morality." *The Journal of Philosophy*, Vol. 63 (1966).

Frankena, William K. "Love and Principle in Christian Ethics," in Alvin Plantinga, ed., *Faith and Philosophy: Philosophical Studies in Religion and Ethics* (Grand Rapids, MI: Eerdmans, 1964)

Gallie, W. B. *Philosophers of Peace and War: Kant, Clausewitz, Marx, Engels and Tolstoy*. Cambridge: Cambridge University Press, 1978.

Gallie, W. B. *Understanding War*. New York: Routledge, 1991.

Gan, Barry. *Violence and Nonviolence: An Introduction*. Lanham, MD: Rowman & Littlefield, 2013.

Gandhi, Mohandas. *The Moral and Political Writings of Mahatma Gandhi*, Vols 2 and 3, ed. Raghavan Iyer. Oxford: Clarendon Press, 1987.

Giap, Vo Nguyen. *People's War, People's Army: The Viet Cong Insurrection Manual for Underdeveloped Countries*. New York: Bantam Books, 1968.

Gillis, John R (ed.). *The Militarization of the Western World*. New Brunswick, NJ: Rutgers University Press, 1989.

Gordon, Joy. *Invisible War: The United States and the Iraq Sanctions*. Cambridge, MA: Harvard University Press, 2010.

Grossman, Dave. *On Killing: The Psychological Cost of Learning to Kill in War and Society*, rev. ed. New York: Little, Brown and Company, 2009.

Hagen, William W. "The Balkans' Lethal Nationalism." *Foreign Affairs*, Vol. 78, No. 4 (July/August 1999).

Halberstam, David. *The Making of a Quagmire*. New York: Random House, 1965.

Hashmi, Sohail H. and Steven P. Lee. *Ethics and Weapons of Mass Destruction: Religious and Secular Perspectives*. Cambridge: Cambridge University Press, 2004.

Hedges, Chris. *War Is a Force that Gives Us Meaning*. New York: BBS Public Affairs, 2002.

Holmes, Arthur F. (ed.). *War and Christian Ethics*, 2nd ed. Grand Rapids, MI: Baker Academic, 2005.

Holmes, Robert L. and Gan, Barry (eds). *Nonviolence in Theory and Practice*, 3rd ed. Long Grove, IL: Waveland Press, 2012.

Holmes, Robert L. *The Ethics of Nonviolence: Essays by Robert L. Holmes*, ed. Predrag Cicovacki. New York: Bloomsbury, 2013.

Holmes, Robert L. *On War and Morality*. Princeton: Princeton University Press, Princeton Legacy Library, [1989]2014.

Johnson, James Turner. *Just War Tradition and the Restraint of War: A Moral and Historical Inquiry*. Princeton: Princeton University Press, 1981.

Johnson, James Turner. *Can Modern War Be Just?* New Haven, CT: Yale University Press, 1984.

Johnson, James Turner. *Morality and Contemporary Warfare*. New Haven, CT: Yale University Press, 1999.

Johnson, James Turner and Weigel, George. *Just War and the Gulf War*. Washington, DC: Ethics and Public Policy Center, 1991.

Kaeuper, Richard .*War, Justice and Public Order: England and France in the Later Middle Ages*. Oxford, UK: Clarendon Press, 1988.

Kahin, George McTurnan and Lewis, John W. *The United States in Vietnam: An Analysis in Depth of the History of America's Involvement in Vietnam*. A Delta Book, 1967.

Karnow, Stanley. *Vietnam: A History*. New York: Penguin Books, 1984.

Kelsay, John and Johnson, James Turner (eds). *Just War and Jihad: Historical and Theoretical Perspectives on War and Peace in Western and Islamic Traditions*. New York: Greenwood Press, 1991.

Kennedy, David M. "War and the American Character." *The Stanford Magazine*, Vol. 3, No. 1 (Spring/Summer 1975).

Ketwig, John. *...and a hard rain fell: A GI's True Story of the War in Vietnam*. Naperville, IL: Sourcebooks, 2008.

King-Hall, Stephen. *Defense in the Nuclear Age*. Nyack, NY: Fellowship Publications, 1959.

Kunkel, Joseph C. and Klein, Kenneth H. *Issues in War and Peace: Philosophical Inquiries*. Wolfeboro, NH: Longwood Academic, 1989.

Kurlansky, Mark. *Nonviolence: Twenty-Five Lessons from the History of a Dangerous Idea*. New York: Modern Library, 2006.

Lackey, Douglas P. *The Ethics of War and Peace*. Englewood, New Jersey: Prentice-Hall, 1989.

Lackey, Douglas. "The Moral Irrelevance of the Counterforce/Countervalue Distinction." *The Monist*, Vol. 70 (1987).

Lacouture, Jean. *Vietnam: Between Two Truces*. New York: Random House, 1966.

Lake, David A. "Powerful Pacifists: Democratic States and War." *American Political Science Review*, Vol. 86, No. 1 (March 1992).

Laqueur, Walter. *No End to War: Terrorism in the Twenty-First Century*. New York: Continuum, 2003.

Lee, Steven P. *Ethics and War: An Introduction*. Cambridge: Cambridge University Press, 2012.

Lider, Julian. *On the Nature of War*. Westmead, England: Saxon House, 1977.

Lind, Michael. *Vietnam: The Necessary War: A Reinterpretation of America's Most Disastrous Military Conflict*. New York: Simon & Schuster, 1999.

Luban, David. "Just War and Human Rights." *Philosophy and Public Affairs*, Vol. 9 (1980).

Lynd, Staughton. *Nonviolence in America: A Documentary History*. Indianapolis, IN: The Bobbs-Merrill Company, 1966.

Lynd, Staughton. *The Pentagon Papers: The Secret History of the Vietnam War as Published by the* New York Times. New York: Bantam Books, 1971.

Maclear, Michael. *The Ten Thousand Day War: Vietnam 1945-1975*. New York: St. Martin's Press, 1981.

Moyar, Mark. *Triumph Forsaken: The Vietnam War, 1954-1965*. Cambridge: Cambridge University Press, 2006.

May, Larry (ed.). *War: Essays in Political Philosophy*. Cambridge: Cambridge University Press, 2008.

May, Larry. *Aggression and Crimes against Peace*. Cambridge: Cambridge University Press, 2008.

May, Larry, Rovie, Eric and Viner, Steve (eds). *The Morality of War: Classical and Contemporary Readings*. Upper Saddle River, NJ: Prentice Hall, 2006.

May, Todd. *Nonviolent Resistance: A Philosophical Introduction*. Cambridge: Polity, 2015.

McMahan, Jeff. *The Ethics of Killing: Problems at the Margins of Life*. Oxford: Oxford University Press, 2002.

McMahan, Jeff. *Killing in War*. Oxford: Clarendon Press, 2009.

Merton, Thomas. *The Nonviolent Alternative*, ed. Gordon C. Zahn. New York: Farrar-Straus-Giroux, 1980.

Mueller, John. *Retreat from Doomsday: The Obsolescence of War*. New York: Basic Books, 1989.

Murphy, Jeffrie. "The Killing of the Innocent." *The Monist*, Vol. 57, No. 4 (October 1973), pp. 527–551.

Nardin, Terry (ed.). *The Ethics of War and Peace: Religious and Secular Perspectives*. Princeton: Princeton University Press, 1996.

Narveson, Jan. "Pacifism: A Philosophical Analysis," in ed. Richard Wasserstrom. *War and Morality*. Belmont, CA: Wadsworth.

Neitzel, Sönke and Harald Welzer. *Soldaten: On Fighting, Killing, and Dying, The Secret World War II Transcripts of German POWs*. New York: Alfred A. Knopf, 2012.

Norman, Richard. *Ethics, Killing and War*. Cambridge: Cambridge University Press, 1995.

O'Brien, William V. *The Conduct of Just and Limited War*. New York: Praeger, 1983.

O'Neill, William G. *Kosovo: An Unfinished Peace*. Boulder, CO: Lynne Rienner, 2002.

Orend, Brian. *The Morality of War*. Toronto: Broadview Press, 2006.

Paige, Glenn D., Satha-Anand, Chaiwat and Gilliatt, Sarah (eds). *Islam and Nonviolence*. Honolulu, HI: Center for Global Nonviolence, Matsunaga Institute for Peace, University of Hawaii, 1993.

Parkin, Nicholas Edward. *Pacifism, Innocence, and Modern War*, PhD dissertation, Centre for Applied Philosophy and Public Ethics, Department of Philosophy, The University of Melbourne, September 2012.

Polner, Murray and Goodman, Naomi (eds). *The Challenge of Shalom*. Philadelphia, PA: New Society Publishers, 1994.

Ramsey, Paul. *The Just War: Force and Political Responsibility*. Lanham, MD: University Press of America, 1968.

Regan, Richard J. *Just War: Principles and Cases*. Washington, DC: The Catholic University of America Press, 1996.

Reichberg, Gregory M., Syse, Henrik and Begby, Endre (eds). *The Ethics of War: Classic and Contemporary Readings*. Oxford: Blackwell, 2006.

Reitan, Eric. "The Irreconcilability of Pacifism and Just War Theory: A Response to Sterba." *Social Theory and Practice*, Vol. 20, No. 2 (Summer 1994).

Roberts, Adam (ed.). *Civilian Resistance as a National Defense: Non-Violent Action against Aggression*. Baltimore, MD: Penguin Books, 1969.

Rodin, David. *War and Self-Defense*. Oxford: Oxford University Press, 2002.

Rodin, David and Shue, Henry (eds). *Just and Unjust Warriors: The Moral and Legal Status of Soldiers*. Oxford: University Press, 2008.

Romaya, Bassam. *The Iraq War: A Philosophical Analysis*. New York: Palgrave Macmillan, 2012.

Russell, Frederick H. *The Just War in the Middle Ages*. Cambridge: Cambridge University Press, 1975.

Ryan, Cheney. *The Chickenhawk Syndrome: War, Sacrifice, and Personal Responsibility*. New York: Rowman & Littlefield, 2009.

Ryan, Cheney C. "Self-Defense, Pacifism, and the Possibility of Killing." *Ethics*, Vol. 93, No. 3 (April 1983).

Sagan, Scott D. "Realist Perspectives on Ethical Norms and Weapons of Mass Destruction," in ed. Sohail H. Hashmi and Steven P. Lee. *Ethics and Weapons of Mass Destruction: Religious and Secular Perspectives*. Cambridge: Cambridge University Press, 2004.

Sharp, Gene. *The Politics of Nonviolent Action*. Boston, MA: Porter Sargent, 1973.

Sharp, Gene. "Making the Abolition of War a Realistic Goal." *World without War Issues Center Midwest Newsletter*. December 1980.

Sharp, Gene. *Social Power and Political Freedom*. Boston, MA: Porter Sargent, 1980.

Sharp, Gene. *Civilian-Based Defense: A Post-Military Weapons System*. Princeton: Princeton University Press, 1990.

Sharp, Gene. *Waging Nonviolent Struggle: 20th Century Practice and 21st Century Potential*. Boston, MA: Porter Sargent, 2005.

Sheehan, Neil. *A Bright Shining Lie: John Paul Vann and America in Vietnam*. New York: Vintage Books, 1989.

Sherman, Nancy. *After War: Healing the Moral Wounds of Our Soldiers*. Oxford: Oxford University Press, 2015.

Singer, P. W. *Wired for War: The Robotics Revolution and Conflict in the 21st Century*. New York: Penguin Books, 2010.

Smith, David Livingstone. *The Most Dangerous Animal: Human Nature and the Origins of War*. New York: St. Martin's Press, 2007.

Sorabji, Richard and Rodin, David (eds). *The Ethics of War: Shared Problems in Different Traditions*. Aldershot: Ashgate, 2006.

Sparrow, James T. *Warfare State: World War II Americans and the Age of Big Government*. Oxford: University Press, 2011.

Sterba, James P. *"From Just War Theory to Pacifism,"* in ed. James P. Sterba. *Justice for Here and Now.* Cambridge: Cambridge University Press, 1998, pp. 151–172.

Sterba, James P. "Reconciling Pacifists and Just War Theorists." *Social Theory and Practice,* Vol. 18, No. 1 (Spring 1992).

Stern, Jessica. *Terror in the Name of God: Why Religious Militants Kill.* New York: HarperCollins, 2003.

Stevenson, William R. Jr. *Christian Love and Just War: Moral Paradox and Political Life in St. Augustine and His Modern Interpreters.* Macon, GA: Mercer University Press, 1987.

Syse, Henrik and Reichberg, Gregory M. (eds). *Ethics, Nationalism, and Just War: Medieval and Contemporary Perspectives.* Washington, DC: The Catholic University of America Press, 2007.

Teichman, Jenny. *Pacifism and the Just War.* Oxford: Blackwell, 1986.

Temes, Peter S. *The Just War: An American Reflection on the Morality of War in Our Time.* Chicago: Ivan R. Dee, 2003.

Tesón, Fernando R. *Humanitarian Intervention: An Inquiry into Law and Morality.* New York: Transnational Publishers, 1988.

Tolstoy, Leo. *The Kingdom of God Is Within You.* New York: Farrar, Straus and Cudahy, 1961.

Tolstoy, Leo. *The Law of Love and the Law of Violence.* New York: Holt, Rinehart and Winston, 1970.

Tolstoy, Leo. *Government Is Violence: Essays on Anarchism and Pacifism.* London: Phoenix Press, 1990.

Turse, Nick. *KILL ANYTHING THAT MOVES: The Real American War in Vietnam.* New York: A Metropolitan Book, 2013.

Vorabej, Mark. "Pacifism and Wartime Innocence." *Social Theory and Practice,* Vol. 20, No. 2 (Summer 1994).

Walzer, Michael. *Just and Unjust Wars: A Moral Argument with Historical Illustrations.* New York: Basic Books, 1977.

Walzer, Michael. *Arguing about War.* New Haven, CT: Yale University Press, 2004.

Wasserstrom, Richard A. (ed.). *War and Morality.* Belmont, CA: Wadsworth, 1970.

Weigel, George. *Against the Grain: Christianity and Democracy, War and Peace.* New York: The Crossroad Publishing Company, 2008.

Werner, Richard. "Pragmatism for Pacifists." *Contemporary Pragmatism,* Vol. 4, No. 2 (December 2007), pp. 93–115.

Wink, Walter (ed.). *Peace Is the Way: Writings on Nonviolence from the Fellowship of Reconciliation.* Maryknoll, NY: Orbis Books, 2006.

Wright, Quincy. *A Study of War,* 2nd ed. Chicago, IL: University of Chicago Press, 1965.

Yoder, John Howard. *When War Is Unjust: Being Honest in Just-War Thinking,* 2nd ed. Eugene, OR: Wipf & Stock, 2001.

Zahn, Franklin. *Alternatives to the Pentagon: Nonviolent Methods of Defending a Nation.* Nyack, NY: Fellowship Publications, 1996.

Zupan, Daniel S. *War, Morality, and Autonomy: An Investigation in Just War Theory.* Hampshire: Ashgate, 2004.

Index